Advanced SOAP for Web Professionals

ISBN 0-13-035655-7

Advanced SOAP for Web Professionals

Dan Livingston

Prentice Hall PTR
Upper Saddle River, NJ 07458
www.phptr.com

Library of Congress Cataloging-in-Publication Data

Livingston, Dan.
Advanced SOAP for Web development / Dan Livingston
p. cm.
ISBN 0-13-035655-7
1. Web site development. 2. Internet programming. 3. Object oriented programming. I. Title: Advanced Simple Object Oriented Protocol for Web development. II. Title.

TK5105.888.L57 2002
005.2'76--dc21 2002020195

Editorial/Production Supervision: *Donna Cullen-Dolce*
Senior Managing Editor: *Karen McLean*
Cover Design Director: *Jerry Votta*
Cover Design: *Talar Boorujy*
Manufacturing Manager: *Alexis Heydt-Long*
Marketing Manager: *Jim Keogh*
Editorial Assistant: *Richard Winkler*
Series Design: *Gail Cocker-Bogusz*

A division of Pearson Education, Inc.
Upper Saddle River, NJ 07458

Prentice Hall books are widely used by corporations and government agencies for training, marketing, and resale.

The publisher offers discounts on this book when ordered in bulk quantities.
For more information, contact: Corporate Sales Department, Phone: 800-382-3419;
Fax: 201-236-7141; E-mail: corpsales@prenhall.com; or write: Prentice Hall PTR,
Corp. Sales Dept., One Lake Street, Upper Saddle River, NJ 07458.

Printed in the United States of America

10 9 8 7 6 5 4 3 2 1

ISBN 0-13-035655-7

Pearson Education LTD.
Pearson Education Australia PTY, Limited
Pearson Education Singapore, Pte. Ltd.
Pearson Education North Asia Ltd.
Pearson Education Canada, Ltd.
Pearson Educación de Mexico, S.A. de C.V.
Pearson Education—Japan
Pearson Education Malaysia, Pte. Ltd.

Contents

CHAPTER 2

CHAPTER 3

CHAPTER 4

CHAPTER 6

CHAPTER 7

Preface

Many people have called XML the Next Big Thing, but when pressed for reasons why, it can be difficult to get a clear answer out of them. SOAP may be the answer, though: It has the potential to be the killer app of XML. SOAP is the best method yet of transferring data from any application to any other application across the Internet.

Who This Book Is For

This book is for anyone who wants to keep their job in the field of Web technology, or is curious about XML and .NET. Seriously, the best way to survive in this economic climate is to constantly update your marketable skills and know all you can.

This book is aimed at Web developers and programmers. It will help if you know some XML already, but it's not necessary (there are some primers at the back of the book). You don't have to know anything about DCOM or Java or distributed architectures or activating objects. If you know those things, then your understanding of SOAP will be a deeper one than if you're a graphic designer who dabbles in ActionScript. The designers will not be at a severe disadvantage, though—everything is explained in full.

What You Will Learn

The goal of this book is to teach you everything you need to know about SOAP and its related technologies like WSDL and UDDI, as well as SOAP's place in Microsoft's .NET strategy. Everything in this book is focused on that goal. When you're done with this tome, you'll know what SOAP is, how it works, its strengths, and its weaknesses, as well as related technologies like WSDL, UDDI, and XML-RPC, and security extensions via SSL and XML Digital Signature. Of course, we'll also discuss Web services in general and .NET in some detail.

The examples in this book are available at www.wireman.com/soap, and you can write me at soap-dan@wireman.com with your comments, questions, huzzahs, and flames.

What You Will Not Learn

This is a SOAP book, not a programming book. By that, I mean that this book is dedicated to focusing on SOAP. Since SOAP is a platform- and language-independent technology, I wanted to stay away from tons of code in C++ or Java, and focus just on SOAP. Since SOAP can fulfill an incredible number of programming needs, the odds of my using an example that you specifically would find useful are pretty slim. So I decided against puffing up the book with code you'd never use, and used that room to dig deeper into what SOAP really is.

1

Why SOAP? Web Services and .NET

In This Chapter

- A Peek at SOAP
- Web Services and Internet 3.0
- .NET: How Evil Is It?

It appears the Internet is evolving again, and SOAP is playing a major part in that evolution. Before we dive into what SOAP is and why it's useful, we need to step back and look at the larger picture of what's happening on the Internet, and how it's related to Microsoft's latest attempt at world domination (.NET). We need a larger picture in order to put SOAP in the proper context. SOAP itself is simple enough so that its actual structure isn't the most interesting part of the story.

A Peek at SOAP

Briefly, Simple Object Access Protocol (SOAP) is a way to structure data so that any computer program in any language can read SOAP and send messages in SOAP.

If you're like me, you're impatient when it comes to new technology—you want to know all the gritty details and the big picture all at once. To sate your appetite, I'll show you two example SOAP packets here, a request for data and a response to that request, but I won't go into any detail yet. That will have to wait until Chapter 2.

The classic SOAP example involves an application needing to know the latest stock price for a certain company. Your application sends a request for information to a remote computer that has the stock price information. That remote computer hears your request via SOAP, and returns the stock price. This type of interaction is known as request-response, and it's how the Web currently works (you ask a server for a Web page, and the server gives it to you).

Here's all the code for the two messages. Example 1–1 shows the request.

EXAMPLE 1–1 Example SOAP request

```
<env:Envelope
  xmlns:env="http://www.w3.org/2001/06/soap-
envelope">
  <env:Body>
      <m:getStockPrice
      env:encodingStyle="http://www.w3.org/2001/06/
      soap-encoding" xmlns:m="http://www.wire-
      man.com/services/stockquotes">
        <symbol>PSFT</symbol>
      </m:getStockPrice>
  </env:Body>
<env:Envelope>
```

Example 1–2 shows what the response might look like:

EXAMPLE 1–2 Example of SOAP response

```
<env:Envelope xmlns:env="http://www.w3.org/2001/06/
soap-envelope">
     <env:Body>
       <m:getStockPriceResponse
       env:encodingStyle="http://www.w3.org/2001/06/
       soap-encoding" xmlns:m="http://www.wire-
       man.com/services/stockquotes">
       <price>45.89</price>
       </m:getStockPriceResponse>
     </env:Body>
</env:Envelope>
```

These examples will have to hold you until the next chapter, when we dive headfirst into the details of SOAP. The rest of this chapter covers something more important: SOAP's place in the universe—why it exists and why you should care. Here's a preview: Many people think SOAP is the killer app of XML.

Web Services and Internet 3.0

SOAP exists because of an idea called Web services. Web services are new, and there aren't a whole lot of them out there right now. However, they're growing in number daily and have the same potential for explosion that Web pages had back in 1996 (maybe even greater). To get a strong idea of what Web services are, and why they're part of the next phase of the Internet, it's useful to cover a bit of Internet history to get some context.

A Brief History of the Internet

The Internet began as an American military experiment called ARPANET, whose goal was to build an interconnected computer network that could continue to function even if some nodes (that is, some computers) were destroyed or rendered inoperable by, say, a nuclear strike. Clearly, this experiment worked (without having to test exactly what effect a nuclear explosion would have), and ARPANET grew until it became known as the Internet. Most serious geeks knew about it and started playing with something called email, even though everyone at the time knew that phones were more convenient. Some folks have called this Internet 1.0.

Then in 1991, a guy called Tim Berners-Lee came up with a way for Swiss physicists to post their scientific papers on this Internet so they could read each other's papers easily. This idea caught on quickly and bloomed into the World Wide Web. Initially, the Web was used for people to communicate with each other, sharing such things as scientific papers, personal Web sites, marketing sites for companies, and pornography. In the beginning, the Web was mainly a static environment used mostly for person-to-person communication.

As more serious developers started learning about the Web and a new technology called Common Gateway Interface (CGI), they were able to create programs that allowed people to actually accomplish some things over the Web, such as buying books, reserving airline tickets, and transferring money across bank accounts. In this fashion, a large portion of the Web became devoted to people-machine communication and interaction. People interacted with software programs in order to accomplish things. This phase has been called Internet 2.0.

Many people think the next step in using the Internet will involve software applications communicating with each other over the Internet. These programs will use each other's components, modules, and methods in order to accomplish their tasks. For example, you could write a program in Java that does something, but your program needs to get some information that lives on another machine, a remote computer. Your Java app must be able to communicate with this remote machine in order to get its work done. It must be able to ask that computer for the data it needs, and be able to receive and understand that data. The remote machine must be able to listen for your Java app's cry for help, process the request, and return the information in such a way that your Java program can actually read it.

This next use of the Internet that focuses on machine-machine communication has been called Internet 3.0.

So What's a Web Service?

A Web service is the name for a method or function that is available for other applications to access over the Internet. To use a classic example, say that you have a program that needs to find out the latest stock price for a certain company, and that information lives on another computer. This remote computer has been configured in such a way that if you send it a request for a stock price, it will respond with that company's current price. In this case, the remote computer is hosting a *Web service*. It's just a method or function that can be accessed by other programs over the Web.

Another way to look at it: When people want some information, they look for certain Web pages and get that information in HTML form. When applications want information, they look for certain Web services and get that information by requesting it from another computer.

People receive Web pages in the form of Hypertext Markup Language (HTML). Computers receive information from Web services in the form of SOAP. SOAP is HTML for computer-computer interaction over the Web.

The goal of Web services is a seamless integration of services across the hardware and software barriers that exist on the Internet. In this system, much of the Internet could become repackaging of other bits and pieces out there.

MONEY AND WEB SERVICES

Why would you bother to write a Web service? The story to get developers such as yourself onto the Web services wagon is that you could write a Web service, expose it to the world, and then charge people who used your Web service, either on a per-use basis or subscription basis. It's certainly an appealing idea: Write something brilliant, even a small thing, and people will flock to you to use your program and drive truckloads of cash to your front door. This has not actually happened yet, but honestly, the potential is there. The next few years will be interesting.

EVOLUTION FROM SOFTWARE TO SERVICES

Right now, the idea of software is that of a discrete process. A consumer buys a shrink-wrapped package with a manual and a CD. They install the CD's program on their machine, and it runs without anyone else on the planet knowing about it. Then the person usually "loans" the CD to someone who asks nicely.

In the Web services view of the world, this process disappears. Instead, you buy access to a Web service for a certain amount of time. For example, instead of buying Word at the store, you'll buy the access rights from Microsoft for, say, a year. You download some components from the Microsoft Web site, but otherwise, your Word program mostly lives on some server at Microsoft. If Word needs to be updated, Microsoft simply upgrades the program on their server, and your program is updated without your even being aware of it. This upgrade is free for you—it's part of the subscription price. After a year, you must renew your subscription.

Notice you don't have a CD to loan to anyone else. Part of the push for Web services is that they will cut down substantially on software piracy (at least for a while, anyway). With less piracy, more people will actually have to buy software, and software companies will make more money.

Though this probably rankles some of you, this has aspects of fairness to it—you pay for what you use. Most of us more or less adhere to the philosophy of using something for free if you're using it to learn, but paying for it once you're using the software in a way that makes money for you.

And this is one big reason why Microsoft is putting so much of their weight behind Web services and making it easy for developers (and themselves) to create Web services: In the long run, they think they will make more money.

REQUIREMENTS FOR WEB SERVICES

Initially, a lot of people will be experimenting with creating their own Web services, and many of those services will break from time to time. However, if you want your Web service to be used by anyone who will actually pay money for it, there are some things you must remember. Your Web service:

- Must be 100% reliable. It must always work, and always work in the same way.
- Can also use other Web services, which means that everything must be working or a whole chain of services could go down.
- Must be extremely available—that is, highly scalable and always on.
- Must be able to handle unexpected inputs (usually returning a fault is adequate).
- Must not affect the availability of any other Web service, even if those Web services share common components.
- Must be secured so that only authorized systems and users can use it.

That's a high-level look at what will be required of Web services in order to become used and (hopefully) profitable.

From a more granular point of view, what do Web services need in order to be able to communicate with each other and announce themselves to the world? Here's a list of some other requirements. We'll go into more detail about these later (actually, the whole book is devoted to understanding how the following requirements are implemented, so don't worry if the list below isn't 100% clear; it will be).

- A standard way to represent data, so the services know what to look for.
- A common, extensible message format.
- A common, extensible service description language.
- A way to discover services located on a particular Web site.
- A way to discover service providers.

SOME CONCERNS ABOUT WEB SERVICES

Famed software interface guy Bruce "Tog" Tognazinni recently exposed a potential abuse of Web services. He signed up with a digital TV recording service (ReplayTV), and one of the reasons he signed up was because he could record TV without the commercials. He paid the subscription price and received the service. Partway into the year he signed up for, the company changed its service, and he could no longer record without commercials. Essentially, he paid for a service that was now significantly less valuable to him, and there was nothing he could do about it.

ReplayTV has since changed their policy and reverted back to their original functionality, but this raises a legitimate concern: How well do you trust the company that is providing a Web service? In an exaggerated example, suppose you're using a Microsoft Web service to use Word, and one day they decide they don't like Word anymore and you find the only thing the program does is run Tetris.

As with many other aspects of Web services, we'll have to see how this issue plays itself out. I can already picture attorneys wringing their hands in happy anticipation of conflict.

FINDING WEB SERVICES

We'll cover this in more detail later, but much work has been done to define exactly how someone can locate a Web service they need, how they can find out what sort of input parameters that Web service needs, and how to structure those parameters. The current plan is for all Web services to register in a big list called the Universal Discovery, Description and Integration Registry (UDDI Registry). Inside this registry you'll find all the information you need to connect to and interact with a particular Web service. We'll cover this in more detail in Chapter 6, when we cover UDDI.

Once you find the Web service you want to use, your application will also have to know what sort of information to pass to this Web service. A whole new language called, appropriately, Web Services Description Language (WSDL) is being developed that spells out exactly what sort of information a Web service needs in order to work.

WEB SERVICES AND RPC

The request-response form of communication between a local computer and a remote one is often called a Remote Procedure Call (RPC), because it involves a program invoking a method, or function, that lives on a remote computer. RPC is not new—people have been doing it for about 20 years in one form or another. Sun Microsystems is usually given credit for being the first to create a generic way for applications to call methods on remote machines.

This method of software applications talking to each other over the Internet, machine-to-machine communication, will likely be the next big use of the Web, and may surpass all others in significance. Will it actually happen? Probably—many developers are excited by the idea, and incidentally, Microsoft has bet the company's future that it will.

This kind of system is also known as "distributed." That is, the system is distributed over several computers. It could be said that part of your application lives in a separate place (even though you can also say that your application is simply calling another application). In any case, this is known as a distributed architecture.

A view of how this works is illustrated in Figure 1–1.

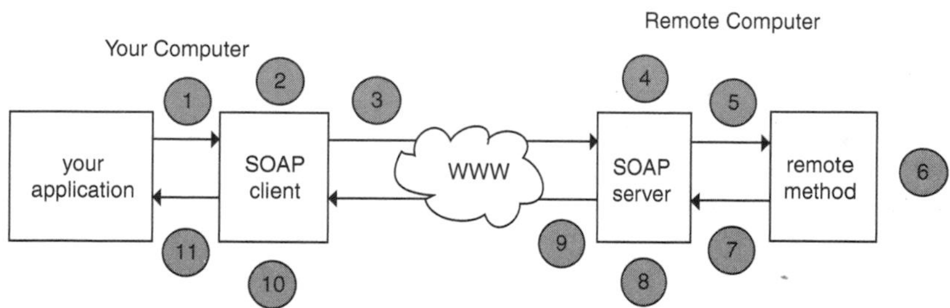

FIGURE 1–1 A Web service using SOAP

In this scenario, your application wants some information that lives on a remote computer somewhere.

1. Your application sends out a request for data, and the first stop on its journey is the SOAP client (which might also live on your computer).
2. This SOAP client takes in the request for data and translates the parameters into a SOAP message, like we saw at the beginning of the chapter.
3. The client then sends this SOAP message on its way to the remote computer, which has a SOAP server running at all times, listening for incoming SOAP messages.

4. The job of this SOAP server is to listen for SOAP messages, take the input data in those SOAP messages, and translate it into something the remote method can understand.
5. It then passes the input data to the remote method.
6. The method does its thing and comes up with some data.
7. This data is given back to the SOAP server.
8. The SOAP server then acts as a SOAP client, in that it takes the returned data and turns it back into SOAP.
9. It then sends this response back to the original SOAP client on your computer.
10. Your SOAP client then translates the SOAP data into something your application can understand.
11. And finally, your application gets the data it needs in a form it can understand.

A vital facet of Web services is that it doesn't matter what platform the requesting or responding computer is. It could be a Mac calling a method on a Linux box, or a Palm requesting something from a Windows machine. Not only do Web services not care about platforms, they don't even know. This is like the Web: When you download a Web page, do you know what kind of server that it came from? Not without doing a little research. And really, you don't care—you just want your Web page. Web services have a similar goal and so must be platform-independent.

Web services take this concept one step further—they don't even care what language the remote methods are in. C# can talk to Perl, which can talk to Python, which can talk to PHP, which can talk to a really fast guy with an abacus. It doesn't matter. The only thing these programs need to have in common is their ability to read and write SOAP messages. Some of you may remember when people were trying to make a new language called Esperanto, a language that everyone on the planet would learn to speak and read so everyone would be able to talk to each other. It failed miserably. Fortunately, computers are more malleable than people, and we can force computers to all speak the same language, and that language can be SOAP.

TRANSPARENCY AND PLUMBING

A Web service using SOAP is an example of a loosely connected application. Connections are said to be tight or loose. The looser the connection is, the less one application knows about the other. Web services are very loose—methods only know what other methods do, not what platform they're on or even what language they're written in. Loose connections generally go through an intermediate step. In the case of Web services, SOAP is this intermediate step.

The details of the connections between applications are known as plumbing. The tighter a connection, the more you, the programmer, must know about plumbing. Plumbing is usually a pain, and most developers avoid it if possible. That may be one reason why connections have become looser and looser over the years: No one wants to program plumbing.

Looser connections generally provide more flexibility for developers.

SUPPORT FOR WEB SERVICES

Companies like Microsoft, Oracle, IBM, Hewlett-Packard and Sun are running to create their own Web services. In fact, that's what Microsoft's HailStorm project is: a bunch of Web services.

Part of the Web services plan is for people never to install software on their computers, but instead just access the programs over the Internet. For now, "Web services" just means invoking methods over the Internet: My computer makes your computer run a little program for me and return the results.

You can create Web services right now. You don't need to wait for anyone, including Microsoft. This is important: .NET is not necessary to create a fully functional Web service. Some .NET tools (like Visual Studio.NET) are designed to make it easy to create Web services, but that's it—no one, not you or anyone, has to go through Microsoft to create or use Web services.

In general, it's expected that a number of individual developers will slowly start experimenting and creating their own Web services until some sort of critical mass is reached. At that point, an explosion of Web services is expected to arise as businesses eventually decide that Web services are a solid technology to invest IT capital in.

For clarification, it's important to note that Java and C# compile code into bytecode that's understood as native language by a virtual (imaginary) machine. Visual Basic, similarly, compiles into pseudocode that an interpreter executes. C++ compiles into native machine language. In this sense, C++ does not have a runtime environment other than the operating system itself.

Intermediate Language

A huge part of the .NET program is the creation of a common intermediate language. What does this mean? First, an intermediate language is the computer-friendly language your source code is compiled into. When you compile a program using a .NET compiler (like the upcoming Visual Studio.NET), your source code is compiled into a language called Microsoft Intermediate Language (IL). .NET compilers compile all languages into this Intermediate Language, and it tacks on a little metadata as well. Figure 1–2 illustrates this:

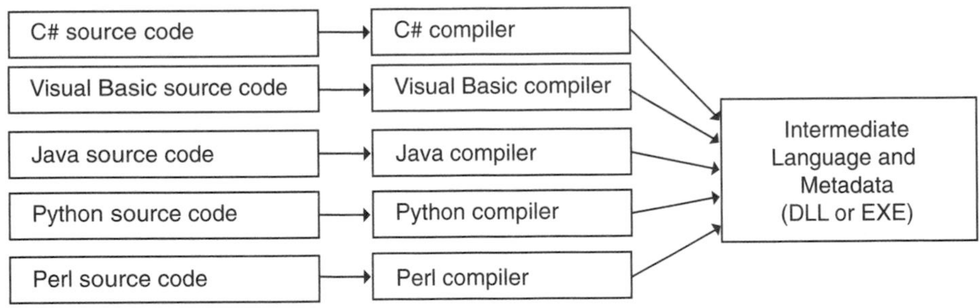

FIGURE 1–2 Compiling source code into a common intermediate language

New languages are being added to this list all the time. At last count, there are 18 languages that can be compiled into IL, and by the time you read this, hopefully a few dozen more.

How do you get a hold of one of these compilers for your language of choice? A number of vendors are creating .NET-aware compilers, so by now, the most common languages have several .NET-aware compilers available.

As you can see from Figure 1–2, the IL files are given the extension DLL or EXE. This is just like a COM (Component Object Model) binary, but internally, the two are nothing alike.

METADATA AND ASSEMBLIES

When some source code is compiled into IL, a .NET-aware compiler does a little bit more than just a translation into IL. It also creates some metadata, or data about the compiled program. This metadata describes in exhaustive detail all of the types of data that are in your code, including base classes, methods, properties, and events. You don't have to worry about creating this metadata yourself—a .NET-aware compiler will do it for you.

When a .NET compiler translates your source code into IL and creates some metadata, this creates something called an *assembly*. We won't be going into more detail here about assemblies.

For those of you with experience in Windows programming, you know about a metadata language called IDL, which sometimes was present and sometimes wasn't. This ambiguity isn't part of .NET—you must have metadata. In fact, you can't help it, since the compiler always creates it.

Common Language Runtime

Since all .NET source code is compiled into a single intermediate language, IL, it should only require a single runtime to execute anything in that intermediate language, right? That is, since a runtime can only run a certain kind of compiled code, if you compile different languages into that same compiled code, then a runtime could execute all of them. You would have a single runtime that could execute compiled code from multiple languages. In fact, the runtime wouldn't even care if the compiled code started out as C#, Eiffel, or COBOL. The runtime just sees the IL and runs that. This runtime is called the Common Language Runtime (CLR), and it's a hugely important part of .NET.

The CLR basically has two components: an engine and a base class library.

CLR ENGINE

One component of the CLR is the actual execution engine (also known as mscoree.dll). This engine examines the metadata of the assembly, makes sure everything is where it should be, and then compiles the IL instructions into something that's platform-specific (for example, into something that's Windows-based or UNIX-based), which is then finally executed.

BASE CLASS LIBRARY

The CLR's base class library essentially contains all the rules for all allowable kinds of data types. In other words, every data type that is in any compiled IL file has to have some equivalent in the base class library. A language can't have any old data type it wants and then expect the CLR to be able to run it. .NET languages have to follow certain rules, and the base class library contains most of those rules. That means that some languages will have to be tweaked slightly in order for them to compile into IL properly. However, this isn't expected to be much of a problem—the base class library has many, many types in it, so whatever language you're working in, chances are you're fine.

Common Type System (CTS)

The CTS describes all of the data types that the CLR can understand. That is, since the Common Language Runtime isn't all-knowing and can only understand a limited number of data types, the CTS is needed to define exactly what types the CLR understands. In addition, it also defines how those types interact with each other and how they should appear in the metadata.

To get a more thorough understanding of what this actually means, let's look at some broad categories of data types that are part of the CTS. These include:

- Class types: The notion of a "class" is necessary for any object-oriented programming, so it's logical that classes are supported by the CTS. A class is composed of any number of methods, properties, and events.
- Structure types: Structures are also supported by the CTS.

- Interface types: Interfaces are collections of methods, properties, and event descriptions—they're more abstract than classes.
- Type members: A member is either a method, a property, a field, or an event.
- Enumeration types: An enumeration allows you to create a list of variables that can exist under a single name.
- Delegate types: For those of you from the C world, this is the equivalent of a type-safe C style function pointer.
- Intrinsic data types: These data types are different forms of integers, strings, Booleans, objects, decimal numbers, and so on.

Common Language Specification

Different computer languages can have different levels of functionality. Some will let you overload operators or will support unsigned data types, while others will not. However, in order for the IL and Common Language Runtime to work, all languages must share at least a certain subset of functionality. The purpose of the Common Language Specification is to define a set of explicit rules that provides a baseline for all languages that wish to be .NET-aware.

Rules of the CLS include how to represent text strings, how to use static types, how enumerations are represented, and so on.

.NET and SOAP

So .NET involves a common intermediate language and a common language runtime (among some other things). What does this have to do with SOAP?

Well, one thing we didn't cover is how to actually create Web services in your .NET-aware language. As it turns out, this is amazingly easy in most languages. In some cases, all you have to do is add a single line of code:

```
[WebMethod]
your method code
```

When you add this code, you automatically create a method that is capable of acting as a Web service. Well, the compiler and the runtime actually make your method a Web service. Now this Web service can read and write SOAP messages. Microsoft decided to use SOAP as their way of communicating between Web services. For example, if you want your .NET web services to communicate, they must communicate via SOAP messages. Microsoft has decided that SOAP is the glue that will hold Web services together.

NOTE .NET and HailStorm

You may have heard about HailStorm but not completely understood it. HailStorm is a bunch of Web services that Microsoft is developing. These Web services have different functions, like keeping track of calendar events, schedules, contacts, document storage, email and voicemail inboxes, and so on. Microsoft would like you to keep all of your important information with them, and that you would communicate with this information via Web services. The fact you're using a Web service shouldn't be part of the experience, though.

The upshot of the above is that if you only plan to use Microsoft's tools, you don't really need to know anything about SOAP—Microsoft will take care of it for you. While this will save you time, you'll be stuck in case anything goes wrong, because you won't know enough to debug anything. Besides, how much do you trust any software vendor to know what's best for you? Learning SOAP gives you another tool in your programming tool chest, and as most of us know, the more tools we have, the better off we usually are.

Recap

.NET is an aggregation of several things, but its most interesting feature is the ability to write programs in any language. Since they're all compiled into the same intermediate language, these programs can now talk to each other as Web services, and it doesn't matter what language they were written in, where the applications are, or what platform they're on.

2

Basic SOAP

IN THIS CHAPTER

- What Is SOAP?
- What SOAP Can and Can't Do
- Advantages and Disadvantages
- Serializing and SOAP
- Basic SOAP Structure

SOAP is a communication protocol that uses established Web technologies—XML and HTTP—to achieve something entirely new: true interoperability among applications on any computer platform and written in any language over the Internet. The demand for something like SOAP has existed for some time now. In fact, one of the reasons XML was invented was that it would facilitate an application like SOAP. While it's possible you'll never have to write a line of SOAP in your life, it's important to understand what it can do and what its limitations are.

What Is SOAP?

SOAP is a data format—it's a way to represent data as text. If you want to send a remote method some input parameters that include an integer, a string, and an array, the SOAP specification tells you what the text in the SOAP message should look like. SOAP exists only as a specification. SOAP is just a document put together by some people who thought, "Hey! This is a pretty good idea." It's up to brilliant programmers like yourself to actually write the applications that can read, write, and send SOAP messages.

Overview

SOAP is a flavor of XML, which means that everything in SOAP is 100% XML.

SOAP = XML

The major goal of SOAP is to be able to invoke remote procedure calls over the Web. Remember remote procedure calls from the last chapter? They're also known as RPCs. Every SOAP document contains XML and nothing but. SOAP is a way to communicate input parameters, which can be integers, multidimensional arrays, structures, strings, and so on, as XML.

SOAP = XML + RPC

Therefore, a SOAP document is an XML document designed to invoke methods on remote computers. Great—how does it get from a computer that needs the method run to the computer that actually has the method? The answer is, any way you want. The original design of SOAP demanded that HTTP be used to transmit SOAP messages, but the latest round of the specification opened it up to any protocol, such as FTP or SMTP. However, we'll only be looking at SOAP over HTTP, since that's how most of the world will be moving SOAP around.

SOAP = XML + RPC + HTTP

Goals of SOAP

Parts of SOAP can seem strange if you don't know why the inventors made the decisions they did. Let's look at some of the goals of SOAP—these are the things that were running around in the heads of the people who sat down and decided what this SOAP thing should be.

SIMPLICITY AND EXTENSIBILITY

Their first goal was "simplicity and extensibility." This doesn't sound earth shattering, but it's pretty important. Let's look at the simplicity first.

The inventors wanted SOAP to be easy to learn. The specific goal was that someone who only knew HTML would be able to look at a SOAP message and not only figure out what was going on, but be able to fix the easier problems. SOAP is also intended to be easy to implement. It shouldn't take a genius to program an application that makes use of SOAP.

SOAP also needed to be extensible. Extensible means, "You can make up your own tags." SOAP is extensible because the inventors knew they couldn't predict the future and didn't want to try. They wanted SOAP to solve a few problems really well, but they left the specification open enough so that it could be added to when problems arose or people wanted new features. It was important to be able to make these changes without having to rewrite the entire specification. They decided to make their SOAP house out of wood, so rooms could be added without having to rebuild the whole house, as opposed to forming it from a single piece of plastic. Because SOAP is extensible, it can grow and problems can be solved as they become clearer, without severely impacting existing applications.

REMOTE PROCEDURE CALLS

SOAP has to be able to efficiently handle remote procedure calls. These calls involve transient documents (the requests and responses are never actually saved) that trigger responses on remote hosts. SOAP must be able to handle all sorts of input parameters and responses as well. The inventors decided to minimize the number of times remote computers had to talk to each other in order to communicate. They ended up with a simple request-response model. That is, your application asks the remote method for something, the remote method responds, and the two of you forget each other's existence.

This request-response model meshed perfectly with HTTP: After all, it's how the Web works. Here are the three steps:

1. Request
2. Response
3. Amnesia

This type of connection is also called *stateless*, since the state of neither the client nor the server is maintained past the initial response.

SOLVE ISSUES WITH CURRENT DISTRIBUTED ARCHITECTURES

There are systems out there that do what SOAP does, such as DCOM, RMI, and CORBA (see Appendix C for details). However, these systems are much harder to work with, might run on proprietary networks, and are more expensive to install. While these systems have more features than SOAP, the inventors decided that SOAP would solve just a few of those issues, but solve them well. Other technologies would have to solve what SOAP would ignore (for example, SOAP doesn't touch security or garbage collection).

INTEROPERABILITY

Interoperability (frequently shortened to *interop*) is the ability of an application to interact with very different systems. One of SOAP's goals is to facilitate a purely platform-agnostic interoperability among applications. That is, SOAP doesn't care if the machine is a Windows machine, a Linux PDA, or an Apple iBook. In fact, there's no way for it to know. SOAP's nonspecificity is vital because SOAP is intended for use over the Internet, and you never know what someone has installed as their server machine: For all you know, you're connecting to an Amiga.

OPEN TO ALL

If there was any discussion about SOAP belonging to a single company, the idea was squashed early. SOAP was designed to be an open standard that no one could own. Even Microsoft, who helped write SOAP, agreed to this. Why? Most likely because of a wariness many developers have of all things with the Microsoft label; an open standard would be much more quickly adopted than a Microsoft-only one. Besides, Dave Winer, a seriously vocal advocate of open standards, was part of the team that wrote SOAP.

As it stands, no one owns SOAP, not even Microsoft.

A Short History of SOAP

Work on SOAP started way back in 1997, back when many people were just discovering how image rollovers worked. People from Microsoft, DevelopMentor (a spinoff of Lucent), and Userland Software (a small software company) sat down and started figuring out what this SOAP thing should be.

It was quickly apparent that XML would be a logical choice. Structured data was becoming a de facto standard of communication, and XML was the best, most accessible structured-data format out there. XML also offered a rich, extensible structure.

One of the biggest challenges in creating SOAP was deciding which different kinds of data (that is, data types) would be represented. What would an array look like? A structure? An array of structures? The inventors started creating their own system, but then noticed something called XML Data. This turned into XML Schema, and it solved most of the data-typing problems they were having except the array one. Not overeager to reinvent the wheel, they decided that XML Schema would be the base for all of the data typing in SOAP. If there was any place that XML Schema did not solve a data-typing problem, the SOAP inventors made something up.

A year later, in 1998, SOAP was ready to be released to the world. However, internal conflicts at Microsoft continually delayed the project. Around this time, SOAP co-inventor Dave Winer decided to stop waiting and wrote his own stripped-

SECURITY

There is nothing in the SOAP specification that defines how a SOAP message could be secure. However, since SOAP can travel over HTTP, it is often assumed that SOAP can travel via Secure Sockets Layer (SSL). It is possible to include security information by placing XML Signature data in the SOAP header (see Chapter 7 for more on this).

GARBAGE COLLECTION

SOAP doesn't concern itself with clearing up objects that are no longer needed and are taking up valuable memory space. Garbage collection is left to the applications that call SOAP into action, not to SOAP itself.

BOXCARING

Boxcaring involves placing multiple method invocations in a single message, like a string of boxcars in a train. SOAP can only request one method at a time. There's no way to enclose multiple method invocations into a single SOAP message.

OBJECTS BY REFERENCE

All the data in a SOAP message must actually be explicitly spelled out in the SOAP message. It's not possible to have code in a SOAP message that refers, or points, to some external data source (thus, an object by reference). It's possible that this will be included in a future version of SOAP, but not yet.

REMOTE OBJECT ACTIVATION

Distributed object systems are designed to hold tons of long-lived objects. However, it doesn't make sense for objects to be alive and taking up memory all the time. They should only be awake when they're needed. Waking up objects is known as activation. When you wake up an object on another computer, this is known as remote object activation, and it's a common occurrence in the programming world. However, there is nothing in SOAP that explicitly activates an object. It's up to the receiving host to do any necessary object activation.

Advantages and Disadvantages

Creating any new technology always involves trade-offs. For every choice, there is usually good news and bad news, and the choices made when creating SOAP are no different.

Advantages

Clearly, the inventors of SOAP thought its advantages heavily outweighed its disadvantages. Here are some of them.

BUILT ON OPEN TECHNOLOGIES

The fact that SOAP is open to the world and belongs to no one solves several problems. First, developers are more likely to trust and adopt open standards than something that's proprietary. Also, open standards are exposed, which means that more people can pick them apart and come up with solutions. When you have thousands of brains trying to solve a problem, you often get some pretty good answers.

Also, since SOAP is built on XML and XML Schema, its inventors didn't have to come up with everything themselves. They were able to stand on the shoulders of giants, as it were, and apply the work that other people had done.

CAN MOVE OVER HTTP

Currently, HTTP networks are nearly ubiquitous—almost every company and many homes have networks where HTTP flows freely. This means that SOAP can travel over existing networks—no one has to build anything new. This makes life easier for developers, since most of us don't enjoy writing plumbing code.

SOAP WILL WORK RIGHT NOW

You don't have to wait for any company to come out with any product to start using SOAP—you can start now, and many people already have. There are dozens of Web services working right now that use SOAP to communicate.

ENCOURAGES LOOSELY COUPLED APPLICATIONS

Loosely coupled applications make your life easier. Loosely coupled means that you don't have to know much about what you're connecting to. An example of a loosely coupled application is, well, this book. I don't know anything about you (except that you make wise choices when purchasing books, and are undoubtedly very good-looking), and you don't know much about me. But I'm able to communicate with you anyway. That's loosely coupled. If everyone on the planet spoke their own individual language, I'd have to speak to each of my readers individually, and know a lot about each individual. In that case, the application would be tightly coupled.

SOAP doesn't care about the receiver of a SOAP message. It's up to the receiver to parse through and understand a SOAP message. Loose coupling allows for much more flexibility in communication. It usually involves more work on the receiving end to understand the message, but the gains in ease of programming and flexibility are usually worth it.

Disadvantages

Of course, SOAP is not perfect. All strengths can be weaknesses and vice versa, depending on your perspective. Here are some of the weaknesses people see in SOAP.

HTTP IS SLOW

HTTP is not the speediest protocol out there. It became popular mostly because it was relatively easy to implement, not because it was the world's best protocol. SOAP doesn't have to travel over HTTP, but it's accepted that the vast majority of SOAP traffic will go over HTTP, so concerns with HTTP definitely concern SOAP.

HTTP IS STATELESS

Stateless refers to the way applications interact over HTTP. We've seen this before:

1. Request
2. Respond
3. Amnesia

If more connections are required, the requesting application must reintroduce itself as if it had never connected to the other application. While this is helpful in freeing up memory quickly, it's hard to keep track of what a user does over the course of several Web pages, since there's no way to remember what they did before. That's why people started using cookies to keep track of users. Keeping track like this is known as maintaining the state of a connection. The amnesia step is bypassed.

Some people say this statelessness is a good thing: After all, an application shouldn't have to call a Web service many times in a row. Others see it as a weakness. If a situation arises where state is important to maintain, the developer has to come up with some kind of workaround (it turns out you can use the SOAP Header for this, but we'll cover that later).

UNLIMITED NUMBER OF DATA TYPE SCHEMAS

SOAP is based on XML Schema to define its data types such as integers, strings, and such. However, you don't have to use SOAP's encoding scheme: You can use any data-type encoding scheme you want. SOAP processors are only required to know XML Schema and SOAP's own encoding, so there's no guarantee that if you use some obscure encoding mechanism, the SOAP receiver will be able to understand. Thus, most people will probably stick to SOAP's encoding rules.

However, this openness to any data schema could turn out to be problematic—too many schemas could result in confusion. Will this really become a problem? Who knows? It doesn't seem like it would, but the technology world has proven to be a bit unpredictable.

SERIALIZATION BY VALUE, NOT BY REFERENCE

We've touched on this before. All the data that exists in a SOAP message must be physically present within that SOAP message. There's no way that you can point to an external data source and say, "Use this." The data has to be in the SOAP message itself. This can be clunky, as it's sometimes easier to not have to serialize everything into a SOAP message. It's generally expected that this will change with future versions of SOAP.

Serializing and SOAP

Those of you straight from the Web development world may be a little fuzzy on serialization. Therefore we'll spend a few paragraphs examining exactly what this serialization thing is.

Most computer languages have ways to specify whether a certain variable is a number, string, Boolean, and so on. This is known as data typing: It specifies what type of data a variable is. Each language stores this typing information internally in a certain way. A Java program's internal representation of a string looks different than a Python representation of a string. Nevertheless, if you want your Java application to talk to the Python application, you have three choices:

1. Alter your internal representation of a string to match Python's.
2. Alter the Python program to understand Java's internal representation.
3. Create an intermediate step. Your Java application spits out something neutral, say plain text, which Python can read easily. Python can then take that text and transform it into something Python understands as data types.

You probably guessed that step 3 is what SOAP does. The process where Java translates its internal representation of a string into something neutral (plain text) is known as serialization. Serialization is translation of something into something else, usually so that it will be understood by another application. Often, serialization involves turning something into plain text. Taking that plain text and creating a native internal representation is known as deserialization—this is what the Python application in our example would have to do.

As a side note, step 3 is an example of a loosely coupled application. Steps 1 and 2 are tightly coupled.

Basic SOAP Structure

All SOAP messages can have three parts: an envelope that contains the entire SOAP message, an optional header that contains metadata, and the body, which contains the actual data being transmitted, including the name of the method to be invoked and the input parameters.

Figure 2–1 illustrates the basic structure of a SOAP message.

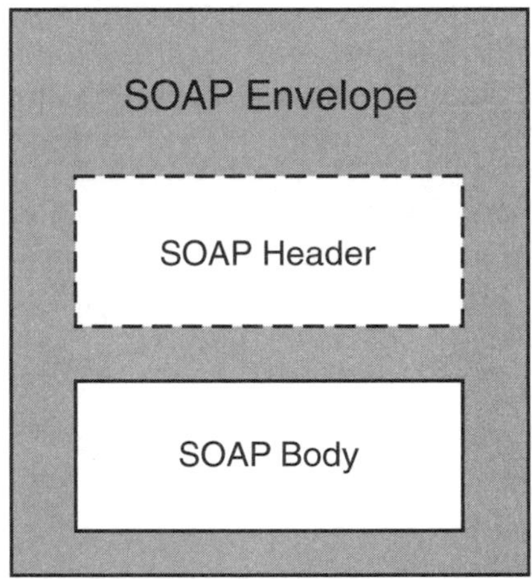

FIGURE 2–1 Basic SOAP message structure

Let's look at these parts in more detail.

SOAP Envelope

All SOAP messages must have an Envelope element (and yes, it has to be capitalized). The Envelope element must also have a namespace that defines which version of SOAP is being used.

```
<env:Envelope
  xmlns:env="http://www.w3.org/2001/06/soap-envelope">
    ... rest of SOAP message ...
</env:Envelope>
```

The namespace is necessary. As I'm writing this, many people have already implemented SOAP 1.1, whose namespace looks a little different:

```
<SOAP-ENV:Envelope
  xmlns:SOAP-ENV="http://schemas.xmlsoap.org/soap/envelope">
    ... rest of SOAP message ...
</SOAP-ENV:Envelope>
```

Remember that the prefixes of namespaces (env and SOAP-ENV in these examples) don't matter. The only thing the SOAP receiver cares about is the URI section of the namespace.

You should note that SOAP messages cannot contain DTDs, references to DTDs, or processing instructions.

SOAP Header

The header section of a SOAP message is optional. Its purpose in life is to provide additional information or instructions for the SOAP processor. Why would you bother with such a thing? Here are some examples of information a header could provide:

- Transactions
- Payments
- Definitions of elements referred to in the SOAP body
- Authentication
- Actors (we'll get to this)

Using information in the header is one way to get around the statelessness of HTTP. For example, you could state information, such as a user ID, in the SOAP Header.

Information in the header is only good for out-of-band information that modifies the SOAP request in some way, or passes nonvital information.

If a header is in your SOAP message, it must be the first child element in the envelope. Header information is wrapped by a Header element like so:

```
<env:Envelope
  xmlns:env="http://www.w3.org/2001/06/soap-envelope">
  <env:Header>
      <shel:transaction
      xmlns:shel="http://www.shelleybiotech.com/medserv/">
      7
      </shel:transaction>
  </env:Header>
  … rest of SOAP message, including SOAP body …
</env:Envelope>
```

How the Code Works

Notice that the Header element is capitalized: `<env:Header>`. Our header has one child element: `<shel:transaction>`. This child element is scoped to its own namespace, which is actually necessary. All immediate child elements of the SOAP Header must be namespace-qualified.

As it is right now, the SOAP processor may or may not understand what this header information means. If it doesn't, the header will be ignored. But what if this transaction information was really important? If it's necessary that the SOAP processor understand this information, you can add a mustUnderstand attribute like so:

```
<shel:transaction
xmlns:shel="http://www.shelleybiotech.com/medserv/"
mustUnderstand="1">
  7
</shel:transaction>
```

How the Code Works

The mustUnderstand attribute can have a value of 0 or 1, with 0 being the default. If you use mustUnderstand="1", this tells the SOAP processor that if it doesn't know what to do with the transaction information, then don't bother with the rest of the SOAP message. In this case, the SOAP processor would return a special fault SOAP message.

You can have as many elements as you want in the header, and as many child elements as you want.

SOAP ACTORS

We've been working on the assumption that there are two computers involved in our distributed system: a requesting machine and a receiving machine. In the real world, there are usually several intermediate machines that accept the SOAP message and move it along its path until it reaches its ultimate destination. These intermediate machines are called *SOAP nodes*. The SOAP message travels a path among these SOAP nodes until it reaches its ultimate SOAP receiver. Figure 2–2 shows an example.

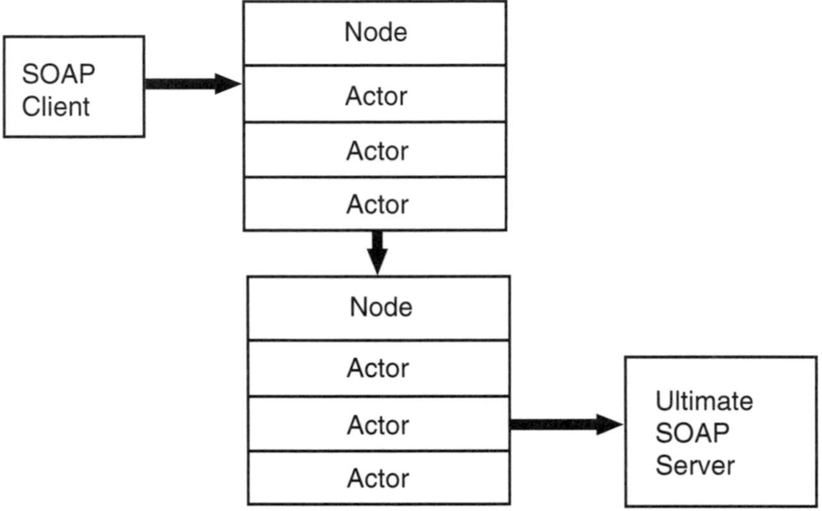

FIGURE 2–2 SOAP message moves along its message path through various SOAP nodes

One would expect that these SOAP nodes don't really do anything except forward the SOAP message to the next SOAP node. However, they may be more functional than that. It's possible to place some information in your SOAP header that needs to be processed in a certain way, and it doesn't matter whether the ultimate SOAP receiver does this processing or one of the SOAP nodes along the way does the processing. The SOAP node that can perform the processing is said to be an *actor*. Odd, huh? Hold onto your gray matter—it gets stranger.

A SOAP node can contain any number of actors. That is, if a SOAP node can run seven specific chunks of processing, it has seven SOAP actors. In other words, the SOAP node can play the role of seven different SOAP actors.

Actor role = SOAP node functionality

A specific chunk of functionality is not necessarily limited to a single computer. A chunk of processing, a bit of functionality, can be running on several different machines at once. For example, most of us probably have Word on our computers. Our computers share a piece of functionality. This situation can also exist in the SOAP world, which means that multiple SOAP nodes can play the role of the same actor.

So, what would the SOAP message code look like?

```
<env:Envelope
  xmlns:env="http://www.w3.org/2001/06/soap-envelope">
  <env:Header>
      <shel:transaction
      xmlns:shel="http://www.shelleybiotech.com/medserv/"
      env:Actor="http://somewhere.org/soap/actor/do_it">
              7
      </shel:transaction>
  </env:Header>
  ... rest of SOAP message, including SOAP body ...
</env:Envelope>
```

How the Code Works

I highlighted the attribute that alerts the SOAP node that this piece of header information is designed to be processed by a SOAP node, not the ultimate SOAP receiver. Any header block with the env:Actor attribute should be processed by the first appropriate actor it finds. A header block without the env:Actor attribute is meant to be processed by the ultimate SOAP receiver. Actors are identified by URIs. This particular SOAP message is looking for the actor with the label of "http://somewhere.org/soap/actor/do_it". The SOAP message doesn't care which SOAP node contains this actor, this bit of functionality.

When an actor sees a Header element that has its name, it processes that header block, and can either completely remove it from the SOAP message or insert its own header in its place. Actors do not forward header blocks intended for that actor.

There is a special actor known as "http://www.w3.org/2001/06/soap-envelope/actor/next". Use of this actor indicates that the SOAP header block is intended for the next SOAP node that processes the message.

That's our SOAP request. The SOAP processor receives this message, runs its method, and returns a SOAP response. What would this response look like?

RESPONSE

A response to our request for a patient's medical history could look something like Example 2–2.

EXAMPLE 2–2 SOAP Response

```
<env:Envelope
  xmlns:env="http://www.w3.org/2001/06/soap-
  envelope">
  1.<env:Body>
      2.<shel:getPatientHistoryResponse
      xmlns:shel="http://www.shelleybiotech.com/
      medserv"
      3.env:encodingStyle="http://www.w3.org/2001/
      06/soap-encoding">
          4.<history>perfectly healthy</history>
      </shel:getPatientHistoryResponse>
  </env:Body>
</env:Envelope>
```

How the Code Works

You can see that this looks almost exactly like the requesting SOAP message. There are important differences, though.

1. The Body element looks exactly the same.
2. Notice that this element contains the method name with "Response" added to the end. This is necessary: Every SOAP response message must contain the name of the method with "Response" tacked on the end of it. This is really the only way to tell that this is a response instead of a request (almost true: You could look at the HTTP header, but we'll save that for another chapter).
3. We're using SOAP's encoding style, just like the request message.
4. An actual medical history would probably be longer, but you get the idea.

Occasionally, of course, errors happen and the SOAP processor can't return the output of a method for some reason. When that happens, a SOAP fault message must be returned.

FAULTS

The third kind of SOAP message is the fault message, which is used to carry error or status information (usually error). Here's a quick look:

```
<env:Envelope xmlns:env="http://www.w3.org/2001/06/soap-
envelope">
    <env:Body>
      <env:Fault>
        ...fault information...
      </env:Fault>
    </env:Body>
</env:Envelope>
```

As with the Header and Body, the Fault element must be capitalized. Also, the Fault element must appear once and only once inside the SOAP Body: It isn't possible to have two Faults in a SOAP message.

Within the Fault tag, you can use four different elements:

- faultcode (must use)
- faultstring (must use)
- faultactor (optional)
- detail (sometimes optional; depends on the type of error)

FAULT CODES

Currently, there are only four types of faults that can be defined by SOAP. They are

- VersionMismatch
- MustUnderstand
- Client
- Server

VERSIONMISMATCH • This VersionMismatch fault code is used when an invalid envelope namespace is used. According to the SOAP 1.2 specification, the only valid namespace for the SOAP envelope is "http://www.w3.org/2001/06/soap-envelope". Any other namespace must cause an error. The most common cause of this error will probably be an application using the namespace from SOAP version 1.1: "http://schemas.xmlsoap.org/soap/envelope/".

MustUnderstand • In the case where a SOAP Header element contains a child element with a mustUnderstand="1" attribute, and the receiving SOAP processor is unable to process that header (that is, the Header doesn't understand), then a MustUnderstand fault message must be returned. For example, say this SOAP message was passed to a SOAP processor:

```
<env:Envelope xmlns:env="http://www.w3.org/2001/06/soap-
envelope">
    <env:Header>
      <w1:someData xmlns:w1="http://www.wire-man.com/ns/
      soap1/" env:mustUnderstand="1"/>
      <w2:someData xmlns:w2="http://www.wire-man.com/ns/
      soap2/" env:mustUnderstand="1"/>
    </env:Header>
    <env:Body>
      … body information …
    </env:Body>
</env:Envelope>
```

Notice that there are two header blocks that must be understood by the SOAP processor. If the SOAP server isn't able to understand those headers, it cannot continue processing the message, but must instead stop dead in its tracks and fire off a fault message to the requesting SOAP client.

```
<env:Envelope xmlns:env="http://www.w3.org/2001/06/soap-
envelope">
    <env:Body>
      <env:Fault>
        <faultcode>MustUnderstand</faultcode>
        <faultstring>One or more necessary headers were not
        understood</faultstring>
      </env:Fault>
    </env:Body>
</env:Envelope>
```

Client • If an incoming SOAP message from a SOAP client is incorrectly formed or is lacking enough information to be processed accurately (for example, no payment or authentication information), then the SOAP server must return a fault message with a Client fault code. This implies that the SOAP message should be changed in some way before being resent.

Server • If a SOAP message can't be processed because of problems with the SOAP processor and not the contents of the message, then a fault message with a Server fault code must be returned. For example, the SOAP server could be improperly programmed or need to contact another SOAP node that doesn't respond.

If an error occurs while processing a request, the SOAP HTTP server must issue a HTTP 500 "Internal Server Error" response and include the SOAP fault message.

EXTENDING FAULT CODES

Fault codes are designed to be extensible, which is fortunate since having only four types of errors isn't particularly useful. Here are a few examples of extended fault codes:

- Client.Authentication
- Client.Authentication.Expired
- MustUnderstand.Payment
- VersionMismatch.OldVersion

You can create your own extensions to the four generic fault codes. Generally, the values that occur later (in this example, "Expired" and "Payment") are more specific than the first values (for example, "Client" and "VersionMismatch").

FAULTSTRING

The faultstring is a human-readable explanation of the fault. It isn't intended to be processed, only displayed. There must be a faultstring element in every SOAP fault message. You saw a faultstring in action above, and here's another example:

```
<env:Envelope xmlns:env="http://www.w3.org/2001/06/soap-
envelope">
    <env:Body>
      <env:Fault>
        <faultcode>Client</faultcode>
        <faultstring>Authentication incomplete: must have
        username and password</faultstring>
      </env:Fault>
    </env:Body>
</env:Envelope>
```

FAULTACTOR

Since the SOAP message may be processed by any number of SOAP nodes along the way to the ultimate SOAP receiver, and any one of them may stop the message in its tracks and return a fault message, it can be useful to know which SOAP node (that is, which actor) saw the error.

```
<env:Envelope xmlns:env="http://www.w3.org/2001/06/soap-
envelope">
    <env:Body>
      <env:Fault>
        <faultcode>Client</faultcode>
        <faultstring>Authentication incomplete: must have
        username and password</faultstring>
        <faultactor>http://www.wire-man.com/soap/actor/
        145</faultactor>
      </env:Fault>
    </env:Body>
</env:Envelope>
```

This code describes that the SOAP node that was playing the role of http://www.wire-man.com/soap/actor/145 said there was a fault with the content of the SOAP message.

DETAIL

If the source of the error is in the SOAP message body, then information about that error is in the detail element. In fact, when the error is in the SOAP Body, the detail element must be present. Its purpose in life is to carry application-specific error information relating to the SOAP Body. It's so specific that it isn't allowed to contain any information about what happened in the header of the message, only the body of the SOAP message. If there is no detail element in a SOAP Fault, then it is safe to assume that the error did not occur in the SOAP Body.

```
<env:Envelope xmlns:env="http://www.w3.org/2001/06/soap-
envelope">
    <env:Body>
      <env:Fault>
        <faultcode>ServerClient</faultcode>
        <faultstring>Server Error</faultstring>
        <faultactor>http://www.wire-man.com/soap/actor/
        145</faultactor>
        <detail>
          <oops:faultDetails xmlns:oops="http://www.wire-
          man.com/soap/faults">
            <message>The server blew up. Boom!</message>
            <errorcode>002</errorcode>
          </oops:faultDetails>
        </detail>
      </env:Fault>
    </env:Body>
</env:Envelope>
```

Notice that the detail entry is namespace-qualified. All such entries must have a namespace qualification.

PLACING ERROR INFO IN HEADERS

To further add to the error information in a message, you can place more detailed error information in the SOAP Header, like so:

```
<env:Envelope xmlns:env="http://www.w3.org/2001/06/soap-
envelope" xmlns:oops="http://www.w3.org/2001/06/soap-
faults">
    <env:Header>
      <oops:didNotUnderstand attrName="w1:someData"
      xmlns:w1="http://www.wire-man.com/ns/soap1/"
      <oops:didNotUnderstand attrName="w2:someData"
      xmlns:w2="http://www.wire-man.com/ns/soap2/" />
    </env:Header>
    <env:Body>
      <env:Fault>
        <faultcode>MustUnderstand</faultcode>
```

```
        <faultstring>One or more necessary headers were not
understood</faultstring>
      </env:Fault>
    </env:Body>
</env:Envelope>
```

Recap

Well, that's how SOAP is put together. All SOAP messages encapsulate requests, responses, or faults. There's a chance that future versions will incorporate messaging (for Instant Messenger systems and such), but that hasn't happened as of this writing.

Now that we know how to put together a SOAP message, let's check out how to serialize our input parameters into SOAP-friendly XML.

3

SOAP Data Types: Encoding and XML Schema

IN THIS CHAPTER

- Overview
- Simple Types
- Compound Types

If your application is going to communicate with another application, there must be some way to encode your data in a way that the other application understands. SOAP does provide a way to do this, but you aren't limited to SOAP's encoding scheme. As long as the other application understands the message you send it, you can encode your data in any crazy way you want to, and it's still a SOAP message. Since SOAP processors are required to understand SOAP's method of encoding, it's best if you encode your data in the SOAP-specified way, because more applications out there will be able to understand you. We'll spend this chapter looking at how this data encoding is done and how it ties into XML Schema.

Overview

It may seem odd to some of you that data type encoding is needed at all. For example, if you have the following SOAP message:

```
<env:Envelope
  xmlns:env="http://www.w3.org/2001/06/soap-envelope">
  <env:Body>
    <w:addNum
    xmlns:w="http://www.shelleybiotech.com/medical/
    services">
      <number1>7</number1>
      <number2>6</number2>
    </w:addNum>
  </env:Body>
</env:Envelope>
```

It sure looks like the two input parameters, number1 and number2, are integers and not strings. However, we're dealing with dumb computers that aren't capable of common sense. They only know what we tell them, so we have to be completely explicit.

Simple and Compound Types

SOAP sees the world of data in two colors: simple and compound. Examples of simple data types are integers, decimal numbers, URIs, and strings. Essentially, a simple type is anything that can be represented like this:

```
<someElement>someValue</someElement>
```

Simple types don't have any subelements. They're also known as scalar values.

Compound types involve a group of simple types collected together. Examples of compound types are arrays and structures. Compound types usually have subelements. Here, patient uses a compound data type.

```
<patient>
     <name>Irving Archbite</name>
     <age>32</age>
     <birthday>1970-01-28</birthday>
</patient>
```

Compound types can also involve other compound types. For example, patientList is a compound type list, the information for a photographer named Irving Archbite and his performance artist girlfriend, Fuji Persimmon.

```
<patientList>
     <patient>
       <name>Irving Archbite</name>
       <age>32</age>
       <birthday>1970-01-28</birthday>
</patient>
<patient>
       <name>Fuji Persimmon</name>
       <age>28</age>
       <birthday>1973-11-28</birthday>
</patient>
<patientList>
```

In this case, the compound type patientList contains two other patient compound types, which in turn contain three simple types.

Multireference Values

You can also encode data in your SOAP message to refer to other parts of the message, like so:

```
<env:Envelope
  xmlns:env="http://www.w3.org/2001/06/soap-envelope">
  <env:Body>
    <w:getPatientHistory>
    xmlns:w="http://www.wire-man.com/medical/services">
      <patient href="#patient-1" />
      <someGuy id="patient-1">
```

```
            <name>Irving Archbite</name>
            <age>32</age>
            <birthday>1970-01-28</birthday>
        </someGuy>
    </w:getPatientHistory>
  </env:Body>
</env:Envelope>
```

We'll get into this more later in the chapter, but I wanted you to see this quickly. The value that the patient element contains is held in whatever element has an ID of "patient-1", which in this case is someGuy. You could even do something like this:

```
<patient href="#patient-1"/>
<anotherPatient href="#patient-1"/>
<someGuy id="patient-1">
    <name>Irving Archbite</name>
    <age>32</age>
    <birthday>1970-01-28</birthday>
</someGuy>
```

In this case, the patient and anotherPatient elements both point to the same place. You wouldn't want to use this example, but you get the idea. It's a shorter way of coding this:

```
<patient
    <name>Irving Archbite</name>
    <age>32</age>
    <birthday>1970-01-28</birthday>
</patient>
<anotherPatient>
    <name>Irving Archbite</name>
    <age>32</age>
    <birthday>1970-01-28</birthday>
</anotherPatient>
```

Encoding and XML Schema

In order for something like SOAP to exist, it must have some method, some precise, computer-understandable means for serializing data and producing data types. The SOAP inventors, realizing this need, decided that creating a separate language, distinct from SOAP, would be the best way to accomplish this. Having to know both SOAP and this other data-type language placed a burden on developers, but it would make everyone's life easier in the long run, since the two functionalities are separated. Wrapping all imaginable data typing into SOAP would make it overly massive and unwieldy.

The SOAP inventors thus created Component Description Language (CDL). Partway though figuring out what CDL should look like, something called XML Data (now XML Schema) appeared. In the spirit of using open, existing Internet technology, the SOAP people decided to drop CDL in favor of XML Schema. There was also much overlap in what CDL and XML Schema were trying to accomplish. That's how XML Schema became the basis for data typing in SOAP messages.

However, XML Schema doesn't do everything that SOAP needs. For example, XML Schema doesn't address arrays. Instead of waiting for XML Schema to come around and specify how arrays should work, the SOAP guys decided to keep moving and solve the array issue themselves. Thus, there are pieces of data typing, such as arrays and structures, spelled out in the SOAP specification.

In other words, serialization (also known as encoding or marshalling) in SOAP is based on XML Schema, except for the bits that XML Schema doesn't cover. In those few cases, SOAP uses its own data-typing rules. (Check out Appendix B for a quick primer on XML Schema if you need one. If you want a more comprehensive look at XML, by all means feel free to check out *Essential XML for Web Professionals* by yours truly.)

Example 3–1 shows XML Schema and SOAP.

EXAMPLE 3–1 Patient XML Schema

```
<!-- schema document -->
<xsd:schema xmlns:xsd="http://www.w3.org/2001/
XMLSchema">
    <xsd:element name="name" type="xsd:string"/>
    <xsd:element name="age" type="xsd:integer"/>
    <xsd:element name="birthdate" type="xsd:date"/>
</xsd:schema>
```

Valid instances of this schema could include:

```
<name>Colt West</name>
<age>1</age>
<birthday>2000-06-12</birthday>
```

You can connect an XML Schema document and a SOAP message by using namespaces. It's up to the SOAP processor to have the relevant XML Schema document and to be able to connect a namespace in your SOAP message with the namespace in the XML Schema document.

```
<xsd:schema xmlns:xsd="http://www.w3.org/2001/XMLSchema"
targetNamespace="http://www.shelleybiotech.com/services/
medical">
    <xsd:element name="name" type="xsd:string"/>
    <xsd:element name="age" type="xsd:integer"/>
    <xsd:element name="birthdate" type="xsd:date"/>
</xsd:schema>
```

And here's the entire SOAP message.

```
<env:Envelope xmlns:env="http://www.w3.org/2001/06/soap-
envelope">
    <env:Body>
      <shel:patientInfo
      xmlns:shel="http://www.shelleybiotech.com/services/
      medical">
          <name>Colt West</name>
          <age>1</age>
          <birthday>2000-06-12</birthday>
      </shel:patientInfo>
    </env:Body>
</env:Envelope>
```

How the Code Works

Notice the bold sections in the XML Schema and the SOAP message. The XML Schema document names itself with the targetNamespace attribute, and the SOAP message uses the same namespace when it sets the shel namespace. This kind of connection can be confusing because the files only share a namespace, but the SOAP message doesn't actually spell out the name of the XML Schema document—there's no reference to "patient.xsd." It's up to the SOAP processor to know what to do with the SOAP message's namespace.

Simple Types

Since SOAP uses XML Schema, it's useful to quickly look at what kind of simple types XML Schema actually provides for use. Figure 3–1 lists all of the types available in XML Schema and their hierarchy. This image is derived from the XML Schema specification.

We won't go into detail here what all those simple types mean, or how to format them.

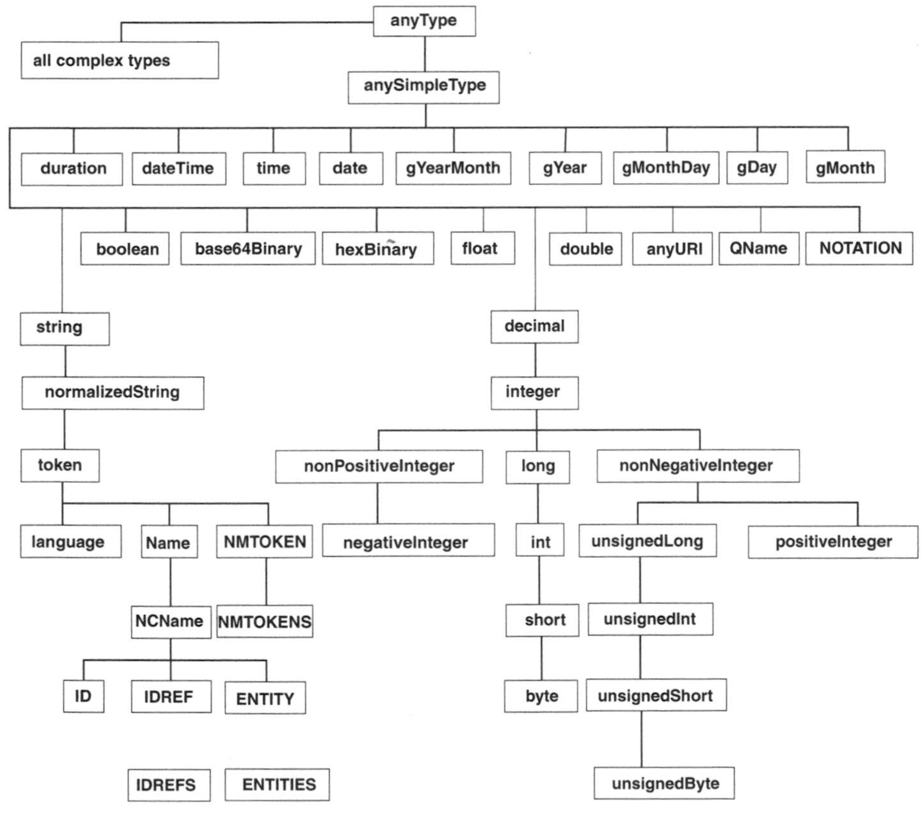

FIGURE 3–1 XML Schema data-type hierarchy

So, if you have some simple types in your SOAP message, how do you encode them? There are two ways to specify what kind of simple types you're using:

1. Specify the type of the element in a separate XML Schema document, as in the example above, or
2. Use SOAP encoding.

SOAP encoding? What does that mean? In a sense, it means not bothering with an external XML Schema document. This is shown in Example 3–2.

EXAMPLE 3–2 Encoding within the SOAP message

```
<env:Envelope xmlns:env="http://www.w3.org/2001/06/
soap-envelope">
     <env:Body>
       <shel:patientInfo xmlns:shel="http://
       www.shelleybiotech.com/services/medical"
       1.xmlns:enc="http://www.w3.org/2001/06/soap-
       encoding">
              2.<enc:string>Colt West</enc:string>
              3.<enc:int>1</enc:int>
              4.<enc:date>2000-06-12</enc:date>
       </shel:patientInfo>
     </env:Body>
</env:Envelope>
```

How the Code Works

1. We added a new namespace here, an official SOAP namespace: http://www.w3.org/2001/06/soap-encoding. Use of this namespace lets the SOAP processor know that the elements that are a part of this encoding namespace are encoding according to the SOAP specification. That is, they are taken mostly from XML Schema and parts from the SOAP specification.
2. We're calling this element enc:string. Notice from Figure 3–1 that "string" is one of the simple types from XML Schema. Since it's part of XML Schema and SOAP uses XML Schema, "string" is also part of SOAP's encoding scheme. Using the namespace in this fashion

lets the SOAP processor know that this element is an official string data type.

3. This is similar to enc:string in the line above. XML Schema has a simple type called "int," and by placing an element called "int" in the namespace of SOAP's encoding, we're telling the SOAP processor that this input parameter is an integer.
4. Same as #2 and #3. By using the name of an XML simple type—"date"—and placing that element in a namespace equal to SOAP encoding, the SOAP processor knows that the value of this chunk of data had better be a properly formatted date value.

All of the simple types listed in Figure 3–1 will work more or less in the same fashion. Table 3–1 contains a list of all of XML Schema's simple types.

TABLE 3–1 XML Schema Simple Data Types

anyType	ENTITIES	Integer	positiveInteger
anySimpleType	Float	Language	QName
anyURI	Gday	Long	short
base64Binary	GMonth	Name	string
boolean	gMonthDay	NCName	time
Byte	Gyear	NegativeInteger	unsignedByte
decimal	gYearMonth	NMTOKEN	unsignedInt
duration	hexBinary	NMTOKENS	unsignedLong
dateTime	ID	NonNegativeInteger	unsignedShort
Date	IDREF	NonPositiveInteger	
double	IDREFS	NormalizedString	
ENTITY	Int	NOTATION	

Enumerations

XML Schema allows for something called enumerations, which means that elements can be limited to contain one item from a list of acceptable options. For example, let's say there are a certain number of patient types: outpatient, inpatient, and clinical trial. Here's an example of some data that uses patientType:

```
<name>Amanda Muller</name>
<patientType>outpatient</patientType>
<age>26</age>
<birthday>1975-06-12</birthday>
```

In the case of enumerations, you have to use an external XML Schema document—there isn't a way to encode the possible values of an enumeration in a SOAP message. Let's look at Example 3–3, an XML Schema and SOAP message that would use an enumeration.

EXAMPLE 3–3 XML Schema enumeration

```
<xsd:schema xmlns:xsd="http://www.w3.org/2001/
XMLSchema"
  1.xmlns:tns="http://www.shelbiotech.com/services/
  medical"
  2.targetNamespace="http://www.shelbiotech.com/
  services/medical">

  <!-- define simple type -->
  3.<xsd:simpleType name="patientType">
      <xsd:restriction base="xsd:string">
        <xsd:enumeration value="inpatient"/>
        <xsd:enumeration value="outpatient"/>
        <xsd:enumeration value="clinical trial"/>
      </xsd:restriction>
    </xsd:simpleType>

    <!-- define elements -->
    <xsd:element name="name" type="xsd:string"/>
    4.<xsd:element name="patientType"
    type="tns:patientType"/>
    <xsd:element name="age" type="xsd:integer"/>
    <xsd:element name="birthdate" type="xsd:date"/>

</xsd:schema>
```

How the Code Works

1. We're using a new namespace here: tns. Tns stands for "this namespace" and it's pretty common. It isn't usually necessary: Its real function is to aid readability
2. Our targetNamespace is the same as it's always been.
3. We're defining our enumeration simple type here and calling it "patientType."
4. Here, we define the patientType element and link it to the simple type of the same name we created earlier.

Example 3–4 shows what the SOAP message would look like:

EXAMPLE 3–4 SOAP message with enumeration

```
<env:Envelope xmlns:env="http://www.w3.org/2001/06/
soap-envelope">
  <env:Body>
    1.<shel:patientInfo xmlns:shel="http://
    www.shelleybiotech.com/services/medical">
          <shel:name>Amanda Muller</shel:name>
          2.<shel:patientType>outpatient
          </shel:patientType>
          <shel:age>26</shel:age>
          <shel:birthday>1975-06-12</shel:birthday>
    </shel:patientInfo>
  </env:Body>
</env:Envelope>
```

How the Code Works

1. We use the same namespace as before, linking to the targetNamespace in the XML Schema document.
2. We don't require anything different when using the patientType element. All the work was done in XML Schema. As far as the SOAP message is concerned, patientType is just another element.

Byte Arrays

You can encode binary information into a SOAP message using something called byte arrays. These binary objects require a special kind of encoding, and base64 is usually recommended (base64Binary is the XML Schema simple type). Consider Example 3–5:

EXAMPLE 3–5 SOAP message with a byte array

```
<env:Envelope xmlns:env="http://www.w3.org/2001/06/
soap-envelope">
    <env:Body>
      <shel:patientInfo xmlns:shel="http://
      www.shelleybiotech.com/services/medical">
          <shel:xRayImage>aG93IG5vDyBicm==
          </shel:xRayImage>
          <shel:patientType>
              outpatient
          </shel:patientType>
          <shel:age>26</shel:age>
          <shel:birthday>1975-06-12</shel:birthday>
      </shel:patientInfo>
    </env:Body>
</env:Envelope>
```

How the Code Works

If we had a very simple image, we could turn that image into text by encoding the information into base64 notation, as this byte array demonstrates.

Polymorphism

Many computer languages allow you to have variables that can be one of several different values, with each of these values being of a different data type. The specific data type isn't chosen until runtime. When a variable can be different kinds of data types, it is called "polymorphic."

You are allowed to have polymorphic variables (variables are also called "accessors") in a SOAP message. However, you need to be extra-specific when dealing with polymorphic accessors: You must include an xsi:type attribute.

For example, let's say that a patient's birthday may be either an XML Schema date type, or it can be a string like "January 5, 1946." In this case, the birthday variable is a polymorphic accessor. Since a SOAP message has to have a specific value, Example 3–6 shows what it would look like:

EXAMPLE 3–6 Polymorphic accessor

```
<env:Envelope xmlns:env="http://www.w3.org/2001/06/
soap-envelope">
  <env:Body>
    <shel:patientInfo xmlns:shel="http://
www.shelleybiotech.com/services/medical"
xmlns:xsd="http://www.w3.org/2001/XMLSchema"
xmlns:xsi="http://www.w3.org/2001/XMLSchema-
instance">
          <shel:name>Barney Gum</shel:name>
          <shel:patientType>outpatient
          </shel:patientType>
          <shel:age>26</shel:age>
          <shel:birthday xsi:type="xsd:date">1975-
          06-12</shel:birthday>
    </shel:patientInfo>
  </env:Body>
</env:Envelope>
```

How the Code Works

Notice the two blocks of code in boldface. First, we declare two namespace for XML Schema and XML Schema-Instance. The only place we use these namespaces is in the birthday element, and they're both needed there. In the second block of code, we unequivocally state that the birthday element is a date data type. We could have used:

```
<shel:birthday xsi:type="xsd:string">June 6,
1975</shel:birthday>
```

if we had decided to send a string value instead of a strict date value. Remember, xsi:type is only needed if you're using a polymorphic accessor. If you're not, don't worry about it.

You may be asking: Why is this sort of thing necessary? Isn't there an easier way to set a variable's data type? The answer is: no, not when it's a polymorphic accessor. If it isn't, then all of the techniques we discussed earlier are just fine, and you don't need to use xsi:type.

In the XML Schema for this element, it's been set up to accept either a date or a string. Since the value can handle both, it's known as a polymorphic accessor, and we're using the xsi:type attribute to spell out which data type is being used.

Custom Simple Types

One of the advantages of XML Schema over Document Type Definitions (DTD) is that XML Schema allows you to create your own simple types based on existing, predefined simple types. For example, if you wanted to require that some data was a phone number with area code, Example 3–7 shows you how you could do that.

EXAMPLE 3–7 New custom simple type

```
<xsd:schema xmlns:xsd="http://www.w3.org/2001/
XMLSchema"
xmlns:tns="http://www.shelbiotech.com/services/
medical" targetNamespace="http://
www.shelbiotech.com/services/medical">

<!-- define simple type -->
<xsd:simpleType name="patientType">
      <xsd:restriction base="xsd:string">
        <xsd:enumeration value="inpatient"/>
        <xsd:enumeration value="outpatient"/>
        <xsd:enumeration value="clinical trial"/>
      </xsd:restriction>
</xsd:simpleType>

1.<xsd:simpleType name="phoneNumType">
<xsd:restriction base="xsd:string">
        <xsd:pattern value="(\d{3})\s\d{3}-\d{4}" />
      </xsd:restriction>
</xsd:simpleType>


    <!-- define elements -->
    <xsd:element name="name" type="xsd:string"/>
    <xsd:element name="patientType"
```

EXAMPLE 3–7 New custom simple type (Continued)

```
    type="tns:patientType"/>
    2.<xsd:element name="phoneNumber"
    type="tns:phoneNumType"/>
    <xsd:element name="age" type="xsd:integer"/>
    <xsd:element name="birthdate" type="xsd:date"/>

</xsd:schema>
```

How the Code Works

1. We're creating a new simple type called phoneNumType that forces a string to look like (123) 456-7890.
2. Here's where we add the new phone number element with our new type.

Simple Type Recap

That covers how to encode your simple data types into a SOAP message. Remember that a simple type, also known as a scalar, is a single value that can live inside an XML element, like so:

```
<pants>blue</pants>
```

You don't get to use attributes to define the value of your simple type. For example,

```
<pants cut="low">blue</pants>
```

won't work in SOAP. If this is the information you want to send, it has to be structured in a different way. There are currently 45 different simple data types to choose from, including integers, strings, URIs, and floating-point numbers, so chances are good you'll find something you can use.

In order to define these data types, you can spell them out in an external XML document and use namespaces to link to your SOAP message, or you can declare the SOAP encoding namespace in the SOAP message itself, which is almost like importing XML Schema into your SOAP message.

There are also ways to encode enumerations (which require an external XML Schema document) as well as byte arrays and polymorphic accessors (which don't require an external XML Schema document).

Now let's get a little more complicated and start looking at structures and arrays.

Compound Types

In the SOAP world, a compound data type is anything that has more than one value. Structures and arrays are examples of compound data types. XML Schema allows for compound types in general, but doesn't differentiate between different varieties of compound types. You can create something that looks like an array in XML Schema, but there isn't anything in XML Schema that lets you explicitly say, "This is an array." The same goes for structures. Thus, the inventors of SOAP decided to create a way to explicitly say, "This is an array" and "This is a structure." How exactly that happens is the subject of this section.

Structures

Structures, also known as structs, are a collection of name-value pairs. The only thing these pairs have in common is that they are all prefixed by the same name. For example, Example 3–8 is a patient struct:

EXAMPLE 3–8 A struct

```
patient.name = "Gaylord Moxon"
patient.age = 79
patient.city = "Davis"
patient.state = "CA"
```

Structs can also contain other structs, as in Example 3–9.

EXAMPLE 3–9 Nested structs

```
outpatients.patient.name.first = "Gaylord"
outpatients.patient.name.middle = "Emery"
outpatients.patient.name.last = "Moxon"
outpatients.patient.age = 79
outpatients.patient.city = "Davis"
outpatients.patient.state = "CA"
```

So, what does a structure look like in SOAP? As Example 3–10 shows, it's simpler than you'd think.

EXAMPLE 3–10 A structure inside a SOAP message

```
<env:Envelope xmlns:env="http://www.w3.org/2001/06/
soap-envelope">
    <env:Body>
      <shel:getPatientInfo xmlns:shel="http://
      www.shelleybiotech.com/services/med">
        <p:patient
        xmlns:shel="http://www.shelleybiotech.com/
        ns/patients">
            <name>Gaylord Moxon</name>
            <age>79</age>
            <city>Davis</city>
            <state>CA</state>
        </p:patient>
      </shel:getPatientInfo>
    </env:Body>
</env:Envelope>
```

How the Code Works

For this example, we're passing a structure named "patient" to a method named "getPatientInfo." This structure has four elements: name, age, city, and state. How can we tell this is a structure when it looks like normal XML? We can tell because of the p namespace:

```
<p:patient xmlns:shel="http://www.shelleybiotech.com/ns/
patients">
    <name>Gaylord Moxon</name>
    <age>79</age>
    <city>Mariposa</city>
    <state>CA</state>
</p:patient>
```

By wrapping a namespace around patient and all of its contents, you're declaring this is a structure. Every containing element (patient, in this example) must be qualified by a namespace. If we wanted a structure that contained other structures, as in Example 3–9, it might look like this:

```
<o:outpatients
xmlns:o="http://www.shelleybiotech.com/ns/out">
  <p:patient
  xmlns:shel="http://www.shelleybiotech.com/ns/patients">
      <n:name
      xmlns:n="http://www.shelleybiotech.com/ns/names">
              <first>Gaylord</first>
              <midle>Emery</middle>
              <last>Moxon</last>
        </n:name>
        <age>79</age>
        <city>Mariposa</city>
        <state>CA</state>
  </p:patient>
</o:outpatients>
```

How the Code Works

There are three container elements: outpatients, patient, and name. We used three namespaces to qualify those elements, which set them apart from other elements as containing elements. Did you notice that noncontainer elements like first, middle, last, age, city, and state aren't namespace-qualified? That's because they don't need to be—the rules of namespaces and scoping dictate that everything inside of a namespace-qualified element automatically becomes a part of that namespace. In other words, the elements first, middle, and last are a part of the o, p, and n namespaces even though they don't have prefixes. Age and city are a part of the o and p namespaces, but not n.

It's also possible to avoid an overly nested structure by referencing elements as in Example 3–11.

EXAMPLE 3–11 Coding a complex structure using references

```
<o:outpatients
xmlns:o="http://www.shelleybiotech.com/ns/out">
  <patient href="#patient-1"/>
</o:outpatient>

<o:patient id="patient-1"
xmlns:shel="http://www.shelleybiotech.com/ns/out">
  <name href="#name-1"/>
```

EXAMPLE 3–11 Coding a complex structure using references (Continued)

```
  <age>79</age>
  <city>Mariposa</city>
  <state>CA</state>
</o:patient>

<o:name id="name-1" xmlns:o="http://
www.shelleybiotech.com/ns/out">
  <first>Gaylord</first>
  <midle>Emery</middle>
  <last>Moxon</last>
</o:name>
```

How the Code Works

I introduced a few new things here. First, all the elements are using the same prefix and namespace—o and http://www.shelleybiotech.com/ns/out. This is fine—you don't need to create new namespaces for each nested structure. As long as the container element is namespace-qualified, you're fine.

Which method should you use? It doesn't really matter. I find the second method a little easier to handle, but it's up to your personal preference.

Since we've been talking about XML Schema so much, it'd be wrong not to include the schema for the above structures. Example 3–12 contains the XML Schema fragment that describes our buddy Gaylord.

EXAMPLE 3–12 XML Schema for nest structures

```
<!-- define types -->
<xsd:complexType name="patientType">
    <xsd:sequence>
      <xsd:element name="name" type="nameType"/>
      <xsd:element name="age" type="xsd:integer"/>
      <xsd:element name="city" type="xsd:string"/>
      <xsd:element name="state" type="xsd:string"/>
    </xsd:sequence>
</xsd:complexType>

<xsd:complexType name="nameType">
    <xsd:sequence>
```

Example 3–12 XML Schema for nest structures (Continued)

```
        <xsd:element name="first" type="xsd:string"/>
        <xsd:element name="middle" type="xsd:string"/>
        <xsd:element name="last" type="xsd:string"/>
    </xsd:sequence>
</xsd:complexType>

<!-- define main element -->
<xsd:element name="outpatient" xmlns:xsd="http://
www.w3.org/2001/XMLSchema">
    <xsd:complexType>
        <xsd:sequence>
            <xsd:element name="patient"
            type="patientType"/>
        </xsd:sequence>
    </xsd:complexType>
</xsd:element>
```

I'll let you decipher the XML Schema yourself (remember, Appendix B has a quick primer). This is all you really need in order to place structures in your SOAP message.

Arrays

Arrays in SOAP look almost exactly like structures, the only real difference being that the head element of an array has a special attribute that says, "The following is an array, not a structure!" This special attribute is the arrayType attribute, and we'll cover how to use it in detail. Arrays in SOAP can contain any sort of element, including other arrays. SOAP arrays can also differentiate between nested arrays (arrays of arrays) and true multidimensional arrays. Example 3–13 shows an array called patientList that contains two names as its elements.

Example 3–13 An array in SOAP

```
<env:Envelope xmlns:env="http://www.w3.org/2001/06/
soap-envelope">
  <env:Body>
    1.<shel:getPatientInfo
    xmlns:shel="http://www.shelleybiotech.com/
    services/med"
```

EXAMPLE 3–13 An array in SOAP (Continued)

```
    xmlns:xsd="http://www.w3.org.2001/XMLSchema"
    xmlns:enc="http://www.w3.org/2001/06/soap-
    encoding">
          2.<patientList
          enc:arrayType="xsd:string[2]">
              3.<patient>Irving Archbite</patient>
              <patient>Fuji Persimmon</patient>
          </patientList>
      </shel:getPatientInfo>
    </env:Body>
</env:Envelope>
```

How the Code Works

1. We're setting a few more namespaces in the method name element. Not only the namespace for Shelley Biotech, but also for XML Schema and SOAP's encoding namespace. We need these in order to properly define our array.
2. This element defines the array, and it does so using the enc:arrayType attribute. This attribute proclaims, "The following is an array." The value of the attribute defines what kind of information can be in the array, as well as how many elements may be in the array. In this case, all the elements in the array must be strings and there may only be two elements in the array. Since we're referring to XML Schema's definition of a string, we have to prefix "string" with "xsd."
3. Here's where we spell out the contents of the two elements of the array.

Another way to view this array:

```
patientList[0] = "Irving Archbite"
patientList[1] = "Fuji Persimmon"
```

In this case, we've set the length of the array to two elements. But what if you're not sure of the final size, or you want the array to be unbounded? Simple: change

```
enc:arrayType = "xsd:string[2]"
```

to

```
enc:arrayType = "xsd:string[]"
```

Just omit the number in the square brackets and you can add as many elements as you want.

Pretty simple, right? So far, yes—we'll get more complicated in a moment. For right now, let's look at Example 3–14, which shows how you could define a SOAP array within XML Schema.

EXAMPLE 3–14 Defining an array in XML Schema

```
1.<xsd:schema xmlns:xsd="http://www.w3.org/2001/
XMLSchema" xmlns:enc="http://www.w3.org/2001/06/
soap-encoding">
    2.<xsd:import namespace="http://www.w3.org/
    2001/06/soap-encoding"/>
    3.<xsd:element name="patientList"
    type="enc:Array"/>
</xsd:schema>
```

How the Code Works

1. We're declaring a namespace we don't usually bother with in an XML Schema document: SOAP's encoding namespace. We need this namespace declared in order to define the array type. This is because XML Schema doesn't have an array type, so we need to bring it in from somewhere else.
2. Using import is how we physically bring SOAP's encoding scheme (which includes a definition for arrays) into our XML Schema document. Remember, since XML Schema doesn't have the foggiest idea what an array is, we have to bring in the idea of an array from somewhere else, and SOAP's encoding scheme is the place from where we bring it.
3. Finally, we define the array by making its type enc:Array. Usually this is xsd:string or xsd:phoneNumType, something that comes predefined within XML Schema (xsd:string) or that you can define yourself

within an XML Schema document (xsd:phoneNum-Type). Since the definition of an array lives somewhere else, we must use a different namespace to define it.

DEFINING ARRAY ELEMENT DATA TYPES

So, is your array full of strings, integers, or what? Above we saw one way to specify that an array has two strings as its elements. In general, there are three ways to specify what your array is made of. Example 3–15 repeats a fragment of Example 3–13 as a reminder.

EXAMPLE 3–15 Fragment of Example 3–13

```
<shel:getPatientInfo
xmlns:shel="http://www.shelleybiotech.com/services/med"
xmlns:xsd="http://www.w3.org.2001/XMLSchema"
xmlns:enc="http://www.w3.org/2001/06/soap-encoding">
  <patientList enc:arrayType="xsd:string[2]">
      <patient>Irving Archbite</patient>
      <patient>Fuji Persimmon</patient>
  </patientList>
</shel:getPatientInfo>
```

We don't need to use the names "patientList" or "patient." After all, we're just passing data and the method doesn't necessarily care what the names of the array and its elements are. If we remove these names, we can focus on the data types themselves, as Example 3–16 shows.

EXAMPLE 3–16 An array without element names

```
1.<enc:Array xmlns:xsd="http://www.w3.org.2001/
XMLSchema" xmlns:enc="http://www.w3.org/2001/06/
soap-encoding" enc:arrayType="xsd:string[2]">
      2.<enc:string>Irving Archbite</enc:string>
      <enc:string>Fuji Persimmon</enc:string>
</enc:Array>
```

How the Code Works

1. We've replaced "patientList" with "enc:Array," so we're making sure the enc namespace is defined. Instead of giving the containing element of the array a special name, we're just saying, "This is an array." You don't have to code this way, but it's a way to be more explicit than the code in Example 3–15.
2. Instead of "patient," we're spelling out what the array element contains. In this case, they're both strings. Note that you can use any kind of type defined in XML Schema here, since SOAP's encoding is based on XML Schema. This means that everything in XML Schema is part of SOAP's encoding scheme, which is why we can use enc:string instead of xsd:string at certain points.

You can get even more verbose and explicit in your array definitions, as you can see in Example 3–17.

EXAMPLE 3–17 Verbose data-type definitions

```
1.<enc:Array xmlns:xsd="http://www.w3.org.2001/
XMLSchema" xmlns:xsi="http://www.w3.org/2001/
XMLSchema-instance" xmlns:enc="http://www.w3.org/
2001/06/soap-encoding"
enc:arrayType="xsd:string[2]">
    2.<element xsi:type="xsd:string">Irving
    Archbite</element>
    <element xsi:type="xsd:string">Fuji Persimmon</
    element>
</enc:Array>
```

How the Code Works

1. The only thing different about this line is that we're declaring another namespace: XML Schema-instance.
2. Here, the name of the element isn't important—the way the type is being defined is via the xsi:type attribute. We saw this briefly earlier when we looked at polymorphic accessors. It's simply another way to define a data type within SOAP.

ARRAYS OF DIFFERENT DATA TYPES

Arrays don't have to be just strings or integers. They can contain all sorts of different data types, as shown in Example 3–18.

EXAMPLE 3–18 Different data types in an array

```
<enc:Array xmlns:xsd="http://www.w3.org.2001/
XMLSchema" xmlns:enc="http://www.w3.org/2001/06/
soap-encoding"
1.enc:arrayType="xsd:anyType[5]">
    2.<enc:string>David Warmbier</enc:string>
    <enc:int>29</enc:int>
    <enc:date>1971-10-15</enc:date>
    <enc:string>San Diego</enc:string>
    <enc:string>CA</enc:string>
</enc:Array>
```

How the Code Works

1. We're allowing for anything to appear in our array by setting its type to "anyType," which means that anything goes—just about anything can appear in our array.
2. We start with a string, and then move on to inserting an integer, a date, and two more strings.

We can also use data types of our own devising. Suppose we want to send an array of two patients, whose information is coded as so:

```
<patient>
    <name>Irving Archbite</name>
    <age>32</age>
    <homePage>www.irvingarch.com</homePage>
</patient>
<patient>
    <name>Fuji Persimmon</name>
    <age>26</age>
    <homePage>www.syrianbull.com</homePage>
</patient>
```

Therefore, we have two potential array elements (patient) that contain some structs. How do we create this array? It's actually pretty easy, as we can see in Example 3–19.

EXAMPLE 3–19 Array element containing XML

```
<enc:Array xmlns:enc="http://www.w3.org/2001/06/
soap-encoding"
xmlns:shel="http://www.shelleybiotech.com/services/
encoding" enc:arrayType="shel:patient[2]">
     <patient>
          <name>Irving Archbite</name>
          <age>32</age>
          <homePage>www.irvingarch.com</birthday>
     </patient>
     <patient>
          <name>Fuji Persimmon</name>
          <age>26</age>
          <homePage>www.syrianbull.com</homePage>
     </patient>
</enc:Array>
```

This is an array of structs. But how is that possible? The containing elements aren't namespace-qualified! Actually, they are, and that qualification happens in `enc:arrayType="shel:patient[2]"`. It's in this attribute that the elements of the array are placed in the shel namespace, so we don't have to spell the namespace out again when the actual elements are listed—they're already part of the namespace.

CUSTOM DATA TYPES AS ARRAYS

You could also create a custom type within XML Schema, and use that type for the value of your arrayType attribute. For example, imagine that you want an array of Social Security numbers, which must be formatted in a certain way. Example 3–20 shows what the XML Schema could look like.

EXAMPLE 3–20 Custom array type

```
<xsd:schema xmlns:xsd="http://www.w3.org/2001/
XMLSchema"
xmlns:tns="http://www.shelleybiotech.com/services/
encoding"
xmlns:enc="http://www.w3.org/2001/06/soap-encoding"
targetNamespace="http://www.shelleybiotech.com/
services/encoding">

<!-- define types -->
1.<xsd:simpleType name="ssnType">
    <xsd:restriction base="xsd:string">
      <xsd:pattern value="\d{3}-\d{2}-\d{4}" />
    </xsd:restriction>
</xsd:simpleType>

2.<xsd:complexType name="ssnArrayType">
    <xsd:complexContent>
      <xsd:restriction base="enc:Array">
        <xsd:sequence>
          <xsd:element name="ssn"
          type="tns:ssnType" maxOccurs="unbounded"/>
        </xsd:sequence>
      </xsd:restriction>
    </xsd:complexContent>
</xsd:complexType>

<!—define element -->
3.<xsd:element name="ssnArray" type="ssnArayType"/>

</xsd:schema>
```

How the Code Works

1. We start by creating a custom simple type to contain our Social Security numbers. We've created a pattern that must look like 555-55-5555, and called it "ssnType."
2. Here's where we create a custom complex type that is based on the array type from the SOAP specification. That's why our base type is enc:Array instead of xsd:Array—XML Schema doesn't know anything about arrays. We create a sequence of elements called "ssn," and there can be any number of them.

3. Finally, we define the element that contains the actual array.

Whew! Now let's look at Example 3–21, which shows what a SOAP message based on the above schema could look like.

EXAMPLE 3–21 Custom array type in a SOAP message

```
<shel:ssnArray
xmlns:shel="http://www.shelleybiotech.com/services/
encoding"
xmlns:enc="http://www.w3.org/2001/06/soap-encoding"
enc:arrayType="shel:ssnType[]">
    <ssn>555-55-5555</ssn>
    <ssn>000-00-0002</ssn>
    <ssn>123-45-6789</ssn>
</shel:ssnArray>
```

Notice the enc:arrayType attribute. The value of the type is that of ssnType, not arrayType, as you might expect. This makes sense, though. We want the elements in the array to be Social Security numbers, not more arrays.

NESTED ARRAYS

SOAP also allows you to create nested arrays. That is, an array where one or more of the elements of that array is itself another array. There's a slightly different notation to describe nested arrays. Suppose you had an array of three elements. Defining this array would look like this:

```
enc:arrayType = "xsd:anyType[3]"
```

Now suppose that each element in this array was also an array, and each of these subarrays had four elements. In this case, the definition would look like

```
enc:arrayType = "xsd:anyType[4][3]"
```

That's right—the length of the subarrays comes before the length of the main array. This is a little counterintuitive (it was for me, anyway), so it might help to see it like this:

```
(anyType[4])[3]
```

That is, we start with an array of four elements. Then, we define that there are three instances of that four-element array. Let's look at Example 3–22.

EXAMPLE 3–22 Nested array

```
<enc:Array xmlns:enc="http://www.w3.org/2001/06/
soap-encoding" xmlns:enc="http://www.w3.org/2001/
XMLSchema"
1.enc:arrayType="xsd:anyType[3][2]">
    2.<patient href="#patient-1"/>
    <patient href="#patient-2"/>
</enc:Array>

3.<enc:Array id="patient-1" xmlns:enc="http://
www.w3.org/2001/06/soap-encoding" xmlns:xsd="http:/
/www.w3.org/2001/XMLSchema"
enc:arrayType="xsd:anyType[3]>
    <enc:string>Irving Archbite</enc:string>
    <enc:int>32</enc:int>
    <enc:anyURI>http://www.irvingarch.com
    </enc:anyURI>
</enc:Array>

<enc:Array id="patient-2" xmlns:enc="http://
www.w3.org/2001/06/soap-encoding" xmlns:xsd="http:/
/www.w3.org/2001/XMLSchema"
enc:arrayType="xsd:anyType[3]>
    <enc:string>Fuji Persimmon</enc:string>
    <enc:int>26</enc:int>
    <enc:anyURI>http://www.syrianbull.com</enc:anyURI>
</enc:Array>
```

How the Code Works

1. The arrayType attribute defines an array with two main elements, with each of those elements containing a three-element array.
2. Instead of placing the subarrays directly inside the main array, we're referencing them. This can make the document a little more readable.
3. Here's where we define the actual subarrays.

It's entirely permissible to have a nested array where the numbers of elements in the subarrays are different from each other. For example, say you have an array with three main elements. Each of these main elements is an array, but the first element is a two-element array, the second element is a four-element array, and the third main element is a 1000-element array. How would you code this? Simple.

```
enc:arrayType = "xsd:anyType[][3]"
```

That's it. By removing the number from the first set of brackets, you leave that value open to be anything.

MULTIDIMENSIONAL ARRAYS

SOAP also allows you to create true multidimensional arrays, where you specify the row and column. For example, if you want to create an array with four columns and two rows, it might look something like Example 3–23.

EXAMPLE 3–23 Multidimensional array

```
<enc:Array xmlns:enc="http://www.w3.org/2001/06/
soap-encoding" xmlns:enc="http://www.w3.org/2001/
XMLSchema" enc:arrayType="xsd:string[2,4]">
    <element>row1, column1</element>
    <element>row1, column2</element>
    <element>row1, column3</element>
    <element>row1, column4</element>
    <element>row2, column1</element>
    <element>row2, column2</element>
    <element>row2, column3</element>
    <element>row2, column4</element>
</enc:Array>
```

How the Code Works

This doesn't require much explanation. The syntax for a multidimensional array is

```
enc:arrayType="xsd:datatype[numberRows, numberColumns]"
```

When you list out your elements, they are placed into the array by filling each row, one at a time, starting at the first column.

To create a multidimensional array with an unlimited number of rows and columns, you can omit both numbers in the brackets, but must keep the comma.

```
enc:arrayType="xsd:string[,]">
```

As we'll see soon, you can specify exactly where in this big array a value is.

PARTIALLY TRANSMITTED ARRAYS

Sometimes you don't want to send an entire array. Say you have an array with 17 elements, but the method you're trying to invoke only needs the sixth and seventh elements. The remote method also needs to know that those two chunks of data are the sixth and seventh elements of an array–you can't just send a two-element array. You can accomplish this by using a new attribute, offset, which is shown in Example 3–24.

EXAMPLE 3–24 Partially transmitted array

```
<enc:Array xmlns:enc="http://www.w3.org/2001/06/
soap-encoding" xmlns:enc="http://www.w3.org/2001/
XMLSchema" enc:arrayType="xsd:string[17]"
enc:offset="[5]">
    <enc:string>the sixth element</enc:string>
    <enc:string>the seventh element</enc:string>
</enc:Array>
```

How the Code Works

The offset attribute determines which element is first in line. In this case, the element in the [5] position is the first element in the listed array. The default value for offset is zero, so it's usually assumed that the element in the [0] position is the first element listed.

Partially transmitted arrays are also known as *varying arrays*.

SPARSE ARRAYS

You can also specify exactly which elements to send in an array, even if those items aren't next to each other. This is also known as a *sparse array*. You can use the position attribute to accomplish this. Let's say we have another array with 17 elements, but we only want three elements: those in positions [0], [5], and [12]. Example 3–25 shows what that would look like.

EXAMPLE 3–25 Sparse array

```
<enc:Array xmlns:enc="http://www.w3.org/2001/06/
soap-encoding" xmlns:enc="http://www.w3.org/2001/
XMLSchema" enc:arrayType="xsd:string[17]">
  <item enc:position="[0]">the first element</item>
  <item enc:position="[5]">the sixth element</item>
  <item enc:position="[12]">the thirteenth
  element</item>
</enc:Array>
```

Now let's get a little nuts. Imagine we have an array of seven elements. Each of those elements is a multidimensional array of an unknown number of rows and columns. Got it? Now imagine that we only want three elements out of this big mess. Such a thing might look like Example 3–26.

EXAMPLE 3–26 Multidimensional sparse array

```
<enc:Array xmlns:enc="http://www.w3.org/2001/06/
soap-encoding" xmlns:enc="http://www.w3.org/2001/
XMLSchema"
1.enc:arrayType="xsd:string[,][7]">
  <enc:Array href="#multiDimArray"
  enc:position="[3]"/>
</enc:Array>

2.<enc:Array id="multiDimArray" xmlns:enc="http://
www.w3.org/2001/06/soap-encoding" xmlns:enc="http:/
/www.w3.org/2001/XMLSchema"
enc:arrayType="xsd:string[8,9]">
    3.<item enc:position="[2,3]">3rd row,
        4th column</item>
    <item enc:position="[4,4]">5th row,
        5th column</item>
    <item enc:position="[6,0]">7th row,
        1st column</item>
</enc:Array>
```

How the Code Works

1. This is how we describe an array containing another set of multidimensional arrays: [,][7]. We're also referring to a multidimensional array, and we're saying that this array is in position [3], which means that we're looking at the fourth element in the main array. Notice that the enc:position attribute lives inside of the array's elements, not in the main element like enc:offset does.
2. Here's where we define the multidimensional array that's the fourth nested array inside the main array. This particular array happens to have eight rows and nine columns. Other multidimensional arrays in the main array may have any number of rows and columns.
3. Finally, we pull the three elements out of the multidimensional array.

And that's arrays in SOAP.

Recap

A lot of code was thrown at you in this chapter, but you now have a strong understanding of how SOAP uses XML Schema to determine the format for data types, and how SOAP adds its own data-encoding rules when XML Schema falls short.

4

HTTP and SOAP

IN THIS CHAPTER

- Purpose of HTTP
- Internet Communication
- HTTP Message Structure
- HTTP and Security
- Secure Sockets Layer (SSL)
- Advantages and Disadvantages of HTTP
- SOAPAction

The amount of HTTP you must know in order to create SOAP messages isn't much—not enough to fill an entire chapter, certainly. So, if you're short on time, skip to the last two sections in this chapter. However, since the majority of your SOAP messages will undoubtedly travel over HTTP, this means they will inherit both the capabilities and limitations of HTTP. So to properly understand what your SOAP messages can and can't do on the wire, it's helpful to have some understanding of what HTTP really is and how it works. I recommend that you read this whole chapter—the HTTP story is actually a pretty interesting one.

Purpose of HTTP

The goal of HTTP is to make communications between systems easy by giving them some rules of conversation, including requests and responses. If HTTP were a part of English, it would involve saying, "Hello," and "Goodbye," among other things. We'll only look at a few of these other features, focusing on security.

History

Many moons ago, back when Tim Berners-Lee was creating the World Wide Web, he needed a way for Web browsers to regulate their communications—that is, they needed a way to have simple conversations. He, along with a guy named Robert Cailliau created a protocol they called Hypertext Transfer Protocol (HTTP).

The first specification for HTTP came in at 656 words and fit on a few pages (it's listed in Appendix H if you're curious). The current specification takes up several documents, one of which weighs in at 176 pages. We won't get into that much detail here.

One of the great things about HTTP is that it doesn't care what kind of information it's carrying: It can be text, images, sounds, or program files. This kind of flexibility has helped make HTTP as popular as it is.

Internet Communication

So how does HTTP actually work? How does it regulate conversations and where does this happen, exactly? To answer this in a useful way, we need to look at how HTTP fits into the whole picture of how the Internet works.

Communication across the Internet happens in several layers, and there's a protocol for each layer. For communication across the Web, the protocols used are HTTP, Transmission

Control Protocol (TCP) and Internet Protocol (IP), and the actual network technology, like Ethernet, that moves the bits across the wire. Figure 4–1 shows the structure of this communication system.

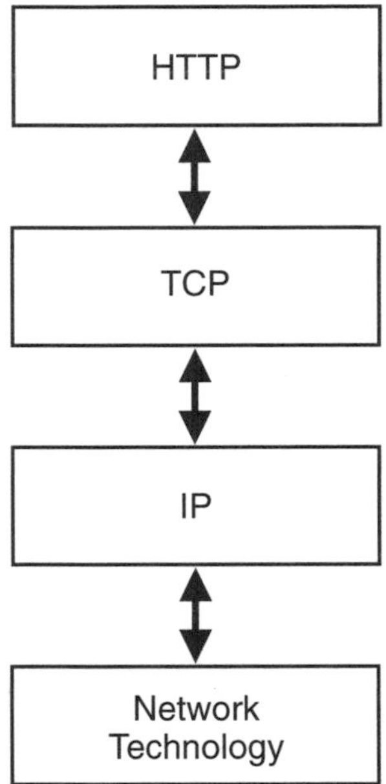

FIGURE 4–1 Internet communication protocols

Each layer has its own specific job, and the advantage of dividing these jobs into entirely separate protocols is greater flexibility. This communication is loosely coupled, a concept we've already examined. This flexibility is important, because one of the Internet's great strengths is its ability to connect all forms of disparate systems and network technologies. Because of this flexibility, HTTP can travel over any kind of network connection—HTTP doesn't even know and it certainly doesn't care.

How do HTTP, TCP, and IP fit into the picture?

IP

IP actually deserves the grand name of Internet Protocol—every computer or system that uses the Internet uses IP to communicate on some level. IP's purpose in life is to take individual packets of information and forward them to their final destination. IP takes responsibility for all the packets transferred.

TCP

TCP's job is to make IP reliable. In other words, TCP must ensure that packets arrive in the right order, that none of them are lost in transit, and that no errors appear.

HTTP

As we've seen, HTTP's job is to do something meaningful with the information in the packets, including organizing those exchanges into something that looks like a conversation.

Figure 4–2 shows a closer look at how these protocols interact.

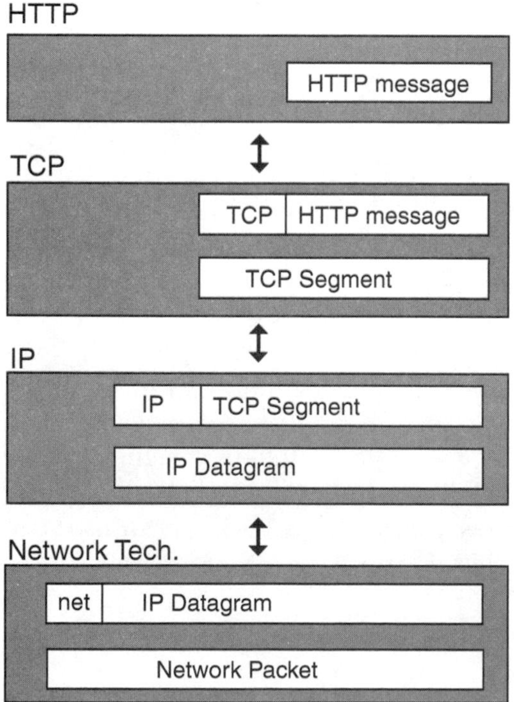

FIGURE 4–2 How the protocols interact

CLIENTS AND SERVERS

HTTP requires the presence of applications that act as either clients or servers. The difference is quite important and easy to distinguish, since clients and servers follow different rules and procedures. For example, clients always initiate HTTP communication. In fact, if an application initiates a HTTP contact, that's enough for it to be called a client. Servers can't initiate contact—they can only respond to requests from clients. Servers are only supposed to do what clients ask them to. Clients act and servers react.

Connections

In order for HTTP to communicate, it must travel over an open TCP connection. That means that when a client initiates an HTTP communication, it must also create a TCP connection. Here's the sequence of a simple HTTP communication.

1. Client to server over TCP: Hi there.
2. Server to client over TCP: Hello. I see you.
3. Client to server over TCP: I see you too.
4. Client to server over HTTP: I want this web page.
5. Server to client over HTTP: Here it is.
6. Server to client over TCP: Goodbye.
7. Client to server over TCP: Goodbye.

There are more technical terms for what's happening here, but you get the idea. After the client tells the server "Goodbye," the two completely forget about each other. This forgetfulness is known as a *stateless* connection. That is, neither the client nor the server remember what state the other is in, or even where the connection is coming from. Once the transaction is over, it's over. We'll look more closely at statelessness a few sections down.

The first three steps where the client and server get synchronized and say "Hello" are known collectively as a *handshake*. In earlier versions of HTTP, clients had to reestablish TCP connections every time they contacted a server. This wasn't a big problem in the early days of the Web when Web pages were simple. However, as Web pages became more complex and could have dozens of images on them, retrieving each image required a whole new TCP connection. This caused a performance hit, as clients kept having to open and close connections.

PERSISTENCE

People decided that having to constantly open and close TCP connections was inefficient, and they created a new version of HTTP and called it HTTP/1.1. This version had a new feature called *persistence* that allowed a TCP connection to stay open while multiple HTTP requests were made. This sped up performance. Here's what a conversation using persistence could look like:

1. Client to server over TCP: Hi there.
2. Server to client over TCP: Hello. I see you.
3. Client to server over TCP: I see you too.
4. Client to server over HTTP: I want this web page.
5. Server to client over HTTP: Here it is.
6. Client to server over HTTP: I want this image.
7. Server to client over HTTP: Here is your image.
8. Client to server over HTTP: I want this Flash movie.
9. Server to client over HTTP: Here is your Flash movie.
10. Server to client over TCP: Goodbye.
11. Client to server over TCP: Goodbye.

As you can see, we were able to make three HTTP requests over a single TCP connection. Unlike HTTP/1.0, the server is not allowed to close the connection after the client's initial HTTP request. Persistence significantly increases the speed of downloading an entire web page.

PIPELINING

There's another speed trick in HTTP/1.1 called *pipelining*. This trick allows the client to make all of its requests without having to wait for the server to respond. In the examples above, did you notice that the client had to wait until it received something from the server in order to make the next request? By using pipelining, the client can fire off all of its requests at once, and then wait for the server to give it everything. This method also speeds performance. Here's what a combination of persistence and pipelining might look like:

1. Client to server over TCP: Hi there.
2. Server to client over TCP: Hello. I see you.
3. Client to server over TCP: I see you too.
4. Client to server over HTTP: I want this HTML page.
5. Client to server over HTTP: I want this image.
6. Client to server over HTTP: I want this Flash movie.
7. Server to client over HTTP: Here is your HTML page.
8. Server to client over HTTP: Here is your image.
9. Server to client over HTTP: Here is your Flash movie.
10. Server to client over TCP: Goodbye.
11. Client to server over TCP: Goodbye.

Basic HTTP Operations

An HTTP message can request four basic things from a server (there are more, but we'll just look at the basic ones right now): GET, POST, PUT, and DELETE. Let's go over them briefly.

GET

GET is a simple two-message exchange. The HTTP message identifies the object the client wishes to get via a URL, and if the server can return the object, it does, along with a "200 OK" status message.

POST

POST is also a two-way message, but in addition to asking for an object via a URL, the message also contains a number of variables and values. This collection of variables is known as a *payload*. Remember the XML payload from Chapter 2? This is the same kind of thing. So when a client identifies that it's asking for a POST, it's sending both a URL and a data payload.

PUT

The idea behind PUT is to allow a user to upload a file on a remote server. This is not used when you've a browser to upload a file—that technique uses the POST method. PUT isn't used because it's problematic to handle authentication.

DELETE

This method acts the same as PUT, but instead instructs the server to delete the indicated file. This method is generally not used because, like PUT, it's problematic to handle authentication.

Some of the other methods available to HTTP clients are OPTIONS, HEAD, TRACE, and CONNECT, but we won't be going over them here.

Cookies and Statelessness

Part of HTTP's statelessness is that each HTTP message acts as if each client request is completely independent of all other client requests in the world, ever. The amnesia is complete: Nothing of the previous request is remembered and no future request is anticipated.

Statelessness is generally seen as a good thing, because maintaining client state (that is, remembering who the client is and what they wanted) takes up server resources like memory and processing time. However, sometimes as a Web developer, you want the client state to be preserved. You want the server to remember who the user is and what they've done. In order for this to happen, servers must be able to somehow associate one HTTP request with another. There are several ways to do this, but HTTP has actually provided a way called *cookies*.

Cookies are essentially name-value pairs that a server creates and sends to the client, who has the choice of storing the cookie locally, or rejecting the cookie—no client ever has to accept a cookie. When the client recontacts the server, it sends along the cookie information, so the server can use that information to identify the specific user and what he or she has done. Some users like cookies, as they can sometimes enhance user experience and allow a Web site to react in a more personal way to a user's actions. Others see cookies as an invasion of privacy.

HTTP Message Structure

Unlike most communication protocols, HTTP messages consist mostly of English text, which makes this chapter much easier to read than it could be. So let's start looking at the details of an HTTP message.

HTTP is a two-message system, request and response, and the structure of HTTP messages mirrors that dichotomy. That is, there is a request HTTP message structure and a response HTTP message structure. Let's start by looking at requests, or what the clients initiate contact with.

Requests

Requests are structured like Figure 4–3.

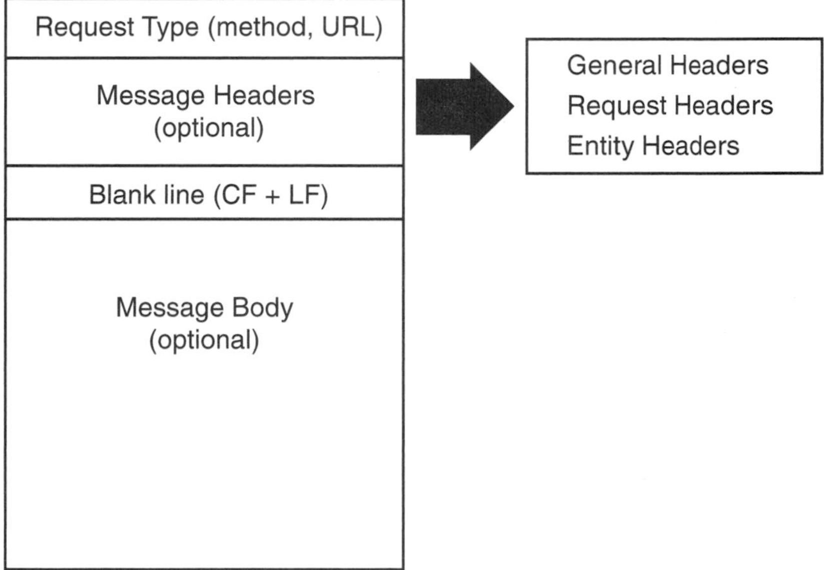

FIGURE 4–3 HTTP request message structure

Example 4–1 is a request to see the (fictional) Shelley Biotechnologies home page.

EXAMPLE 4–1 Request for home page

```
GET / HTTP/1.1
Accept: */*
Accept-Language: en-us
Accept-Encoding: gzip
User-Agent: Mozilla/4.0 (compatible; MSIE 5.5;
Windows NT 5.0)
Host: www.shelleybiotech.com
```

The top line is the Request line, which contains three things:

1. The method (`GET`)
2. The URL (`/`)
3. The version of HTTP (`HTTP/1.1`)

In this case, there are five message headers, though there could be any number of them. We then have a blank line and no message body. We don't need a message body, since we're just asking for a page, not sending any information. Even though there isn't a message body, we still have to have a blank line. The line is the signal to the server that the headers for the request have ended.

Responses

Responses look much like requests, with some small but significant differences. This is shown in Figure 4–4.

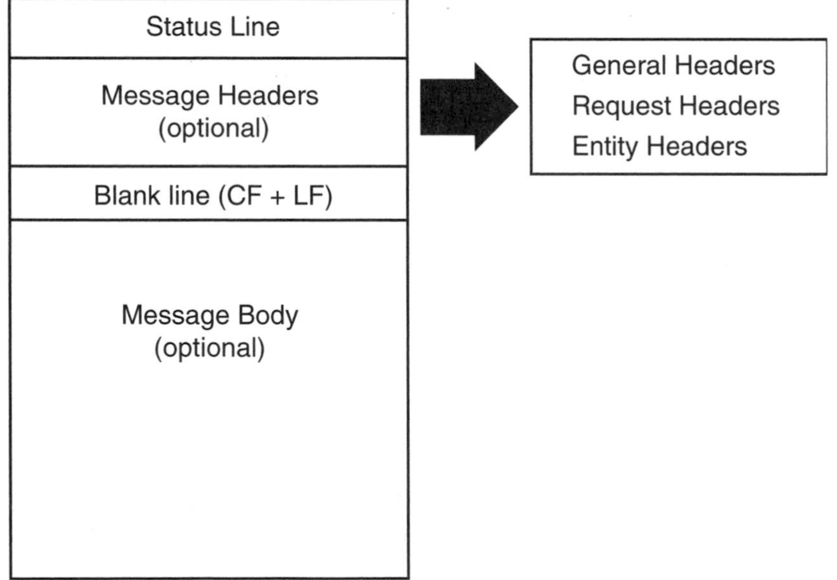

FIGURE 4–4 HTTP response message

The actual response from our fictional company's server might look like Example 4–2.

EXAMPLE 4–2 Response from Shelley

```
HTTP/1.1 200 OK
Date: Mon, 10 Sep 2001 16:46:54 GMT
Server: Apache/1.3.20 (Unix) FrontPage/4.0.4.3
X-Powered-By: PHP/3.0.16
Connection: close
Content-Type: text/html

<html>…</html>
```

How the Code Works

The top line, otherwise known as the status line, contains the version of HTTP being used (`HTTP/1.1`), a numerical code describing the status of the server response (`200`), and a string describing the status (`OK`). This is followed by a number of headers. HTTP has a large number of predefined headers that clients and servers are allowed to use—way more than we'll look at in this book. However, if you decide that you want to add extra information in your HTTP header that isn't covered by one of the predefined HTTP headers, you can include one of your own by prefacing it with a "X-", as in the "X-Powered-By" header in the above example. There is no "X-Powered-By" header in the HTTP specification, but the people who set up this specific server felt it was important to add this header, so they did.

HTTP and Security

Not everyone with a computer and an Internet connection is made of sweetness and light. There are people who merrily pit their technical skills against networks and try to gain access to information that is certainly not theirs. These people would love to look at your bank account balance or credit card numbers. Thus, some form of security is necessary for certain applications that communicate across the Internet. The most popular method of securing HTTP connections is something called Secure Sockets Layer (SSL), which is actually a separate protocol that's similar to HTTP. However, HTTP has a few security methods of its own, and we'll look at those in the next section. After all, your SOAP messages will move over HTTP, and it's likely security will be a necessary factor you'll have to think about. So here's what HTTP can offer you.

There are essentially three forms of security:

1. Identity authentication: making sure the server and the client are who they say they are.
2. Message integrity: ensuring that the message that was sent is the same message that was received.
3. Message confidentiality: ensuring that no one else can read the message except for its intended recipient.

Basic Authentication

The simplest form of HTTP security is Basic Authentication, which allows the server to send a request for a username and password. Here's what the sequence looks like:

1. Client to server: I want an HTML page.
2. Server to client: Oh yeah? You're unauthorized.
3. Client reconnects to server.
4. Client to server: I want an HTML page.
5. Client to server: Here's my username and password.
6. Server to client: Here is the HTML page.

Example 4–3 shows what the first two steps would actually look like.

EXAMPLE 4–3 Basic Authentication

```
GET /clientArea/ HTTP/1.1
Accept: */*
Accept-Language: en-us
Accept-Encoding: gzip
User-Agent: Mozilla/4.0 (compatible; MSIE 5.5;
Windows NT 5.0)
Host: www.shelleybiotech.com

HTTP/1.1 401 Unauthorized
WWW-Authenticate: Basic
realm="clients@shelleybiotech.com"
```

How the Code Works

Our request looks just like the earlier example, except that we're now trying to access a directory called "clientArea." The server responds with a 401 status, saying in essence that it needs to know who we are and that it doesn't yet. By using the WWW-Authenticate header and making its value "Basic," the server is saying that it only needs a username and password. Usually, you know this happens because a small dialog box pops up that asks for your username and password, as in Figure 4–5.

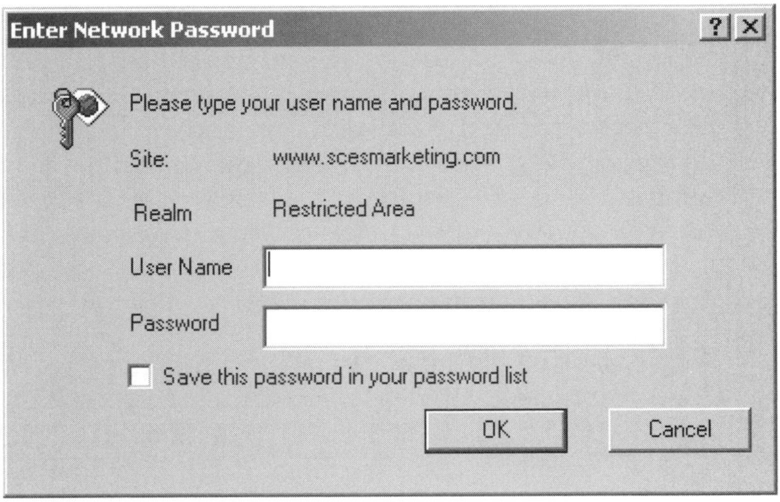

FIGURE 4–5 Simple username and password

When you enter in that information and press the "OK" button, HTTP requires that the username and password be encoded before being sent to the server. This encoding method is called Base64, and it's a way to encode binary sequences into plain text as well as to encrypt text sequences.

When the username and password are encoded, they are set in a GET request that looks something like Example 4–4:

EXAMPLE 4–4 Basic Authenitcation reply

```
GET /clientArea/ HTTP/1.1
Authorization: Basic QWEsdfSgfdDfgDfg34defg==
```

How the Code Works

The request is simplified here to focus on the Authorization header. We say, "Here's the basic authorization, nice and encoded." In all future communications with the server, the client can include this authorization line, shunting past the Unauthorized response from the server.

So what's wrong with this form of security? Well, the username and password are being sent across the public Internet, and anyone who knows how to listen would be able to pluck your username and password out, and probably decode it. Since most people use the same username and password for a number of sites, this could be disastrous. The lack of real security is why you don't see this level of security very often.

Original Digest Authentication

Since Basic Authentication wasn't providing any real security, a new form of security was devised called Digest Authentication. HTTP/1.0 has a version of this, and HTTP/1.1 made some improvements, so I'm calling the 1.0 version "Original" Digest Authentication and the 1.1 version "Improved" Digest Authentication.

Original Digest Authentication addresses the fundamental weakness of Basic Authentication, namely the transmission of passwords across the Internet.

Digest Authentication works by the client proving to the server that it knows that password in question without having to actually send that password to the server. How does such a thing happen? First, the server sends a special value to the client, and the client combines the password and this special value, the result of which is a chunk of encoded text called a *message digest*. The client then sends this digest back to the server. The server reproduces this digest and sees if the digest the client created and sent matches the digest the server created itself. If the digests match, then both the server and client used the same values to create the digest and thus the client used the same password the server did.

Sounds a little like the Basic Authentication, doesn't it? A password is combined with something and sent to the server. However, the value that the password is combined with is crucial to the system's overall security. And the server must choose a different value each time. Let's look at some code in Example 4–5.

EXAMPLE 4–5 First steps of Digest Authentication

```
GET /clientArea/ HTTP/1.1
Accept: */*
Accept-Language: en-us
Accept-Encoding: gzip
User-Agent: Mozilla/4.0 (compatible; MSIE 5.5;
Windows NT 5.0)
Host: www.shelleybiotech.com

HTTP/1.1 401 Unauthorized
WWW-Authenticate: Digest
realm="clients@shelleybiotech.com",
nonce="dsfsf345egfsdDS34rdf3SF345srfw44jh435jhg4353DF"
```

How the Code Works

The only things to look at here are the "Digest" value of WWW-Authenticate and the nonce attribute. In this case, the server is requesting a digest form of authentication, not Basic. The nonce parameter is the value the client is to combine with the password. Servers can create any value they want to make up their nonce, but the HTTP specification suggests that the value be a combination of a timestamp and a message that contains three more parts: the timestamp (again), the ETag value (don't worry about this), and a secret value known only to the server. The complicated scheme to create the nonce ensures that someone intercepting these messages won't be able to decode them. If they could figure out the timestamps, they wouldn't know the secret value the server uses to create the nonce, so they wouldn't be able to decode it.

NOTE Where does "nonce" come from?

"Nonce" is a term that's mostly used by people who put dictionaries together. A nonce-word is a word that's only in use temporarily. If you lived in England a couple hundred years ago, you'd use the phrase "for the nonce" to mean "temporarily." Since the value of the nonce parameter is used only temporarily, it's a pretty appropriate term. For example, it's likely "phat" is a nonce-word, but who knows? "Bitchin" has been around longer than anyone would have guessed.

Though it's the same word, I am assuming that there is no connection to "nonce" and the British criminals' slang word for a sexual offender.

Now, let's assume our client knows how to deal with the server's request for a Digest Authentication. Example 4–6 shows what the response might look like:

EXAMPLE 4–6 Client's original Digest Authentication

```
GET /clientArea/ HTTP/1.1
Authorization: Digest username="jake",
  realm="clients@shelleybiotech.com",
  nonce="dsfsf345egfsdDS34rdf3SF345srfw44jh435jhg
4353DF",
  uri="/clientArea/",
  response="sdhg34hg34jkhg43kjh43n3453kja09dak3b3"
```

How the Code Works

The client returns the user's username, the realm, and the nonce that was passed by the server. In addition, the URI is returned (in case there's a proxy server in the way that altered the URL), as well as the client's response to the authentication request. That is, the value of the response parameter is the combination of the nonce with the user's password. Once the server gets this response, it combines the nonce with the password it holds in its memory and sees if it's the same as what the client has sent.

Using this method, the server can reliably determine that the client is who it says it is. However, it doesn't allow the client to determine who the server is, nor does it allow anyone to be sure that the message wasn't altered somewhere between the client and the server. These shortcomings were corrected in HTTP/1.1 in the Improved Digest Authentication.

Improved Digest Authentication

The arrival of HTTP/1.1 brought improved security in the form of Improved Digest Authentication. The enhancements include:

- Defense against replay attacks
- Support for mutual authentication
- Better security for frequent clients
- Message integrity protection

To indicate that the server supports these enhancements, the server message includes a new parameter, qop, which mean "quality of protection." Here's Example 4–7:

EXAMPLE 4–7 qop parameter

```
HTTP/1.1 401 Unauthorized
WWW-Authenticate: Digest
  realm="clients@shelleybiotech.com",
  qop="auth",
nonce="dsfsf345egfsdDS34rdf3SF345srfw44jh435jhg4353DF"
```

The value of the qop parameter can be "auth," "auth-int," or "auth,auth-int." We'll look at all of these. "Auth" means that only authentication is required, while "auth-int" means that message integrity is also required.

DEFENSE AGAINST REPLAY ATTACKS

In a replay attack, an adversary (say, a hacker) fools the server into thinking it has a valid password. The adversary does this by copying the client's authorization message, and sending that valid message later to the server. That is, it "replays" the client's message to the server.

To combat this, a new parameter is being added to the Authorization field in the header: nc. The nc value gets incremented each time a client issues a request with the same nonce value. Example 4–8 shows the nc parameter in action.

EXAMPLE 4–8 Defending against replay attacks

```
GET /clientArea/ HTTP/1.1
Authorization: Digest username="jake",
  realm="clients@shelleybiotech.com",
  qop="auth",
  nc=00000001,
  nonce="dsfsf345egfsdDS34rdf3SF345srfw44jh435jhg
4353DF",
  uri="/clientArea/",
  response="sdhg34hg34jkhg43kjh43n3453kja09dak3b3"
```

How the Code Works

The lines of code in bold tell the server that Improved Digest Authorization is being used (from the qop parameter), and that this is the first time the client has issued a request with that particular nonce value. Note that the nc value always has eight digits.

For this scheme to work, the server has to actually keep track of the nc values it receives, so it knows if it has received a duplicate.

The more hack-minded of you may be thinking that a replay attack would still be easy to accomplish here: All you have to do is copy the message and increment the nc value, right? Not quite—the nc value is part of the response digest, so the digest response is based partially on the nc value. If the hacker copies the message and increments the nc value, the authentication still won't work, because the hacker didn't change the digest response.

MUTUAL AUTHENTICATION

Original Digest Authentication doesn't give clients a way to properly authenticate a server, even though it allows a server to ID a client. This can be corrected with just a few modifications.

Server authentication is just like client authentication, but backwards. The server creates a digest containing the user's password, and returns that digest along with the requested object. The client verifies the digest before accepting and displaying the object. In other words, Mutual Authentication can look like this:

1. Client to Server: Send me an HTML page.
2. Server to Client: Unauthorized: who are you?
3. Client to Server: This is who I am. I still want that HTML page.
4. Server to Client: Here is the HTML page, and confirmation that I am who I say I am.

The server triggers the mutual authentication process by including a qop parameter. If the client supports this method, then it is *required* to initiate server authentication. That is, Mutual Authentication is a mandatory part of HTTP/1.1. How exactly does that happen? Let's look at Example 4–9.

EXAMPLE 4–9 Mutual Authentication

```
--- Initial request
---
GET /clientArea/ HTTP/1.1
Accept: */*
Accept-Language: en-us
Accept-Encoding: gzip
User-Agent: Mozilla/4.0 (compatible; MSIE 5.5;
Windows NT 5.0)
Host: www.shelleybiotech.com

--- Server response
---
HTTP/1.1 401 Unauthorized
WWW-Authenticate: Digest
realm="clients@shelleybiotech.com",
  nonce="dsfsf345egfsdDS34rdf3SF345srfw44jh435jhg
4353DF"

--- Client authentication
---
GET /clientArea/ HTTP/1.1
Authorization: Digest username="jake",
  realm="clients@shelleybiotech.com",
  qop="auth",
  nc=00000001,
  nonce="dsfsf345egfsdDS34rdf3SF345srfw44jh435jhg
4353DF",
```

EXAMPLE 4–9 Mutual Authentication (Continued)

```
  1.cnonce="234kj234kjh879kjhds98cxmn435bnisdf",
  uri="/clientArea/",
  response="sdhg34hg34jkhg43kjh43n3453kja09dak3b3"

--- Server authentication
---
HTTP/1.1 200 OK
2.Authentication-Info: qop="auth",
    3.rspauth="85fgh456edr34rsfw43454gsdf3tdfbji1",
    4.cnonce="234kj234kjh879kjhds98cxmn435bnisdf",
    5.nc=00000001
```

How the Code Works

1. In the HTTP message where the client authenticates itself, it adds a new parameter: cnonce, which stands for "client nonce." This is a value the client creates and sends to the server. Remember how the server creates a parameter called "nonce" and sends it to the client, so that the client can combine that value with the password to create a digest and send it back to the server? Well, cnonce is for the server to create a digest to return to the client.
2. When the server is returning its own authentication, it uses the Authentication-Info header.
3. The rspauth (response authentication) parameter is the server's version of the client responce parameter. That is, the client hands cnonce to the server. The server combines this value with the user's password and returns rspauth. The client then combines cnonce with the password and makes sure the resulting digest is the same as the rspauth.
4. The server also returns the cnonce value.
5. The server also returns the nc value.

SECURITY FOR FREQUENT CLIENTS

While replay protection and Mutual Authentication are mandatory features of HTTP/1.1, the other security features, security for frequent clients and message integrity, are optional.

A frequent client is a client that makes many requests of the same HTTP server. The security issue that frequent clients face is that the more times they contact a server, the more likely it is that those messages will be intercepted.

To examine the root of this problem, let's back up a little bit. The method that an application uses to combine a password and a nonce to create a digest is called a *key*. For example, many HTTP digests involve combining the username, realm, and password. These values never change no matter how many requests are made.

A possible solution to this problem is to change the key occasionally. That is, change the way the digest is made. By forcing clients to occasionally change their keys, servers prevent adversaries from accumulating a substantial amount of useful data. Let's look at Example 4–10.

EXAMPLE 4–10 Changing keys

```
HTTP/1.1 401 Unauthorized
WWW-Authenticate: Digest
  realm="clients@shelleybiotech.com",
  qop="auth",
  algorithm=MD5,
  nonce="dsfsf345egfsdDS34rdf3SF345srfw44jh435jhg
4353DF"


GET /clientArea/ HTTP/1.1
Authorization: Digest username="jake",
  realm="clients@shelleybiotech.com",
  qop="auth",
  algorithm=MD5,
  nc=00000001,
  nonce="dsfsf345egfsdDS34rdf3SF345srfw44jh435jhg
4353DF",
  cnonce="234kj234kjh879kjhds98cxmn435bnisdf",
  uri="/clientArea/",
  response="sdhg34hg34jkhg43kjh43n3453kja09dak3b3"
```

How the Code Works

The bold sections of the code display a new parameter: algorithm. Use this parameter to tell the client to use a certain kind of encoding. MD5 is popular, but MD5-sess is stronger.

MESSAGE INTEGRITY

The last kind of HTTP-specific security we'll look at is maintaining message integrity. Here's a scenario: You're trying to pay off your credit card bill, which has reached $4000. You've been a frugal consumer, and you're ready to pay the bill online. Without your knowledge, someone has set up a computer between you and the credit card company. You connect to this evil adversary, and send them all your information—it's mostly encoded, so the adversary can't take anything directly. However, it does tweak some of the information and forwards that tweaked message to your credit card company. In the end, $4000 goes to the adversary's bank account, not to your credit card payment. This kind of attack is called the *man-in-the-middle* attack, because the adversary poses as a server to you and as a client to the real server. The adversary changed nothing in the HTTP header, only the content of the message itself.

This is a serious vulnerability, but fortunately it's pretty easy to protect against. If the entire content of the message itself is encoded into the message digest, then the adversary can't modify any of the content without having to create a whole new digest.

How do you trigger message integrity? Easily—check out Example 4–11:

EXAMPLE 4–11 Triggering message integrity

```
HTTP/1.1 401 Unauthorized
WWW-Authenticate: Digest
  realm="clients@shelleybiotech.com",
  qop="auth-int",
  algorithm=MD5,
  nonce="dsfsf345egfsdDS34rdf3SF345srfw44jh435jhg
4353DF"
```

EXAMPLE 4–11 Triggering message integrity (Continued)

```
GET /clientArea/ HTTP/1.1
Authorization: Digest username="jake",
  realm="clients@shelleybiotech.com",
  qop="auth-int",
  algorithm=MD5,
  nc=00000001,
  nonce="dsfsf345egfsdDS34rdf3SF345srfw44jh435jhg
4353DF",
  cnonce="234kj234kjh879kjhds98cxmn435bnisdf",
  uri="/clientArea/",
  response="sdhg34hg34jkhg43kjh43n3453kja09dak3b3"
```

How the Code Works

That's it! Just change the value of the qop parameter to auth-int, and the client and server applications do the rest.

That's about it for Improved Digest Authentication, and that's as far as using only HTTP can take you, as far as security goes. There is one major facet that the above doesn't cover: keeping people from eavesdropping on and pulling the messages from your HTTP conversations. Most applications want that level of security (especially if the message is, say, your credit card number), and that means that you have to use SSL (or something close to it).

Secure Sockets Layer (SSL)

As we've seen, HTTP offers some, but not complete, security. In particular, there's no way to encrypt the messages themselves. That's bad, because the Internet is public and no matter how well your identity is authorized, if your message is still in plain English, all a hacker has to do is pull the message contents, and do with it what he or she wills.

This is such a big deal that if there were no way to encrypt messages, e-commerce (even to the point of the existence of credit cards) wouldn't exist. To solve this, some people at Netscape (remember them? They used to make browsers) created something called Secure Sockets Layer (SSL). SSL isn't a part of HTTP. It's its own layer, entirely separate from HTTP.

The Netscape folks included this proprietary software inside their software, and just about everyone followed suit, even Microsoft. In fact, right now SSL is the most popular network security protocol in the world.

Figure 4–6 shows where SSL lives in relation to the other communication protocols.

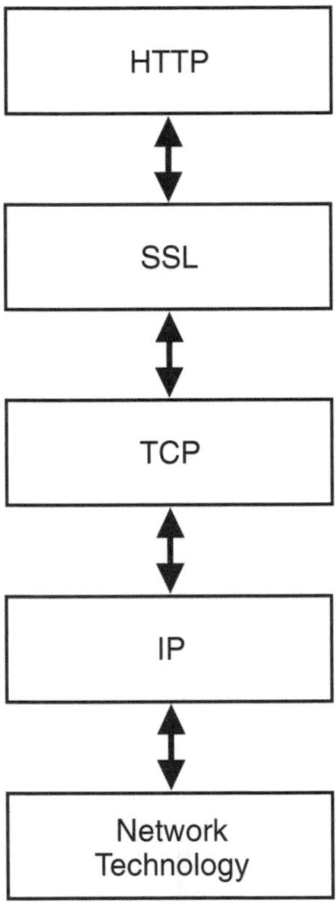

FIGURE 4–6 Where SSL lives

HTTP communicates only with SSL, instead of with TCP as before. Clients can elect to use SSL, and a URL beginning with HTTPS usually means that a secure server is being used. However, this isn't standard, so the only way to tell for sure is to look at the little padlock icon on your browser. If it's locked, then SSL is being used.

HTTP over SSL has a default port of 443, as opposed to HTTP's default port of 80. This means that many applications will have to have two default ports: 80 and 443.

So how does this SSL thing work? It involves something you've probably heard of before: public key cryptography.

Public Key Cryptography

SSL relies completely on public key cryptography, which solves the problem of key management, a fundamental problem in cryptography in general.[1]

KEY MANAGEMENT

When two entities decide to communicate in coded messages, they share a secret value called a *key*. In the case of the digests discussed above, the shared key is the user's password. Both the client and the server must know the user's password in order to send the information securely. An adversary that obtains a key, like the password, can pretend to be both client and server.

This presents a problem: How do the parties agree on an exchange of the value of the key? Sending the key along with the message isn't a very secure way to do it. This is part of the problem of key management.

TWO KEYS

Public key cryptography solves this problem of exchanging keys by involving two keys per coded message instead of just one. For example, one key can be used to encode information, but another key must be used to decode it. The two keys are certainly related, but the relationship is usually so mathematically complex that one can't be derived from the other. Imagine a door that requires one key to lock it, and a different key to unlock it.

---

1. A great novel that combines action, smarts, and cryptography: *Cryptonomicon* by Neal Stephenson. Nine thumbs up.

PUBLIC AND PRIVATE

The use of two keys allows for an interesting solution: One of the keys can be freely published, so anyone has access to it. This key is known as the *public key.* The other key, however, is closely guarded, kept secret, and not sent over any network, ever. This is known as the *private key.*

Generally, a server that supports SSL will have two keys: its public key and its private key. This server will send its public key to any client that asks. However, it won't send its private key to anyone for any reason.

Here's how it works:

1. Client asks server for public key.
2. Server sends client the public key.
3. Client encodes the data (including the message itself), using the public key.
4. Client sends encoded data to server.
5. Server receives data, and decodes it, using its private key.

In this scenario, the client sends an encoded message to the server. What if the opposite must happen? That is, how does the server send an encoded message to the client? Here's how that works:

1. Client contains its own private and public key.
2. Server asks client for encoded message.
3. Client encodes its information using its private key.
4. Client sends encoded information and public key to the server.
5. Server uses client's public key to decode the information. If the value makes sense, it means the client sent the message.

Here's another way to look at it:

- A server's public key encodes information.
- A server's private key decodes information.
- A client's private key encodes information.
- A client's public key decodes information.

Read the above bullet points a few times until it makes sense. Done? Great. Think you're done with public key cryptography? Not quite.

PUBLIC KEY CERTIFICATES

Here's a complication: How can you be sure of the authenticity of a received public key? How do you know a public key comes from where it says it comes from? There is no easy answer to this question. The best people came up with was to create something called Public Key Certificates issued by Certification Authorities.

A Certification Authority is an authority that clients and servers both trust, and that issues Public Key Certificates. How does one go about getting this vaunted Certificate?

1. You present your public key to the Certification Authority along with proof of the server's identity.
2. The Certification Authority then encrypts the server's public key using its own private key. This process is known as *signing*.
3. This encrypted public key is stored in a digital certificate. It is this certificate that the server sends to clients. Those clients who know the Certification Authority's public key can then decrypt the public key, thus verifying that the Certification Authority did indeed give that particular public key its stamp of approval.

Great. Now how do clients get a Certification Authority's public key? There are many of these Authorities. If a client tries to get these public keys over an insecure network, we're back at the beginning, with an adversary laying in wait, ready to transmit a phony public key. The solution: Preload browsers with all the Certification Authority public keys. Your browser has them right now. If you go to your browser's preferences, and look under "security" or something similar, you should see a list of Certification Authorities. That means your browser holds the public keys for all of those Authorities.

A disadvantage of public key cryptography is that it's slow. It takes up processing power and time. There are ways to speed it up, but those are beyond the scope of this book.

SSL Operation

SSL offers three services:

1. Identity authentication
2. Message integrity
3. Confidentiality

In general, the negotiation between client and server involved in SSL takes nine steps and occurs before any HTTP communication happens.

1. Client to server: Hello.
2. Server to client: Hi there.
3. Server to client: Here's my certificate.
4. Server to client: I'm through saying Hello now.
5. Client to server: Here's my public key
6. Client to server: Here's my cipher specification.
7. Client to server: Goodbye.
8. Server to client: Changing cipher specification.
9. Server to client: Goodbye.

Don't worry about the cipher specification—that's just part of the negotiation, and we won't go into it here.

Open Source

SSL is technically proprietary, so there's an effort underway to create something called Transport Layer Security (TLS), which is just SSL, but released to the world. In fact, version 1.0 of TLS is just an incremented version of SSL.

There is also a volunteer group of coders who have created something called OpenSSL, which has become very popular. As of this writing, this project is very close to releasing version 1.0 of OpenSSL.

Advantages and Disadvantages of HTTP

There are many developers out there arguing that HTTP is the perfect way for SOAP messages to travel, and other arguing that HTTP is a horrible way to move SOAP messages. Both sides have good points. Let's look at a few of them:

ADVANTAGES

- HTTP is everywhere—not much new infrastructure will have to be built
- HTTP is stateless, and SOAP messages are mostly involved with RPC, where statelessness is fine.

DISADVANTAGES

- HTTP is slow
- HTTP is insecure—too many HTTP holes are punched through firewalls for something as potentially damaging as remote procedure calls.

Regardless of which side is right, SOAP messages—lots of them—will be traveling over HTTP. We'll just have to wait and see what happens.

SOAPAction

So, what exactly do you have to know about HTTP in order to create your SOAP systems? Not much at all. You have to add a single SOAPAction header to your HTTP header, as in Example 4–12, that contains a URI of where the actual method is.

EXAMPLE 4–12 SOAPAction in action

```
GET /shelleyServ/ HTTP/1.1
User-Agent: Mozilla/4.0 (compatible; MSIE 5.5;
Windows NT 5.0)
Host: www.shelleybiotech.com
SOAPAction: "HTTP://www.shelleybiotech.com/
shelleyServ/"

<env:Envelope
  xmlns:env="HTTP://www.w3.org/2001/06/soap-envelope">
  <env:Body>
      <w:getPatientHistory xmlns:w="HTTP://
    www.wire-man.com/medical/services"
    env:encodingStyle="HTTP://www.w3.org/2001/06/
    soap-encoding">
           <SSN>555-55-5555</SSN>
      </w:getPatientHistory>
  </env:Body>
</env:Envelope>
```

How the Code Works

The bold line in the HTTP header is all you need to worry about. All SOAP client requests must contain a SOAPAction header, but as to what that header can contain, well, it has to either be some form of URI or be blank. Example 4–13 contains some acceptable SOAPAction headers:

EXAMPLE 4–13 SOAPAction headers

```
SOAPAction: "HTTP://www.shelleybiotech.com/
shelleyServ/"
SOAPAction: "find_patient/ssn.class"
SOAPAction: ""
SOAPAction:
```

The only real purpose of the SOAPAction header is to allow servers, such as firewalls, to appropriately filter SOAP messages.

Recap

So that's SOAP and HTTP. There isn't much direct connection between them beyond the mandatory use of the SOAPAction header by SOAP clients. Most of this chapter concerned itself with how HTTP actually worked, and what kind of security is available to SOAP messages traveling over HTTP (and maybe SSL).

5

SOAP Security Extensions

IN THIS CHAPTER

- Security for SOAP
- Introduction to XML Signature
- Core Generation and Validation
- Detailed Syntax
- XML Signature in SOAP Messages

SSL is great for securely transporting SOAP messages, as long as they're traveling over HTTP and all of your intermediaries (remember actors?) are completely trusted. However, this isn't always the case, and you can't guarantee that any SOAP message will be able to rely completely on SSL to keep it 100% confidential and unchanged. Recognizing the need for SOAP to have some additional security features, some folks got together and created a specification for SOAP Security Extensions. This specification is currently a submitted

Note to the W3C, which means that it could change significantly in the future. However, these extensions rely heavily on another specification called XML Signature, which is in a much more stable state.

Security for SOAP

The goal of adding security measures to SOAP messages themselves is to ensure, by a variety of means, true end-to-end security to the sending, transport, and reception of a SOAP message. SSL/TLS is great for ensuring secure transport over HTTP, but that's it (actually, SSL can apply to any protocol, including FTP, and even ssh, which is telnet over SSL). As mentioned above, your SOAP messages may not travel over HTTP, and there may be untrustworthy actors ready to intercept and inappropriately process your message before it gets to its ultimate destination. It's generally agreed that the best place for security information to live in a SOAP message is in the header. Security extensions are expected to live here, and they're essentially placing something called XML Signature into a SOAP header. What does this mean and what does XML Signature do? Well, that deserves a section all of its own.

Introduction to XML Signature

The specification for XML Signature is a way to ensure several forms of security to a SOAP message:

1. Message integrity: what you sent is what they received
2. Message authentication: message is what you think it is
3. Sender authentication: you are who you say you are

XML Signature works by encoding a bunch of relevant information and associating that information with a certain key. XML Signatures are applied to almost any kind of digital content, also called data objects. Data objects are digested (remember, a digest is an encoded piece of text; the data objects are not actually eaten). This digest is then combined with other information, and that combination is digested again. This second digest is then cryptographically signed. These Signatures are represented by the Signature element in the SOAP header (if you're signing a SOAP message, of course).

Let's look at Example 5–1, which shows the overall structure of a digital signature as defined by XML Signature.

EXAMPLE 5–1 XML Signature structure

```
<Signature>
    1.<SignedInfo>
      2.(CanonicalizationMethod)
      3.(SignatureMethod)
      4.(<Reference 5.(URI=)? >
        6.(Transitions)?
        7.(DigestMethod)
        8.(DigestValue)
      </Reference>)+
    </SignedInfo>
    9.(SignatureValue)
    10.(KeyInfo)?
    11.(<Object>
      12.(SignatureProperties)?
      13.(Manifest)?
    </Object>)*
</Signature>
```

How the Code Works

First, we're taking some notation from DTDs: "?" means "zero or one occurrences," "*" means "zero or more occurrences," and "+" means "one or more occurrences."

1. As you could have predicted, the SignedInfo element is the information that is actually signed. When this reaches its destination, the SignedInfo element must undergo core validation, which involves two processes: validation of the Signature over the SignedInfo element and validation of each Reference digest within the SignedInfo element.

2. The CanonicalizationMethod is the algorithm used to canonicalize[1] the SignedInfo element before it is digested.
3. Once the SignedInfo is canonicalized, then the SignatureMethod element supplies the algorithm used to digest everything into the SignatureValue. This digestion actually involves several algorithms. At minimum, it involves a digest algorithm and a key-dependent algorithm. Other algorithms are certainly possible as well.
4. The Reference element(s) contains the digest method and resulting digest value over some data object. In other words, the Reference element contains a pointer to a data object, the method of its encryption, and the resulting encrypted value. To sign a data object, a signature is applied (more on exactly what that means later) to the digest value.
5. The URI value in the Reference element points to the actual data object to be signed. If there are multiple Reference elements, at most only one of them may choose to omit this attribute.
6. The Transforms element contains an optional list of processing steps that were applied to the data object before digestion occurred. These transformations can include canonicalization, encoding, decoding, compression, inflation, XSLT, XPath, and XML Schema validation, and so on.

---

1. Canonicalization is a method that breaks an XML document or fragment down into its logical parts. For example, let's say we have two XML documents that contain the same information but with small differences, like the attributes are in a different order. The two documents are not byte-for-byte identical, because the attributes are in slightly different places. However, if both of the documents were canonicalized, and those canonical forms were compared, they would be identical. Why? Because the canonical form of an XML document contains its basic information, and since the two documents contain the same information, their canonical forms would be identical.

7. The DigestionMethod element details the algorithm applied to the data after everything listed in the Transforms element has run its course.
8. When the DigestionMethod does its thing on the data object, a value is yielded, and that value is the DigestionValue.
9. The SignatureValue is the result of applying the SignatureMethod to everything in the SignedInfo element.
10. The KeyInfo is the key to be used to validate the signature. Almost anything can serve in this capacity, including certificates, key names, key agreement algorithms, and so on. Did you notice that this element is optional? This may seem counterintuitive, but there are two reasons for it: The signer may not wish to reveal the key information to all applications that will process the SOAP message (including actors), and the key information may already be known by the receiving application, so it doesn't need to be stated explicitly in the SOAP message itself.
11. The Object element is an optional one. It provides a way to include data objects in the signature document itself or in an external file.
12. SignatureProperties is a list of separate SignatureProperty elements. These properties can include such information as the time of signing. They can be optionally signed by referring to them from inside a Reference element.
13. Objects may also include a Manifest, which is a list of data objects to be included for signing. While this is quite similar to simply having multiple Reference objects, there is a difference. For example, if you don't want some references to be a part of the core validation, then you would list them in a Manifest instead of including them as regular References. A Manifest is also useful if you have a large number of Signatures that need to be applied to a large number of documents. You could have an enormous SignedInfo element with a ton of References, and a bunch of Signatures applied to that document. Using Manifest to hold many Refer-

ences and referring to that Manifest from multiple Signature elements is a more efficient approach.

Let's look at Example 5–2, which contains some sample code for this.

EXAMPLE 5–2 Sample XML Signature

```
<Signature Id="ShelleyBioSignature"
xmlns="http://www.w3.org/2000/09/xmldsig#">
<SignedInfo>
  <CanonicalizationMethod Algorithm="
  http://www.w3.org/TR/2000/CR-xml-c14n-20001026"/>
  <SignatureMethod
    Algorithm="http://www.w3.org/2000/09/
    xmldsig#dsa-sha1"/>
  <Reference URI="http://www.shelleybiotech.com/
  ms_sig23">
       <Transforms>
            <Transform
            Algorithm="http://www.w3.org/TR/2000/CR-
            xml-c14n-20001026"/>
       </Transforms>
       <DigestMethod
            Algorithm="http://www.w3.org/2000/09/
            xmldsig#sha1"/>
       <DigestValue>
            3jhg4589de92334j3h34h4rnk=
       </DigestValue>
  </Reference>
</SignedInfo>
<SignatureValue>SDF235GG9DRGRgdfGd55GEDFG…</
SignatureValue>
<KeyInfo>
  <KeyValue>
       <DSAKeyValue>
            <P>…</P>
            <Q>…</Q>
            <G>…</G>
            <Y>…</y>
       </DSAKeyValue>
  </KeyValue>
</KeyInfo>
<Object>
  <SignatureProperties>
       <SignatureProperty Id="timeOfSigning"
```

EXAMPLE 5–2 Sample XML Signature (Continued)

```
Target="#thisSignature">
        <timestamp
xmlns="http://www.shelleybiotech.com/dsig/timestamp">
            <date>2002-02-27</date>
            <time>13:42:05+08:00</time>
        </timestamp>
      </SignatureProperty>
  </SignatureProperties>
</Object>
</Signature>
```

We won't dissect this code just yet, but it's useful to have an actual look at it. You may have noticed that we used SignatureProperties in the Object element, but we didn't include a Manifest. If we do that, we also have to change the Reference element, as in Example 5–3.

EXAMPLE 5–3 Manifest

```
<Signature ...>
<SignedInfo>
  <CanonicalizationMethod...>
  <SignatureMethod...>
  <Reference URI="#ShelleyManifest839"
    Type="http://www.w3.org/2000/09/
    xmldsig#Manifest">
        <DigestMethod Algorithm="http://www.w3.org/
        2000/09/xmldsig#sha1"/>

        <DigestValue>
            3jhg4589de92334j3h34h4rnk=
        </DigestValue>
  </Reference>
  ...
</SignedInfo>
<Object>
    <Manifest ID="ShelleyManifest839">
      <Reference>...</Reference>
      <Reference>...</Reference>
    </Manifest>
</Object>
</Signature>
```

Did you notice in the first reference that the URI referred to the Manifest within the Object element? That's how you can apply a signature to a multitude of objects simply.

Now that we've looked at all the pieces of XML Signature, let's look at how it works.

Core Generation and Validation

The "core" of XML Signature refers to the combination of the digestion of the data objects with the generation of the actual signature. The generation of this core must follow certain specific processes. Also, the receiver of such a signature must follow certain rules in order to validate that the signature is correct.

Core Generation

Core Generation involves two steps: Reference generation and Signature generation.

REFERENCE GENERATION

There are three steps to generate References:

1. Apply the transformation (in the Transforms element) to the data object.
2. Calculate the digest value of the transformed data object. In other words, digest it.
3. Create the actual Reference element, including the identification of the data and any optional Transformation elements, the digest algorithm (the DigestMethod element), and the actual value of the digest (placed in the DigestValue element).

SIGNATURE GENERATION

There are also three steps to generate the actual Signature:

1. Create the SignedInfo element with the SignatureMethod, CanonicalizationMethod, and any Reference elements.
2. Canonicalize and calculate the SignatureValue over SignedInfo, based on encryption algorithms specified in the SignedInfo element.

3. Finally, create the Signature, which includes the SignedInfo, any Object elements, KeyInfo, and SignatureValue elements.

Core Validation

On the receiving end, the digital signature must be examined to see if it's real.

SIGNATURE VALIDATION

1. Key information should be retrieved from the KeyInfo element or from some external source, in case the KeyInfo is absent.
2. Obtain the canonical form from the SignatureMethod, using the CanonicalizationMethod element and use the result to confirm the SignatureValue over the SignedInfo element.

REFERENCE VALIDATION

1. Canonicalize the SignedInfo element, based on the CanonicalizationMethod in the SignedInfo element.
2. For each Reference element, obtain the actual data object that was digested and digest it using the DigestionMethod in the Reference section. Then compare the obtained digest value with the value in the DigestValue method.

Detailed Syntax

Hopefully, you now have a semisolid understanding of how XML Signature is structured and how it works. That's good for an overview, but not enough for us—we need to know some of the implementation details. Thus, we'll be looking closely at many of the requirements of the elements and attributes of XML Signature.

Signature Element

As you've seen, the Signature element is the root element of XML Signature. Example 5–4 lets us examine the XML Schema of this element.

EXAMPLE 5–4 Signature element

```
<schema xmlns="http://www.w3.org/2001/XMLSchema"
  xmlns:ds="http://www.w3.org/2000/09/xmldsig#"
  targetNamespace="http://www.w3.org/2000/09/
  xmldsig#"
  elementFormDefault="qualified">

  <element name="signature" type="ds:SignatureType"/>
  <complexType name="SignatureType">
    <sequence>
      <element ref="ds:SignedInfo"/>
      <element ref="ds:SignatureValue"/>
      <element ref="ds:KeyInfo" minOccurs="0"/>
      <element ref="ds:Object" minOccurs="0"
            maxOccurs="unbounded"/>
    </sequence>
  </complexType>

</schema>
```

The Signature element doesn't do much but act as a container. We'll be examining the other elements right now.

SignatureValue Element

As shown in Example 5–5, this element contains the actual value of the digital signature. If this value doesn't validate, then the signature is unacceptable.

EXAMPLE 5–5 SignatureValue schema

```
<element name="SignatureValue"
  type="ds:SignatureValueType"/>
<complexType name="SignatureValueType">
  <simpleContent>
      <extension base="base64Binary">
```

EXAMPLE 5–5 SignatureValue schema (Continued)

```
        <attribute name="Id" type="ID"
            use="optional"/>
    </extension>
  </simpleContent>
</complexType>
```

SignedInfo Element

The SignedInfo element, seen in Example 5–6, contains the information needed to create the digital signature. That is, the canonicalization algorithm, the signature algorithm, and any references that exist.

EXAMPLE 5–6 SignedInfo schema

```
<element name="SignedInfo"
type="ds:SignedInfoType"/>
<complexType name="SignedInfoType">
  <sequence>
      <element ref="ds:CanonicalizationMethod"/>
      <element ref="ds:SignatureMethod"/>
      <element ref="ds:Reference"
            maxOccurs="unbounded"/>
  </sequence>
  <attribute name="Id" type="ID" use="optional"/>
</complexType>
```

CanonicalizationMethod Element

This element is required, as canonicalization is a necessary step in creating the digital signature. It is strongly recommended that you use an XML-based canonicalization as opposed to a text-based one.

An application needs to be careful in accepting and executing any canonicalization method it comes across. These methods could have many negative effects, including:

- Rewriting the URIs
- Converting the signature into something trivial by using a known key
- Modification or deletion of the SignedInfo element

Example 5–7 shows the schema for a canonicalization method.

EXAMPLE 5–7 CanonicalizationMethod schema

```
<element name="CanonicalizationMethod"
  type="ds:CanonicalizationMethodType">
<complexType name="CanonicalizationMethodType"
  mixed="true">
  <sequence>
      <any namespace="##any" minOccurs="0"
            maxOccurs="unbounded"/>
  </sequence>
  <attribute name="Algorithm" type="anyURI"
      use="required"/>
</complexType>
```

SignatureMethod Element

This element is also required, as it contains a necessary algorithm used to create the digital signature. All of the cryptographic functions (public keys, hashing, and so on) are defined by the SignatureMethod element. Example 5–8 shows its schema.

EXAMPLE 5–8 SignatureMethod schema

```
<element name="SignatureMethod"
  type="ds:SignatureMethodType"/>
<complexType name="SignatureMethodType"
mixed="true"/>
<sequence>
  <element name="HMACOutputLength" minOccurs="0"
        type="ds:HMACOutputLngth"/>
  <any namespace="##other" minOccurs="0"
        maxOccurs="unbounded"/>
</sequence>
<attribute name="Algorithm" type="anyURI"
    use="required"/>
</complexType>
```

Reference Element

The Reference element, predictably, refers to an actual piece of digital content (also called a *data object*). Since there can be more than one chunk of digital content, there can be more than one Reference element. This element, the schema of which appears in Example 5–9, uses a URI to identify where the digital content actually is, as well as any possible transformations that are to be run before the Reference's digest is created (see next section).

EXAMPLE 5–9 Reference schema

```
<element name="Reference" type="ds:ReferenceType"/>
<complexType name="ReferenceType">
  <sequence>
      <element ref="ds:Transforms" minOccurs="0"/>
      <element ref="ds:DigestMethod"/>
      <element ref="ds:DigestValue"/>
  </sequence>
  <attribute name="Id" type="ID" use="optional"/>
  <attribute name="URI" type="anyURI" use="optional"/>
  <attribute name="Type" type="anyURI" use="optional"/>
</complexType>
```

Transforms and Transforms Elements

The Transforms element simply contains a number of Transform elements. Each Transform specifies an algorithm that was run on the data object before the digest was created. There can be more than one Transform for each Reference element, and it is understood that the output of one Transform is the input of the next Transform element. The schema for the Transforms and Transform elements appears in Example 5–10.

These transformations don't necessarily apply to the entire data object. Sometimes, a transformation applies only to a certain part of a data object, and that's what the XPath element is for: It defines a node-set that the transformation is to be applied to.

EXAMPLE 5–10 Transforms and Transform schemas

```
<element name="Transforms" type="ds:TransformsType"/>
<complexType name="TransformType">
  <sequence>
      <element ref="ds:Transform"
          maxOccurs="unbounded"/>
  </sequence>
</complexType>

<element name="Transform" type="ds:TransformType"/>
<complexType name="TransformType" mixed="true"/>
  <choice minOccurs="0" maxOccurs="unbounded">
      <any namespace="##other"
          processContents="lax"/>
      <element name="XPath" type="string"/>
  </choice>
  <attribute name="Algorithm" type="anyURI"
      use="required"/>
</complexType>
```

DigestMethod Element

This element specifies the algorithm that is used to create the digest of the Reference. Example 5–11 shows the schema.

EXAMPLE 5–11 DigestMethod schema

```
<element name="DigestMethod"
type="ds:DigestMethodType"/>
<complexType name="DigestMethodType" mixed="true">
  <sequence>
      <any namespace="##other" processContent="lax"
            minOccurs="0" maxOccurs="unbounded"/>
  </sequence>
</complexType>
```

DigestValue Element

This element is the result of applying the algorithm in the DigestMethod element to the Reference. Its schema is shown in Example 5–12. Remember, the DigestMethod is applied after all the transformations have been applied. The result of this digestion is placed in the DigestValue element.

EXAMPLE 5–12 DigestValue schema

```
<element name="DigestValue"
type="ds:DigestValueType"/>
<simpleType name="DigestValueType">
    <restriction base="base64Binary"/>
</simpleType>
```

KeyInfo Element

The optional KeyInfo element exists to allow the recipients of the digital signature the keys needed to validate the signature—that is, prove the signature is authentic and the message has arrived unmolested. This element can contain information such as keys, names, certificates, or other information.

If this element doesn't exist, it's assumed that the recipient will know the proper keys to use to validate the signature. Example 5–13 shows the schema of this element.

EXAMPLE 5–13 KeyInfo schema

```
<element name="KeyInfo" type="ds:KeyInfoType"/>
<complexType name="KeyInfoType" mixed="true">
    <choice maxOccurs="unbounded">
      <element ref="ds:KeyName"/>
      <element ref="ds:KeyValue"/>
      <element ref="ds:RetrievalMethod"/>
      <element ref="ds:X509Data"/>
      <element ref="ds:PGPData"/>
      <element ref="ds:SPKIData"/>
      <element ref="ds:MgmtData"/>
      <any processContents="lax"
          namespace="##other"/>
    </choice>
    <attribute name="Id" type="ID" use="optional"/>
</complexType>
```

KeyName Element

This element, its schema shown in Example 5–14, lives inside the KeyInfo element and relates the identifier of the key to be used. Common values are names of keys, email addresses, a key index, and so on.

EXAMPLE 5–14 KeyName schema

```
<element name="KeyName" type="string"/>
```

KeyValue Element

This element contains the value of a single public key. The formats for these key values must be in DSA or RSA form (see Example 5–15).

EXAMPLE 5–15 KeyValue schema

```
<element name="KeyValue" type="ds:KeyValueType"/>
<complexType name="KeyValueType" mixed="true">
    <choice>
      <element ref="ds:DSAKeyValue"/>
      <element ref="ds:RSAKeyValue"/>
      <any namespace="##other"
            processContents="lax"/>
    </choice>
</complexType>
```

DSAKeyValue Element

DSA public key values can have the following fields:

- P: a prime modulus (can be public)
- Q: an integer in the range of 2^{159} and 2^{160} that is a prime divisor of P-1 (can be public)
- G: an integer with certain properties (we won't get into them here) with respect to P and Q (can be public)
- J: (P-1) / Q (included solely for efficiency)
- Y: G^X mod P (where X is part of the private key)

Example 5–16 shows the schema for the DSAKeyValue element.

EXAMPLE 5–16 DSAKeyValue schema

```
<element name="DSAKeyValue"
type="ds:DSAKeyValueType"/>
<complexType name="DSAKeyValueType">
    <sequence>
      <sequence minOccurs="0">
        <element name="P" type="ds:CryptoBinary"/>
        <element name="Q" type="ds:CryptoBinary"/>
      </sequence>
      <element name="J" type="ds:CryptoBinary"
            minOccurs="0"/>
      <element name="G" type="ds:CryptoBinary"
            minOccurs="0"/>
      <element name="Y" type="ds:CryptoBinary"/>
      <sequence minOccurs="0">
            <element name="Seed"
              type="ds:CryproBinary"/>
        <element name="PgenCounter"
              type="ds:CryptoBinary"/>
      </sequence>
    </sequence>
</complexType>
```

RSAKeyValue Element

RSA Key values have only two fields: Modulus and Exponent, both in base64 form. Example 5–17 shows the schema of the RSAKeyValue element.

EXAMPLE 5–17 RSAKeyValue schema

```
<element name="RSAKeyValue"
type="ds:RSAKeyValueType"/>
<complexType name="RSAKeyValueType">
  <sequence>
      <element name="Modulus"
          type="ds:CryptoBinary"/>
      <element name="Exponent"
          type="ds:CryptoBinary"/>
    </sequence>
</complexType>
```

RetrievalMethod Element

If this element is inside a KeyInfo element, then it's a reference to KeyInfo information that's stored in another location (for example, in another document). Its schema is contained in Example 5–18.

Example 5–18 RetrievalMethod schema

```
<element name="RetrievalMethod"
  type="ds:RetrievalMethodType"/>
<complexType name="RetrievalMethodType">
  <sequence>
  <element name="Transforms" type="ds:TransformsType"
        minOccurs="0"/>
  </sequence>
  <attribute name="URI" type="anyURI"/>
  <attribute name="Type" type="anyURI"/>
</complexType>
```

X509Data Element

The X509Data element (see Example 5–19) contains one or more identifiers of keys or X509 certificates. We could get into much more detail here, but it's beyond the scope of this book.

Example 5–19 X509Data schema

```
<element name="X509Data" type="ds:X509DataType"/>
<complexType name="X509DataType">
  <sequence maxOccurs="unbounded">
    <choice>
      <element name="X509IssuerSerial"
          type="ds:X509IssuerSerialType"/>
      <element name="X509SKI"
          type="base64Binary"/>
      <element name="X509SubjectName"
          type="string"/>
      <element name="X509Certificate"
          type="base64Binary"/>
      <element name="X509CRL"
          type="base64Binary"/>
```

EXAMPLE 5–19 X509Data schema (Continued)

```
      <any namespace="##other"
          processContents="lax"/>
    </choice>
  </sequence>
</complexType>

<complexType name="X509IssuerSerialType">
  <sequence>
    <element name="X509IssuerName" type="string"/>
    <element name="X509SerialNumber"
        type="integer"/>
  </sequence>
</complexType>
```

PGPData Element

Any information about PGP public keys is conveyed here (see Example 5–20).

EXAMPLE 5–20 PGPData schema

```
<element name="PGPData" type="ds:PGPDataType"/>
<complexType name="PGPDataType">
  <choice>
    <sequence>
      <element name="PGPKeyID"
          type="base64Binary"/>
      <element name="PGPKeyPacket"
          type="base64Binary" minOccurs="0"/>
      <any namespace="##other"
          processContents="lax" minOccurs="0"
          maxOccurs="unbounded"/>
    </sequence>
    <sequence>
      <element name="PGPKeyPacket"
          type="base64Binary"/>
      <any namespace="##other"
          processContents="lax" minOccurs="0"
          maxOccurs="unbounded"/>
    </sequence>
  </choice>
</complexType>
```

SPKIData Element

Any information about SPKI public key pairs, certificates, and any other SPKI data is listed here (see Example 5–21).

EXAMPLE 5–21 SPKIData schema

```
<element name="SPKIData" type="SPKIDataType"/>
<complexType name="SPKIDataType">
  <sequence maxOccurs="unbounded">
    <element name="SPKISexp" type="base64Binary"/>
    <any namespace="##other" processContents="lax"
          minOccurs="0"/>
  </sequence>
</complexType>
```

MgmtData Element

Any in-band information, such as key distribution or agreement data, goes here. This can include DH key exchanges and RSA key encryptions. However, use of this element, the schema of which can be seen in Example 5–22, is definitely *not* recommended.

EXAMPLE 5–22 MgmtData schema

```
<element name="MgmtData" type="string"/>
```

Object Element

The Object element (see Example 5–23) can contain all sorts of things, but it's mostly used to point to references that occur outside the current document or references that are to be treated differently than those in the SignedInfo element.

EXAMPLE 5–23 Object schema

```
<element name="Object" type="ds:ObjectType"/>
<complexType name="ObjectType" mixed="true">
  <sequence minOccurs="0" maxOccurs="unbounded">
    <any namespace="##any" processContents="lax"/>
```

EXAMPLE 5–23 Object schema (Continued)

```
  </sequence>
  <attribute name="Id" type="ID" use="optional"/>
  <attribute name="MimeType" type="string"
        use="optional"/>
  <attribute name="Encoding" type="anyURI"
        use="optional"/>
</complexType>
```

Manifest Element

The Manifest element's purpose in life is to contain a list of Reference elements. If a SignedInfo element points to a Manifest, then the validation of the Manifest elements occurs during signature validation, not reference validation. The Manifest element's schema is shown in Example 5–24.

EXAMPLE 5–24 SignatureValue schema

```
<element name="Manifest" type="ds:ManifestType"/>
<complexType name="ManifestType">
  <sequence>
    <element ref="ds:Reference"
          maxOccurs="unbounded"/>
  </sequence>
  <attribute name="Id" type="ID" use="optional"/>
</complexType>
```

SignatureProperties Element

Additional information regarding the generation of signatures, such as the time the signature was generated or some sort of serial number, exists in the SignatureProperties element (see Example 5–25).

EXAMPLE 5–25 SignatureValue schema

```
<element name="SignatureProperties"
  type="ds:SignaturePropertiesType"/>
<complexType name="SignaturePropertiesType">
  <sequence>
```

EXAMPLE 5–25 SignatureValue schema (Continued)

```
    <element ref="ds:SignatureProperty"
          maxOccurs="unbounded"/>
  </sequence>
  <attribute name="Id" type="ID" use="optional"/>
</complexType>

<element name="SignatureProperty"
type="ds:SignaturePropertyType"/>
<complexType name="SignaturePropertyType"
mixed="true">
  <choice maxOccurs="unbounded">
    <any namespace="##other" processContents="lax"/>
  </choice>
  <attribute name="Target" type="anyURI"
  use="required"/>
  <attribute name="Id" type="ID" use="optional"/>
</complexType>
```

XML Signature in SOAP Messages

Well, now you've certainly been exposed to XML Signature. How exactly does all of this fit into a SOAP message? Example 5–26 shows us one way.

EXAMPLE 5–26 Digital signature in a SOAP Message

```
<env:Envelope
  xmlns:env="http://schemas.xmlsoap.org/soap/
  envelope/">
  <env:Header>
    <sec:Signature
        xmlns:sec="http://schemas.xmlsoap.org/soap/
        security/2000-12"
      env:actor="some-URI"
      env:mustUnderstand="1">
      <ds:Signature
          xmlns:ds="http://www.w3.org/2000/09/
          xmldsig#">
        <ds:SignedInfo>
          <ds:CanonicalizationMethod
            Algorithm="http://www.w3.org/TR/2000/
```

Example 5–26 Digital signature in a SOAP Message (Continued)

```
            CR-xml-c14n-20001026">
          </ds:CanonicalizationMethod>
          <ds:SignatureMethod
            Algorithm="http://www.w3.org/2000/09/
            xmldsig#dsa-sha1"/>
        <ds:Reference URI="#Body">
          <ds:Transforms>
            <ds:Transform
              Algorithm="http://www.w3.org/TR/
              2000/CR-xml-c14n-20001026"/>
          </ds:Transforms>
          <ds:DigestMethod
            Algorithm="http://www.w3.org/2000/09/
            xmldsig#sha1"/>
          <ds:DigestValue>
            j6lwx3rvEPO0vKtMup4NbeVu8nk=
          </ds:DigestValue>
        </ds:Reference>
        </ds:SignedInfo>
        <ds:SignatureValue>
              MC0CFFrVLtRlk=...
        </ds:SignatureValue>
      </ds:Signature>
    </sec:Signature>
  </env:Header>
  <env:Body
    xmlns:sec="http://schemas.xmlsoap.org/soap/
    security/2000-12" sec:id="Body">
      <w:getPatientHistory
        xmlns:w="http://www.wire-man.com/medical/
        services" env:encodingStyle="http://
        www.w3.org/2001/06/soap-encoding">
              <SSN>555-55-5555</SSN>
    </w:getPatientHistory>
  </env:Body>
</env:Envelope>
```

How the Code Works

There's good news here—all we really have to do is place a chunk of XML Signature inside the SOAP header block, and we're done! Nothing really special has to be done here. The only thing you must be sure to do is actually link a Reference element to an ID'd part of your SOAP message. In the example above, the relevant code is in bold.

Recap

SOAP messages travel well and securely enough over SSL, but you can't guarantee that your SOAP messages will always travel over HTTP or that all the intermediaries that will receive your SOAP messages are completely trustworthy. To combat this, you can include a digital signature in your SOAP header. The going standard for digital signatures in XML documents is a specification called XML Signature, and we've covered most of it in this chapter.

6

WSDL: Describing Web Services

IN THIS CHAPTER

- What Is WSDL?
- What Does WSDL Do?
- Structure of a WSDL Document
- Data Types
- Messages
- Part Names
- Operations
- Port Types
- Binding
- Services
- SOAP Extensions
- HTTP Extensions
- MIME Extensions
- Multiple Files

So you've created a brilliant Web service that uses SOAP messages. It will make you millions, it's so brilliant. Great! Now what? How do you get people to actually use your Web service? How will they know how to structure their input parameters so your service will know what to do with it?

What Is WSDL?

Web Services Description Language (WSDL) is an XML-based language whose goal is to describe, in a computer-readable form, Web services. The hope is that an application will read a WSDL file and know everything it needs in order to communicate with the Web service successfully. For example, your application needs to know the structure of input parameters, which data format the Web service can understand, where the Web service lives, and so on.

WSDL isn't the first time someone has tried to come up with a scheme for describing Web services. Earlier efforts include languages like IBM's NASSL and Microsoft's SCL. As a side note, WSDL was written by folks from both IBM and Microsoft.

WSDL is extensible, which means you can create your own tags to describe whatever data format you like (like SOAP) and your transfer protocol of choice (like HTTP). In fact, if you're going to use anything besides HTTP and SOAP, you have to make up your own tags—the WSDL specification doesn't cover anything else.

WSDL exists because it's vital. Not describing and not documenting a Web service is like constructing your Web service in a secret place and not telling anyone where it is or what's in it, much less giving them the keys to the front door.

Status

At the time I'm writing this, WSDL's current status with the W3C is just that of a submitted Note—that is, some folks have submitted their idea of what WSDL should be to the W3C. That means the W3C hasn't sunk their teeth into it yet (well, I'm sure they're digging into it right now, and hopefully by the time you read this something beyond a Note will be available).

What Does WSDL Do?

How does one go about describing a Web service? Here's what WSDL covers when it's describing a Web service:

1. Data types: The data types your method is expecting, such as integers, strings, arrays, or something more complicated that you created yourself. These data types are defined inside the <types> element or in an external XML Schema document.
2. Structure of the input and output parameters: For example, should the SOAP request message contain

   ```
   <getPrice>
      <symbol>PSFT</symbol>
   </getPrice>
   ```

   or

   ```
   <getLastTradePrice>PSFT</getLastTradePrice>
   ```

   The structure of these parameters can also be in a separate document. We'll see an example of this later. WSDL uses the <message> and <part> elements to determine this structure.
3. Input and output parameters: Once the messages themselves are defined, WSDL must describe what's an input and what's an output. This type of definition is known as an *operation*. Elements used are <operation>, <input>, and <output>.
4. Pairing of inputs and outputs: It's possible to define any number of input and output parameters, so a necessary part of WSDL is to define what input and output parameters are associated with each other. These groups are known as *port types*.
5. Transport protocol and data format: The association of port types with protocols and data formats is known as *binding*. In most of our examples, the protocol is HTTP and the data format is SOAP. The WSDL spec specifies what to do in the case of SOAP and HTTP, but not in any others.
6. Web address of the Web service: The actual URL address is known as a *port*, and the part of WSDL that defines a port is known as a service.

If this isn't clear to you right now, don't worry—we'll be going over everything in detail. The above list serves mostly to give you a taste of what's ahead.

Concepts and Terminology

Much of WSDL is concerned with what is abstract and what is concrete. These concepts take a little while to get used to if you haven't seen them before, but knowing them will make understanding the rest of WSDL significantly easier.

An abstract definition is something that describes what could be, but isn't yet. More to the point, when WSDL describes the input and output parameters of a Web service, those are abstract descriptions because only what should be in those SOAP messages is described, not the actual content of the messages. A recipe is an abstract description: It specifies what the parts are and how to put them together, but you have to create the finished product yourself.

So, what counts as concrete in the WSDL world? Transport protocols and data formats are concrete. In our examples, that means HTTP and SOAP. In WSDL, protocols and data formats are spelled out, which makes them concrete. A vital step in describing a Web service is connecting the input and output parameters that the Web service knows how to use with the transport protocol and data format the Web service can understand. This connection of the abstract (parameters) and the concrete (protocols and data formats) is known as binding.

When WSDL goes about defining all the parts of a Web service, it must specify these parts in a certain order:

Data types ➤ Messages ➤ Operations ➤ portTypes ➤ Bindings ➤ Services

Structure of a WSDL Document

Imagine you're the CTO of a clothing store in downtown San Francisco called Stitch. When the store starts to run low on an item, that item is reordered from the supplier automatically. In this example, the Stitch store is running low on Dexter Dean low-cut jeans. Dexter Dean has recently created a Web service solely for the use of their biggest client, Stitch. All you have to do is send a SOAP message to the Dexter Dean Web service ordering more jeans, and they'll be shipped automatically. The Stitch computer system has to be able to read the WSDL file that accompanies the Dexter Dean Web service in order to know how to format their request.

Resulting SOAP Messages

Here's what the request and response SOAP messages should look like (minus the envelope and body). Example 6–1 shows a possible request message.

EXAMPLE 6–1 Request from Stitch store to Dexter Dean for more jeans

```
<s:placeStitchOrder
xmlns:s="http://www.dexterdean.com/serv/stitch">
  <jeans>low-cut</jeans>
  <quantity>70</quantity>
</s:placeStitchOrder>
```

The response from Dexter Dean might look like Example 6–2.

EXAMPLE 6–2 Response from Dexter Dean

```
<s:placeStitchOrderResponse
xmlns:s="http://www.dexterdean.com/serv/stitch">
  <status>order received</status>
  <shipDate>2002-03-14</shipDate>
</s:placeStitchOrderResponse>
```

Root WSDL Element

What will this WSDL document look like? All WSDL documents look something like Example 6–3:

EXAMPLE 6–3 Structure of Dexter Dean WSDL document

```
<?xml version="1.0"?>
<definitions name="StitchOrder"
xmlns="http://schemas.xmlsoap.org/wsdl/">
  1. Define data types
  2. Define messages (parameters)
  3. Define operations (what's input and what's
     output)
  4. Define port types (combine operations into a
     group)
  5. Define bindings (connect port types to a
     protocol and data format)
  6. Define location of service
</definitions>
```

Everything in a WSDL file is wrapped inside the <definitions> element. The name of the document (StitchOrder in this case) doesn't really matter—WSDL doesn't use it for anything.

Data Types

Now, you'll want to define what kinds of data types will be part of your Web service. All data type definitions belong either in an external XML Schema document or within the <types> tags, as shown in Example 6–4.

EXAMPLE 6–4 Defining data types

```
<?xml version="1.0"?>
<definitions name="StitchOrder" xmlns:tns="http://
www.dexterdean.com/serv/stitch">

  <types>
    <xsd:schema
    xmlns:xsd="http://www.w3.org/2000/10/XMLSchema">
      <xsd:element name="jeans" type="xsd:string"/>
      <xsd:element name="quantity" type="xsd:int"/>
      <xsd:element name="status" type="xsd:string"/>
      <xsd:element name="shipDate" type="xsd:date"/>
    </xsd:schema>
  </types>

  ... a bunch of other definitions ...

</definitions>
```

How the Code Works

We're defining four elements here: jeans, quantity, status, and shipDate. At this point we don't know what's an input parameter or what's an output parameter. All we know is that four elements have been defined.

You may have also noticed that we included a namespace in the <definitions> element. We don't use it here, but we will later. Remember that tns stands for "this namespace."

Messages

Messages are a little strange: They can contain one or more *parts*, where a part is a vaguely named element that can either represent an element (like jeans or status from the example above), or a simple or complex type. So messages contain parts, and parts can be either elements or types. Let's look at Example 6–5, which shows parts that are elements.

EXAMPLE 6–5 Message parts

```
<?xml version="1.0"?>
<definitions name="StitchOrder"
1.xmlns:tns="http://www.dexterdean.com/serv/stitch">

    <types>…</types>

    2.<message name="StitchOrderInput">
        3.<part name="body1" element="tns:jeans"/>
        <part name="body2" element="tns:quantity"/>
    </message>

    4.<message name="StitchOrderOutput">
        <part name="body1" element="tns:status"/>
        <part name="body2" element="tns:shipDate"/>
    </message>

    … a bunch of other definitions …

</definitions>
```

How the Code Works

1. As in the earlier example, we're declaring a namespace called tns, standing for "this namespace," just to clearly distinguish between elements defined in this document and elsewhere.
2. We're creating our first message here, and we're calling it "StitchOrderInput." Notice that there's no way to know that this message is an input parameter other than the presence of "Input" in the message's name.
3. The two parts of this message are the jeans and quantity elements. The names of these parts are unimportant—they aren't really used anywhere. Both of these parts are elements, since they are defined as elements in the types section of the WSDL document.
4. Finally, we create the message containing the two output parameters: status and shipDate. The names of the parts are again unimportant, but the fact that they're both elements is important.

So, how does a message contain a type instead of an element? How does that work? To examine this, imagine that the Stitch store buys more than jeans from Dexter Dean. They also buy T-shirts, sweatshirts, and hats. However, the Dexter Dean Web service can only handle orders of a single type of clothing item. That item can be jeans or T-shirts or sweatshirts or hats, but not any combination of them.

First, in Example 6–6, let's code this in the types section of our WSDL document.

EXAMPLE 6–6 Complex type

```
<definitions name="StitchOrder" xmlns:tns="http://
www.dexterdean.com/serv/stitch">

  <types>
    <xsd:schema
xmlns:xsd="http://www.w3.org/2000/10/XMLSchema">
      <xsd:complexType name="clothingType">
        <xsd:choice>
          <xsd:element name="jeans"
```

EXAMPLE 6–6 Complex type (Continued)

```
                type="xsd:string"/>
            <xsd:element name="tshirts"
                type="xsd:string"/>
            <xsd:element name="sweatshirts"
                type="xsd:string"/>
            <xsd:element name="hats"
                type="xsd:string"/>
          </xsd:choice>
        </xsd:complexType>

        <xsd:element name="quantity" type="xsd:int"/>
        <xsd:element name="status" type="xsd:string"/>
        <xsd:element name="shipDate" type="xsd:date"/>
      </xsd:schema>
    </types>

    … a bunch of other definitions …

  </definitions>
```

How the Code Works

As you can see from the section in bold, we've created a complex type called "clothing" that can contain one of four different elements. This complex type isn't used anywhere else in the document right now.

In order for our message to take advantage of this more flexible definition, we have to make one of the elements a type definition, as in Example 6–7.

EXAMPLE 6–7 Using a complex type in a message

```
<definitions name="StitchOrder"
xmlns:tns="http://www.dexterdean.com/serv/stitch">

  <types>
    …
  </types>

  <message name="StitchOrderInput">
      <part name="body1" type="tns:clothingType"/>
      <part name="body2" element="tns:quantity"/>
  </message>
```

EXAMPLE 6–7 Using a complex type in a message (Continued)

```
  <message name="StitchOrderOutput">
      <part name="body1" element="tns:status"/>
      <part name="body2" element="tns:shipDate"/>
  </message>

  … a bunch of other definitions …

</definitions>
```

How the Code Works

We didn't change much in this part of the code. We altered a part element slightly, making it a type instead of an element (you can only use one or the other), and made it equal to the name of the complex type we defined.

That about wraps it up for messages. Not too bad, I hope. Messages are collections of elements. If the elements are part of a complex type, then in the WSDL view of the world, that element is really a type.

Part Names

The only thing you really have to know about part names is that all parts within a single message must have different names. However, parts in different messages can have the same name.

Bad

```
<message name="StitchOrderInput">
      <part name="body" element="tns:jeans"/>
      <part name="body" element="tns:quantity"/>
</message>
```

Fine

```
<message name="StitchOrderInput">
      <part name="body1" element="tns:jeans"/>
      <part name="body2" element="tns:quantity"/>
</message>
```

```
<message name="StitchOrderOutput">
      <part name="body1" element="tns:status"/>
      <part name="body2" element="tns:shipDate"/>
</message>
```

Operations

Just as a message is a collection of parts, an operation is a collection of one or more messages. The purpose of a collection is to define which messages are inputs and which are outputs of the remote method. In the example above, the input message is named "StitchOrderInput" and the output message is named "StitchOrderOutput." Example 6–8 shows an operation definition in action.

EXAMPLE 6–8 Defining an operation

```
<definitions name="StitchOrder"
xmlns:tns="http://www.dexterdean.com/serv/stitch">

  <types>...</types>

  <message>...</message>
  <message>...</message>

  <operation name="PlaceStitchOrder">
      <input message="tns:StitchOrderInput"/>
      <output message="tns:StitchOrderOutput"/>
  </operation>

  ... some other definitions ...

</definitions>
```

How the Code Works

We're creating an operation called "PlaceStitchOrder," and inside this operation we're spelling out which message is the input parameter and which message is the output parameter. This is the only way in WSDL to explicitly describe inputs and outputs.

There are three allowable elements inside of <operation>: <input>, <output>, and <fault>. The fault element is optional, and is only used if you want to include a certain message type when a fault occurs, in addition to the usual fault information that is provided. In other words, if <faultstring>, <faultcode>, <faultactor>, and <detail> aren't enough information, you can add a fault element to an operation to specify that additional information must be sent.

This is a good time to mention that at this point in our WSDL, we know what the input and output parameters are and how they're structured, but we don't know what actual data format they're in, what transport protocol they're moving over, or even where they're supposed to go.

Operation Syntax

All operations have a syntax they must adhere to. Here it is in Example 6–9:

EXAMPLE 6–9 Operation syntax

```
<operation name="NMTOKEN" parameterOrder="NMTOKENS"?>
  <input name="NMTOKEN"? message="QName"/>?
  <output name="NMTOKEN"? message="QName"/>?
  <fault name="NMTOKEN"? message="QName"/>*
</operation>
```

The question marks and asterisk are notation and not part of the actual element. A question mark means the element or attribute can appear zero or one time—it either appears once or not at all. The asterisk means that the element can appear any number of times or not at all. You may be asking yourself, how can input and output be optional? Aren't they kind of necessary? The quick, semihelpful answer is: sometimes. We'll answer this in a clearer way in the next section.

Kinds of Operations

There are more options for operations than to contain an input and an output. In fact, there are four kinds of operations:

1. Request-response: The endpoint receives a message and responds with a corresponding message.
2. One-way: The endpoint receives a message.
3. Solicit-response: The endpoint sends a message and receives a corresponding message.
4. Notification: The endpoint sends a message.

As you might have guessed, the kind of operation we just saw in Example 6–9 was a request-response: We're sending some input to an endpoint and receiving some output from that endpoint.

REQUEST-RESPONSE SYNTAX

Example 6–10 shows how all request-response operations (like the one in Example 6–9) must look:

EXAMPLE 6–10 Request-response syntax

```
<operation name="NMTOKEN" parameterOrder="NMTOKENS"?>
  <input name="NMTOKEN"? message="QName"/>
  <output name="NMTOKEN"? message="QName"/>
  <fault name="NMTOKEN"? message="QName"/>*
</operation>
```

How the Code Works

Both an input and an output element are required for request-response systems. Only a single input or a single output may be a part of an operation: There isn't a way in WSDL to ever have more than a single output and a single input in an operation.

ONE-WAY SYNTAX

One-way operations, as in Example 6–11, simply send some data to a remote location, and don't receive a response. These can be used to invoke operations on remote computers that don't require responses, or as part of an instant messaging system.

EXAMPLE 6–11 One-way syntax

```
<operation name="NMTOKEN">
    <input name="NMTOKEN"? message="QName"/>
</operation>
```

How the Code Works

This is pretty simple—there's a single input element in the operation and nothing else. There's no reason to have an output or a fault element, since the endpoint isn't meant to communicate back to your application. That's why it's called "one-way."

SOLICIT-RESPONSE SYNTAX

Solicit-response, as shown in Example 6–12, is exactly the opposite of request-response: The endpoint initiates contact, and your application responds with an appropriate message.

EXAMPLE 6–12 Solicit-response syntax

```
<operation name="NMTOKEN" parameterOrder="NMTOKENS"?>
  <output name="NMTOKEN"? message="QName"/>
  <input name="NMTOKEN"? message="QName"/>
  <fault name="NMTOKEN"? message="QName"/>*
</operation>
```

How the Code Works

The only difference between this syntax and request-response is that the order of the input and output elements is reversed. That's it.

You may be asking yourself how a solicit-response system would actually work: After all, isn't it just request-response from another perspective? The answer is: maybe. Not too helpful, but remember that all we're building here is an abstract concept of a solicit-response system. It isn't the job of an operation to decide how something will be done. The job of the operation is to spell out what should be done, not how. It's up to the specific binding to decide exactly how a solicit-response system will work.

NOTIFICATION SYNTAX

A notification, seen here in Example 6–13, involves the endpoint sending a message, but not requiring a response. It's the opposite of a one-way system.

EXAMPLE 6–13 Notification syntax

```
<operation name="NMTOKEN">
  <output name="NMTOKEN"? message="QName"/>
</operation>
```

How the Code Works

Again, pretty simple—the endpoint sends a message, and it's over.

Parameter Order

Did you notice the attribute parameterOrder that appeared in a few operations? This is used to spell out in what order the parameters are listed: It's a white space-separated list.

Port Types

Time for another collection! Port types are collections of operations. Example 6–14 is a port type:

EXAMPLE 6–14 Port type containing an operation

```
<portType name="stitchOrderPortType">
  <operation name="PlaceStitchOrder"/>
</portType>
```

In all of our examples, we're just going to place a single operation in a port type. This is because something that involves multiple operations is beyond the scope of this book. Since our examples are only going to involve a single operation, we can wrap the port type element around the operation, like Example 6–15:

EXAMPLE 6–15 Nesting an operation definition inside a port type

```
<portType name="stitchOrderPortType">
  <operation name="PlaceStitchOrder">
    <input message="tns:StitchOrderInput"/>
    <output message="tns:StitchOrderOutput"/>
  </operation>
</portType>
```

How the Code Works

Since there's only one operation inside the port type, it doesn't seem like the port type has much of a function. And in our code, it doesn't. However, the content of a port type is the only thing that can be tied to a real data format and real transport protocol. In other words, the port type contains all of the abstract information in the WSDL document. It is this port type that is connected to the concrete information of protocol and data format.

Quick Review

Confused yet? Let's do a quick review: Our WSDL document begins by defining the data types that are used by the input and output parameters. Those elements and/or types become something called parts. These parts are now grouped into messages. These messages are then grouped into operations. At this point, we know what the input and output parameters are, and we've combined these parameters into an operation and into a port type. This port type contains all of the abstract information in our WSDL document.

Let's look at Example 6–16, which combines everything we've built so far:

EXAMPLE 6–16 All the abstract info

```
<definitions name="StitchOrder"
xmlns:tns="http://www.dexterdean.com/serv/stitch">

  <!-- Define data types -->
  <types>
    <xsd:schema
xmlns:xsd="http://www.w3.org/2000/10/XMLSchema">
      <xsd:complexType name="clothingType">
        <xsd:choice>
          <xsd:element name="jeans"
              type="xsd:string"/>
          <xsd:element name="tshirts"
              type="xsd:string"/>
          <xsd:element name="sweatshirts"
              type="xsd:string"/>
```

EXAMPLE 6–16 All the abstract info (Continued)

```
          <xsd:element name="hats"
              type="xsd:string"/>
        </xsd:choice>
      </xsd:complexType>

      <xsd:element name="quantity" type="xsd:int"/>
      <xsd:element name="status" type="xsd:string"/>
      <xsd:element name="shipDate" type="xsd:date"/>
    </xsd:schema>
  </types>

  <!-- Define messages -->
  <message name="StitchOrderInput">
      <part name="body1" type="tns:clothingType"/>
      <part name="body2" element="tns:quantity"/>
  </message>

  <message name="StitchOrderOutput">
      <part name="body1" element="tns:status"/>
      <part name="body2" element="tns:shipDate"/>
  </message>

  <!-- Define operation and port type -->
  <portType name="stitchOrderPortType">
      <operation name="PlaceStitchOrder">
        <input message="tns:StitchOrderInput"/>
        <output message="tns:StitchOrderOutput"/>
</operation>
    </portType>

    ... concrete definitions ...

</definitions>
```

Binding

Binding is the necessary step of associating a transport protocol and a data format with a bunch of messages, operations, and port types. In other words, binding nails down the abstract onto something concrete.

In our examples, we'll be looking at HTTP as the chosen transport protocol and SOAP as the chosen data format. However, you could use anything, like VoiceXML over BEEP (Blocks Extensible Exchange Protocol). Heck, you could use smoke signals to communicate across a canyon and WSDL wouldn't care.

Technically, WSDL doesn't provide any tags to define what kind of protocols or data format you're using. In order to specify any protocol or data format, you must make up your own tags and place them into your WSDL document (this is also known as *extending* WSDL). The good news is that the inventors of WSDL decided to make our lives easier and extended WSDL to create ways to bind a port type to both HTTP and SOAP.

Why would WSDL be designed this way? Doesn't this mean the spec is incomplete? Actually, no—it's a smart decision. The inventors of WSDL knew there was no way they'd be able to keep up with all of the new protocols and data formats that are quickly appearing these days. If those definitions were a part of the official WSDL specification, it would have to be rewritten every time someone created a new protocol or data format that people wanted to use. By putting the responsibility on developers to create their own tags, the inventors of WSDL have allowed room for a more organic growth.

Example 6–17 shows what a binding to HTTP and SOAP might look like.

EXAMPLE 6–17 Binding

```
1.<binding name="stitchOrderBinding"
2.type="stitchOrderPortType">
      3.<soap:binding style="document"
transport="http://schemas.xmlsoap.org/soap/http"/>

    4.<operation name="PlaceStitchOrder">
        5.<soap:operation
soapAction="http://www.dexterdean.com/stitchOrder"/>
      6.<input>
        7.<soap:body use="literal"/>
      </input>
      8.<output>
        <soap:body use="literal"/>
      </output>
    </operation>
</binding>
```

How the Code Works

First of all, don't worry much about anything that begins with "soap":—we'll look at them quickly here, and examine them in depth a little later. For now, concentrate on what's being accomplished instead of how to do it yourself.

1. All information about binding goes in the binding element. You have to name your binding (it gets used later), and you must also provide the name of the port type that you're associating with this binding.
2. Notice that the value of the type attribute is the same value as the name of the port type we defined earlier.
3. This is one of the special extensions of WSDL that's included in the specification. The soap:binding element allows us to specify HTTP as the transfer protocol that must be used.
4. What?! Another operation element? But we already defined one! Yes, we did, but we have to use it again, for a different reason: We need to contain all the information about the body of the message and how it will be formatted. Notice this operation has the same name as the operation element we used earlier.
5. The soap:operation element is used to define the value of the SOAPAction field in the HTTP header.
6. We must specify what the input part of our message will be.
7. Here, we say, "We're using SOAP!" The use attribute determines that we're using plain, vanilla XML Schema to define our data types, and that we didn't need to use any fancy SOAP definitions, like we would for an array.
8. We must do the same for the output parameters.

So this is one example of a binding, but what's a more general structure? How would you go about creating a binding? Example 6–18 contains the basic syntax of the binding element:

Example 6–18 Binding syntax

```
1.<binding name="NMTOKEN" type="QName">
    2.<!-- extensible element goes here -->
    3.<operation name="NMTOKEN">
      4.<!-- extensible element goes here -->
      <input name="NMTOKEN">
        5.<!-- extensible element goes here -->
      </input>
      <output>
        6.<!-- extensible element goes here -->
      </output>
      <fault name="NMTOKEN">
        7.<!-- extensible element goes here -->
      </fault>
    </operation>
</binding>
```

How the Code Works

1. The name of the binding is needed later, when we associate the binding to the actual location on the Web of the method. The value of the type attribute is the name of the port type.
2. The element in this position sets some information that applies to the entire binding. In Example 6–17, we set the transfer protocol to be HTTP, but we could have inserted some other information instead.
3. Even though you've already specified which port type is to be used, you must also specify which operation within that port type is to be used, since port types may have more than one operation. This is redundant for us, since all of the port types in our examples contain a single operation. The name attribute must be equal to the name of the operation we want to use.
4. The optional element in this position can specify some information that applies only to this operation, not to the binding as a whole. It may appear that you could have a binding-specific protocol and an operation-specific protocol, but that isn't true: A binding must specify exactly one protocol.

5. The element in this position specifies concrete grammar for the input message. That is, it defines the data format to be used.
6. The element in this position specifies concrete grammar for the output message. That is, it defines the data format to be used.
7. The element in this position specifies concrete grammar for the fault message, if there is one. That is, it defines the data format to be used.

You should note that specific address information, where the Web service actually lives, must *not* be a part of the binding information.

This is as closely as we'll look at binding right now. The extensions to WSDL that cover SOAP and HTTP will be examined fully later in the chapter.

Services

Well, we have almost everything now—all the abstract information in the form of data types, messages, operations, and so on, as well as the concrete information of which transfer protocol must be used and the data formats of the messages. We've described everything this Web service needs to be used except for one thing: Where is it? We start with defining a *port*, the actual location of the Web service. Example 6–19 shows its syntax.

EXAMPLE 6–19 Port syntax

```
<port name="NMTOKEN" binding="QName">
  <!-- extensible element with web service address -->
</port>
```

How the Code Works

Not a whole lot to a port, is there? It associates a location with a binding via the binding attribute. Then, it's up to you to come up with a way to extend WSDL (remember, that means make up your own tag) to describe where your Web service actually lives. Again, the folks who created WSDL have done this for us, in the case that we're using SOAP. The port of the example we've been working on looks like Example 6–20.

EXAMPLE 6–20 Dexter Dean port

```
<port name="stitchOrderPort"
  binding="stitchOrderBinding">
  <soap:address location="http://
  www.dexterdean.com/serv/stitch/order"/>
</port>
```

How the Code Works

Notice that we used the name of the binding element as the value of the binding attribute here. We then used a new extension called soap:address that allowed us to specify the location of Dexter Dean's service for Stitch. As with the other extensions of soap:body, soap:binding, and so on, soap:address will be examined in detail later.

Placing the Port

Now that we have a port we need to place it inside a service element, as in Example 6–21.

EXAMPLE 6–21 Service

```
<service name="stitchOrderService">
  <port name="stitchOrderPort"
  binding="stitchOrderBinding">
          <soap:address location="http://
  www.dexterdean/serv/stitch/order"/>
  </port>
</service>
```

How the Code Works

As you can see, the port element was simply placed inside the service element. The service element is given a name of "stitchOrderService," which isn't used by WSDL right now. It should be noted that services could contain one or more ports, since different ports can be attached to different bindings (we'll see more complex examples in the last section of the chapter).

The Whole Code

Well, now we're done. We've defined everything we needed to. Just to have it in one place, Example 6–22 shows our WSDL document in its entirety.

EXAMPLE 6–22 The whole WSDL document

```
<definitions name="StitchOrder"
xmlns:tns="http://www.dexterdean.com/serv/stitch">

  <!-- Define data types -->
  <types>
    <xsd:schema
xmlns:xsd="http://www.w3.org/2000/10/XMLSchema">
      <xsd:complexType name="clothingType">
        <xsd:choice>
          <xsd:element name="jeans"
              type="xsd:string"/>
          <xsd:element name="tshirts"
              type="xsd:string"/>
          <xsd:element name="sweatshirts"
              type="xsd:string"/>
          <xsd:element name="hats"
              type="xsd:string"/>
        </xsd:choice>
      </xsd:complexType>

      <xsd:element name="quantity" type="xsd:int"/>
      <xsd:element name="status" type="xsd:string"/>
      <xsd:element name="shipDate" type="xsd:date"/>
    </xsd:schema>
  </types>

  <!-- Define messages -->
  <message name="StitchOrderInput">
      <part name="body1" type="tns:clothingType"/>
      <part name="body2" element="tns:quantity"/>
  </message>

  <message name="StitchOrderOutput">
      <part name="body1" element="tns:status"/>
      <part name="body2" element="tns:shipDate"/>
  </message>
```

EXAMPLE 6–22 The whole WSDL document (Continued)

```
  <!-- Define operation and port type -->
  <portType name="stitchOrderPortType">
      <operation name="PlaceStitchOrder">
        <input message="tns:StitchOrderInput"/>
        <output message="tns:StitchOrderOutput"/>
      </operation>
  </portType>

  <!--
  --- Concrete definitions ---
  -->
<binding name="stitchOrderBinding"
  type="stitchOrderPortType">
      <soap:binding style="rpc"
transport=
"http://schemas.xmlsoap.org/soap/http"/>

      <operation name="PlaceStitchOrder">
          <soap:operation
soapAction=
"http://www.dexterdean.com/stitchOrder"/>
      <input>
          <soap:body use="literal"/>
      <output>
          <soap:body use="literal"/>
      </output>
    </operation>
  </binding>

  <service name="stitchOrderService">
      <port name="stitchOrderPort"
          binding="stitchOrderBinding">
          <soap:address
location="http://www.dexterdean/serv/stitch/order"/>
      </port>
  </service>

</definitions>
```

SOAP Extensions

The inventors of WSDL were kind enough to include extensions that cover the SOAP data format. Specifically, the following are supported:

- A way to connect a binding to the SOAP protocol
- The URI for the SOAPAction field in the HTTP header
- A list of definitions for SOAP headers

In order to accomplish this, WSDL comes with the following SOAP elements:

- soap:binding—defines transport protocol
- soap:operation—defines URI for SOAPAction field in HTTP header
- soap:body—specifies how message parts appear inside SOAP body
- soap:header—specifies some or all of the headers to appear inside the SOAP message
- soap:headerfault—specifies some or all of the faults placed in the SOAP header
- soap:fault—specifies how message parts appear inside the SOAP fault
- soap:address—specifies the address of the Web service

Let's start with a big code listing in Example 6–23, covering the syntax of all these elements, so you can see where they would go and their relationship to each other. Then we'll go over each one.

EXAMPLE 6–23 Syntax of SOAP extensions

```
<definitions>
  … other definitions …
  <binding>
        <soap:binding style="rpc|document"
        transport="uri"/>
      <operation>
        <soap:operation soapAction="uri"?
        style="rpc|document"?>?
        <input>
```

EXAMPLE 6–23 Syntax of SOAP extensions (Continued)

```
            <soap:body parts="nmtokens"?
use="literal|encoded" encodingStyle="uri-list"?
namespace="uri"?/>
          <soap:header message="QName"
part="nmtoken" use="literal|encoded"
encodingStyle="uri-list"? namespace="uri"?/>*
              <soap:headerfault message="QName"
use="literal|encoded" encodingStyle="uri-list"?
namespace="uri"?/>*
          </soap:header>
        </input>
        <output>
            <soap:body parts="nmtokens"?
use="literal|encoded" encodingStyle="uri-list"?
namespace="uri"?/>
          <soap:header message="QName"
part="nmtoken" use="literal|encoded"
encodingStyle="uri-list"? namespace="uri"?/>*
              <soap:headerfault message="QName"
use="literal|encoded" encodingStyle="uri-list"?
namespace="uri"?/>*
          </soap:header>
        </output>
        <fault>*
            <soap:fault name="nmtoken"
use="literal|encoded" encodingSytle="uri-list"?
namespace="uri"?/>
        </fault>
      </operation>
    </binding>

    <port>
      <soap:address location="uri"/>
    </port>
</definitions>
```

How the Code Works

The SOAP extensions are in bold. Remember our syntax notation? Question marks mean the element or attribute can appear once or not at all. The asterisk means the element or attribute may appear any number of times, from zero to some very large number. Values in italics represent what kind of value should go there. A vertical bar (|) means "or."

Now let's get into the details!

soap:binding

The purpose of the soap:binding element is to announce that the binding is bound to the SOAP data format. It also indicates which transport protocol is being used. Here's the syntax:

```
<soap:binding transport="uri" style="rpc|document"? />
```

The value of the required transport attribute is a URI that corresponds to the transport protocol this SOAP message is to travel over. The WSDL specification only states that the URI for HTTP is "http://schemas.xmlsoap.org/soap/http." To use another protocol, such as SMTP or BEEP, you'll have to create your own URI, such as "http://www.dexterdean.com/soap/beep."

The style attribute is optional, and its value must be either "rpc" or "document." Style indicates whether the operation is RPC-oriented (that is, messages containing input and output parameters) or document-oriented (messages containing one or more documents). Our example is a single document defining input and output parameters, so our style is definitely "rpc." Thus, our soap:binding looks like this:

```
<soap:binding transport="http://schemas.xml-
soap.org/soap/http" style="rpc" />
```

If your message is to be in SOAP, then the soap:binding element is mandatory.

soap:operation

The soap:operation element is optional, and its most important job is to define the URI of the SOAPAction field in the HTTP header. The syntax for this element is:

```
<soap:operation soapAction="uri"? style="rpc|document"? />?
```

For example, if this was our element:

```
<soap:operation soapAction="http://www.dexter-
dean.com/stitchOrder"/>
```

then our HTTP header could look something like Example 6–24:

EXAMPLE 6–24 stichOrder HTTP header

```
POST /stitchOrder HTTP/1.1
Content-Type: text/xml; charset="utf-8"
Content-Length: nnnn
SOAPAction: "http://www.dexterdean.com/stitchOrder"
```

The style attribute is also optional—you only need to use it if you want the style to be different than what's set in the soap:binding element. The default value is "document," but only if you don't set anything in the soap:binding element.

soap:body

The soap:body element specifies how the message parts appear inside the SOAP body—that is, how to assemble the different parts inside the body of a SOAP message.

```
<soap:body parts="nmtokens"? use="literal|encoded" encoding-
Style="uri-list"? namespace="uri"? />
```

USE AND ENCODINGSTYLE ATTRIBUTES

The only required attribute is use, which specifies how the parts of the message are defined; that is, are the data types of the parts defined by XML Schema only, or were more encoding rules (such as SOAP) involved? In our Dexter Dean example, all of our data types were defined using only XML Schema. As a reminder, Example 6–25 contains the data types we used.

EXAMPLE 6–25 Data types

```
<!-- Define data types -->
<types>
  <xsd:schema
xmlns:xsd="http://www.w3.org/2000/10/XMLSchema">
    <xsd:complexType name="clothingType">
      <xsd:choice>
        <xsd:element name="jeans"
            type="xsd:string"/>
```

EXAMPLE 6–25 Data types (Continued)

```
        <xsd:element name="tshirts"
            type="xsd:string"/>
        <xsd:element name="sweatshirts"
            type="xsd:string"/>
        <xsd:element name="hats"
            type="xsd:string"/>
      </xsd:choice>
    </xsd:complexType>

    <xsd:element name="quantity" type="xsd:int"/>
    <xsd:element name="status" type="xsd:string"/>
    <xsd:element name="shipDate" type="xsd:date"/>
  </xsd:schema>
</types>
```

All of these data types are completely defined within XML Schema. We have a derived clothingType that we created by combining predefined data types, and we created three more elements using predefined XML Schema data types. We didn't use any SOAP encoding here: no arrays, no special structures.

Because we relied solely on XML Schema to define our data types, the use attribute in the soap:body element is "literal." If we had used any other method to define these data types, such as SOAP encoding, the value would be "encoded," and we would have to specify what kind of encoding in the encodingStype attribute. Clear as mud, right? Let's go through an example.

Say Dexter Dean decides they're only selling jeans, and they need us to pass an array whose first element is the quantity, and the next element is the size. For example, Dexter Dean needs this array:

```
jeans[0] = 70
jeans[1] = "XL"
```

In this case, we'd set up our WSDL like Example 6–26:

EXAMPLE 6–26 Dexter Dean with an array

```
<types>
  <xsd:schema
  xmlns:xsd="http://www.w3.org/2000/10/XMLSchema"
  1.xmlns:enc="http://www.w3.org/2001/06/soap-
  encoding">
    2.<xsd:import
namespace="http://www.w3.org/2001/06/soap-encoding"/>
      3.<xsd:element name="jeans" type="enc:Array"/>
      <xsd:element name="quantity" type="xsd:int"/>
      <xsd:element name="status" type="xsd:string"/>
      <xsd:element name="shipDate" type="xsd:date"/>
  </xsd:schema>
</types>
```

How the Code Works

1. In our WSDL document, the first thing we do is declare the SOAP encoding namespace.
2. Next, we actually import the namespace, so it's clear that we'll be using data types from the SOAP specification
3. Since we now have a namespace and have imported the data type information, we can declare that we have an array named "jeans" and its type is enc:Array.

Since we're using an encoding scheme beyond XML Schema, we have to disclose this fact in the soap:body element. In the example, it would look like this

```
<soap:body use="encoded" encodingStyle="http://
schemas/xmlsoap.org/soap/encoding"/>
```

You have noticed that the namespace for SOAP encoding is from the old SOAP 1.1 version, not the latest, SOAP 1.2. The latest version of WSDL was built on SOAP 1.1, so it's not surprising that they used the old namespace. However, the value of encodingStyle will soon be updated to http://www.w3 .org/2001/06/soap-encoding, hopefully by the time this book hits the shelves.

PARTS ATTRIBUTE

This attribute contains a space-separated list of which parts appear in the body of the SOAP message. Other parts may appear in the header, or other portions of the message, in case you're doing something fancy, like using SOAP in conjunction with Multipurpose Internet Mail Exchange (MIME) binding. If you don't include this attribute, it's assumed that all parts are located in the SOAP body element.

NAMESPACE ATTRIBUTE

This attribute is a little odd, and we have to look at an actual SOAP message to see where this attribute comes in. Suppose Stitch's SOAP message to Dexter Dean looks something like Example 6–27.

EXAMPLE 6–27 SOAP message to Dexter Dean

```
<env:Envelope xmlns:env="http://www.w3.org/2001/06/
soap-envelope">
  <env:Body>
    <dex:placeStitchOrder
xmlns:dex="http://www.dexterdean.com/serv/stitch"
xmlns:xsd="http://www.w3.org.2001/XMLSchema"
xmlns:enc="http://www.w3.org/2001/06/soap-encoding">
             <jeans enc:arrayType="xsd:string[2]">
               <quantity>70</quantity>
               <size>XML</size>
             </jeans>
      </dex:placeStitchOrder>
  </env:Body>
</env:Envelope>
```

That means that our soap:body element might look like this:

```
<soap:body use="encoded"
encodingStyle="http://schemas/xmlsoap.org/soap/encoding"
namespace="http://www.dexterdean.com/serv/stitch" />
```

Notice that the namespace we used in the SOAP element that contains the method name (placeStitchOrder) is the same as the namespace attribute in the soap:body element. The namespace attribute can only be used if your SOAP message is going to be RPC-oriented, which ours is. If your SOAP message is document-oriented, then this attribute should not be present.

Is this attribute mandatory or optional? Unfortunately, the WSDL specification isn't clear on this point. Until it becomes clearer in future versions, I'd recommend including it in your WSDL documents. It can't hurt.

soap:fault

Use soap:fault to define how the fault elements in the SOAP message should be formatted, in case there is one. This element is patterned almost exactly like soap:body. Here's the syntax:

```
<operation .... >
    <fault>*
<soap:fault name="nmtoken" use="literal|encoded"
encodingStyle="uri-list"? namespace="uri"?>
    </fault>
</operation>
```

soap:header and soap:headerfault

Use soap:header and soap:headerfault to define how SOAP header elements appear in the SOAP message. These elements work almost exactly like the soap:body element. Note that it isn't necessary to list every header element that could appear in the SOAP message. Example 6–28 shows the syntax for soap:head and soap:headerfault.

EXAMPLE 6–28 Syntax of soap:header and soap:headerfault

```
<definitions>
<binding>
<operation>
  <input>
    <soap:header message="QName" part="nmtoken"
    use="literal|encoded" encodingStyle="uri-list"?
    namespace="uri"?/>*
            <soap:headerfault message="QName"
    use="literal|encoded" encodingStyle="uri-list"?
    namespace="uri"?/>*
    </soap:header>
```

Example 6–28 Syntax of soap:header and soap:headerfault (Continued)

```
    </input>
    <output>
      <soap:header message="QName" part="nmtoken"
      use="literal|encoded" encodingStyle="uri-list"?
      namespace="uri"?/>*
            <soap:headerfault message="QName"
      use="literal|encoded" encodingStyle="uri-list"?
      namespace="uri"?/>*
      </soap:header>
    </output>
  </operation>
  </binding>
  </definitions>
```

How the Code Works

The attributes use, encodingStyle, and namespace mean the same thing here as they do for soap:body. However, there is no style attribute, since header elements don't contain method parameters—and since style would always be "document," there's no point to including it.

The message and part attributes are both needed to specify which message and part define the data type to be included in the header.

The soap:headerfault is optional and has exactly the same syntax as soap:header. The only reason this element exists is because the SOAP specification requires that errors pertaining to header elements must be returned in headers. The soap:headerfault is how you can format those header-based errors.

soap:address

The purpose of soap:address is just to define the actual location of a Web service. The format is:

```
<definitions>
    <port>
        <binding>
            <soap:address location="uri"/>
        </binding>
    </port>
</definitions>
```

How the Code Works

No big mystery here. The value of the location attribute is the URL of where the Web service is.

Table 6–1 summarizes all the SOAP extensions to WSDL.

TABLE 6–1 SOAP Extensions

EXTENSION	DESCRIPTION
soap:address	Defines location of Web service.
soap:binding	Defines data format as SOAP, as well as defining transport protocol to be used.
soap:body	Defines how data in SOAP body is encoded.
soap:fault	Defines how data in SOAP fault, if present, is encoded.
soap:header	Defines how SOAP header appears.
soap:headerfault	Defines how fault related to a header element appears.
soap:operation	Defines value of SOAPAction field in HTTP header.

HTTP Extensions

WSDL also has a way to bind your messages to HTTP without having to use the soap:binding element. That is, you can use HTTP as your transfer protocol without having to tie it to a certain data format.

Using WSDL's HTTP extensions, you can send your data via the GET method—that is, in the URL—or you can send it via POST. We'll get a little fancy in this section and introduce a few new concepts in addition to HTTP extensions.

In our example, let's say Dexter Dean can accept messages through one of three different ports. All three ports are HTTP-based. The first two ports can accept data via the URL—that is, GET—while the third can accept data via POST.

The data we'll be passing will be three variables: clothing, color, and size.

```
clothing = "jeans"
color = "red"
size = "XL"
```

Here's what the data to the three ports might look like:

```
port 1: GET, URL="http://www.dexterdean.com/
stitch/CjeansCred/XL"

port 2: GET, URL="http://www.dexterdean.com/
stitch?clothing=jeans&color=red&size=XL"

port 3: POST, URL="http://www.dexterdean.com/
stitch" PAYLOAD="clothing=jeans&color=red&size=XL"
```

In Example 6–29, Dexter Dean will return an image of the specified clothing item instead of a text-based string. So in the code below, we'll not only introduce the HTTP extensions, but we'll also look at having several different ports, as well as seeing what outputting an image looks like. It's a few things to absorb at once, but if you've made it this far in the book, you have a good chance of understanding it.

EXAMPLE 6–29 Code for HTTP extensions<definitions ...>

```
<!-- Define messages -->
1.<message name="ClothesImageInput">
    <part name="clothing" type="xsd:string"/>
    <part name="color" type="xsd:string"/>
    <part name="size" type="xsd:string"/>
</message>

2.<message name="ClothesImageOutput">
    <part name="clothingImage" type="xsd:binary">
</message>

3.<portType name="ClothesImagePortType">
    <operation name="ClothesImageOperation">
        <input message="tns:ClothesImageInput"/>
        <output message="tns:ClothesImageOutput"/>
  </operation>
  </portType>

4.<binding name="binding1"
  type="ClothesImagePortType">
      5.<http:binding verb="GET"/>
      <operation name="ClothesImageOperation">
```

EXAMPLE 6–29 Code for HTTP extensions<definitions …> (Continued)

```
        6.<http:operation location="stitch/
        C(clothing)C(color)/(size)"/>
        <input>
            7.<http:urlReplacement/>
        </input>
        <output>
            8.<mime:content type="image/gif"/>
            <mime:content type="image/jpeg"/>
        </output>
      </operation>
  </binding>

  9.<binding name="binding2"
  type="ClothesImagePortType">
      10.<http:binding verb="GET"/>
      <operation name="ClothesImageOperation">
          11.<http:operation location="stitch"/>
          <input>
              12.<http:urlEncoded/>
          </input>
          <output>
              13.<mime:content type="image/gif"/>
              <mime:content type="image/jpeg"/>
          </output>
        </operation>
      </binding>

  14.<binding name="binding3"
  type="ClothesImagePortType">
      15.<http:binding verb="POST"/>
      <operation name="ClothesImageOperation">
        16.<http:operation location="stitch"/>
        <input>
          17.<mime:content type="application/x-
          www-form-urlencoded"/>
        </input>
        <output>
          18.<mime:content type="image/gif"/>
          <mime:content type="image/jpeg"/>
           </output>
        </operation>

 <service name="service1">
```

EXAMPLE 6–29 Code for HTTP extensions<definitions ...> (Continued)

```
          19.<port name="port1" binding="tns:binding1">
              20.<http:address location="http://
              www.dexterdean.com/"/>
          </port>
          21.<port name="port2" binding="tns:binding2">
              <http:address location="http://
              www.dexterdean.com/"/>
          </port>
          22.<port name="port3" binding="tns:binding3">
              <http:address location="http://
              www.dexterdean.com/"/>
          </port>
     </service>

</definitions>
```

How the Code Works

1. We begin this large chunk of code by doing something familiar, defining three elements as the input message: clothes, color, and size. All three are simple strings.
2. The output, instead of the usual text that we've seen, will be an image of the item of clothing we specified in the input message. We'll be getting back a picture of a big pair of red jeans. Notice that its type is binary, so we don't yet know that it's an image. At this point, it could be anything, even an executable.
3. You've seen this before: We're specifying which message is input and which is output by placing them in an operation, and then nesting that operation inside a portType.
4. We're creating a binding, just as we've done before. However, since we have three different ports we can send our data to, we'll be creating three different bindings. Each binding will link to the same port type, though.
5. This is new: We use http:binding to announce that our messages must travel over HTTP. The value of the verb attribute must either be GET or POST.
6. Another new element: http:operation. The value of the location attribute must be a relative URL. You also

notice that something funky is going on in this URL: We're using parentheses and part names. What is all this? When we're encoding information in a URL using a nonstandard method (the standard being foo.html/ p=1&o=2), we type out the URL, replacing the parts that are the values of the variables with the name of the variable surrounded by parentheses. That's why it looks like "stitch/C(clothing)C(color)/(size)". This will turn into "stitch/CjeansCred/XL" in the actual message. How does your application know that it has to replace the variable names surrounded by parentheses into their actual values? Check out #7.

7. The http:urlReplacement element's only job is to tell your application to replace the parentheses in the http:operation element with the actual values of those variables. You should note that if you replace a variable with a value that has parentheses in it, another replacement will not happen. For example, if the value of your clothes part was "jeans(lowcut)," there would not be any attempt to search for a message part called "lowcut."
8. Here's where we specify that an image is the output. This involves MIME extensions to WSDL, which we'll be examining in the next section. For now, just blip over this code—it'll be explained later.
9. We're creating a second binding here—also something that we haven't done before. We're still tying it to the single port type that we defined earlier.
10. As in the first binding, we're tying this to HTTP and requiring that the GET method be used.
11. Our http:operation is simpler here: We're only looking at the relative URL to send the data to.
12. Since we're using the standard method to send data in a URL—that is, using question marks and ampersands—we only need to specify that the URL is to be encoded, so we use http:urlEncoded. That's it.
13. Even though this is a different binding, the output of an image is still the same, so we again use these MIME extensions.
14. On to the third and final binding!

15. We define the method of this http:binding as POST, since we're sending the information as if it came from an HTML form.
16. As before, the location is a simple relative URL.
17. Notice this input is different: We have to use a MIME extension to send our data as if it were from a form, just like HTML: `application/x-www-form-urlencoded`.
18. Again, we output an image.
19. We've finished defining our three different kinds of binding, and now it's time to tie them into actual locations. We do this by defining three different ports within a single service. After all, the service does the same thing no matter which port we use—the only difference is how the input data is formatted, so we tie our first port to our first binding: binding1.
20. We use our final HTTP extension, http:address, to locate the actual place on the Web where the Dexter Dean Web service is.
21. Our second port definition looks almost exactly like the first, except that we tie it to a different binding. The location is the same
22. Our final port also looks just like the other two, with the only difference being the specified binding. They all still go to the same place.

Table 6–2 summarizes all the HTTP extensions to WSDL.

TABLE 6–2 HTTP Extensions

EXTENSION	DESCRIPTION
http:address	Defines the actual location of the Web service.
http:binding	Indicates that HTTP is the transfer protocol and defines which method, GET or POST, is to be used.
http:operation	Defines the relative URL for the operation.
http:urlEncoded	Indicates that standard URL-encoding is to be used to encode the data.
http:urlReplacement	Indicates that nonstandard encoding is to be used. Specifically, values in the location attribute of http:operation that appear in parentheses are to be replaced by their actual values.

MIME Extensions

In addition to SOAP and HTTP, WSDL also includes some extensions that allow you to define elements as certain MIME types. You saw some examples of this in Example 6–29. You can bind the following MIME types:

- text/xml
- application/x-www-form-urlencoded (the format used to submit an HTML form)
- multipart/related
- other (defined by the type string, like image/gif and image/jpeg)

When would we want to use such a thing other than responding with an image? Well, let's say we want to ask the Dexter Dean store if they have a certain item in stock, such as an XML pair of red jeans. Dexter Dean's Web service is so helpful that not only do they respond with a regular SOAP message containing the answer, but they also include some VoiceXML for speaking browsers, as well as an image of the clothing item in question. So three pieces are being returned by the Dexter Dean Web service. Example 6–30 shows what the WSDL describing that service might look like.

EXAMPLE 6–30 WSDL with MIME extensions

```
<defininitions ...>

<types>
  <xsd:schema ...>

    <!-- SOAP response -->
    1.<xsd:element name="inStock">
      <xsd:simpleType>
        <xsd:restriction base="xsd:string">
        <xsd:enumeration value="item is in stock"/>
        <xsd:enumeration value="item is not in
        stock"/>
        </xsd:restriction>
      </xsd:simpleType>
    </xsd:element>
    <!-- Defining VoiceXML response -->
```

EXAMPLE 6–30 WSDL with MIME extensions (Continued)

```
2.<xsd:complexType name="voiceXMLForm">
    <xsd:element name="form">
      <xsd:complexType>
      <xsd:element name="block" type="xsd:string"/>
      </xsd:complexType>
    </xsd:element>
  </complexType>

  <xsd:element name="vxml">
    <xsd:complexType>
    <xsd:attribute name="version" type="xsd:int"/>
    <xsd:element name="form"
    type="xsd:voiceXMLForm"/>
    </complexType>
  </xsd:element>

  </xsd:schema>
</types>

3.<message name="dexterDeanInput">
  <part name="clothes" type="xsd:string"/>
  <part name="color" type="xsd:string"/>
  <part name="size" type="xsd:string"/>
</message>

4.<message name="dexterDeanOutput">
  <part name="body" element="tns:inStock"/>
  <part name="voice" element="tns:vxml"/>
  <part name="picture" type="xsd:binary"/>
</message>

5.<portType name="dexterDeanPortType">
  <operation name="DexterDeanOp">
    <input message="dexterDeanInput"/>
    <output message="dexterDeanOutput"/>
  </operation>
</portType>

<binding name="DexterDeanBinding"
type="tns:dexterDeanPortType">
  <operation name="DexterDeanOp">
    <soap:operation soapAction="http://
    www.dexterdean.com/inStock"/>
```

Example 6–30 WSDL with MIME extensions (Continued)

```
    6.<input>
        <soap:body use="literal"/>
    </input>
    <output>
        7.<mime:multipartRelated>
            8.<mime:part>
                9.<soap:body parts="body"
                use="literal"/>
            </mime:part>
            <mime:part>
                10.<mime:mimeXml part="voice"/>
            </mime:part>
            <mime:part>
                11.<mime:content part="picture"
                type="image/jpeg"/>
            </mime:part>
        </mime:multipartRelated>
    </output>
  </operation>
</binding>

12.<service name="DexterDeanService">
  <port name="CompanyInfoPort"
  binding="tns:DexterDeanBinding">
        <soap:addresslocation="http://
        www.dexterdean.com/inStock"/>
  </port>
</service>

</definitions>
```

How the Code Works

1. We begin by defining the first output element—that is, what the SOAP response message may contain. We've defined an element called inStock that can have two values: "item is in stock" or "item is not in stock."
2. We then define the second part of our reponse: the VoiceXML. As of this writing, VoiceXML is a submitted Note to the W3C, and it's intended to be a standard way to code for browsers that can speak, as well as lis-

ten for particular responses. Our VoiceXML will be a simple description of the item. For example, our VoiceXML will look something like:

```
<vxml version="1.0">
   <form>
     <block>extra large red jeans</block>
   </form>
</vxml>
```

3. We define our input message to be the three parts we've used earlier: clothes, color, and size. They're all strings.
4. We create the output message in a similar way to the input message: We assign the message three parts. Two of them have formats that were defined in the <types> section, while the third (the image) is simply a binary type. Notice that we haven't had to use any MIME extensions yet.
5. As usual, we define the operation, explicitly defining what the input and output messages are, and place that operation inside a port type.
6. You've seen this before: The input message is bound to the SOAP data format, which is what we wanted.
7. Here's where the MIME comes in. In this case, our output message has three parts, so we use the mime:multipartRelated element to contain everything.
8. Since our output has three parts, we must use three mime:part elements. These elements are the only children of mime:multipartRelated elements.
9. The first part of the output message is a basic SOAP message, so we just use good ol' soap:body. It's plain text/xml, so we don't need to do anything fancy with it.
10. The next part of our output, the VoiceXML, is a little different. Since it's a different flavor of XML, we announce that fact by using mime:mimeXml, which says that it's some sort of XML that isn't SOAP. We then use the part attribute to link the element to its proper message part.
11. Finally, we tack on an image using mime:content. Anything can go in the mime:content type attribute:

an image, a Flash movie, or an HTML form. We're sending a JPEG of the clothing item, so we have type="image/jpeg".

12. To link the binding to a location on the Web, we use the same old port and service elements that we've seen before. No big whoop.

Table 6–3 contains a summary of WSDL's MIME extensions.

TABLE 6–3 MIME Extensions

EXTENSION	DESCRIPTION
mime:content	Describes any sort of MIME content, such as text/HTML or image/png.
mime:multipartRelated	Groups together a set of any number or kind of MIME elements.
mime:part	Defines a part of a group of MIME elements, grouped together by being nested inside mime:multipartRelated.
mime:mimeXml	Defines a chunk of text as being some kind of XML besides SOAP.

Multiple Files

As you've seen, sometimes WSDL can become pretty long. Fortunately, there's a way to split one long WSDL file into several pieces. In this section, we'll be taking the code from Example 6–22 (the big one) and splitting it into three separate files. For example, you could split a single WSDL document into three documents: one containing the data type definitions, one containing the messages and port types, and the last containing the binding and service definitions.

We can start by placing all of the type definitions into an XML Schema document, as in Example 6–31.

EXAMPLE 6–31 http://www.dexterdean.com/stitchOrder/stitchorder.xsd

```
<?xml version="1.0"?>

<schema xmlns="http://www.w3.org/2000/10/XMLSchema"
targetNamespace="http://www.dexterdean.com/serv/
schemas">


  <complexType name="clothingType">
    <choice>
        <element name="jeans" type="string"/>
        <element name="tshirts" type="string"/>
        <element name="sweatshirts" type="string"/>
        <element name="hats" type="string"/>
    </choice>
  </complexType>

  <element name="quantity" type="int"/>
  <element name="status" type="string"/>
  <element name="shipDate" type="date"/>
</schema>
```

Notice the targetNamespace of this document. We'll be referring to it later. Next we have Example 6–32.

EXAMPLE 6–32 http://www.dexterdean.com/stitchOrder/stitchorder.wsdl

```
1.<definitions name="stitchOrder"
targetNamespace="http://www.dexterdean.com/
stitchOrder/definitions" xmlns:tns="http://
www.dexterdean.com/stitchOrder/definitions"
xmlns:myXsd="http://www.dexterdean.com/stitchOrder/
schemas" xmlns="http://schemas.xmlsoap.org/wsdl/">

  2.<import namespace="http://www.dexterdean.com/
  stitchOrder/schemas" location="http://
  www.dexterdean.com/stitchOrder/stitchorder.xsd"/>

  <!-- Define messages -->
  <message name="StitchOrderInput">
      3.<part name="body1"
      type="myXsd:clothingType"/>
```

EXAMPLE 6–32 http://www.dexterdean.com/stitchOrder/stitchorder.wsdl (Continued)

```
        <part name="body2" element="myXsd:quantity"/>
    </message>

    <message name="StitchOrderOutput">
        <part name="body1" element="myXsd:status"/>
        <part name="body2" element="myXsd:shipDate"/>
    </message>

    <!-- Define operation and port type -->
    <portType name="stitchOrderPortType">
        <operation name="PlaceStitchOrder">
            <input message="tns:StitchOrderInput"/>
            <output message="tns:StitchOrderOutput"/>
        </operation>
    </portType>

</definitions>
```

How the Code Works

1. We begin this WSDL document like all others, with a definitions element. Notice the targetNamespace attribute: We'll be seeing it in the next document. We're setting a namespace here that we haven't seen before: myXsd. This namespace is the same value as our XML Schema document's targetNamespace. By declaring this namespace, we can refer to any element or type in the XML Schema document by using the myXsd prefix.
2. The import statement is necessary to actually bring in the data types from the XML Schema document into this one. Declaring the namespace in the definitions element didn't bring in any data—it just declared the namespace that gave a way to refer to those elements. We need the import statement to actually make those elements available, and we have to use both the namespace and location attributes to make it work properly. The location has to be present to actually find the file, and the namespace says that all the elements from that external file are a part of that namespace.

3. When we define the parts of the messages, we use elements and types from the XML Schema document. Thus, to make sure there's no confusion as to where those elements and types are defined, we place them in the namespace reserved for that XML Schema document.

Almost done! Let's look at Example 6–33, the final document that defines the binding and the services.

EXAMPLE 6–33 http://www.dexterdean.com/stitchOrder/stitchservice.wsdl

```
1.<definitions name="stitchOrder"
targetNamespace="http://www.dexterdean.com/
stitchOrder/services" xmlns:tns="http://
www.dexterdean.com/stitchOrder/services"
xmlns:soap="http://schemas.xmlsoap.org/wsdl/soap"
xmlns:defs="http://www.dexterdean.com/stitchOrder/
definitions" xmlns="http://schemas.xmlsoap.org/
wsdl/">

2.<import namespace="http://www.dexterdean.com/
stitchOrder/definitions"
location="http://www.dexterdean.com/sitichOrder/
stitchorder.wsdl"/>


  <!--
  --- Concrete definitions ---
  -->
  3.<binding name="stitchOrderBinding"
  type="defs:stitchOrderPortType">
    <soap:binding style="rpc"
    transport="http://schemas.xmlsoap.org/soap/
    http"/>

    <operation name="PlaceStitchOrder">
        <soap:operation
        soapAction="http://www.dexterdean.com/
        stitchOrder"/>
        <input>
            <soap:body use="literal"/>
        <output>
            <soap:body use="literal"/>
```

EXAMPLE 6–33 http://www.dexterdean.com/stitchOrder/stitchservice.wsdl (Continued)

```
        </output>
      </operation>
  </binding>

  <service name="stitchOrderService">
      <port name="stitchOrderPort"
      binding="stitchOrderBinding">
          <soap:address location="http://
          www.dexterdean.com/serv/stitch/order"/>
        </port>
  </service>

</definitions>
```

How the Code Works

1. As usual, we begin with the definitions element and a bunch of namespaces. There's a new one here: defs. This namespace is tied to the targetNamespace of the messages and port type document.
2. As before, we import the previous document. So, all of the messages and port types are imported into this final document, and those are placed in the indicated namespace (the same one defs is tied to, as it must be).
3. Notice that here is the only place we use the defs namespace, and that's to specify the name of the port type. That's it—that's the only time you'll need that namespace in this document.

That's it! You now have three documents instead of one, so now any one of these documents can be used multiple times by other documents, which can be useful if you have a number of related Web services.

Recap

Long chapter, huh? Well, you made it. Good job. WSDL is the way for Web services to describe themselves in computer-friendly ways. WSDL documents explicitly spell out what kind of input parameters are expected and how they're structured, as well as what the output parameters should look like, what data formats are acceptable, and what the transfer protocol should be. Chances are you may never actually have to write a line of WSDL in your life. Many tools, including Microsoft's .NET ones, will be able to look at your Web service and automatically write the WSDL for you. Don't despair that you just wasted time reading this chapter. After all, you want to know how Microsoft is going to be describing your code, right?

Next, we look at how someone could actually find your wonderful Web service through something called UDDI.

7

UDDI

In This Chapter

- The Case for UDDI
- High-Level View
- UDDI Business Registry
- UDDI Business Registry Security
- UDDI Data Types
- Inquiry and Publishing Functions
- Error Handling

How do you find a Web service? Right now, it's pretty easy because there aren't very many of them yet. A little surfing or talking to friends and you'll likely find the Web service you need (or discover that you'll have to write it yourself). However, many companies are completely convinced that there will soon be millions upon millions of Web services available over the Internet. In that case, some sort of central list of all the Web services out there will be needed. Some folks, like Ariba, Microsoft, and IBM, got together and came up with a few ideas as to what this central Web service list should look like.

The Case for UDDI

UDDI stands for Universal Description, Discovery, and Integration. Its central goal is to make it easier for businesses to make money. Don't lose sight of that: It's the only reason UDDI exists. That isn't necessarily an evil thing, either. Now to a more interesting question: How does UDDI stand to let businesses make more money? To understand, we need a little background.

Assumptions

The creators of UDDI worked with several assumptions:

- Since Web services are the next form of business-to-business (B2B) e-commerce, you can make a lot of money if you have a popular Web service.
- Given the right environment, Web services in general will become wildly popular, perhaps equaling Web pages in number.
- The existing infrastructure of the Internet is severely limiting the widespread use or rapid growth of Web services.
- If the infrastructure is improved, that will significantly contribute to the widespread use of Web services, and of global B2B e-commerce everywhere. Many people will make a lot of money.

Thus, if you provide a solid infrastructure that will allow a simple deployment of Web services, they will become popular in general, and Microsoft (did I say that? I meant "everyone") stands to make a lot of money.

As I said, this isn't bad. In fact, it gives us developers a good impetus (and excuse) to start working on some cool Web services.

What Businesses Need

Given the assumption that Web services will become popular (and remember, Microsoft has bet their company that they will, so there's a pretty good chance Web services will be around for a while), businesses will have several needs, such as to:

- Discover (that is, locate) each other's Web services
- Expose their own Web services to the world in such a way that other businesses can find and use (and eventually pay for) them
- Make the needs and capabilities of Web services known

It is generally assumed that the build-up of Web services will happen slowly at first, as brave individual developers such as yourself start playing with and deploying them. As confidence grows that Web services will work well, the number of Web services will increase until a critical mass is reached. At that point, the more business-minded people who control the budgets of the world will be convinced of the usefulness of Web services, and will have many more built. This last stage will result in some sort of explosion of Web services, and millions of them could result.

There are several things keeping Web services from becoming widely deployed right now:

- Many existing systems that connect businesses take completely different and incompatible paths. That is, they can't communicate with each other without a lot of extra work.
- Businesses have to make large investments of time and money in order to securely connect their business, and only businesses that happened to invest in the same technology can communicate with each other.

The inventors of UDDI realized that their future wasn't in self-contained, single-platform boxes, but rather in the embracing of all of the diverse platforms, operating systems, and languages that exist on the Internet.

UDDI Goals of Meeting Business Needs

The main charter of the folks who wrote the myriad UDDI specifications is to make Web services discoverable—that is, to provide a programmatic way for people to find and use a certain Web service.

UDDI is the first cross-industry attempt to address the current limitations afflicting the spread of Web services. Not only does it provide a way for Web services to be discovered and used, but it's also built on open standards. That is, all communication with UDDI is done via SOAP messages over HTTP. That's good news: It means UDDI is using open standards to get its work done, and since you already know a lot about SOAP and HTTP, you're well set up to take advantage of this.

Why SOAP? Besides being open, SOAP also deals with RPC. Web services are essentially remote procedure calls, which are often the weakest link in many large architectures. In fact, the Gartner Group recently projected that 5% of major companies implementing enterprise software will experience some sort of failure in the coming year, an example being the heavily reported problems Nike had with i2's software.[1] I hope that the use of UDDI and Web services will bring that failure percentage down.

What a Solid Infrastructure Would Do

UDDI is designed to provide an infrastructure that would allow Web services to flourish. Specifically, UDDI was created to provide a way for businesses to list not only their Web service, but also:

- Basic business information, like business name, address, contact info, and the like.
- Information about the categories the business is in. Is it a robotics company or do they make doughnuts?
- Technical information about the Web service: How exactly does an application contact the Web service and receive information from it? This often takes the form of a WSDL file.

Ideally, absolutely everything you need to know about a business and how to call and get information from its Web service will be available through a business's entry in the UDDI Business Registry.

Here are some other big-word ways to say this:

- UDDI is a standard for registering and discovering Web services.

1. Full disclosure: My wife is a User Experience Architect for PeopleSoft, a competitor of i2.

- UDDI is a service-based architecture for describing Web services.
- You get the idea. If you want to find a Web service and a way to talk to it, go through UDDI.

What does this new infrastructure look like? UDDI provides a way for businesses of any size to register their Web services in a single place. This single place is called the UDDI Business Registry. The information about your business that lives in the UDDI Business Registry can be broken down into three basic categories: white pages, yellow pages, and green pages. We'll look at those in more detail later.

Use Case

Let's look at how, ideally, someone would use UDDI. If you needed to find a Web service that accomplished something specific for you, you would go to some search engine that could tap into the UDDI Business Registry and would show you an appropriate Web service. You would then create a program that would connect to this Web service and feed it information in a way that the service can understand.

High-Level View

Now that you know that UDDI is a specification that allows businesses to both register and look for Web services, let's look more closely. The descriptions of Web services and their businesses live in a place called the UDDI Business Registry. There are two reasons why someone would want to communicate with a Business Registry:

1. To register a Web service—that is, list the business and what it does, along with the Web service and its interface (how to communicate with the Web service). This is known as *publishing*.
2. To find a Web service according to some set of parameters. This is known as *inquiring*.

That's it: publishing and inquiring. All messages that flow to and from a Business Registry deal with publishing a Web service or inquiring about one. What do these messages actually look like? Fortunately, you already know: They're SOAP messages. UDDI Business Registries can only communicate via SOAP messages: It's the only language they know. To get even more detailed, there are about 40 possible kinds of SOAP messages. That is, there are about 25 different methods that concern themselves with publishing and about 15 that deal with inquiring. Remember, SOAP messages are all about invoking remote methods, and since UDDI has a certain number of methods that are part of its specification, there are a corresponding number of SOAP messages.

Table 7–1 illustrates how UDDI fits into the whole Web services system.

TABLE 7–1 Interop Stack

Interop Stack	Universal Service Interop Protocol (not defined yet, but will probably be WSDL)
	UDDI
	SOAP
	XML
	HTTP

This table is from a technical paper at *www.uddi.org*, the current official source of UDDI information.

White, Yellow, and Green Pages

As we saw earlier, the parts of an entry in a UDDI Business Registry can be conceptually placed into three areas:

- White pages: for basic business information
- Yellow pages: for business and service classification
- Green pages: for technical and interface information

Let's look at more closely at these concepts.

WHITE PAGES

The white pages contain information about the business, like the business name, location, contact information, telephone number, URLs, and so on. The white pages are the place where the Web service provider publishes information about itself. Known identifiers like a Dun & Bradstreet number are also part of the white pages. No information about the Web service itself is part of the white pages.

> **NOTE** Dun & Bradstreet numbers are assigned by a company called, predictably, Dun & Bradstreet. The full name is D&B D-U-N-S number (Data Universal Numbering System). Each business that applies for one gets a D&B number. Getting a D&B number is recommended by most large trade organizations.
>
> The number itself is simply a nine-digit number. There are about 62 million D&B numbers already assigned.

YELLOW PAGES

The yellow pages contain further classification information about the business. This classification is done through the release of various product and service indices, industry codes, and geographic indices. All the information in the yellow pages is from standards that already exist, like the North American Industry Classification System and the Universal Standard Products and Services Codes.

The information in the yellow pages is used to find the appropriate business. It can also be used to describe a group of Web services.

GREEN PAGES

The green pages contain all the detailed technical information. The information here allows your application to bind, or connect to and interact with, a certain Web service. All of the technical details on how to communicate with a Web service are contained in the green pages. This information includes URLs, method names, argument types, and so on.

Metadata about the services themselves is also available.

Well, that's about it for the big-picture view of how UDDI is set. Now let's look at UDDI Business Registries, so you understand how these things are put together and propagated.

UDDI Business Registry

The existence of UDDI Business Registries is central to the whole concept of UDDI. Without the Business Registries, UDDI is almost worthless.

Up until now, it probably sounded like everyone's data would be stored in one massive central location, one single UDDI Business Registry. Fortunately, that isn't true: Business Registries copy themselves in a manner much like DNS.

It starts like this: Anyone can create a UDDI Business Registry. Anyone can create one, and any client can access any one of those registries. Of course, it wouldn't do anyone any good if there were a million of these registries but they were all different. Fortunately, all the Business Registries are designed to be the same, no matter how many of them there are.

It happens like this: Say there are bunches of UDDI Business Registries out there, including the one you have. Someone from the Stitch IT department creates a Web service and registers that Web service on your Business Registry. Then, through a number of requests and confirmations, the information of the Stitch Web service is replicated to all of the other UDDI Business Registries in the world. A close examination of how this replication happens is beyond the scope of this book, but we'll look at it using a certain scenario.

But before we examine our Business Registry scenario, it's time for some terminology. Ready?

- Operator site: a UDDI Business Registry
- Node operator site: same as operator site
- Operator cloud: all of the UDDI Business Registries that are publicly accessible
- Publisher: the individual who publishes information about a Web service

Well and good. Now let's imagine that we have two clothing companies, Stitch and Dexter Dean. These two have decided they have complementary business models and decide to merge in order to ride out the stagnant economy. However, they both have Web services in different Business Registries that need to be combined. This is known as a custody change. How does this happen?

First, we have to look at the roles involved in this transfer. We'll abstract them a little bit.

- Source publisher: the original person who published a certain Web service
- Target publisher: the person who will from now on be responsible for that Web service
- Source operator: the operator site that currently holds the Web service's information
- Target operator: the operator site that is supposed to receive the Web service's information
- All operators: all operator sites in the operator cloud

Figure 7–1 shows how the roles interact with each other. Notice that the replication from one operator site to all other operator sites is blithely labeled "replication" without any explanation. It's actually quite a complex process, but more than we're going to get into here. Transferring custody is perhaps a bit advanced for right now, but it should give you an idea of the differences between publishers and operators, and show you visually a number of different operator sites.

About the Figure

1. The source publisher sends a shared secret to the target publisher. This is a verification that the intended destination is actually who they say they are. It's important that this secret be communicated in some out-of-band way, such as a phone call or a fax.
2. The source publisher requests transfer of all or some of its entries. Node operators must provide some kind of user interface that allows the operator to manage all of those entries. The source publisher is also given the option to cancel the entire operation at any point before the final step of replication.
3. Once the source publisher manually confirms the transfer request, the source operator requests a transfer of the target operator. That is, the source operator asks the target operator if it can receive a transfer from the source operator.

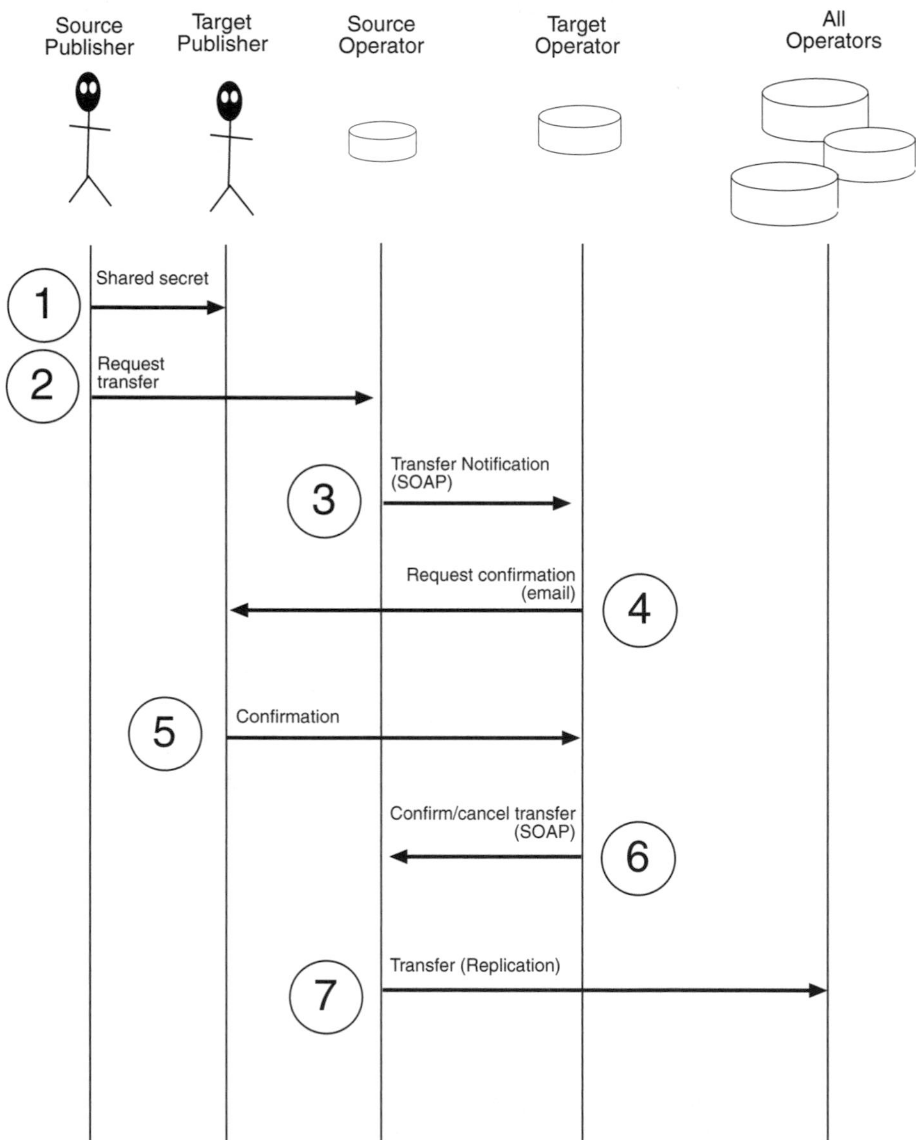

FIGURE 7–1 Transferring custody of Web service information

4. A confirmation email is then sent to the target publisher from the target operator. This email looks like this:

```
To: publisherEMail
Subject: UDDI Transfer Confirmation Request

The following UDDI entity transfer has been requested.
Please confirm the transfer to the publisher account by
following the link below and the instructions provided
there.

Transfer Group Key:

Transfer Group:
Key Type     Key NameKey Value
(type)       (name)(uuid)


...

Source UDDI Node Information
Publisher Name: authorizedName
Publisher Email: publisherEMail
Operator: sourceOperator

Target UDDI Node Information
Operator: targetOperator

Confirmation URL: URL
```

5. The target publisher then clicks the URL in the email (it's the last line of the email), which leads to a Web page that allows the target publisher to either confirm or cancel the transfer. The target publisher also has to enter the shared secret from Step 1. Only five unsuccessful attempts are allowed before the target operator cancels the whole operation.
6. The target operator then sends a SOAP message to the source operator either confirming or canceling the operation.
7. The source operator then relinquishes custody of the data. All subsequent changes to the data occur at the target operator site. This information then spreads to the world via replication.

UDDI Business Registry Security

As I write this, the World Trade Towers were brought down, so in a sad way, I suppose it's appropriate to talk about security. There's also a growing concern about privacy in general, as well as a general anxiety when dealing with any technology that Microsoft is extremely interested in.

The following are three kinds of security issues:

1. Unauthorized access
2. Disclosure of information
3. Denial of service

Each node operator is responsible for implementing his or her own security, but there are some minimum requirements. Each individual in control of an operator site is called an "operator." All operators must clearly state the security policies somewhere on their Web site, in an obvious place. Let's look at these minimal security measures that everyone has to take.

Data Replication

Operator sites must adhere to the UDDI version 2.0 Replication Specification, as well as synchronize their copy of the UDDI registry with new registration data from each of the other adjacent operators at least every 12 hours.

Data Management, Integrity, and Confidentiality

These policies concern themselves with how to store and modify information, as well as who gets to modify the information. Here are some of the less obscure policies (if you're really interested in the gory details, check out the specifications at *www.uddi.org*):

- SSL must be used.
- Operators must implement their own access mechanism (this comes into play in the data custody example above).
- Operators must properly generate UUIDs for keyed entries (more about UUIDs and keys later).
- Operators must associate themselves with the entries in their registry.

Administration and Privacy

Here are some of the more basic policies regarding interaction with the operator site:

- Operators must allow users to register their business on the operator site. Online users must be able to navigate through a graphic interface.
- Operators must provide all appropriate security, privacy, and policy notices.

Availability

Operators must be clear when their sites will be offline.

- Operators must make their policies for service availability known to the public.
- Any planned outage (for, say, maintenance) must be clearly stated.

Auditing

If the UDDI Police batter down your door, they're going to make sure you have a bunch of historical data ready for scrutiny. Here's what you better have (or off to UDDI jail you go):

- All appropriate audit information (detailed below) for the last 12 months.
- All save, update, and delete operations: when it happened, who did it, what it was done to, and the UUIDs involved.
- All new registrations.
- If there was a data custody transfer (like the example above), you better know all the parties involved, as well as all of the UUIDs of all of the pieces of transferred data.
- Change records from replications.
- For all operations, the following must be recorded:
  - Publisher account info (that is, who did it).
  - Timestamp.
  - Name of API (that is, what method was invoked, like `save_business` or `find_tModel`).

- UUID of major players in the operation, including businessKey, serviceKey, bindingKey, and tModelKey. More on these keys later in the chapter.
- Updated email address of the publisher.

Contested (Bogus) Information

No matter how good the security is, someone could figure out a way to post false information on your operator site. If this happens, there's a four-step procedure.

1. The presence of an unauthorized entry is brought to the attention of the operator.
2. The operator decides if the report is worth pursuing. If he or she decides that it is, the operator notifies the business with the unauthorized entry, asking them to remove it or prove that it's real. Or, if he or she is feeling punchy, the operator can simply remove the entry and notify the business.
3. If the business continues to assert that the entry is real, the operator can either decide to delete it anyway or tell the person who reported the entry that some other authority needs to solve the problem.
4. If the operator deletes an entry, that fact must appear in any audit.

Operators are not required to be the mediating authority whenever there's a disagreement about an entry. It's expected that they'll try to assist, but they don't have to, and they can delete any entry they want to, but should do so only if it is clear that a business is being misrepresented.

UDDI Data Types

Oh, we're not done yet. We're just getting started. Everything else in this chapter examines how UDDI stores information and its data model, which will hopefully give you a more solid understanding of this whole UDDI thing. Yes, we're going to see some code now. Finally.

First off, it's important to understand the pages metaphor we looked at earlier—white, yellow and green—are just metaphors. For example, there is no <whitePages> tag. The information in UDDI is contained within five different data types (I've put the name of the actual element in parentheses):

- Business information (businessEntity)
- Service information (businessService)
- Binding information (bindingTemplate)
- Service specification information (tModel)
- Relationships among businesses (publisherAssertion)

These are all complex data types that exist within UDDI Business Registry entries. It is these elements and the information they contain that comprises an entry. Figure 7–2 shows the hierarchy of these different elements.

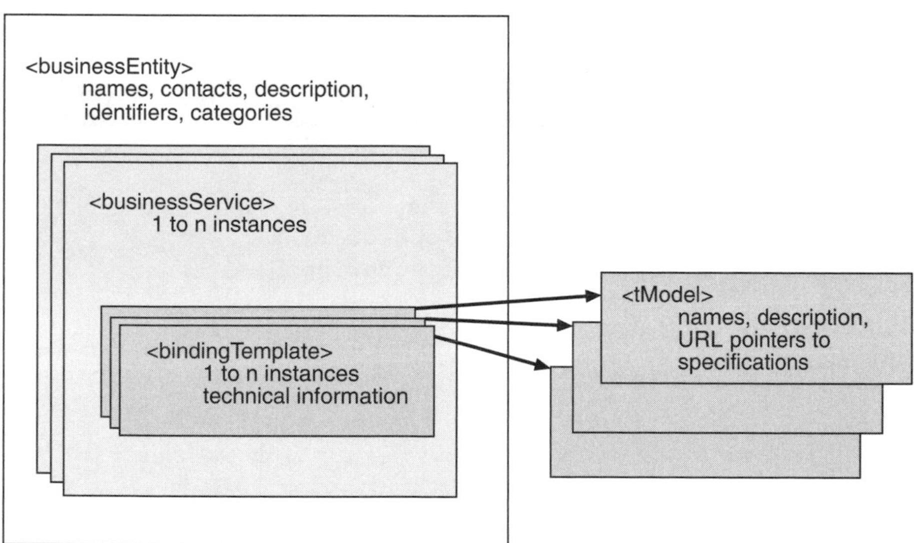

FIGURE 7–2 Hierarchy of UDDI data types

Three elements, businessEntity, businessService, and bindingTemplate, are in a hierarchical relationship. businessEntity contains businessService, which contains bindingTemplate. bindingTemplate then points, in a one-to-one ratio, to tModels. At the top of the figure, a publisherAssertion element spells out the relationship between two businessEntity elements. Don't worry—we'll look at these elements and what they do in detail soon.

As you might expect, the folks who wrote the UDDI specifications needed a way to define exactly how these elements are structured: what kind of data they could contain, which attributes are allowed, and so on. Not surprisingly, they decided to use XML Schema to define these elements. The XML Schema for UDDI data types is in Appendix G. And now, let's start looking at these elements closely.

businessEntity

The businessEntity element contains all the information about a business that has one or more Web services. This element is the top-level element of a Registry entry.

Example 7–1 shows the XML Schema code that determines what the businessEntity can contain.

EXAMPLE 7–1 businessEntity

```
<element name = "businessEntity">
  <complexType>
      1.<attribute ref="businessKey" use="required"/>
      2.<attribute ref="operator"/>
      3.<attribute ref="authorizedName">
      <sequence>
          4.<element ref="discoveryURLs"
              minOccurs="0"/>
          5.<element ref="name"
              maxOccurs="unbounded"/>
          6.<element ref="description" minOccurs="0"
              maxOccurs="unbounded"/>
          7.<element ref="contacts" minOccurs="0"/>
          8.<element ref="businessServices"
              minOccurs="0"/>
          9.<element ref="identifierBag"
              minOccurs="0"/>
          10.<element ref="categoryBag"
              minOccurs="0"/>
      </sequence>
  </complexType>
</element>
```

How the Code Works

1. The businessKey attribute is a UUID that uniquely defines this business among all the other businesses in the world. A UUID is a Universally Unique Identification number. UUIDs must be in this form: XXXXXXXX-XXXX-XXXX-XXXX-XXXXXXXXXXXX (8-4-4-4-12), where each character is a hexadecimal value from the set {A–F,a–f,0–9}. UUIDs are case insensitive (upper and lower case character values are equivalent).
2. The operator is the certified UDDI registry operator name or operator that manages the master businessEntity copy. This information is recorded when the initial save is made.
3. The authorizedName is the actual name of the person who published the businessEntity data.
4. This optional element is a list of URLs that lead to alternate discovery mechanisms (that is, non-UDDI methods of discovery). There isn't any sort of standard right now as to how this should exactly work, but it's anticipated that there will be at some point in the future.
5. The name element is required: It's the human-readable name of the business itself. This information is provided, along with other bits of data, in a find_business call (more on that later). There can be more than one name element.
6. This is a short human-readable business description. There can be more than one description element.
7. The contacts element can contain any number of individual contact points. These contacts can contain a person's name, address, phone, email address, and what sort of contact they are (technical, sales, customer service), as well as a general description.
8. The businessServices element contains, as you would expect, a list of one or more businessService elements, which we'll cover later.
9. The oddly named identifierBag element contains a list of identification numbers for the business. For example, a D&B number or a tax identification number would go in here.

10. The categoryBag element acts much like the identifierBag element, except that this element contains a list of codes that categorize what sort of industry the business is in.

That's businessEntity in a nutshell. Hopefully, you have a more detailed understanding of what sort of data is present in a businessEntity element. Did you notice number 8, businessServices? We're now moving to the businessService element, the next step down in our hierarchy.

businessService

The businessService element exists in order to identify a high-level categorization of the business itself. That is, the element should answer the question, "What kind of business is it?"

Example 7–2 shows the XML Schema specification:

EXAMPLE 7–2 businessService

```
<element name="businessService">
  <complexType>
    1.<attribute ref="serviceKey" use="required"/>
    2.<attribute ref="businessKey"/>
    <sequence>
        3.<element ref="name"
            maxOccurs="unbounded"/>
        4.<element ref="description" minOccurs="0"
            maxOccurs="unbounded"/>
        5.<element ref="bindingTemplates"/>
        6.<element ref="categoryBag"
            minOccurs="0"/>
    </sequence>
  </complexType>
</element>
```

How the Code Works

1. Each businessService must have its own unique key, a UUID that distinguishes it from all the other business services in the world.
2. The businessKey attribute is optional. If the businessEntity element that contains the businessService element has its own businessKey, then there doesn't need to be one in the businessService element. However, it's possi-

ble that a business will want to reuse a certain service for several different business entities. In this case, called a *service projection*, the same businessService would exist under a few different businessEntity elements. Those businessService elements would have different UUIDs, but since they point back to the same businessEntity, they would have the same businessKey. Thus, it's possible for a businessService to have a different businessKey than the businessEntity that contains that service. It's a little convoluted, but it works.

3. As before, the name element is a human-readable name that helps people to identify the service.
4. The description element provides a longer, human-readable description of the business service (which may contain a number of related Web services).
5. The bindingTemplates element contains a list of bindingTemplate elements, which we'll examine in the next section.
6. The categoryBag element acts just like the categoryBag element in the businessEntity element. That is, it contains classification info about the service, based on existing standards.

And that's your basic businessService. Let's dive into some more detail and see what these bindingTemplates are all about.

bindingTemplate

The bindingTemplate element specifies where a certain Web service lives, as well as pointing to the technical information that describes how to actually interact with a Web service. These smaller tidbits of technical data are called tModels (apparently, no one likes this name, but the UDDI folks couldn't come up with anything better).

The bindingTemplate essentially contains pointers to other chunks of data. Example 7–3 shows its schema:

EXAMPLE 7–3 bindingTemplate

```
<element name="bindingTemplate">
  <complexType>
    1.<attribute ref="bindingKey" use="required"/>
    2.<attribute ref="serviceKey"/>
    <sequence>
    3.<element ref="description" minOccurs="0"
          maxOccurs="unbounded"/>
    4.<choice>
        5.<element ref="accessPoint"
              minOccurs="0"/>
        6.<element ref="hostingRedirector"
            minOccurs="0"/>
    </choice>
    7.<element ref="tModelInstanceDetails"/>
    </sequence>
  </complexType>
</element>
```

How the Code Works

1. Each bindingTemplate gets its own key, which is a UUID, thus distinguishing a bindingTemplate from all others.
2. If the bindingTemplate is located inside a businessService element, then the serviceKey attribute is optional. However, if the bindingTemplate is located somewhere apart from a businessService element, then this attribute must be present.
3. The description element is a human-readable string that describes the bindingTemplate.
4. One of the following two elements must be present: If accessPoint is unavailable, then hostingRedirector must be used.
5. The accessPoint element is a text field containing the entry point address suitable for calling a particular Web service. This may be a URL, an email address, a telephone number, or even a fax number.
6. The hostingRedirector element sends the application to another bindingTemplate altogether. You might want to do this if you want a certain bindingTemplate to be available to a number of different services. By redirecting a service to a different bindingTemplate, several services can share the same information.

7. This structure is just a container for tModelInstanceInfo elements. What are tModelInstanceInfo elements? The answer won't mean much until you read the next section, on tModel. Essentially, the tModelInstanceInfo elements describe the tModels as well as give the tModel keys. This will make more sense soon, I promise.

tModel

Apparently, tModel stands for "TypeModel," and the tModel moniker was the name that the inventors of UDDI all agreed upon. Even though no one really likes it, it was the least offensive choice overall.

tModels aren't part of a bindingTemplate in a hierarchical sense. BindingTemplates link to tModels, but the two do not have a parent-child relationship.

tModels define the interface of underlying service implementations. In other words, tModels define a particular service type. Any number of bindingTemplates can point to a single tModel. tModels provide the ability to describe compliance with a specification, a concept, or a shared design. tModels have various uses in the UDDI registry. Right now, let's look at tModels representing technical specifications like wire protocols, interchange formats, and sequencing rules.

For example, a tModel can point to a specific WSDL document that describes how to interact with a Web service.

tModels have such a vague job description that it can be difficult to understand what exactly they're for. Let's look at their XML Schema to ground us a little (Example 7–4).

EXAMPLE 7–4 tModel

```
<element name="tModel">
  <complexType>
    1.<attribute ref="tModelKey" use="required"/>
    2.<attribute ref="operator"/>
    3.<attribute ref="authorizedName"/>
    <sequence>
        4.<element ref="name"/>
        5.<element ref="description" minOccurs="0"
            maxOccurs="unbounded"/>
```

Example 7–4 tModel (Continued)

```
        6.<element ref="overviewDoc"
            minOccurs="0"/>
        7.<element ref="identifierBag"
            minOccurs="0"/>
        8.<element ref="categoryBag"
            minOccurs="0"/>
    </sequence>
  </complexType>
</element>
```

How the Code Works

1. As with all of the other elements we've seen, tModels get their own UUID, or key.
2. The operator attribute is the certified name of the UDDI registry site operator that manages the master copy of the tModel data.
3. The authorizedName attribute is the name of the individual responsible for publishing the information.
4. The name element is a human-readable name that should very briefly describe what the tModel does.
5. The description element here acts the same as in all other UDDI elements—it's a human-readable string describing what the tModel is for.
6. The overviewDoc element refers to remote descriptive information or instructions related to the tModel, such as WSDL documents. Note that this information can also live in the tModelInstanceInfo in the businessService element.
7. The identifierBag element is similar to what you've already seen: an optional list of name-value pairs that can be used to record identification numbers for a tModel.
8. The categoryBag element is similar to what you've already seen, an optional list of name-value pairs that are used to tag a tModel with specific taxonomy information (e.g. industry, product, or geographic codes).

Chances are the most your tModels will ever really do is point to more exact documents on the Web. Example 7–5 and Example 7–6 both show the tModel element in action.

EXAMPLE 7–5 tModel

```
<tModel>
  <name>dexterdean.com:address:1.0</name>
  <description xml:lang="en">
      Codes for Clothing Types
  </description>
  <overviewDoc>
      http://www.dexterdean.com/clothing/codes.html
  </overviewDoc>
</tModel>
```

EXAMPLE 7–6 Another tModel example

```
<tModel authorizedName="..." operator="..."
tModelKey="...">
  <name>StitchOrder Service</name>
  <description xml:lang="en">
      WSDL description of Dexter Dean's order-
      taking service for Stitch
  </description>
  <overviewDoc>
      <description xml:lang="en">
          WSDL source document.
      </description>
      <overviewURL>
          http://stockquote-definitions/stq.wsdl
      </overviewURL>
  </overviewDoc>
  <categoryBag>
      <keyedReference tModelKey="UUID:..."
          keyName="uddi-org:types"
          keyValue="wsdlSpec"/>
  </categoryBag>
</tModel>
```

Almost done! Only one more data type to go!

publisherAssertion

It is expected that most large companies won't be able to easily, or accurately, define their business with a single businessEntity. In fact, it's recommended that large companies or those with divergent product lines register multiple businessEntities. However, it would be nice to have a way to associate those multiple businessEntities in some sort of meaningful way. UDDI provides a way to associate these scattered businessEntities using the publisherAssertion element. Example 7–7 shows its structure:

EXAMPLE 7–7 publisherAssertion

```
<element name="publisherAssertion">
  <complexType>
      <sequence>
          1.<element ref="fromKey"/>
          2.<element ref="toKey"/>
          3.<element ref="keyedReference"/>
      </sequence>
  </complexType>
</element>
```

How the Code Works

1. The UUID of the first businessEntity this assertion is for. Think of an assertion as a claim that a relationship exists.
2. The UUID of the second businessEntity involved in the relationship.
3. The type of relationship this is.

That's about it for publisherAssertion. There's not a whole lot going on for this data type.

The UDDI API XML Schema, in its entirety, is listed in Appendix G. Feel free to peruse it at your leisure.

Inquiry and Publishing Functions

Now that we've looked at the data model for UDDI entries in Business Registries, let's look at how one would actually construct the SOAP messages to either inquire about a certain Web service or publish an entry.

First, a quick SOAP review. SOAP messages look something like Example 7–8:

EXAMPLE 7–8 Sample SOAP message

```
<env:Envelope
  xmlns:env="http://www.w3.org/2001/06/soap-
  envelope">
  <env:Body>
      <w:getPatientHistory xmlns:w="http://
      www.wire-man.com/medical/services"
      env:encodingStyle="http://www.w3.org/2001/06/
      soap-encoding">
          <SSN>555-55-5555</SSN>
    </w:getPatientHistory>
  </env:Body>
</env:Envelope>
```

SOAP messages need a method name and some idea of what to place in the XML payload. In this final section, we'll briefly look over all of the functions available to SOAP when communicating with UDDI Business Registries. A thorough look at all of the available functions and how to craft an XML payload for each would make this an unbearably long chapter, so we'll keep it short. If you're really interested, go to *www.uddi.org* and check out the Programming API specification.

Inquiries

We'll begin by looking at all of the functions available to you if you want to look for a Web service and related information. These are listed in Table 7–2, adapted from the UDDI specification.

TABLE 7–2 Inquiry Functions

FUNCTION	DESCRIPTION
find_binding	Used to locate specific bindings within a registered businessService. Returns a bindingDetail message.
find_business	Used to locate information about one or more businesses. Returns a businessList message.
find_relatedBusinesses	Used to locate information about businessEntity registrations that are related to a specific business entity, whose key is passed in the inquiry. The Related Businesses feature is used to manage registration of business units and subsequently relate them based on organizational hierarchies or business partner relationships. Returns a relatedBusinessesList message.
find_service	Used to locate specific services within a registered businessEntity. Returns a serviceList message.
find_tModel	Used to locate one or more tModel information structures. Returns a tModelList structure.
get_bindingDetail	Used to get full bindingTemplate information, suitable for making one or more service requests. Returns a bindingDetail message.
get_businessDetail	Used to get the full businessEntity information for one or more businesses or organizations. Returns a businessDetail message.
get_businessDetailExt	Used to get extended businessEntity information. Returns a businessDetailExt message.
get_serviceDetail	Used to get full details for a given set of registered businessService data. Returns a serviceDetail message.
get_tModelDetail	Used to get full details for a given set of registered tModel data. Returns a tModelDetail message.

That's it! Those are all of the inquiry functions that can be passed to a UDDI Business Registry. And remember, all requests for information must be embedded in a SOAP message and sent over HTTP.

Publishing Functions

There are a few more publishing than inquiring functions available to you. Table 7–3 has the whole lot of them.

TABLE 7–3 Publishing Functions

FUNCTION	DESCRIPTION
add_publisherAssertions	Used to add relationship assertions to the existing set of assertions.
delete_binding	Used to remove an existing bindingTemplate from the bindingTemplates collection that is part of a specified businessService structure.
delete_business	Used to delete registered businessEntity information from the registry.
delete_publisherAssertions	Used to delete specific publisher assertions from the assertion collection controlled by a particular publisher account. Deleting assertions from the assertion collection will affect the visibility of business relationships. Deleting an assertion will cause any relationships based on that assertion to be invalidated.
delete_service	Used to delete an existing businessService from the businessServices collection that is part of a specified businessEntity.
delete_tModel	Used to hide registered information about a tModel. Any tModel hidden in this way is still usable for reference purposes and accessible via the get_tModelDetail message, but is simply hidden from find_tModel result sets. There is no way to actually cause a tModel to be deleted, except by administrative petition.
discard_authToken	Used to inform an operator site that a previously provided authentication token is no longer valid and should be considered invalid if used after this message is received and until such time as an authToken value is recycled or reactivated at an operator's discretion. See get_authToken.

Table 7–3 Publishing Functions (Continued)

Function	Description
get_assertionStatusReport	Used to get a status report containing publisher assertions and status information. This report is useful to help an administrator manage active and tentative publisher assertions. Publisher assertions are used in UDDI to manage publicly visible relationships between businessEntity structures. Relationships are a feature introduced in generic 2.0 that helps manage complex business structures requiring more than one businessEntity or more than one publisher account to manage parts of a businessEntity. Returns an assertionStatusReport that includes the status of all assertions made involving any businessEntity controlled by the requesting publisher account.
get_authToken	Used to request an authentication token from an operator site. Authentication tokens are required when using all other APIs defined in the publisher's API. This function serves as the program's equivalent of a login request.
get_publisherAssertions	Used to get a list of active publisher assertions that are controlled by an individual publisher account. Returns a publisherAssertions message of all publisher assertions associated with a specific publisher account. Publisher assertions are used to control publicly visible business relationships.
get_registeredInfo	Used to request an abbreviated synopsis of all information currently managed by a given individual.
save_binding	Used to register new bindingTemplate information or update existing bindingTemplate information. Use this to control information about technical capabilities exposed by a registered business.

TABLE 7–3 Publishing Functions (Continued)

FUNCTION	DESCRIPTION
save_business	Used to register new businessEntity information or update existing businessEntity information. Use this to control the overall information about the entire business. Of the save_xx APIs this one has the broadest effect. In UDDI v.2, a feature is introduced where save_business can be used to reference a businessService that is parented by another businessEntity.
save_service	Used to register or update complete information about a businessService exposed by a specified businessEntity.
save_tModel	Used to register or update complete information about a tModel.
set_publisherAssertions	Used to save the complete set of publisher assertions for an individual publisher account. Replaces any existing assertions, and causes any old assertions that are not reasserted to be removed from the registry. Publisher assertions are used to control publicly visible business relationships.

Error Handling

If something breaks, is missing, dies, or is just formatted wrong, the operator site can return an error message encased within a SOAP Fault message. In this section, we'll look at all of the error messages that you might accidentally bring forth.

To start things off simple, let's first look at a successful message, as shown in Example 7–9:

EXAMPLE 7–9 Successful SOAP message<?xml version="1.0" encoding="UTF-8" ?>

```
<Envelope
xmlns="http://schemas.xmlsoaporg.org/soap/envelope/">
  <Body>
     1.<dispositionReport generic="2.0"
       operator="OperatorURI"
```

EXAMPLE 7–9 Successful SOAP message<?xml version="1.0" encoding="UTF-8" ?> (Continued)

```
        xmlns="urn:uddi-org:api_v2" >
          2.<result errno="0" >
              3.<errInfo errCode="E_success" />
          </result>
      </dispositionReport>
  </Body>
</Envelope>
```

How the Code Works

1. The first line of the SOAP body contains the dispositionReport element, which contains the version of UDDI (in the "generic" attribute), the URL of the operator site, and the namespace of the version of UDDI in use.
2. Each result gets an error number. If the number is zero, then no error has occurred.
3. Each error also has a specific code that corresponds with a single error number.

Well and good. Now let's look at an Example 7–10, a returned error.

EXAMPLE 7–10 SOAP error message

```
<?xml version="1.0" encoding="UTF-8" ?>
<Envelope
xmlns="http://schemas.xmlsoaporg.org/soap/envelope/">
<Body>
  <Fault>
    <faultcode>Client</faultcode>
    <faultstring>Client Error</faultstring>
    <detail>
      <dispositionReport generic="2.0"
        operator="OperatorURI"
        xmlns="urn:uddi-org:api_v2" >
        <result errno="10050" >
            <errInfo
              errCode="E_fatalError">
              The findQualifier value
              passed is unrecognized:
```

EXAMPLE 7–10 SOAP error message (Continued)

```
                    XYZ
                </errInfo>
            </result>
        </dispositionReport>
    </detail>
  </Fault>
</Body>
</Envelope>
```

How the Code Works

The only new code here is in bold. Notice our error number is now something besides zero, and our errInfo actually contains some text. That's really the only difference.

Let's wrap this chapter up with a quick look at all of the possible errors and a quick description (Table 7–4). Hopefully, skimming this list will help you get a better grasp of how all the pieces of UDDI work together.

TABLE 7–4 UDDI Error codes

ERROR CODE	ERROR NUMBER	DESCRIPTION
E_assertionNotFound	30000	Signifies that a particular publisher assertion (consisting of two businessKey values and a keyed reference with three components) cannot be identified in a save or delete operation.
E_authTokenExpired	10110	Signifies that the authentication token information has timed out.
E_authTokenRequired	10120	Signifies that an invalid authentication token was passed to an API call that requires authentication.
E_accountLimitExceeded	10160	Signifies that a save request exceeded the quantity limits for a given data type.
E_busy	10400	Signifies that the request cannot be processed at the current time.

TABLE 7–4 UDDI Error codes (Continued)

ERROR CODE	ERROR NUMBER	DESCRIPTION
E_transferAborted	30200	Signifies that a custody transfer request will not succeed.
E_unrecognizedVersion	10040	Signifies that the value of the generic attribute passed is unsupported by the operator instance being queried.
E_unknownUser	10150	Signifies that the user ID and password pair passed in a get_authToken message is not known to the operator site or is not valid.
E_unsupported	10050	Signifies that the implementer does not support a feature or API.
E_userMismatch	10140	Signifies that an attempt was made to use the publishing API to change data that is controlled by another party.
E_valueNotAllowed	20210	Signifies that a value did not pass validation because of contextual issues. The value may be valid in some contexts, but not in the context used. The error text may contain information about the contextual problem.

Recap

You got all that, right? You're ready to build your own UDDI Business Registry from scratch, right? Well, maybe not quite yet. But you do know what UDDI is (a specification use to create UDDI Business Registries, if you've already forgotten) and its five basic data types (businessEntity, businessService, bindingTemplate, tModel, and publisherAssertion). You've also glanced at all of the functions available to you and your SOAP messages, as well as all of the error messages that might come back at you.

8

SOAP Message Attachments

IN THIS CHAPTER

- Quick MIME Review
- Attaching to SOAP

Web services and businesses cannot live on SOAP alone. Often, other items, such as engineering diagrams, facsimiles of legal forms, and the like, need to be transported along with a SOAP message. The inventors of SOAP decided that a method of attaching a file of undetermined type to a SOAP message was necessary. They looked around for how other people had solved similar problems, and came across the idea of Multipurpose Internet Mail Extension (MIME), a way to transmit all sorts of data formats across the wire. Even though MIME was originally designed for email, it's been pretty useful for other purposes. But before we dive too deep into the specifics, let's have a quick review of what MIME types are, and especially, what a multipart/related MIME type really means.

Quick MIME Review

When you send data over the Internet, it travels in 8-bit (sometimes 7-bit) chunks called bytes. When a server receives a big load of bytes from somewhere, how does it know what kind of data it is? Is it a sound, an image, a movie, or a text file? To make this decision easy, often a few extra bytes are sent that describe what the data is. This is the central job of MIME: to describe what type of data is arriving.

This description takes the form of a few ASCII headers that look a lot like HTTP headers. In fact, HTTP headers incorporate MIME headers (okay, I'll spill: Content-Type is an important one).

MIME can also do a few more things, including define a message as being compound—that is, a message that actually combines several other messages inside of it—and delimiting where those different chunks of data begin and end.

MIME divides the world of data into a few major types: text, image, application, audio, and video. These types can be combined in a super type called multipart, which can contain any number of types.

Each type has a few subtypes. For example, text can have a number of different types: plain, html, and xml. Images can be, for example, gif and jpeg. MIME headers display both type and subtype, separated by a slash:

```
text/plain
text/xml
image/jpeg
audio/midi
application/ps
```

MIME was designed for these types and subtypes to be extensible, so you can send anything you want, like fish/head.

Chances are good no server out there will know what to do with fish/head, but you can send it.

In a sense, you can combine several files into a single file with the data type of multipart/related. This combination is what we'll be looking at in the next section. We could go deeper into MIME, but I don't want you falling asleep on me.

Attaching to SOAP

The inventors of SOAP decided to use technologies and types that currently exist to attach messages to SOAP messages, instead of creating a new version of MIME or creating something like text/soap.

Let's say we have to send a SOAP message for an order, along with a TIFF image of a signed purchase order, and that image is attached to the SOAP message. Example 8–1 shows what this might look like.

EXAMPLE 8–1 SOAP with a single attachment

```
MIME-Version: 1.0
1.Content-Type: multipart/related;
2.boundary=MIME_boundary;
  3.type=multipart/mixed;
4.start="<stitch_order.xml@stitchstore.com>"
5.Content-Description: Optional message description

6.--MIME_boundary
7.Content-Type: text/xml; charset=UTF-8
8.Content-Transfer-Encoding: 8bit
9.Content-ID: <stitch_order.xml@stitchstore.com>

<?xml version="1.0"?>
<env:Envelope
  xmlns:env="http://www.w3.org/2001/06/soap-
  envelope">
  <env:Body>
      . . .
      10.<signedPO
href="cid:stitch_po.jpg@stitchstore.com"/>
      . . .
```

EXAMPLE 8–1 SOAP with a single attachment (Continued)

```
</env:Body>
</env:Envelope>

11.--MIME_boundary
12.Content-Type: image/jpeg
Content-Transfer-Encoding: binary
13.Content-ID: <stitch_po.jpg@stitchstore.com>

14.. . . binary JPEG image . . .
15.--MIME_boundary--
```

How the Code Works

1. We start the whole message (also known as a SOAP message packet) by stating that the type of the document is multipart/related, which means that there are several parts to this message.
2. Then, we define the value of the boundary—we'll be using this value to state where one message ends and another begins.
3. The type of the entire document is the same as the type of the root of the message. The root of the message is the first document. For all SOAP messages with attachments, the SOAP message must always be first, so the type in the first line will always be text/xml.
4. Here, we spell out where the root document begins. This is a new kind of notation, where we spell out the name of the file and where it comes from.
5. If you want, you can add a little description of the whole thing.
6. To set a boundary, use two dashes and the name of the boundary. This says we're now looking at a part of the multipart file.
7. We're looking at the SOAP message right now, so the type is text/xml.
8. Text over the Web is transferred in 8-bit bytes, so that's the encoding we use here.
9. This is new: We create an ID of the item in question. Notice this is the same value you saw in number four.

10. We're finally in the SOAP message here. This element, in addition to any others that may be in the SOAP message, refers to another element somewhere else. We know that it's part of another file because it starts with "cid," short for Content-ID. Also notice that the angle brackets aren't part of the href value. This is where we link to the attachment, although technically, the SOAP message doesn't really know or care that it's an attachment. All the SOAP message sees is a URI.
11. Here, we use the boundary to say that the SOAP message is over, and the next thing is beginning.
12. We're attaching a JPEG image.
13. Here's the CID of that image—notice it's what we use in the SOAP message body.
14. Here's where the actual data for the image would go.
15. And finally, we end it with two dashes, the boundary, and two more dashes.

You don't have to use this notation. By spelling out an absolute URI, you can avoid it, as in Example 8–2.

EXAMPLE 8–2 Absolute URIs

```
MIME-Version: 1.0
Content-Type: Multipart/Related;
boundary=MIME_boundary;
  type=text/xml; start="<http://
  www.stitchstore.com/stitch_order.xml>"
Content-Description: Optional message description
Content-Location: http://www.stitchstore.com/
stitch_order.xml

--MIME_boundary
Content-Type: text/xml; charset=UTF-8
Content-Transfer-Encoding: 8bit
Content-ID: <http://www.stitchstore.com/
stitch_order.xml>
Content-Location:
http://www.stitchstore.com/stitch_order.xml

<?xml version="1.0"?>
<env:Envelope
```

EXAMPLE 8–2 Absolute URIs (Continued)

```
   xmlns:env="http://www.w3.org/2001/06/soap-envelope">
   <env:Body>
       . . .
       <signedPO href="http://www.stitchstore.com/
       stitch_po.jpg"/>
       . . .
   </env:Body>
</env:Envelope>

--MIME_boundary
Content-Type: image/jpeg
Content-Transfer-Encoding: binary
Content-ID: <http://www.stitchstore.com/
stitch_po.jpg>
Content-Location:
http://www.stitchstore.com/stich_po.jpg

. . . binary JPEG image . . .
--MIME_boundary--
```

How the Code Works

All the new code in this example is in bold. We didn't change anything drastic. We added a new field, Content-Location, to describe where these remote files actually are. We also used a URL as the content identifier instead of the cid:filename@domainname format in the first example. Either way is fine, but this latter example is generally more informative.

We can even tweak this example some. We can increase readability by using the Content-Location in the base part of the MIME header to determine the base URL for all the files. Then, we can use relative URLs in the rest of the file. Example 8–3 illustrates this.

EXAMPLE 8–3 Base and relative URLs

```
MIME-Version: 1.0
Content-Type: Multipart/Related;
boundary=MIME_boundary;
   type=text/xml; start="<http://
   www.stitchstore.com/stitch_order.xml>"
Content-Description: Optional message description
```

EXAMPLE 8–3 Base and relative URLs (Continued)

```
Content-Location: http://www.stitchstore.com/

--MIME_boundary
Content-Type: text/xml; charset=UTF-8
Content-Transfer-Encoding: 8bit
Content-ID: <http://www.stitchstore.com/
stich_order.xml>
Content-Location: stitch_order.xml

<?xml version="1.0"?>
<env:Envelope
  xmlns:env="http://www.w3.org/2001/06/soap-
envelope">
  <env:Body>
      . . .
      <signedPO href="stitch_po.jpg"/>
      . . .
  </env:Body>
</env:Envelope>

--MIME_boundary
Content-Type: image/jpeg
Content-Transfer-Encoding: binary
Content-ID: <http://www.stitchstore.com/
stitch_po.jpg>
Content-Location: stitch_po.jpg

. . . binary JPEG image . . .
--MIME_boundary--
```

How the Code Works

Again, the changed code is in bold. In the base part of the SOAP message package, we set overall content location to be http://www.stitchstore.com. All of the other locations then jump off from that point, and simply use a relative URL.

HTTP Binding

The SOAP attachment specification also includes some information on binding to HTTP—that is, moving SOAP message packets across the wire using HTTP. The basic concept: The multipart media type header (the multipart/related line) is placed at the HTTP header level, while all others are confined to specific MIME parts. In other words, all other MIME headers cannot double as HTTP headers. This includes the MIME-Version line. Let's use Example 8–4 to see what this looks like.

EXAMPLE 8–4 HTTP binding

```
POST /stitchOrders HTTP/1.1
Content-Type: multipart/related;
boundary=MIME_boundary;
  type=text/xml;
  start="<stitch_order.xml@stitchstore.com>"
Content-Length: nnnn
SOAPAction: http://www.schemas.dexterdean.com/orders
Content-Description: Optional message description

--MIME_boundary
Content-Type: text/xml; charset=UTF-8
Content-Transfer-Encoding: 8bit
Content-ID: <stich_order.xml@stichstore.com>

<?xml version="1.0"?>
<env:Envelope
  xmlns:env="http://www.w3.org/2001/06/soap-envelope">
  <env:Body>
      . . .
      <signedPO
href="cid:stitch_po.jpg@stitchstore.com"/>
      . . .
  </env:Body>
</env:Envelope>

--MIME_boundary
Content-Type: image/jpeg
Content-Transfer-Encoding: binary
Content-ID: <stitch_po.jpg@stitchstore.com>

. . . binary JPEG image . . .
--MIME_boundary--
```

How the Code Works

As you can tell from the code in bold, we're going back to the original method of identifying bits of the SOAP message packet. That is, we're using the cid notation. Also notice that the MIME-Version header has been replaced by the HTTP POST header. We've also included Content-Length and, of course, the required SOAPAction header.

That's about it—nothing else new is going on here.

Recap

That's about all there is to attaching other files to SOAP messages. In short, use MIME, just like you would when sending an attachment along with an email. If MIME was new to you, then you now know a little more about boundaries, types, and subtypes. You also learned about a new notation: cid.

Next, we'll look at a version of SOAP that's smaller, doesn't use namespaces, and has been both roundly criticized and praised: XML-RPC.

9

XML-RPC: SOAP's Little Runaway Brother

IN THIS CHAPTER

- What Is XML-RPC?
- Structure
- Data Encoding
- What's Missing?

XML-RPC was created because somebody became impatient with the delays in making SOAP available to the world, and decided to do his own version of SOAP. Thus, XML-RPC is a standard that has many of the same goals of SOAP, but is a super-stripped-down version. Also, since it was created by a single guy in 1998, when no one was really an XML expert, some questionable decisions were made. But, XML-RPC has enough of a developer base that I'd be remiss to not include a description in this book.

What Is XML-RPC?

XML-RPC stands for XML-Remote Procedure Call. It's a set of tags that allows applications to communicate with each other by sending remote procedure calls, responses, and fault messages.

Goals

Like SOAP, XML-RPC is a way for applications running on different platforms and in different languages to communicate with each other. The XML-RPC specification is designed to be as simple as possible, and it is much simpler than SOAP. XML-RPC is designed to be used over HTTP-POST, and uses XML to encode data. XML-RPC is a verbose language, but it's definitely easy to read.

What XML-RPC Doesn't Do

Data typing in XML-RPC is not based on XML Schema. It has its own simplified way of encoding data, and there is no way to extend it. That is, you can't create your own data types like you can with SOAP—XML-RPC is not extensible. There are also no attributes anywhere in an XML-RPC document. This is deliberate, since it simplifies the document, and it also means that there's no such thing as a namespace in XML-RPC.

There are a number of other things missing in XML-RPC, but we'll look at those later in the chapter.

History

Back in 1998, an outspoken programmer named Dave Winer was working on something like SOAP that he called simply RPC. He hooked up with someone called Don Box and some folks from Microsoft and they started working on SOAP. Dave left his RPC format alone for a while in favor of working on SOAP. He's a smart guy, and he was working with other smart guys, and they were coming up with some pretty good ideas.

However, Microsoft was acting like a standards body as far as SOAP was concerned. That is, there were many discussions, opinions, feedback, arguments, and so on. The process of creating SOAP dragged on slowly. This drove Dave nuts—he was impatient to actually create something.

It finally got to be too much and Dave decided to take what he had learned in the discussions about SOAP and apply it to the RPC format he had been working on. He called this new format XML-RPC and, fully expecting to be squashed like a bug by Microsoft, released XML-RPC to the world.

However, Microsoft didn't squash him, but kept him involved in discussions about SOAP. However, SOAP was evolving into something much more complex than XML-RPC, and the two ended up not looking much alike.

So today we have an evolving SOAP specification and a static XML-RPC specification. There are good and bad points to both situations. XML-RPC is popular enough to have a number of implementations in many languages, and for simpler applications, it may be a more appropriate tool than SOAP.

A common complaint about SOAP is that it's been afflicted with specification creep, which is why the "S" in SOAP doesn't really stand for "Simple" anymore. The XML-RPC spec was frozen over three years ago, so there has been zero specification creep. Unlike SOAP, XML-RPC requires that HTTP be used as the transport protocol.

Structure

Like SOAP, XML-RPC messages come in three flavors: request, response, and fault. Unlike SOAP, there is no header section in XML-RPC.

All XML-RPC messages are sent over HTTP and always use the POST method. Let's look at each one.

Request

Example 9–1 shows a simple remote procedure call:

EXAMPLE 9–1 Simple XML-RPC request

```
<?xml version="1.0"?>
1.<methodCall>
    2.<methodName>placeStitchOrder</methodName>
    3.<params>
```

EXAMPLE 9–1 Simple XML-RPC request (Continued)

```
        4.<param>
            5.<value>jeans</value>
        </param>
        <param>
            <value>red</value>
        </param>
        <param>
            <value>XL</value>
        </param>
    </params>
</methodCall>
```

How the Code Works

Not too much confusion about what's going on here, is there?

1. For a request, everything is wrapped inside a methodCall element.
2. The name of the method is in the methodName element.
3. All of the parameters belong inside of a single params element.
4. Each parameter is spelled out individually by being wrapped by a param element.
5. This is the data encoding part of XML-RPC. All values have a <value> element around them, but we'll get into more detail on data encoding later.

Response

A message response is also simple and verbose, as in Example 9–2.

EXAMPLE 9–2 Simple XML-RPC response

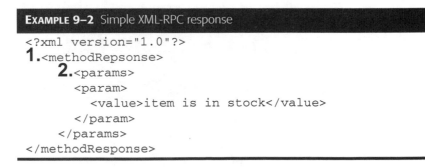

```
<?xml version="1.0"?>
1.<methodRepsonse>
    2.<params>
        <param>
            <value>item is in stock</value>
        </param>
    </params>
</methodResponse>
```

How the Code Works

1. We know this XML-RPC message is a response by the presence of an all-encompassing methodResponse element. Notice that the name of the method does not appear in this message.
2. Just like the request, the returned value(s) are wrapped inside a value element, wrapped inside a param element, wrapped inside a params element.

One limitation of XML-RPC is that only a single value can be returned from a method invocation. Thus, all responses in XML-RPC have the syntax of Example 9–3:

EXAMPLE 9–3 XML-RPC response message syntax

```
<?xml version="1.0"?>
<methodRepsonse>
    <params>
      <param>
        ... a single value ...
      </param>
    </params>
</methodResponse>
```

It seems a little odd to have a params element when it's specified that there can only be a single parameter, but XML-RPC has a few minor oversights like this.

The requirement that XML-RPC must have one and exactly one returning value can be problematic occasionally, since some methods do not return a value. Thus, developers are required to devise some sort of workaround. Here are some solutions that developers are using:

- Returning a success value, like "true" or "1". Unfortunately, this often means hard-coding values into responses—danger!
- Returning the nil value of <nil/> (more on this later).
- Returning some special value that the client will interpret as meaningless. This could be anything from "NoResp0" to "IEatDogFood"—it can be anything that your XML-RPC client will understand to represent a nonexistent response.

Faults

As with SOAP, something can always go wrong on either the server or client side. In either case, there must be some way to tell the client that something has gone wrong and the remote method isn't able to return the desired response. XML-RPC handles this situation by having a special fault message that looks something like Example 9–4.

EXAMPLE 9–4 Simple XML-RPC fault

```
<?xml version="1.0"?>
1.<methodResponse>
    2.<fault>
      3.<value>
        4.<struct>
          5.<member>
              <name>faultCode</name>
              <value><int>9</int></value>
          </member>
          6.<member>
              <name>faultString</name>
              <value>Bad parameters</value>
          </members>
        </struct>
      </value>
    </fault>
</methodReponse>
```

How the Code Works

1. As in the regular response, we begin our message with the methodResponse element.
2. We then use the fault element to announce that this is a fault message. Remember that a normal response would have a params element in this position.
3. The fault messages of XML-RPC must always be a value that is a struct.
4. Fault messages contain a struct with two members. We'll cover structs in more detail later.

5. The struct in a fault message always has two members, faultCode and faultString, no more and no less. In this case, the faultCode is an integer of 9.
6. And the faultString member is "bad parameters."

Pretty simple, right? This means the syntax for an XML-RPC fault message, as shown in Example 9–5, is:

EXAMPLE 9–5 Syntax of XML-RPC fault message

```
<?xml version="1.0"?>
<methodResponse>
    <fault>
      <value>
        <struct>
          <member>
            <name>faultCode</name>
            <value>… some integer …</value>
          </member>
          <member>
            <name>faultString</name>
            <value>… some string …</value>
          </members>
        </struct>
      </value>
    </fault>
</methodReponse>
```

So, you may be asking, "What are the standard faultCodes?" The answer is: there are none. There is no definitive list of XML-RPC faultCodes or what they would mean, or their relationship to any faultString. You can't even use the faultCodes from SOAP, because those faultCodes aren't integers (versionMismatch, mustUnderstand, etc.).

No standard of XML-RPC faultCodes has emerged—so far, individual implementations are using the same faultCodes to mean different things. It's unfortunate that XML-RPC didn't provide a set of standard faultCodes, because there's no way to predict what a certain faultCode may mean—you have to read the faultString to understand what the faultCode is trying to tell you.

Data Encoding

Data in XML-RPC comes in two flavors: simple and compound. The simple data types are integers, double-precision floating-point numbers, strings, date-times, Boolean values, and binary data. Compound data types are arrays and structs. That's it. This will suffice for most applications, but there's no way to extend these types.

Simple Data Types

Interestingly, there are two ways to denote a value as an integer and two ways to denote a value as a string, but the way to denote a value as a date-time is so flawed as to render that data type useless. There are a few more surprises along the way, too.

INTEGERS

XML-RPC can handle integers that are 4-octet integers, which means 32-bit numbers. This translates to integers from -2^{31} to $+2^{31}$ (a little over two billion). You can denote values as integers using either <int> or <i4>. The two tags are completely identical in meaning. It's a little surprising that there are two tags that are 100% interchangeable in all situations, but that's XML-RPC. Integer values can be positive and negative. Example 9–6 shows a few examples.

EXAMPLE 9–6 Examples of integers

```
<value><int>7</int></value>
<value><i4>7</int></value>
<value><int>+1000042</int></value>
<value><i4>-2000000000</i4></value>
```

Note that you can include an optional plus sign. Only the digits 0–9 can appear in these values (excluding the leading plus or minus sign). No white space is allowed, and leading zeros are collapsed.

DOUBLE-PRECISION FLOATING POINT NUMBERS

If you want to use numbers with decimals in XML-RPC, then you must use the <double> element. The range of these numbers is $\sim 9^{323.3}$ to $\sim 10^{308.3}$, both positive and negative and including zero, of course. Check out Example 9–7.

EXAMPLE 9–7 Example of double-precision floating point numbers

```
<value><double>7</double></value>
<value><double>0.0000000005</double></value>
<value><double>-234234.23425346525799</double></value>
<value><double>+40325345</double></value>
```

As with integers, a leading plus or minus sign is allowed. A single decimal point is allowed within the number, along with the digits 0–9. No white space is allowed, and leading zeros are removed.

BOOLEAN

In a bit of a departure from the Boolean values most of you may be used to seeing, Booleans in XML-RPC are either "0" or "1", not "true" or "false". Here are the two allowed Boolean values:

```
<value><boolean>0</boolean></value>
<value><boolean>1</boolean></value>
```

To be absolutely clear, "0" equals "false" and "1" equals "true". If you try to use these values:

```
<value><boolean>false</boolean></value>
<value><boolean>true</boolean></value>
```

you will get an error—these are not allowable values. Also, no white space is allowed.

STRINGS

One of the more bizarre parts of the XML-RPC is that the definition of a string can only be ASCII characters, which means that only English can be transmitted in XML-RPC. Not even accented characters, such as é, can be used. According to the

XML specification, all XML parsers should be able to understand Unicode, or at the least lots and lots of non-ASCII characters. Technically, this requirement should overcome XML-RPC's limitation on strings, but it shouldn't be relied upon blindly. Always check to make sure the server can understand a remote method invocation that happens to be in Spanish or Hebrew or German. Dave Winer, inventor of XML-RPC, has expressed some regret at choosing ASCII to define XML-RPC strings, but hasn't amended the specification as of this writing.

In any case, strings are denoted by the <string> element or nothing at all, in which case it is assumed that the value is a string. Example 9–8 shows some examples.

EXAMPLE 9–8 Strings in XML-RPC

```
<value>item is not in stock</value>
<value<string>item is not in stock</string></value>
<value><string>jeans</string></value>
<value>red</value>
```

It doesn't matter whether the <string> element is present or not—it's entirely optional.

The only other restriction on XML-RPC strings is that if your string contains an ampersand (&) or a less-than sign (<), then they must be replaced by & and <.

DATE-TIMES

To specify a date-time value, use the <dateTime.iso8601> tag. The tag is called this because the data format of the tag is based on the ISO 8601 standard. This standard dictates that date-time values are formatted like this:

```
CCYYMMDDTHH:MM:SS
```

- CC = century. For example, if the year is "2002," then the century value is "20."
- YY = year. If the year is 2002, then the year is "02."
- MM = month
- DD = day

- T = doesn't stand for anything. You must have a "T" in the value.
- HH = hour
- MM = minute
- SS = seconds

Here is an example:

```
<dateTime.iso8601>20020305T12:22:32</dateTime.iso8601>
```

So this time is March 3, 2002 at 22 minutes after noon. You may be asking, where? Is that the time in Australia or San Francisco? While the ISO 8601 standard allows for the inclusion of time zone information, XML-RPC does not. There is no way to define time zone information in XML-RPC. Some people have tried to always use Greenwich Mean Time, but this isn't any sort of standard. Unfortunately, any information about time zone must exist outside of XML-RPC, which reduces its usability.

BINARY DATA

You can encode binary data using the base-64 encoding system, just like as in XML Schema. Use the <base64> element to surround the encoded binary data.

```
<value><base64>wesDFSDFSsds234dffTF==</base64></value>
```

Compound Data Types

Compound data types in XML-RPC consist of arrays and structs.

ARRAYS

All arrays in XML-RPC look like Example 9–9:

EXAMPLE 9–9 Syntax of an array

```
<array>
    <data>
      ... a bunch of values ...
    </data>
</array>
```

Oddly, all arrays must have a <data> tag inside of them. The <array> tag never occurs without the <data> tag, and <data> never occurs without <array>. You may be asking yourself why the <data> tag exists at all. Good question. I don't know—it looks pretty superfluous to me. I think we can chalk it up to a single programmer creating a standard without forcing it to go through a standards process. XML-RPC has some strong points, but it was a quick effort by an impatient guy who wasn't an expert in XML. To be fair, no one was an expert in 1998 and no one is writing about a language I created a few years ago, but the flaws in XML-RPC are becoming more apparent, and the <data> tag is an example.

Let's look at Example 9–10, which shows an array.

EXAMPLE 9–10 Array example

```
<array>
  <data>
      <value>jeans</value>
      <value>70</value>
      <value><int>60</int></value>
      <value><i4>55</i4></value>
      <value><boolean>0</boolean></value>
  </data>
</array>
```

How the Code Works

We have a five-element array here. The first two elements are strings, the next two are integers, and the last is a Boolean.

Array elements can be any type, including other arrays. Let's look at Example 9–11, an array of arrays.

EXAMPLE 9–11 An array of arrays

```
<array>
    <data>
      <value>
        <array>
          <data>
            <value>jeans</value>
            <value>red</value>
            <value>XL</value>
```

EXAMPLE 9–11 An array of arrays (Continued)

```
        </data>
      </array>
    </value>
    <value>
      <array>
        <data>
          <value>tshirts</value>
          <value>purple</value>
          <value>M</value>
        </data>
      </array>
    </value>
    <value>
      <array>
        <data>
          <value>cowboyHats</value>
          <value>leather</value>
          <value>M</value>
        </data>
      </array>
    </value>
  </data>
</array>
```

This is also how you would represent a multidimensional array in XML-RPC. It's a little different than SOAP, because SOAP can differentiate between an array of arrays and a true multidimensional array. Note that you also can't denote exact positions in XML-RPC like you can in SOAP: The whole array must be present in XML-RPC.

Also, XML-RPC doesn't allow you to name an array of any of its elements. Usually, the server doesn't care what you call your array, but it can affect readability.

That's all for arrays! Let's look at the last compound data type in XML-RPC: structs.

STRUCTS

For those of you from the C world (or even ColdFusion), structs will look familiar. If not, then just pretend they're recordsets. That is, structures are simply unordered lists of name-value pairs. Here are some examples:

```
stitchOrder.clothes = "jeans"
stitchOrder.color = "red"
stitchOrder.size = "XL"
```

Structs can also contain other structs.

```
stitchOrder.jeans.quantity.total = "40"
stitchOrder.jeans.color = "red"
stitchOrder.jeans.size = "XL"
```

NOTE Structs can also be viewed as a form of associative array (an array that uses strings instead of numbers to identify elements). For example, stitchOrder.clothes = "jeans" is similar to stitchOrder["clothes"] = "jeans."

Here is Example 9–12, a structure based on the first stitchOrder struct above.

EXAMPLE 9–12 Struct example

```
<value>
  <struct>
      <member>
        <name>clothes</name>
        <value>jeans</value>
      </member>
      <member>
        <name>color</name>
        <value>red</value>
      </member>
      <member>
        <name>size</name>
        <value>XML</value>
      </member>
  </struct>
</value>
```

How the Code Works

Structs are defined, predictably, by a <struct> tag. Each name-value pair inside that structure is known as a *member* of that structure. Inside of each <member>, there is always a name and a value element. The name must be a string, but the value can be anything, even another struct or an array.

Let's look at the more complex Example 9–13.

EXAMPLE 9–13 Complex struct

```
<value>
  <struct>
      <member>
        <name>clothes</name>
        <value>
          <array>
            <data>
              <value>jeans</value>
              <value>hats</value>
              <value>shirts</value>
            </data>
          </array>
        </value>
      </member>
      <member>
        <name>sizesAvailable</name>
        <value>
          <struct>
            <member>
              <name>available</name>
              <value>XS, S, M</value>
            </member>
            <member>
              <name>unavailable</name>
              <value>L, XL</value>
            </member>
          </struct>
        </value>
      </member>
  </struct>
</value>
```

How the Code Works

What we have here is a struct with two members. The first member is an array, and the second is another struct. There are a lot of tags and not a huge amount of actual data. XML-RPC is particularly verbose, but its syntax is so simple that it's relatively easy to follow what's happening. Here's another way to picture the data in the above example:

```
unnamedStruct.clothes[0] = "jeans"
unnamedStruct.clothes[1] = "hats"
unnamedStruct.clothes[2] = "shirts"
unnamedStruct.sizesAvailable.available = "XS, S, M"
unnamedStruct.sizesAvailable.unavailable = "L, XL"
```

Since structures are unordered lists, there's no way to impose any sort of order, and it doesn't matter what order the members are in. For example, this struct:

```
<value>
    <struct>
      <member>
        <name>clothes</name>
        <value>jeans</value>
      </member>
      <member>
        <name>color</name>
        <value>red</value>
      </member>
      <member>
        <name>size</name>
        <value>XML</value>
      </member>
  </struct>
</value>
```

is the same as

```
<value>
    <struct>
      <member>
        <name>color</name>
        <value>red</value>
      </member>
      <member>
        <name>size</name>
        <value>XML</value>
      </member>
      <member>
        <name>clothes</name>
        <value>jeans</value>
      </member>
    </struct>
</value>
```

Null Values

Unfortunately, XML-RPC doesn't allow for null values—there's simply no way to represent a null value. This is unexpected, since most languages, like Java, Python, Perl, and even ActionScript,[1] have nulls.

The folks who have been using XML-RPC have created a nonstandard tag: `<nil/>`. There has been a general agreement that this tag represents a null value. It isn't part of the XML-RPC specification, and it's unlikely that it ever will be. However, most XML-RPC processors understand <nil/>, so chances are good you'll be able to use it in your applications. Here's how it looks in the code:

```
<value><nil/></value>
```

HTTP Headers

There is no parallel in XML-RPC to the SOAPAction field in the HTTP header. In fact, there is no standard way to declare in the HTTP header that the message is in XML-RPC. Example 9–14 shows what a typical header might look like:

EXAMPLE 9–14 Same XML-RPC HTTP header

```
POST /stitchOrder HTTP/1.1
User-Agent: PHP XMLRPC 1.0
Host: xmlrpc.dexterdean.com
Content-type: text/xml
Content-length: nnnn
```

The path can be anything you want. There is a growing trend of placing XML-RPC services in a directory called RPC2. The reason for this is to recognize that Dave Winer was working on a version of RPC before he started working on SOAP, so XML-RPC is something of a second version of his original RPC.

---

1. If you want to know more about the wonderful world of Actionscript, the language behind Flash's interactivity, check out *Advanced Flash 5, ActionScript in Action* by yours truly.

You certainly don't have to place your XML-RPC code in that directory, but it will make you look cool.

Notice that the User-Agent field in our HTTP header spells out what the client is, and in this example, we're using a PHP XMLRPC client. This line is usually ignored by XML-RPC servers, though. Despite this, it's been suggested that any extensions you add to XML-RPC (like the <nil/> value) be listed in the User-Agent field, like this:

```
User-Agent: PHP XMLRPC 1.0 (extensions: nil)
```

No other header fields are required by XML-RPC. This causes some folks to worry about security, and rightly so, so you may want to add WWW_Authenticate and Authenticate fields to your HTTP header. You can also create your own header (provided you know the XML-RPC server will understand your header). If you do decide to include your own header, be sure to prefix it with an "X-" to indicate that it isn't an official header. For example:

```
X-MessageFormat: XMLRPC
```

What's Missing?

Here's a list of what many people think is missing from XML-RPC. If you don't need these features, then XML-RPC may the right tool for you.

- Cannot represent positive or negative infinity.
- Cannot represent NaN (not a number).
- Cannot represent a null value (workaround with <nil/>).
- No global list of standard faultCodes.
- No support for time zone information: incomplete ISO 8601 implementation.
- No associative arrays (but structs are similar).
- No attributes, and thus, no namespaces.
- Strings can only be composed of ASCII characters.
- No specification for publishing information about a Web service that uses XML-RPC. It's likely people will start using WSDL to describe both SOAP and XML-RPC-based Web services.

Recap

XML-RPC is a standard born out of impatience with the sometimes-interminable standards process. While this impatience is certainly understandable, it has resulted in a data format that although useful in a number of situations, still has some serious holes. It's possible that XML-RPC may be more appropriate to your application than SOAP, so it's certainly worth looking at. However, I expect to see a lot more SOAP out there than XML-RPC.

10

Setting Up a Web Service

IN THIS CHAPTER

- Supersimple Web Service
- Web Service Client

Now that you have a pretty good idea what a Web service is and why they're useful, you're probably chomping at the bit to actually create one. The good news is that Microsoft has made it almost frighteningly easy to set up a Web service. We'll start simple, with a small "Hello World"-like program, and get more involved from there.

Supersimple Web Service

In order to follow the examples in this section, you must have a machine running Windows 2000 and IIS. I recommend creating a virtual directory where you can place your Web service files.

Virtual Directory on IIS

Did I just lose you? If you're new to Windows or IIS, here's the scoop: Microsoft has placed a free Web server called Internet Information Server (IIS) on your machine. It's a real Web server, and you can access it right now with this URL: http://localhost/. Go ahead and try it.

Now, to create a virtual directory, you must first create a real directory. I was lazy and made a directory on my desktop called "web test." That's all you really need.

To administer IIS, go to the control panel called "Administrative Tools" and choose "Internet Services Manager." It looks like Figure 10–1.

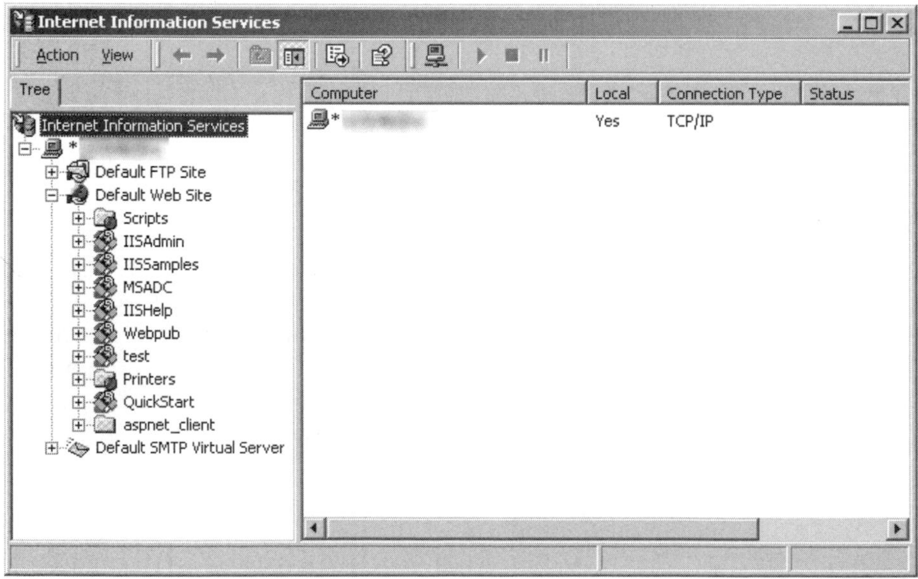

FIGURE 10–1 InternetServices manager

Click the "Default Web Site" icon and choose Action ➤ New ➤ Virtual Directory from the top title bar, as in Figure 10–2.

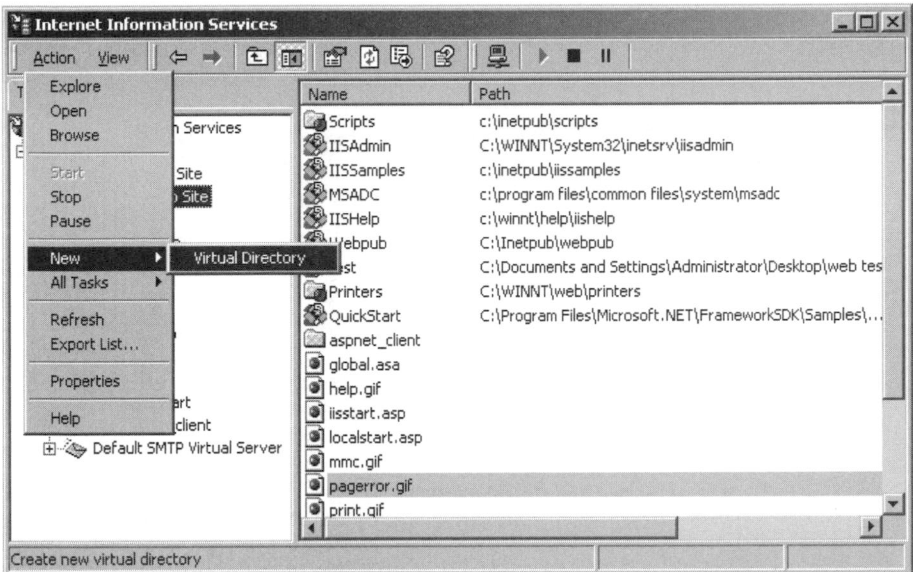

FIGURE 10–2 Creating a virtual directory

A wizard will appear—go ahead and follow its instructions. I was wildly creative and called the virtual directory "test."

You now have a virtual directory! Go ahead and create a little index.html file and place it in the directory.

Downloading Everything

In order for everything to work as I have here, you'll need to download and install three pieces of software (don't worry—it's easy) from Microsoft's Web site: the .NET Framework SDK, the ASP.NET SDK, and the SOAP Toolbox. The location of these programs can shift around a bit, so I recommend visiting *msdn.microsoft.com* and doing some searching.

Once you have these downloaded, installing them is a snap—there are few decisions you have to make.

I'm using the beta 2 version of the .NET Framework SDK, so there may be some differences in what you'll see here and the final version.

Your First Web Service

Here's the bizarrely easy part. Let's start with Example 10–1, a wee Visual Basic program.

EXAMPLE 10–1 Simple VB

```
<%@ WebService Language="VB" Class="GetOrder" %>

Imports System
Imports System.Web.Services

Public Class GetOrder :Inherits WebService

     <WebMethod()> Public Function GetStitchOrder()
As String
          Return("3 size 6 red jeans")
     End Function

End Class
```

How the Code Works

This is a little VB program that only returns a string of "3 size 6 red jeans." Nothing else. Go ahead and save this file as order.asmx. Yes, .asmx: that's .NET's way of saying, "this is a Web service." I used another directory called "services" for all Web service code. Go to your browser and type in http://localhost/test/services/order.asmx and see what happens. It should look something like Figure 10–3.

What the Sam Hill is this? This certainly isn't what you coded. What happened is that IIS noticed that you were accessing a Web service and instead of just serving up an "I don't understand" error, it handed it off to .NET, which did a few things. First, it compiled the program, all by itself. Then, it started it own little Web services tutorial.

Go ahead and click the name of our method, GetStitchOrder. The next screen looks something like Figure 10–4.

Notice you get to see what the requesting and responding SOAP messages will look like. I'll list them in Example 10–2 and Example 10–3.

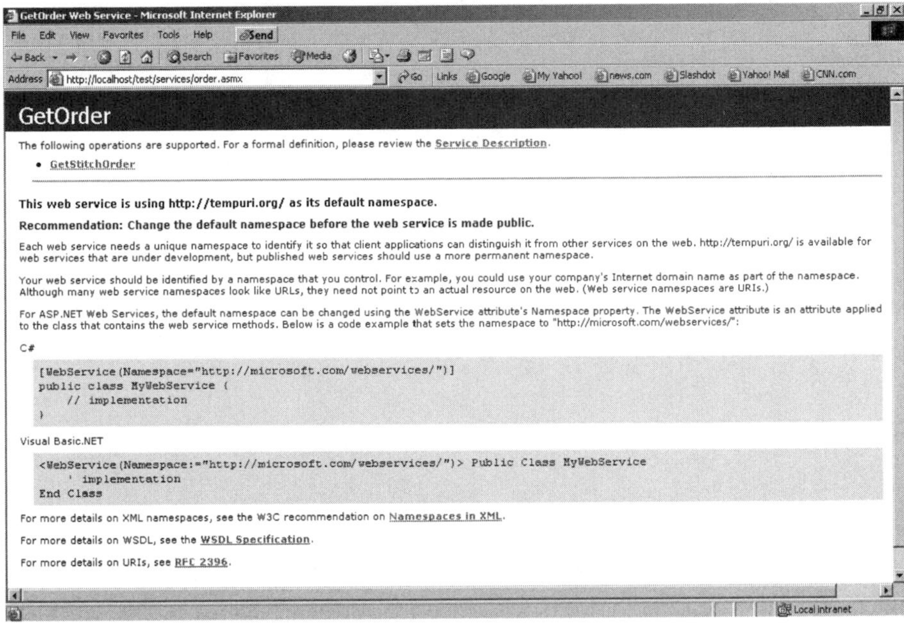

FIGURE 10–3 Microsoft helps out

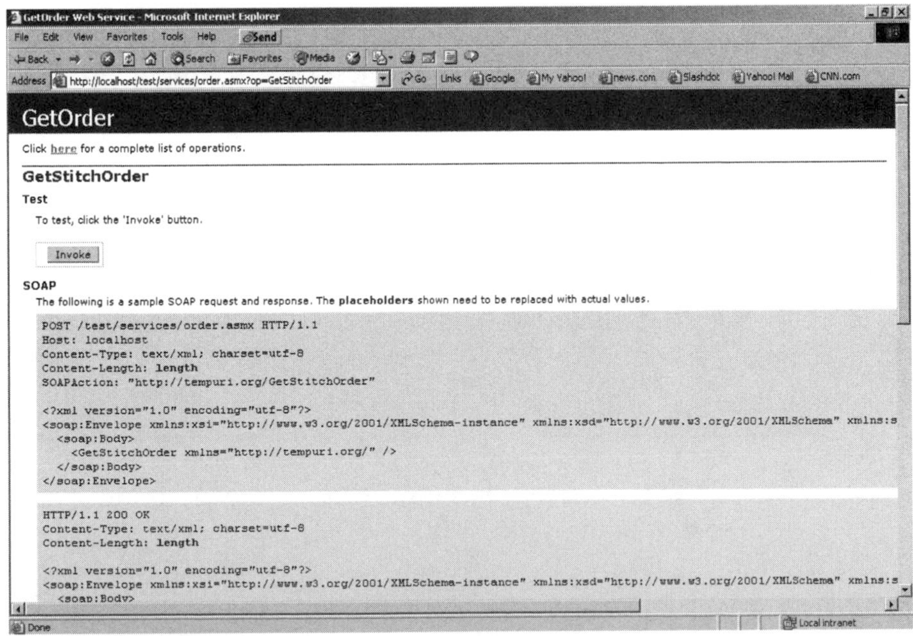

FIGURE 10–4 the GetOrder class

EXAMPLE 10–2 Requesting SOAP message

```
POST /test/services/order.asmx HTTP/1.1
Host: localhost
Content-Type: text/xml; charset=utf-8
Content-Length: nnnn
SOAPAction: "http://tempuri.org/GetStitchOrder"

<?xml version="1.0" encoding="utf-8"?>
<soap:Envelope xmlns:xsi="http://www.w3.org/2001/
XMLSchema-instance" xmlns:xsd="http://www.w3.org/
2001/XMLSchema" xmlns:soap="http://
schemas.xmlsoap.org/soap/envelope/">
  <soap:Body>
    <GetStitchOrder xmlns="http://tempuri.org/" />
  </soap:Body>
</soap:Envelope>
```

EXAMPLE 10–3 Responding SOAP message

```
HTTP/1.1 200 OK
Content-Type: text/xml; charset=utf-8
Content-Length: length

<?xml version="1.0" encoding="utf-8"?>
<soap:Envelope xmlns:xsi="http://www.w3.org/2001/
XMLSchema-instance" xmlns:xsd="http://www.w3.org/
2001/XMLSchema" xmlns:soap="http://
schemas.xmlsoap.org/soap/envelope/">
  <soap:Body>
    <GetStitchOrderResponse xmlns="http://
    tempuri.org/">
      <GetStitchOrderResult>[responce]
      </GetStitchOrderResult>
    </GetStitchOrderResponse>
  </soap:Body>
</soap:Envelope>
```

Cool, eh? Go ahead and press the "Invoke" button. You should end up with some XML, as in Example 10–4.

EXAMPLE 10–4 Responding XML

```
  <?xml version="1.0" encoding="utf-8" ?>
  <string xmlns="http://tempuri.org/">3 size 6 red
jeans</string>
```

Notice the use of the tempuri.org namespace. That's just a placeholder that's used until we put the Web service up in the real world.

Earlier, I mentioned that .NET took care of compiling the program for you. This makes your life easier because you can make changes to your Web service and just save the file—that's it. .NET sees if there have been any changes and if so, recompiles the code. Go ahead and change the code, as in Example 10–5, to handle some big jeans.

EXAMPLE 10–5 Big jeans in VB

```
<%@ WebService Language="VB" Class="GetOrder" %>

Imports System
Imports System.Web.Services

Public Class GetOrder :Inherits WebService

     <WebMethod()> Public Function GetStitchOrder()
As String
          Return("9 waist 46 white jeans")
     End Function

End Class
```

I've bolded the only change to make. Save the file and visit order.asmx in your browser. Invoke the method and notice that, as shown in Example 10–6, the resulting XML has changed!

EXAMPLE 10–6 Resulting big jeans XML

```
  <?xml version="1.0" encoding="utf-8" ?>
  <string xmlns="http://tempuri.org/">9 waist 46
  white jeans</string>
```

In this sense, changing your code is as simple as changing an HTML page. That's the goal anyway. As you bang on this, I'm sure small bugs will begin to appear.

Other Languages

So we know this works in Visual Basic. Just for kicks, replace the code in order.asmx with Example 10–7:

EXAMPLE 10–7 JScript order

```
<%@ WebService Language="JScript" Class="GetOrder" %>

import System;
import System.Web.Services;

public class GetOrder extends WebService {

     WebMethodAttribute public function
     GetStitchOrder() : String {
          return "14 black velvet cowboy hats";
     }

}
```

We're doing the same thing as before, but we're using a different language: JScript. With the advent of .NET, Microsoft has given JScript, its answer to JavaScript, a little boost. Just save order.asx and go ahead and check it out in your browser. Looks exactly like the earlier program, doesn't it? Example 10–8 shows the only difference, the resulting XML:

EXAMPLE 10–8 Resulting XML from JScript program

```
<?xml version="1.0" encoding="utf-8" ?>
<string xmlns="http://tempuri.org/">14 black
velvet cowboy hats</string>
```

Let's do the same thing, but with C#. Paste the code in Example 10–9 into order.asmx and save the file.

EXAMPLE 10–9 Simple C# Web service

```
<%@ WebService Language="C#" Class="GetOrder" %>

using System;
using System.Web.Services;

public class GetOrder : WebService {

     [WebMethod] public String GetStitchOrder() {
          return "19 orange sweatshirts";
     }

}
```

Load the file in your browser and invoke the Web service. It works! Example 10–10 contains the result:

EXAMPLE 10–10 Resulting XML from C# Web service

```
<?xml version="1.0" encoding="utf-8" ?>
  <string xmlns="http://tempuri.org/">19 orange
  sweatshirts</string>
```

And that's a look at the world's simplest Web service.

WSDL

.NET also provides another service: It automatically creates the WSDL needed to describe your Web service. In order to access .NET's interpretation of what your WSDL file should look like, type in http://localhost/test/services/order.asmx?WSDL. The result looks something like Example 10–11.

EXAMPLE 10–11 Generated WSDL file for order.asmx

```
<?xml version="1.0" encoding="utf-8"?>
<definitions xmlns:s="http://www.w3.org/2001/
XMLSchema"
xmlns:http="http://schemas.xmlsoap.org/wsdl/http/"
xmlns:mime="http://schemas.xmlsoap.org/wsdl/mime/"
xmlns:tm="http://microsoft.com/wsdl/mime/
```

EXAMPLE 10–11 Generated WSDL file for order.asmx (Continued)

```
textMatching/" xmlns:soap="http://
schemas.xmlsoap.org/wsdl/soap/"
xmlns:soapenc="http://schemas.xmlsoap.org/soap/
encoding/" xmlns:s0="http://tempuri.org/"
targetNamespace="http://tempuri.org/" xmlns="http://
schemas.xmlsoap.org/wsdl/">
  <types>
    <s:schema attributeFormDefault="qualified"
    elementFormDefault="qualified"
    targetNamespace="http://tempuri.org/">
      <s:element name="GetStitchOrder">
        <s:complexType />
      </s:element>
      <s:element name="GetStitchOrderResponse">
        <s:complexType>
          <s:sequence>
            <s:element minOccurs="1" maxOccurs="1"
  name="GetStitchOrderResult" nillable="true"
  type="s:string" />
          </s:sequence>
        </s:complexType>
      </s:element>
      <s:element name="string" nillable="true"
      type="s:string" />
    </s:schema>
  </types>
  <message name="GetStitchOrderSoapIn">
    <part name="parameters"
    element="s0:GetStitchOrder" />
  </message>
  <message name="GetStitchOrderSoapOut">
    <part name="parameters"
    element="s0:GetStitchOrderResponse" />
  </message>
  <message name="GetStitchOrderHttpGetIn" />
  <message name="GetStitchOrderHttpGetOut">
    <part name="Body" element="s0:string" />
  </message>
  <message name="GetStitchOrderHttpPostIn" />
  <message name="GetStitchOrderHttpPostOut">
    <part name="Body" element="s0:string" />
  </message>
  <portType name="GetOrderSoap">
```

EXAMPLE 10–11 Generated WSDL file for order.asmx (Continued)

```
    <operation name="GetStitchOrder">
      <input message="s0:GetStitchOrderSoapIn" />
      <output message="s0:GetStitchOrderSoapOut" />
    </operation>
  </portType>
  <portType name="GetOrderHttpGet">
    <operation name="GetStitchOrder">
      <input message="s0:GetStitchOrderHttpGetIn" />
      <output message="s0:GetStitchOrderHttpGetOut" />
    </operation>
  </portType>
  <portType name="GetOrderHttpPost">
    <operation name="GetStitchOrder">
      <input message="s0:GetStitchOrderHttpPostIn" />
      <output message="s0:GetStitchOrderHttpPostOut" />
    </operation>
  </portType>
  <binding name="GetOrderSoap"
  type="s0:GetOrderSoap">
    <soap:binding transport="http://
    schemas.xmlsoap.org/soap/http" style="document" />
    <operation name="GetStitchOrder">
      <soap:operation soapAction="http://
      tempuri.org/GetStitchOrder" style="document" />
      <input>
        <soap:body use="literal" />
      </input>
      <output>
        <soap:body use="literal" />
      </output>
    </operation>
  </binding>
  <binding name="GetOrderHttpGet"
  type="s0:GetOrderHttpGet">
    <http:binding verb="GET" />
    <operation name="GetStitchOrder">
      <http:operation location="/GetStitchOrder" />
      <input>
        <http:urlEncoded />
      </input>
      <output>
        <mime:mimeXml part="Body" />
      </output>
```

EXAMPLE 10–11 Generated WSDL file for order.asmx (Continued)

```
    </operation>
  </binding>
  <binding name="GetOrderHttpPost"
  type="s0:GetOrderHttpPost">
    <http:binding verb="POST" />
    <operation name="GetStitchOrder">
      <http:operation location="/GetStitchOrder" />
      <input>
        <mime:content type="application/x-www-form-
        urlencoded" />
      </input>
      <output>
        <mime:mimeXml part="Body" />
      </output>
    </operation>
  </binding>
  <service name="GetOrder">
    <port name="GetOrderSoap"
    binding="s0:GetOrderSoap">
      <soap:address location="http://localhost/test/
      services/order.asmx" />
    </port>
    <port name="GetOrderHttpGet"
    binding="s0:GetOrderHttpGet">
      <http:address location="http://localhost/test/
      services/order.asmx" />
    </port>
    <port name="GetOrderHttpPost"
    binding="s0:GetOrderHttpPost">
      <http:address location="http://localhost/test/
      services/order.asmx" />
    </port>
  </service>
</definitions>
```

Whew! That's one heck of a WSDL document for our little Web service. We won't dissect this WSDL to pieces. You already understand the basics of WSDL, so if you're really interested, feel free to dive in. If you feel like moving on, great! Let's look at a client for a Web service.

Web Service Client

There are many Web service clients already out there in a number of languages: C++, PHP, Java, Perl, Python, and so on. However, I didn't see any ActionScript clients out there. ActionScript is the interactive language behind Flash, and it can send, retrieve, and parse through XML. And since I have some experience with ActionScript,[1] I thought it'd be fun and useful to see if Flash can handle being a SOAP client. As it turns out, it can.

I created a very small Flash movie (downloadable at *www.wire-man.com/soap*) that has a single text box called orderAmount. If we set a variable anywhere in ActionScript called orderAmount, then that value will appear in our Flash movie.

Let's check out the actions of this movie. These are located on the first and only frame of our movie, which means that all the code is executed as soon as the movie loads.

To start simple, the client, as shown in Example 10–12, only retrieves the SOAP response from our Web service. It doesn't send a SOAP request to initiate anything.

EXAMPLE 10–12 Simple Actionscript SOAP client

```
//create XML object
rawXML = new XML();

// load SOAP response into XML object
rawXML.load("http://localhost/test/services/
order.asmx/GetStitchOrder");

// when loading is complete, go to a special function
rawXML.onLoad = loadedXML;

function loadedXML()
{
```

1. *Advanced Flash 5, ActionScript in Action* by yours truly, and *Dan Livingston's Advanced Macromedia Flash Training Course, ActionScript in Action.*

EXAMPLE 10–12 Simple Actionscript SOAP client (Continued)

```
  // loaded XML must remove:
  //    carriage returns
  //    processing instructions
  // to be read correctly by Flash. It's a pain.
  // Hopefully, Flash 6 will correct this.

  // change XML into a string
  stringXML = rawXML.toString();

  // remove carriage returns
  // returns an array, each element being
  // a line of code in the XML
  removeCarriageReturns(stringXML);

  // remove processing instructions
  removeProcessingInstructions(stringArray);

  // create final string from the array
  // returns finalXMLString
  combineArray(stringArray);

  // translate final string into XML
  orderXML = new XML();
  orderXML.parseXML(finalXMLString);

  //extract actual order
  orderAmount =
  orderXML.firstChild.firstChild.toString();
}

function removeCarriageReturns(XMLstring)
{
  stringArray = new Array();
  j=0;
  for(i=0; i<XMLstring.length; i++)
  {
    if (XMLstring.charCodeAt(i) == 13)
    {
      stringArray[j] = stringXML.substring(0,i);
      stringArray[j+1] =
      stringXML.substring(i+2,stringXML.length);
      j = j + 2;
    }
```

EXAMPLE 10–12 Simple Actionscript SOAP client (Continued)

```
  }
  return stringArray;
}

function
removeProcessingInstructions(arrayOfStrings)
{
  // remove processing instructions
  for (i=0; i<arrayOfStrings.length; i++)
  {
    if (arrayOfStrings[i].substr(0,2) == "<?")
    {
      arrayOfStrings[i] = "";
    }
  }
  stringArray = arrayOfStrings;
  return stringArray;
}

function combineArray(arrayToString)
{
  for(i=0; i<arrayToString.length; i++)
  {
    finalXMLString = finalXMLString +
      arrayToString[i];
  }
  return finalXMLString;
}
```

How the Code Works

Since this isn't an ActionScript and XML book, I won't get into the details of the code here. The only part you should look at is the call to the Web service:

```
rawXML = new XML();

// load SOAP response into XML object
rawXML.load("http://localhost/test/services/
order.asmx/GetStitchOrder");
```

Here, we create an XML object, and load whatever GetStitchOrder fires back at us into that object. Oddly enough, what gets returned to ActionScript isn't the SOAP response you'd expect. In fact, it's just the two lines of XML we saw earlier:

```
<?xml version="1.0" encoding="utf-8" ?>
<string xmlns="http://tempuri.org/">19 orange sweatshirts</
string>
```

As you can see, this is a pretty simple example—not a full SOAP client. As it turns out, ActionScript, as of this writing, doesn't have a way to add an HTTP header for the SOAPAction field. Hopefully, by the time you read this, the situation will have changed.

If you're looking for a more full-featured implementation of SOAP, check out *www.soapware.org*, which lists tons of SOAP implementations. There are dozens there right now.

Recap

As you can see, setting up a Web service can be incredibly easy, especially if you go the .NET route. Web services can be written in any language, as can the clients that access them. There are plenty of implementations already out there, in many languages.

11

BizTalk Server and SOAP

In This Chapter

- Purpose of BizTalk
- Structure of BizTalk
- BizTalk Header Elements
- BizTalk Receipts
- BizTalk Attachments
- BizTalk Security

Chances are good that you've never used Microsoft's BizTalk server and that you never will—it's not the world's most popular product. However, what BizTalk accomplishes and how it does it are interesting (it's all in SOAP). Essentially, BizTalk is based on a schema, a specification of a bunch of business-related XML tags. That's it, really. They call it BizTalk Framework. So why should you care about another set of XML tags, when there are already so many out there? It's because, as you starting working more with SOAP and Web services, you'll be dealing more and more with the inner workings of businesses, how they prefer to communicate, and what sort of business processes they need to use. It's not the most exciting stuff on the planet, but given the economy's state, everyone's doing some work they aren't thrilled by. The tags that are a part of BizTalk (at least the concepts behind them) will be useful to you when you have to understand what a bunch of suits are telling you to do. So even if you have zero interest in anything to do with implementing BizTalk, you might want to at least skim through this chapter, and gleam a few business-related ideas from it.

Purpose of BizTalk

As I mentioned above, the goal of BizTalk is to create a set of standard business-related XML tags that will be useful for all companies that want to participate in B2B e-commerce. In that sense, the purpose of BizTalk is quite similar to the current standard, EDI, and the emerging open business standard, ebXML.

These standards are emerging because it has become clear to everyone that no single proprietary solution or middleware platform is going to meet the needs of a complex development environment.

BizTalk doesn't try to address all the issues all businesses must face. It doesn't, for example, cover the following:

- Legal issues
- Arbitration
- Catastrophic failure recovery
- Specific business processes

The BizTalk Framework just provides a set of basic mechanisms for B2B exchanges. Like any specification, BizTalk Framework needs an implementation in order to be of any use. Predictably, Microsoft has released BizTalk Server, which is an application that conforms to the BizTalk Framework. That is, BizTalk Server can read, process, and write the tags that are part of the BizTalk Framework. However, you could write your own server that understands BizTalk if you really wanted to.

Structure of BizTalk

Before diving into the tags themselves and what they mean, we need to quickly look at how BizTalk structures its communications.

First of all, all communication between BizTalk servers is done via SOAP messages. It's assumed that any two business that have decided to use the BizTalk set of tags to communicate will each have at least one BizTalk server. These two businesses, and their servers, communicate by sending SOAP messages back and forth.

The entire SOAP message itself is known as a BizTalk Document (we'll be calling it a "BizTalk SOAP message"). Each BizTalk SOAP message contains one or more independent elements, known as Business Documents (we'll be calling them "independent elements"). Example 11–1 shows a sample BizTalk SOAP message.

EXAMPLE 11–1 Sample BizTalk message

```
<env:Envelope
  xmlns:env="http://www.w3.org/2001/06/soap-
  envelope"
  xmlns:xsi="http://www.w3.org/1999/XMLSchema-
  instance">
<env:Header>
  <end:endpoints env:mustUnderstand="1"
    xmlns:end="http://schemas.biztalk.org/btf-2-0/
    endpoints"
    xmlns:dex="http://www.dexterdean.com/
    datatypes">
    <end:to>
      <end:address xsi:type="dex:department">
        Clothing Orders
      </end:address>
    </end:to>
    <end:from>
      <end:address xsi:type="dex:org">
        Stitch Corporation
      </end:address>
    </end:from>
  </end:endpoints>
```

EXAMPLE 11–1 Sample BizTalk message (Continued)

```
  <prop:properties env:mustUnderstand="1"
    xmlns:prop="http://schemas.biztalk.org/btf-2-0/
    properties">
    <prop:identity>
        uuid:32bc23de-9098-7d3e-aaed-a678d9eab815
    </prop:identity>
    <prop:sendAt>
        2001-09-22T13:55:00+8:00
    </prop:sentAt>
    <prop:expiresAt>
        2001-09-22T14:55:00+8:00
    </prop:expiresAt>
    <prop:topic>
      http://www.dexterdean.com/bizproc/stitchOrder
    </prop:topic>
  </prop:properties>
</env:Header>
<env:Body>
  <so:stitchOrder
    xmlns:so="http://www.dexterdean.com/
    stitchOrder">
    <so:jeans>
        <so:color>red</so:color>
        <so:quantity>17</so:quantity>
        <so:size>6</so:size>
    </so:jeans>
  </so:stitchOrder>
</env:Body>
</env:Envelope>
```

We won't go into the code now. I just wanted to give you a look at what we'll be looking at it more detail.

BizTalk makes extensive use of the SOAP header, so let's take a look at it.

BizTalk Header Elements

The header elements that BizTalk uses cover these concepts:

- Lifetime: the time during which a message is meaningful. After a message's lifetime has expired, it cannot be sent, received, processed, or even acknowledged.
- Identity: BizTalk uses a UUID to identify certain messages.
- Acceptance: the act of accepting a message that was delivered.
- Idempotence (yes, it's a real word): the ability of a SOAP message to be transmitted and accepted more than once and treated as if it was only sent once.
- Receipts: sending a SOAP message back to the source BizTalk server saying essentially, "I got the message" and "I'll process the message."

Here are the five header elements in a BizTalk SOAP message:

- endpoints (required)
- properties (required)
- services (optional)
- manifest (optional)
- process (optional)

Let's go over these one at a time.

endpoints

The message's source and destination are spelled out in the endpoints element. This element must be present and it must be understood. The format of the endpoints element is pretty simple, as you can see in Example 11–2.

EXAMPLE 11–2 endpoints

```
<endpoints env:mustUnderstand="1"
  xmlns="http://schemas.biztalk.org/btf-2-0/
  endpoints"
  xmlns:dex="http://www.dexterdean.com/datatypes"
  xmlns:xsi="http://www.w3.org/1999/XMLSchema-
  instance">
```

EXAMPLE 11–2 endpoints (Continued)

```
  <to>
    <address xsi:type="dex:department">
        Clothing Orders
    </address>
  </to>
  <from>
    <address xsi:type="dex:organization">
        Stitch Corporation
    </address>
  </from>
</endpoints>
```

How the Code Works

We won't get into much detail here, except to point out that there are two subelements, to and from, and each has an address inside. Notice that we're not using a Web address or even a street address. Here, we're just sending the name of a department and an organization. This is fine: It's up to the two BizTalk servers to know what kind of information they'll be sharing.

properties

The properties element in the SOAP header defines the identity of the message, making it unique among all messages, and describes when it was sent, when it should be ignored, and what the message is about. Example 11–3 shows what this could look like.

EXAMPLE 11–3 properties

```
<properties env:mustUnderstand="1"
  xmlns="http://schemas.biztalk.org/btf-2-0/
  properties">
  <identity>
    uuid:32bc23de-9098-7d3e-aaed-a678d9eab815
  </identity>
  <sendAt>2001-09-22T13:55:00+8:00</sentAt>
  <expiresAt>2001-09-22T14:55:00+8:00</expiresAt>
  <topic>
    http://www.stitchstore.com/dexter/order
  </topic>
</properties>
```

How the Code Works

The properties element always contains four subelements: identity, sendAt, expiresAt, and topic. The identity is any kind of URI, and here we've chosen to make this a UUID. The sendAt and expiresAt elements, both timestamps, help keep track of the message. After the time specified in expiresAt, the message becomes a nonentity. If a BizTalk server comes across a message after it has expired, it is to act as if that message doesn't exist and ignore it completely.

The topic element is a little odd: It's a URI whose purpose is to identify the overall purpose of the message. The value of this element is used for routing messages to their correct place on the destination's network. It's recommended that you use the namespace URI of the sending BizTalk server as the value of the topic element.

services

The services element is an optional one, but if it exists, then it must be understood by the receiving BizTalk server. The purpose of the services element is to send messages back to the sending BizTalk server acknowledging that the messages have arrived at the correct destination. The messages that are sent back to the original server are called "receipts" and there are two kinds of them: delivery and commitment. Essentially, they mean "I got the message" and "I commit to processing the message." Example 11–4 shows some code.

EXAMPLE 11–4 services

```
<services
  xmlns="http://schemas.biztalk.org/btf-2-0/services"
  xmlns:dex="http://www.dexterdean.com/datatypes"
  xmlns:xsi="http://www.w3.org/1999/XMLSchema-
  instance"
  xmlns:env="http://www.w3.org/2001/06/soap-envelope"
  env:mustUnderstand="1">
  <deliveryReceiptRequest>
      <sendTo>
        <address xsi:type="dex:URL">
          http://www.stitch.com/receipts
```

EXAMPLE 11–4 services (Continued)

```
         </address>
       </sendTo>
       <sendBy>2001-09-22T15:10:00+8:00</sendBy>
   </deliveryReceiptRequest>
   <committmentRecepitRequest>
       <sendTo>
         <address xsi:type="dex:d_and_b_number">
             55-555-5555
         </address>
       </sendTo>
   </committmentReceiptRequest>
 </services>
```

How the Code Works

As you can see, there are two receipts here that the server must be able to send. The deliveryReceiptMessage element is optional, but if it is present, then the server must send a SOAP message back to the first server.

The committmentReceiptRequest element is optional, but if it is present, then the server must send back a SOAP message saying that the receiving server does indeed intend to actually process the message, beyond just accepting it as a delivery. Did you notice that we used a D&B number instead of a URL in the address field? It's legal—we can do that. However, we better be sure that the server that accepts this message knows what to do with a D&B number.

manifest

SOAP messages, even BizTalk ones, can have attachments and elements that are referred to within the same document. In fact, a message can have a number of parts. The purpose of a manifest element is to list all of those parts—it acts something like a table of contents. If you get a book with nine chapters, and the table of contents says there are sixteen, then you know you're missing something. That's what the manifest is really for—being able to make sure the entire message and all of its parts were delivered. Servers can look through the manifest and make sure that all of the pieces listed in the manifest were actually received. Don't use a manifest unless you have a compound message. Let's look at some code in Example 11–5.

EXAMPLE 11–5 manifest

```
<manifest
  xmlns="http://schemas.biztalk.org/btf-2-0/manifest"
  env:mustUnderstand="1">
  <reference>
    <document href="#order1"/>
    <description>Order for Jeans</description>
  </reference>
  <reference>
    <attachment href="CID:jeans.jpeg@stitch.com"/>
    <description>picture of jeans</description>
  </reference>
  <reference>
    <attachment href="CID:logo.tiff@stitch.com"/>
    <description>logo to place on jeans</
    description>
  </reference>
</manifest>
```

How the Code Works

As you can see, there are three parts to this document. The first is a pointer to a fragment that lives inside the document itself. In other words, there is an element somewhere in the SOAP message with an id="order" attribute.

The other two references are to attachments to the message. In this case, two images are along for the ride, one JPEG and one TIFF. The description element is optional in all cases.

process

Every business has its own process, and the subelements in the process element help the server understand exactly which processes are being used. Processes get their own name, identifier, and possibly some extra detail. Let's use Example 11–6 to see what a process section might look like.

EXAMPLE 11–6 process

```
<process xmlns="http://schemas.biztalk.org/btf-2-0/
  process"
  xmlns:dex="http://www.dexterdean.com/datatypes">
  <type>sales:stitch_order_process</type>
  <instance>sales:stitch_order_process#1242</
  instance>
  <detail>
    <targetPort>stitch_port</targetPort>
  </detail>
</process>
```

How the Code Works

The three basic process subelements are type, instance, and detail. Anything inside the detail element is extensible. That is, it's anything you decide to make up—there isn't any standard to what should be in the detail element.

The other two elements, type and instance, exist to specify which business process is being called into play by the SOAP message. There isn't any set standard for how this information is formatted.

BizTalk Receipts

The receipts we saw when we examined the services element are actually pretty important. It's vital that businesses know whether certain messages reach their destinations or not, and receipts are how BizTalk solves that problem.

Here are some things to keep in mind about receipts:

- The delivery and commitment receipts allow the source server to be sure that the message was actually received and will be processed.
- Since BizTalk deals with some failed messages by resending the original, there is the possibility that the target server will receive several copies of the same message. It will know the messages are duplicates by comparing the value of the identity subelement (inside the properties element). Duplicate messages are discarded.

- If the source server doesn't receive a delivery receipt within the timeout period specified by <sendBy>, a delivery failure report is generated and some sort of action is taken (what this is depends on the implementation).
- There's a small but real possibility that the receipts will be sent, but lost along the way to the source server. The message is processed fully by the receiving server, but the source server thinks the messages were lost and that no action has been taken.

Okay, now let's get into some code in Example 11–7 and look at what the receipts themselves look like.

EXAMPLE 11–7 Delivery receipt

```
<env:Envelope
  xmlns:env="http://schemas.xmlsoap.org/soap/
  envelope"
  xmlns:xsd="http://www.w3.org/2000/08/XMLSchema"
  xmlns:xsi="http://www.w3.org/1999/XMLSchema-
  instance">
<env:Header>
  <endpoints env:mustUnderstand="1"
    xmlns:dex="http://schemas.dexterdean.com/"
    xmlns="http://schemas.biztalk.org/btf-2-0/
    endpoints">
    <to>
        <address xsi:type="dex:URL">
            http://www.stitchstore.com/receipts
        </address>
    </to>
    <from>
        <address xsi:type="dex:department">
              Dexter Dean Sales
        </address>
    </from>
  </endpoints>
  <properties env:mustUnderstand="1"
    xmlns="http://schemas.biztalk.org/btf-2-0/
    properties">
    <identity>
        uuid:24d304a0-b6e1-493a-b457-4b86c684d6f3
    </identity>
```

Example 11–7 Delivery receipt (Continued)

```
    <sentAt>2002-03-12T15:23:00+08:00</sentAt>
    <expiresAt>2002-03-13T08:00:00+08:00</expiresAt>
    <topic>
        http://dexterdean.com/delivery_receipt/
    </topic>
  </properties>
  <deliveryReceipt
    xmlns="http://schemas.biztalk.org/btf-2-0/
    receipts"
    env:mustUnderstand="1">
    <receivedAt>2002-03-12T15:17:00+08:00</
    receivedAt>
    <identity>
        uuid:32bc23de-9098-7d3e-aaed-a678d9eab815</
    identity>
    </deliveryReceipt>
</env:Header>
<env:Body/>
</env:Envelope>
```

How the Code Works

As with all BizTalk SOAP messages, this message must contain both the endpoints and properties elements in the header. In addition to those elements, we also have a new element, in bold here, deliveryReceipt. This element contains two bits of information: when the original message was received and the identity of the original message.

Also notice that the SOAP body element is empty. Receipts always have empty bodies.

Now let's look at Example 11–8, a commitment receipt.

Example 11–8 Commitment receipt

```
<env:Envelope
xmlns:env="http://schemas.xmlsoap.org/soap/envelope"
xmlns:xsd="http://www.w3.org/2000/08/XMLSchema"
xmlns:xsi="http://www.w3.org/1999/XMLSchema-instance">
<env:Header>
<endpoints env:mustUnderstand="1"
    xmlns:dex="http://schemas.dexterdean.com/"
xmlns="http://schemas.biztalk.org/btf-2-0/endpoints">
```

EXAMPLE 11–8 Commitment receipt (Continued)

```
<to>
    <address xsi:type="dex:d_anb_b_number">
            55-555-5555
    </address>
    </to>
    <from>
        <address xsi:type="dex:department">
        Clothing Orders
    </address>
      </from>
    </endpoints>
    <properties env:mustUnderstand="1"
    xmlns="http://schemas.biztalk.org/btf-2-0/
    properties">
      <identity>
        uuid:24d304a0-b6e1-493a-b457-4b86c684d6f7
    </identity>
      <sentAt>2002-03-12T15:23:00+08:00</sentAt>
      <expiresAt>2002-03-13T08:00:00+08:00</
      expiresAt>
    <topic>
      http://dexterdean.com/committment_receipt/
    </topic>
    </properties>
    <committmentReceipt
    xmlns="http://schemas.biztalk.org/btf-2-0/
    receipts"
    xmlns:comm="http://schemas.dexterdean.com/comm"
    env:mustUnderstand="1">
      <decidedAt>2002-03-12T15:43:00+08:00</
      decidedAt>
      <decision>positive</decision>
      <identity>
        uuid:32bc23de-9098-7d3e-aaed-a678d9eab815
      </identity>
      <committmentDetail>
        <comm:expectedShipmentDate>
          2002-03-17
        </comm:expectedShipmentDate>
      </committmentDetail>
  </committmentReceipt>
</env:Header>
<env:Body/>
</env:Envelope>
```

How the Code Works

As with the delivery receipt, the receipt here is shown in bold. The time of the position and the decision itself are shown (the decision must be either positive or negative). The identity is the same as the original message, and the committmentDetail can contain any kind of data you want it to contain.

BizTalk Attachments

As we saw earlier, sometimes it's necessary for attachments to accompany SOAP messages, whether they're images, PDFs, or small executables.

If a BizTalk SOAP message consists of a primary SOAP messages and some attachments, all the content must be in a MIME structure of the mutipart/related MIME media type. Example 11–9 shows an example of a purchase order from Stitch to Dexter Dean. Included are two images: One is a photo of the jeans desired, and the other is the Stitch logo, which needs to be actually stitched onto the jeans themselves. The logo is in TIFF format, and the picture of the jeans is a JPEG, taken with a digital camera.

EXAMPLE 11–9 BizTalk SOAP message with two attachments

```
MIME-Version: 1.0
Content-type: Multipart/Related;
  boundary=biztalk_2_0_related_boundary_example;
  type=text/xml;
  start="<order.xml@stitch.com>"
Content-Description: Optional message description

--biztalk_2_0_related_boundary_example
Content-Type: text/xml; charset=UTF-8
Content-Transfer-Encoding: 8bit
Content-ID: <order.xml@stitch.com>

<?xml version="1.0"?>
<env:Envelope
  xmlns:env="http://www.w3.org/2001/06/soap-envelope"
  xmlns:xsi="http://www.w3.org/1999/XMLSchema-
  instance">
```

EXAMPLE 11–9 BizTalk SOAP message with two attachments (Continued)

```
<env:Header>
  <end:endpoints env:mustUnderstand="1"
    xmlns:end="http://schemas.biztalk.org/btf-2-0/
endpoints"
    xmlns:dex="http://www.dexterdean.com/datatypes">
    <end:to>
      <end:address xsi:type="dex:department">
          Clothing Orders
      </end:address>
    </end:to>
    <end:from>
      <end:address xsi:type="dex:org">
          Stitch Corporation
      </end:address>
    </end:from>
  </end:endpoints>
  <prop:properties env:mustUnderstand="1"
      xmlns:prop="http://schemas.biztalk.org/btf-2-
      0/properties">
      <prop:identity>
          uuid:32bc23de-9098-7d3e-aaed-a678d9eab815
      </prop:identity>
      <prop:sendAt>
          2001-09-22T13:55:00+8:00
      </prop:sentAt>
      <prop:expiresAt>
          2001-09-22T14:55:00+8:00
      </prop:expiresAt>
      <prop:topic>
        http://www.dexterdean.com/bizproc/stitchOrder
      </prop:topic>
    </prop:properties>
    <man:manifest
      xmlns:man="http://schemas.biztalk.org/btf-2-
      0/manifest" env:mustUnderstand="1">
      <man:reference>
        <man:document href="#order1"/>
        <man:description>
          Order for Jeans
        </man:description>
      </man:reference>
      <man:reference>
        <man:attachment
```

EXAMPLE 11–9 BizTalk SOAP message with two attachments (Continued)

```
          href="CID:jeans.jpeg@stitch.com"/>
        <man:description>
          picture of jeans
        </man:description>
      </man:reference>
      <man:reference>
        <man:attachment
          href="CID:logo.tiff@stitch.com"/>
        <man:description>
          logo to place on jeans
        </man:description>
  </man:reference>
</man:manifest>
</env:Header>
<env:Body>
  <so:stitchOrder
    xmlns:so="http://www.dexterdean.com/stitchOrder"
    id="order1">
    <so:jeans>
        <so:color>red</so:color>
        <so:quantity>17</so:quantity>
        <so:size>6</so:size>
    </so:jeans>
  </so:stitchOrder>
</env:Body>
</env:Envelope>

--biztalk_2_0_related_boundary_example
Content-Type: image/jpeg
Content-Transfer-Encoding: binary
Content-ID: <jeans.jpeg@stitch.com>

… raw JPEG image …

--biztalk_2_0_related_boundary_example
Content-Type: image/tiff
Content-Transfer-Encoding: base64
Content-ID: <logo.tiff@stitch.com>

… base64-encoded TIFF image …

--biztalk_2_0_related_boundary_example
```

How the Code Works

We're not overly concerned with how the code works, exactly. I'm sure you can figure most of it out just by reading it. The purpose of this example is just to show you what a BizTalk SOAP message with attachments looks like, so if you ever create one, you'll have some idea what its guts look like.

BizTalk Security

Business messages must often be securely transmitted because they can contain confidential information, like your credit card number. The BizTalk Framework supports S/MIME version 3, a version of MIME that supports encryption.

Why not just use SSL, like we saw in the HTTP chapter? It turns out that SSL is great for single-hop messages, but when a message is looked at, processed by intermediaries, and routed elsewhere, SSL isn't as secure as we'd like. Since BizTalk is designed for only businesses in mind, it needs to support an additional security method that can handle these multihop messages.

S/MIME supports three different forms of security: encryption only, signing only, and both encryption and signing.

Sometimes you'll actually want your header information to be in plain text so that intermediary machines can process the header, but you'll want to keep the actual body of the message encrypted and hidden from view. That is, the headers aren't encrypted, but the body is. S/MIME has a way to do this: The SOAP message itself is in plain text, but the body of it is a single line that refers to an encrypted attachment, which is actually the real information that would otherwise go in the body of the SOAP message. Example 11–10 shows how this might work.

EXAMPLE 11–10 Referring to an encrypted attachment

```
MIME-Version: 1.0
Content-Type: Multipart/Related;
  boundary=biztalk_2_0_related_boundary_example;
  type=text/xml;
  start="<order.xml@stitch.com>"
Content-Description: optional messge description
```

EXAMPLE 11–10 Referring to an encrypted attachment (Continued)

```
--biztalk_2_0_related_boundary_example
Content-Type: text/xml; charset=UTF-8
Content-Transfer-Encoding: 8bit
Content-ID: <order.xml@stitch.com>

<?xml version="1.0"?>
<env:Envelope
  xmlns:env="http://www.w3.org/2001/06/soap-envelope"
  xmlns:xsi="http://www.w3.org/1999/XMLSchema-
  instance">
<env:Header>
  <end:endpoints env:mustUnderstand="1"
    xmlns:end="http://schemas.biztalk.org/btf-2-0/
    endpoints"
    xmlns:dex="http://www.dexterdean.com/datatypes">
    <end:to>
      <end:address xsi:type="dex:department">
          Clothing Orders
      </end:address>
    </end:to>
    <end:from>
      <end:address xsi:type="dex:org">
          Stitch Corporation
      </end:address>
    </end:from>
  </end:endpoints>
  <prop:properties env:mustUnderstand="1"
      xmlns:prop="http://schemas.biztalk.org/btf-2-
      0/properties">
      <prop:identity>
          uuid:32bc23de-9098-7d3e-aaed-a678d9eab815
      </prop:identity>
      <prop:sendAt>
          2001-09-22T13:55:00+8:00
      </prop:sentAt>
      <prop:expiresAt>
          2001-09-22T14:55:00+8:00
      </prop:expiresAt>
      <prop:topic>
          http://www.dexterdean.com/bizproc/
          stitchOrder
      </prop:topic>
    </prop:properties>
```

Example 11–10 Referring to an encrypted attachment (Continued)

```
     <man:manifest
         xmlns:man="http://schemas.biztalk.org/btf-
         2-0/manifest" env:mustUnderstand="1">
     <man:reference>
       <man:attachment href="CID:order1@stitch.com"/>
       <man:description>
           Order for Jeans
       </man:description>
     </man:reference>
     <man:reference>
       <man:attachment
           href="CID:jeans.jpeg@stitch.com"/>
       <man:description>
           picture of jeans
       </man:description>
     </man:reference>
     <man:reference>
       <man:attachment
           href="CID:logo.tiff@stitch.com"/>
       <man:description>
           logo to place on jeans
       </man:description>
   </man:reference>
</man:manifest>
</env:Header>
<env:Body>
  <so:stitchOrder
    xmlns:so="http://www.dexterdean.com/stitchOrder"
      href="CID:order1@stitch.com"/>
</env:Body>
</env:Envelope>

--biztalk_2_0_related_boundary_example
Content-Type: application/pkcs7-mime;
  smime-type=enveloped-data;
  name=smime.p7m
Content-Transfer-Encoding: base64
Content-Description: encrypted jeans order
Content-Disposition: attachement;
  filename=smime.p7m
Content-ID: <order.xml@stitch.com>
```

Example 11–10 Referring to an encrypted attachment (Continued)

```
kjg45jhg45jh45jhg87f6iu23h409erhjmervb54398fdgfg231f
687fg5bn5hg87jvb5v65g4hethef54gswreew8ryesfg4h5hgu4u
y4iihg654o654f6qb4v5cj48ry4ef5tj4fgh8j4df5g4s6r8gydf
4gh8c6fg5h4d8rtyhy6h8s45ry4e658y4e6rtye6r8t

--biztalk_2_0_related_boundary_example
Content-Type: image/jpeg
Content-Transfer-Encoding: binary
Content-ID: <jeans.jpeg@stitch.com>

... raw JPEG image ...

--biztalk_2_0_related_boundary_example
Content-Type: image/tiff
Content-Transfer-Encoding: base64
Content-ID: <logo.tiff@stitch.com>

... base64-encoded TIFF image ...

--biztalk_2_0_related_boundary_example
```

How the Code Works

I've put in bold the three things in this code that have changed. First, instead of the first item of the manifest containing a document element, which refers to a piece of the current document, it's an attachment.

Second, in the body of the SOAP message, we're referring to an attachment using href and a CID notation to find the attachment.

Last, we have the actual encrypted order. This was encrypted using a public key, so the receiving server can then use its private key to unencrypt it.

You can also wrap S/MIME around the whole document, and secure it that way. For example, let's say we simply have the BizTalk SOAP message without any attachments, and we want to send the whole thing via S/MIME. Example 11–11 shows what this would look like.

Example 11–11 S/MIME wrapping

```
MIME-Version: 1.0
Content-Type: Multipart/Related;
  boundary=biztalk_2_0_related_boundary_example;
  type=multipart/signed

--biztalk_2_0_related_boundary_example
Content-Type: Multipart/signed;
  protocol="application/pkcs7-signature";
  micalg-sha1;
  boundary=smime_boundary-1234

--smime-boundary-1234

<?xml version="1.0"?>
<env:Envelope
  xmlns:env="http://www.w3.org/2001/06/soap-envelope"
  xmlns:xsi="http://www.w3.org/1999/XMLSchema-
  instance">
<env:Header>
  <end:endpoints env:mustUnderstand="1"
    xmlns:end="http://schemas.biztalk.org/btf-2-
    0/endpoints"
    xmlns:dex="http://www.dexterdean.com/datatypes">
    <end:to>
      <end:address xsi:type="dex:department">
          Clothing Orders
      </end:address>
    </end:to>
    <end:from>
      <end:address xsi:type="dex:org">
          Stitch Corporation
      </end:address>
    </end:from>
  </end:endpoints>
  <prop:properties env:mustUnderstand="1"
    xmlns:prop="http://schemas.biztalk.org/btf-2-0/
    properties">
    <prop:identity>
        uuid:32bc23de-9098-7d3e-aaed-a678d9eab815
    </prop:identity>
    <prop:sendAt>
        2001-09-22T13:55:00+8:00
    </prop:sentAt>
```

EXAMPLE 11–11 S/MIME wrapping (Continued)

```
    <prop:expiresAt>
        2001-09-22T14:55:00+8:00
    </prop:expiresAt>
    <prop:topic>
        http://www.dexterdean.com/bizproc/
        stitchOrder
    </prop:topic>
  </prop:properties>
  <man:manifest
    xmlns:man="http://schemas.biztalk.org/btf-2-0/
    manifest" env:mustUnderstand="1">
    <man:reference>
      <man:document href="#order1"/>
      <man:description>
          Order for Jeans
      </man:description>
    </man:reference>
    <man:reference>
      <man:attachment
          href="CID:jeans.jpeg@stitch.com"/>
      <man:description>
          picture of jeans
      </man:description>
    </man:reference>
    <man:reference>
      <man:attachment
          href="CID:logo.tiff@stitch.com"/>
      <man:description>
          logo to place on jeans
      </man:description>
  </man:reference>
</man:manifest>
</env:Header>
<env:Body>
  <so:stitchOrder
    xmlns:so="http://www.dexterdean.com/stitchOrder"
    id="order1">
    <so:jeans>
        <so:color>red</so:color>
        <so:quantity>17</so:quantity>
        <so:size>6</so:size>
    </so:jeans>
  </so:stitchOrder>
```

EXAMPLE 11–11 S/MIME wrapping (Continued)

```
</env:Body>
</env:Envelope>
--smime-boundary-1234
Content-Type: application/pkcs7-signature;
  name=smime.p7s
Content-Transfer-Encoding: base64
Content-Disposition: attachment; filename=smime.p7s

.. bas64 encoded detached signature ...

--smime-boundary-1234
--biztalk_2_0_framework_related_boundary_example
```

How the Code Works

Without diving too deep into S/MIME signatures, you should simply look at the sections of code that are in bold. If you're really interested in learning more about the specifics, check out *www.ietf.org/rfc/rfc2633.txt*.

Recap

In this chapter, we looked at some of the issues that businesses are up against, and how BizTalk tries to solve them. We looked at defining endpoints, assigning identity, creating a list of all attachments, demanding and sending receipts, and some security issues. This isn't the most vital chapter in this book, but I hope you found something useful in it.

APPENDIX A

XML Primer

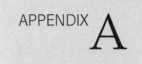

Learning SOAP is a little difficult if you don't know XML. Even if you're just a little rusty or vague on what exactly XML is, you might want to read this chapter. Skim if needed.

What Is XML?

XML is officially the Next Big Thing. And unlike other previous Big Things, it actually has serious staying power. XML stands for Extensible Markup Language, which means it should be called EML, but everyone decided XML was cooler.

There are two parts to that name, "extensible" and "markup language." Let's go over them.

What's a Markup Language?

A markup language is the simplest form of a computer language. HTML is a markup language. Markup languages are comprised of text and tags. That's it. The tags can have attributes. The tags can also be nested within each other. Most tags need closing tags.

The tags themselves exist mainly to describe the text. The tags "mark up" the text.

Since HTML and XML are both markup languages designed to be easily readable by humans, they look pretty similar. Example A–1 shows some XML:

EXAMPLE A–1 Sample XML

```
<?xml version="1.0" ?>
<customer_list>
   <customer number="050">
       <name>Cyndi Lauper</name>
       <customer_since year="1994" />
   </customer>
   <customer number="041">
       <name>Ozzy Osbourne</name>
       <customer_since year="2000" />
   </customer>
</customer_list>
```

Markup languages are simple because they generally don't contain conditional logic, loops, or functions.

What Does Extensible Mean?

Extensible means that you can make up your own tags. This part is critical, because technically, XML isn't a markup language—it's a metamarkup language. In other words, it's a set of rules you use to create your own markup language.

Here's the odd part: Not only are you allowed to create your own tags, you have to. There's no such thing as a pure XML tag—you have to make up your own. Almost anything can be an XML tag:

```
<thisIsALongTagButThatsOkayBecauseXMLisExtensible>
It's true!
</thisIsALongTagButThatsOkayBecauseXMLisExtensible>
```

This also means that technically, no document can be written in XML—it has to be written in a markup language based on XML. All of these made-up languages, including the example above, are called *XML applications*. In other words, you apply the rules of XML, and you end up with your own XML-based language.

If you want to start wading in jargon, XML can also be said to "provide arbitrary structure." In that sense, XML is something like a big bucket of Legos. There are only a certain number of ways things can fit together, but you can build anything you want to out of them.

So why bother with XML? What good does it actually do?

Why XML Is Good

XML is needed because the Internet is an absolute wilderness of different applications, languages, and servers. Some of these computers understand certain languages and other computers understand others. Before XML, there wasn't a way for these machines to talk to each other without knowing who they were talking to and whether the other computer knew their language or not. HTML doesn't count, because it is just a picture of information, not real information. A person can usually figure out what a web site is and what sort of information is on the page, but a computer wouldn't be able to read an image that displayed what kind of information was on the page.

In short, a language needed to exist that all computers on the Internet, no matter what kind of software they were running, could use to communicate with each other. So some really smart people got together and decided what this new language might look like, and they came up with XML.

XML is an open standard, which means that no one owns it. Anyone can use XML without permission from anyone else, like HTML.

XML is plain old text, which just about every computer out there can understand. This aspect of XML holds the promise of being able to write a document once, in a single format, and have other applications format in any way they want. For example, you could create a document in XML, and then other applications, such as a word processing program, a Web publishing program, or a CD writing program, can all access that single XML file. If you need to make a change to that document, you'll be able to make a single change in a single document, and the applications can alter what they have accordingly, instead of having to make changes in several separate documents.

Goals of XML

When XML was developed, the inventors had some goals. Knowing them will help you understand why XML is what it is. These goals were, and still are:

1. XML shall be straightforwardly usable over the Internet.
2. XML shall support a wide variety of applications.
3. XML shall be compatible with SGML. SGML, complicated as it is, is extremely important, and XML cannot afford to totally throw it out the window.
4. It shall be easy to write programs that process XML documents. In this case, "easy" means a graduate student in computer science could write a program in two weeks that can process an XML document.
5. The number of optional features in XML is to be kept to the absolute minimum, ideally zero.
6. XML documents should be human-legible and reasonably clear.
7. The XML design should be prepared quickly.
8. The design of XML shall be formal and concise.
9. XML documents shall be easy to create. This certainly was achieved, since any simple text editor, including SimpleText or NotePad, can create XML documents.
10. Terseness in XML markup is of minimal importance. This is related to number 6, making documents human-readable. Generally, the more terse computer-related data is, the harder it is for people to read it.

Did the inventors of XML achieve their goals? Most people think so, and admirably.

Elements and Nodes

The tags that make up XML have special names. They're called *elements* or *nodes*. The terms are more or less interchangeable (at least as far as we care about here). Example A–2 lets us take another look at the earlier example.

EXAMPLE A–2 Another look

```
<?xml version="1.0" ?>
<customer_list>
   <customer number="050">
       <name>Cyndi Lauper</name>
       <customer_since year="1994" />
   </customer>
   <customer number="041">
       <name>Ozzy Osbourne</name>
       <customer_since year="2000" />
   </customer>
</customer_list>
```

The elements here are a number of customer_list, customer, name, and customer_since elements.

There are different types of elements. For example, any element that lives inside another element is called a *child*. In this example, customer is a child of customer_list, and both name and customer_since are children of customer. Name and customer_since are said to be siblings.

There's also something called a text node. Text nodes are comprised of the text that occurs between an element and its closing tag. For example, in <name>Cyndi Lauper</name>, there are two nodes: name and Cyndi Lauper. "Cyndi Lauper" is the text node.

Did you notice the customer_since elements? They don't contain any text nodes, nor do they have closing tags. When an element doesn't contain anything except attributes, a closing tag is unnecessary if you simply end the element with a single forward slash. The slash says, "This element doesn't need a closing tag."

Structure and Syntax

All XML documents begin with a version declaration that looks something like Example A–3:

EXAMPLE A–3 Version declaration

```
<?xml version="1.0"?>
```

Version declarations are a special kind of XML tag called a processing instruction. Processing instructions aren't really part of the XML information—they're instructions for whatever application is processing the XML document. As of this writing, there's only one version of XML out there, and that's 1.0.

Besides the version declaration, all XML documents have a root element. This element contains all other elements in the document. In the example we've been using, customer_list is the root element. There can only be one root element. Example A–4 is not well-formed XML:

EXAMPLE A–4 Bad XML

```
<?xml version="1.0" ?>
<customer_list>
    <customer number="050">
        <name>Cyndi Lauper</name>
        <customer_since year="1994" />
    </customer>
    <customer number="041">
        <name>Ozzy Osbourne</name>
        <customer_since year="2000" />
    </customer>
</customer_list>
<customer_list>
    <customer number="070">
        <name>Carl Hiaasen</name>
        <customer_since year="1997" />
    </customer>
    <customer number="450">
        <name>Space Ghost</name>
        <customer_since year="2000" />
    </customer>
</customer_list>
```

Notice there are two customer_list elements. Neither one is the root element. Thus, this XML would be rejected by almost any XML application out there—it doesn't follow the rules of well-formed XML.

There are two more rules to cover now: proper nesting and attribute value quoting. Proper nesting means that when an element contains another element, the child element's closing tag must come before the parent's. For example, <a><b>Hi there</b></a> is allowed, where <a><b>Hi there</a></b> is not.

In XML, unlike HTML, all attributes must have quoted values. That's right, no more border=0. It must be border="0".

Attributes or Text Nodes?

It's often debated whether attributes and some text nodes could serve the same purpose. For example, which one of the two bits of code is better?

```
<shirt>
  <size>XXL</size>
</shirt>
```

or

```
<shirt size="XXL" />
```

There is no good answer. It really depends on your application's needs. There is a general consensus that fewer attributes are better because it's easier for most applications to parse through elements than attributes. However, there's no hard-and-fast rule.

The Special Symbols and Comments

Just like HTML, XML has some special characters. However, there are only five of these characters in XML, and they're used to dispel confusion for processing applications, not make little copyright symbols or upside down question marks.

- &—this displays an ampersand (&)
- <—this displays a less than sign (<)
- >—this displays a greater than sign (>)
- "—this display a double quote (")
- '—this displays a single quote (')

Comments in XML look just like HTML: They begin with <!-- and end with -->, and they can take up several lines, as in Example A–5.

EXAMPLE A-5 Commenting in XML

```
<?xml version="1.0" ?>
<!--
   Here's a list of all the current customers
   that are musicians.
-->
<customer_list>
   <!-- Pop representative -->
   <customer number="050">
       <name>Cyndi Lauper</name>
       <customer_since year="1994" />
   </customer>

   <!-- A wee bit harder -->
   <customer number="041">
       <name>Ozzy Ozsbourne</name>
       <customer_since year="2000" />
   </customer>
</customer_list>
```

Recap

That's a brief look at why XML exists, and what it actually is. For a much more in-depth look, feel free to look at *Essential XML for Web Professionals* (by yours truly).

APPENDIX B

XML Schema Primer

Even if you understand the basics of XML, XML Schema can be a little confusing. XML Schema is a special XML-based language designed to describe how certain XML documents should be built. In other words, XML Schema does the same job that Document Type Definitions (DTDs) do. However, XML Schema is much more flexible and powerful, and allows you much more control over XML documents than DTDs. This power comes at a price, though—parts of XML Schema can be challenging to grasp.

Introduction to Namespaces

To learn XML Schema, one must know something about namespaces. If you're like most people, namespaces will seem simple to you. Then, as you think about them some more, you will look for deeper meaning and significance and become quickly confused, for there is none. Then, finally, it will become clear. Hopefully, I'll be able to shortcut this process for you.

Before we dive into details, let's look at the larger picture. Each namespace has two names: a nickname and a real name. The nickname is often short, usually no more than three or four characters. The real name is longer, and is in the form of a URI. So the real name of a namespace would be "http://www.wire-man.com/ns/soap" and that namespace's nickname could be as short as "wire" or even just "w." Here's the confusing part: The real name of the namespace looks a lot like a URL, doesn't it? It isn't: It's just a name, as if your nickname was "Dave Lamb," and your real name was "3746 Robina Avenue, Palmdale, CA." Your real name looks like a real address, doesn't it? Well, it may be, but it doesn't have to be. It's just your real name, and its similarity to a real address could seem confusing.

In other words, if you went to "http://www.wire-man.com/ns/soap," you might find something there, but more likely you'll get a 404 File Not Found error.

Namespaces are used to collect some XML elements into a certain group, as in Example B–1:

EXAMPLE B–1

```
<order xmlns:wire="http://www.wire-man.com/ns/soap">
   <shirt>9 purple</shirt>
   <wire:shirt>5 orange</wire:shirt>
</order>
```

How the Code Works

In the first element, we're using an attribute called xmlns:wire. Xmlns stands for "XML namespace." "Wire" is the nickname and "http://www.wire-man.com/ns/soap" is the real name. What does this exactly do? What is established by creating a namespace? The answer: nothing. All it lets you do is preface elements with the nickname of the namespace. That's it.

So, you may be asking, what's the point? Why would anyone ever bother with namespaces if they don't really accomplish anything? The answer is that namespaces are signals to the applications that will process your XML document. Here's how it's supposed to work: You create an XML document that uses one or more namespaces. You send that document to an XML processor somewhere, and your expectation is that the XML processor will recognize the real names of the namespace you used (it doesn't care what the nickname is), and it will treat elements that are a part of that namespace in a special way. For instance, in the example above, the wire:shirt element will be treated differently than the shirt element. How it will be treated differently depends on which namespace you use and the XML processor you send your XML document to.

Okay, so namespaces are a way to signal an XML processor to treat certain elements in a certain way. What does that have to do with XML Schema? Let's see.

Introduction to XML Schema

XML Schema is nothing but an XML-based language, just like all the others. It's composed of elements, attributes, and text, like all other XML-based languages. An XML processor takes an XML document and its accompanying XML Schema and sees if the XML document adheres to the rules set in the XML Schema. If the XML document passes muster, it is accepted. If not, it's rejected.

Here's Example B–2, which shows what the simplest XML Schema document in the world looks like:

EXAMPLE B–2 Simple XML Schema document

```
<?xml version="1.0" ?>
<xsd:schema
   xmlns:xsd="http://www.w3.org/2000/10/XMLSchema">
</xsd:schema>
```

How the Code Works

As you can see, this is a simple XML document where we've set a namespace called "http://www.w3.org/2000/10/XMLSchema." This is the official namespace for XML Schema. All XML Schema documents must use this namespace, or it isn't really an XML Schema document.

Let's look at Example B–3, a simple XML document and its corresponding XML Schema document.

EXAMPLE B–3 Simple XML document

```
<?xml version="1.0" ?>
<order>
   9 shirts
</order>
```

And Example B–4 shows what the XML Schema document would look like:

EXAMPLE B–4 Corresponding XML Schema document

```
<?xml version="1.0" ?>
<xsd:schema
   xmlns:xsd="http://www.w3.org/2000/10/XMLSchema">
   <xsd:element name="order" type="xsd:string" />
</xsd:schema>
```

How the Code Works

We've added only one new element here in the XML Schema: xsd:element. This XML Schema element states that "an element goes here." The name of the element is "order" and the element can contain plain text that's a string. More on that later.

For now, I confess—I cheated a bit. The XML document has to actually link to an XML Schema document. Here's how that happens (see Example B–5).

EXAMPLE B–5 Complete XML document

```
<?xml version="1.0" ?>
<order xmlns:xsi="http://www.w3.org/2000/10/
XMLSchema-instance"
xsi:noNamespaceSchemaLocation="name_of_xsd_document
.xsd">
   9 shirts
</order>
```

How the Code Works

Since this is just a primer, we're not going to dig too deep into what these attributes mean. For now, just accept that these two attributes are needed to link an XML document to an XML Schema document.

Now, let's get into the guts of XML Schema.

Simple Types

XML Schema sees the world in shades of two types of elements: simple and complex. We'll cover simple-type elements first.

Simple-type elements are elements in this form:

```
<elementName>something</elementName>
```

Simple-type elements are elements that contain only some text, no other elements, and no attributes. The only difference between simple types is what kind of text is inside the elements. If any kind of text can appear in the element, then it's a string (the xsd:string simple type we saw above).

Number-Based Simple Types

Some simple types deal with and only allow numbers. Let's look at them:

Xsd:integer

Description	An element with a simple type of `integer` can be any whole number that's positive, negative, or 0.
Example	`<xsd:element name="price" type="xsd:integer"/>` `<price>31</price>`

xsd:postiveInteger

Description	An element with a simple type of `positiveInteger` can be any whole number that's positive, but not negative or 0.
Example	`<xsd:element name="price" type="xsd:positiveInteger"/>` `<price>1</price>`

xsd:negativeInteger

Description	An element with a simple type of `negativeInteger` can be any whole number that's negative, but not positive or 0.
Example	`<xsd:element name="temperature" type="xsd:negativeInteger"/>` `<temperature>-20</temperature>`

xsd:nonPostiveInteger

Description	An element with a simple type of `nonPostiveInteger` can be any whole number that's negative or 0, but not positive.
Example	`<xsd:element name="temperature" type="xsd:nonPositiveInteger" />` `<temperature>0</temperature>`

xsd:nonNegativeInteger

Description	An element with a simple type of `nonNegativeInteger` can be any whole number that's positive or 0, but not negative.
Example	`<xsd:element name="population" type="xsd:nonNegativeInteger"/>` `<population>17</population>`

xsd:float

Description	An element with a simple type of `float` can be a single-precision 32-bit floating-point number, like 3.5 or 4.5e+8. Also includes positive infinity (`INF`), negative infinity (`-INF`), and not a number (`NaN`).
Example	`<xsd:element name="magnification" type="xsd:float"/>` `<magnification>8e-5</magnification>`

xsd:double

Description	An element with a simple type of `double` can be a double-precision 64-bit floating-point number (see `xsd:float` above).
Example	`<xsd:element name="magnification" type="xsd:double"/>` `<magnification >6e+14</magnification>`

Date- and Time-Based Simple Types

Your simple-type elements can be limited to only contain time and date information. However, date types are predetermined: They must be in the format *YYYY-MM-DD*, so something like "August 7, 2002" isn't allowed. Here are all of the types available:

xsd:date

Description: A date element must be in the format *YYYY-MM-DD*

Example

```
<xsd:element name="birthday" type="xsd:date" />
<birthday>1970-01-28</birthday>
```

xsd:time

Description: A `time` element must be in the form *hh:mm:ss.sss*. You can also add an optional `Z`, +*hh:mm* or –*hh:mm* at the end to indicate a time zone difference. Use `Z` if the time is in UTC (Coordinated Universal Time, or Greenwich Mean Time), or use the additional hours and minutes to indicate difference from the UTC. The hours use the 24-hour clock.

Example

```
<xsd:element name="alarm" type="xsd:time" />
<alarm>05:45:00</alarm>
```

xsd:timeInstant

Description: This type allows you to combine date and time into a single string. The formats are the same except that there's a `T` between the date and the time, *YYYY-MM-DD*T*hh:mm:ss.sss*, along with the optional time zone information described above.

Example

```
<xsd:element name="death"
type="xsd:timeInstant" />
<death>2000-09-12T17:21:35</death>
```

xsd:timeDuration

Description: This type is a little odd. The format is P*n*Y*n*M*n*D*n*TH*n*M*n*S*n*
`P` = Period is mandatory. The other letters stand for what you're used to, except the "`T`"

Example

```
<xsd:element name="timeAloft"
type="xsd:timeDuration"/>
<timeAloft>P2Y3M6D14TH4M12S34</timeAloft>
```

xsd:month

Description: This type specifies a certain month and year. Format is *YYYY-MM*.

Example

```
<xsd:element name="deadline" type="xsd:month" />
<deadline>2001-06</deadline>
```

xsd:year	
Description	This type specifies a year. Format is *YYYY*.
Example	`<xsd:element name="moveToNY" type="xsd:year" />` `<moveToNY>1944</moveToNY>`

xsd:century	
Description	This type specifies a century—it's just the first two digits of a four-digit year. For example, the century of 1969 is "19."

Example	`<xsd:element name="columbus"`
	`type="xsd:century" />`
	`<columbus>14</columbus>`

xsd:recurringDate	
Description	This type specifies a day and a month, but no year. The format is `--`*MM-DD*. Note the double hyphen in front.

Example	`<xsd:element name="birthday"`
	`type="xsd:recurringDate" />`
	`<birthday>--11-28</birthday>`

xsd:recurringDay	
Description	This type specifies a certain day of the month. The format is `---`*DD*. Note the triple hyphen in front.

Example	`<xsd:element name="balanceCheckbook"`
	`type="xsd:recurringDay" />`
	`<balanceCheckbook>---14</balanceCheckbook>`

Miscellaneous Simple Types

There's more out there than just numbers, times, and dates. Here are the rest of the simple types.

xsd:Boolean	
Description	This type specifies true or false (0 or 1 can also be used)

Example	`<xsd:element name="married"`
	`type="xsd:boolean" />`
	`<married>true</married>`

xsd:language	
Description	This type specifies a language, formatted according to the two-character abbreviations in the ISO639. For example, English is `EN`.
Example	`<xsd:element name="spoken" type="xsd:language" />` `<spoken>EN</spoken>`

xsd:uri-reference	
Description	Even though it's `uri`, not `url`, this type specifies a URL.
Example	`<xsd:element name="home" type="xsd:uri-reference" />` `<home>http://www.wire-man.com</home>`

xsd:NMTOKEN	
Description	This type forces the text to be a valid XML name.
Example	`<xsd:element name="name" type="xsd:NMTOKEN" />` `<name>Irving</name>`

That's for basic simple types. But XML Schema doesn't stop there.

Creating Custom Simple Types

It's possible you need to restrict your elements even further than the types above. XML Schema allows you to do this by restricting or extending the basic types. This can include a list of allowable variables, a phone number, or even a date like "August 9, 1813."

Let's start with a list of allowable values. Say, for example, that you have an element <clothes> that can have four values in it: jeans, hats, skirts, and pants. In other words, any of the following would be allowed:

```
<clothes>jeans</clothes>
<clothes>hats</clothes>
<clothes>skirts</clothes>
<clothes>pants</clothes>
```

What would the XML Schema look like to allow such a thing? Example B–6 shows us.

Example B–6 XML enumeration

```
<?xml version="1.0" ?>
<xsd:schema
xmlns:xsd="http://www.w3.org/2000/10/XMLSchema">
   1.<xsd:element name="clothes">
        2.<xsd:simpleType>
          3.<xsd:restriction base="xsd:string">
            4.<xsd:enumeration value="jeans" />
              <xsd:enumeration value="hats" />
              <xsd:enumeration value="skirts" />
              <xsd:enumeration value="pants" />
          </xsd:restriction>
        </xsd:simpleType>
    </xsd:element>
</xsd:schema>
```

How the Code Works

1. We begin by creating the clothes element. Notice down at the bottom of the code, the </xsd:element>? That's new, and all the other elements we'll look at are inside the xsd:element.
2. This element declares that the element clothes will be a simple-type element.
3. Here, we say that the values of the element will be based on a string, and that it will be restricted.
4. Here, we use xsd:enumeration to list each acceptable value that can be inside the clothes element. Since there are four possible elements, there are four xsd:enumeration elements.

That's one way to restrict values using XML Schema. Another way is to force values to fit a certain pattern, like a phone number.

Forcing Text to Fit a Pattern

Forcing text to fit a pattern requires using another language called regular expressions. If you've used Perl before, you've probably used regular expressions. Regex, as it's sometimes called, is too complex to go into any real detail here, but we'll look at it briefly in Example B–7. Let's say our element contains a phone number in the format (415) 555-1212.

EXAMPLE B–7 Using a pattern

```
<xsd:element name="phone_number">
<xsd:simpleType>
   <xsd:restriction base="xsd:string">
       <xsd:pattern value="(\d{3})\s\d{3}-\d{4}" />
   </xsd:restriction>
</xsd:simpleType>
</xsd:element>
```

How the Code Works

The only new thing here is the xsd:pattern. The value of the value attribute is where we use regular expressions. In this case, we start with an open paren, three digits, close paren, a space, three more digits, a dash, and then four more digits. Here's a very quick look at some of the syntax of a regular expression:

\d	any digit
\D	any nondigit
\s	white space, carriage return, new line, or return
\S	any non-white space character
(ab)*	anything in parentheses may appear zero or more times
(ab)+	anything in parentheses may appear one or more times
(ab)?	Anything in parentheses may appear zero or one time
a{n}	"a" must appear n times in a row

You can also limit numerical values to a certain range by restricting an integer type.

Limiting Numerical Values

Say you need an order for clothes to be more than 10 items, but less than 200 (that's all you have). Example B–8 shows how you'd do that.

EXAMPLE B–8 Creating a numerical range

```
<xsd:element name="clothesOrder">
   <xsd:simpleType>
       1.<xsd:restriction base="xsd:integer">
           2.<xsd:maxInclusive value="200" />
           3.<xsd:minInclusive value="10" />
       </xsd:restriction>
   </xsd:simpleType>
</xsd:element>
```

How the Code Works

1. This line bases the value of the element as an integer.
2. As you might guess, the xsd:maxInclusive element allows us to set the upper value of this number to 200. We could also have used xsd:maxExclusive, which would have allowed values up to 199.
3. And minInclusive lets us set the lower value to 10. If we had used minExclusive, then the lowest allowable value would have been 11.

You can also limit how many digits a decimal number may have. This could be useful if your values have to be in dollars. Let's look at Example B–9.

EXAMPLE B–9 Determining precision of your numbers

```
<xsd:element name="orderCost">
   <xsd:simpleType>
       1.<xsd:restriction base="xsd:decimal">
           2.<xsd:precision value="6" />
           3.<xsd:scale value="2" />
       </xsd:restriction>
   </xsd:simpleType>
</xsd:element>
```

How the Code Works

1. We begin by restricting the value inside the orderCost element to be a decimal number.
2. We then set the precision of the number, which determines the total number of digits a number may have, including both sides of the decimal point.
3. The scale element sets the maximum number of digits to the right of the decimal point. Since we want dollars and cents, we'll only allow two digits here.

You can also limit the lengths of strings using XML Schema.

Limiting String Length

If you're taking an order from a customer who lives in the United States, you'll want their state as a part of their address. Since states are usually abbreviated to two characters, you'll have to limit the state element. How to do this? Let's check Example B–10.

EXAMPLE B–10 Limiting string length

```
<xsd:element name="state">
   <xsd:simpleType>
       <xsd:restriction base="xsd:string">
         <xsd:length value="2" />
       </xsd:restriction>
   </xsd:simpleType>
</xsd:element>
```

How the Code Works

I've bolded the code in question. We set the base type of this element as a string, and then restrict its length to two characters using the xsd:length element.

You can also use two other elements, minLength and maxLength, to limit the range of the number of characters that your element can have. Say you will allow your state element to hold anything from a two-character abbreviation to the full name of the state. Example B–11 shows you how to do this.

EXAMPLE B–11 Setting a range of string lengths

```
<xsd:element name="state">
   <xsd:simpleType>
       <xsd:restriction base="xsd:string">
           <xsd:minLength value="2" />
           <xsd:maxLength value="13" />
       </xsd:restriction>
   </xsd:simpleType>
</xsd:element>
```

How the Code Works

Again, the new code is in bold. The two elements, minLength and maxLength, work much like you'd expect them to, setting the minimum and maximum lengths the string inside the state element can be.

You can also create a special kind of string called a list, which is a space-delimited series of strings.

Creating a List

Suppose you want a single element to contain all of the different types of clothing in a customer's order. Using XML Schema, as in Example B–12, you can determine the value of an element to contain such a thing.

EXAMPLE B–12 A list

```
<xsd:element name="clothesTypes">
   <xsd:simpleType>
       <xsd:list itemType="xsd:string" />
   </xsd:simpleType>
</xsd:element>
```

How the Code Works

This is pretty simple: We just use the list element, and set the itemType to string (in this case—it could be any simple type).

Here's what the resulting XML could look like:

```
<clothesTypes>
  jeans hats skirts shirts mittens
</clothesTypes>
```

You can also limit the size of the list by adding more elements inside of it.

```
<xsd:list itemType="xsd:string">
  <xsd:length value="5" />
</xsd:list>
```

This code would set the size of our list to five items, no more and no less. We also could've used:

```
<xsd:list itemType="xsd:string">
  <xsd:minLength value="2" />
  <xsd:maxLength value="7" />
</xsd:list>
```

This would allow for a list that contained at least two items, but no more than seven.

It's possible you'll need more flexibility in your element than a single simple type can provide. If that's the case, you can allow more than one simple type to be allowed inside an element.

Combining Simple Types

Let's say you want an element called <orderItem> be either hold the all-number catalog number of the item, or a text description of the item. You could just use the string simple type, but that wouldn't really help constrain your values. We can combine a simple type of integer with a list of acceptable text values. Example B–13 shows what that looks like.

EXAMPLE B–13 Combining simple types

```
<xsd:element name="orderItem">
<xsd:simpleType>
   <xsd:union>
       <xsd:simpleType>
         <xsd:restriction base="xsd:string">
             <xsd:enumeration value="jeans" />
             <xsd:enumeration value="hats" />
```

EXAMPLE B–13 Combining simple types (Continued)

```
              <xsd:enumeration value="shirts" />
          </xsd:restriction>
        </xsd:simpleType>
        <xsd:simpleType>
          <xsd:restriction base="xsd:integer" />
        </xsd:simpleType>
    </xsd:union>
</xsd:simpleType>
</xsd:element>
```

How the Code Works

We have a new element here: union. This allows us to combine two or more simple types. Notice here that we're combining a simple type that allows three text values with a basic integer simple type. Here are some possible valid XML lines:

```
<orderItem>173</orderItem>
<orderItem>jeans</orderItem>
<orderItem>938</orderItem>
```

Predetermined Content

You can also specify that an element must contain a certain value, or simply give that element a default value:

```
<xsd:element name="color" type="xsd:string" fixed="red" />
<xsd:element name="size" type="xsd:string" default="XL" />
```

Creating and Reusing Custom Simple Types

Let's say you need several phone numbers from a customer: work phone, cell phone, and fax. All of these numbers will be formatted the same, so it seems that you'd have to set them all separately, like Example B–14:

EXAMPLE B–14 The wrong way

```
<xsd:element name="workPhone">
<xsd:simpleType>
   <xsd:restriction base="xsd:string">
       <xsd:pattern value="(\d{3})\s\d{3}-\d{4}" />
```

EXAMPLE B–14 The wrong way (Continued)

```
    </xsd:restriction>
</xsd:simpleType>
</xsd:element>

<xsd:element name="cellPhone">
<xsd:simpleType>
    <xsd:restriction base="xsd:string">
        <xsd:pattern value="(\d{3})\s\d{3}-\d{4}" />
    </xsd:restriction>
</xsd:simpleType>
</xsd:element>

<xsd:element name="fax">
<xsd:simpleType>
    <xsd:restriction base="xsd:string">
        <xsd:pattern value="(\d{3})\s\d{3}-\d{4}" />
    </xsd:restriction>
</xsd:simpleType>
</xsd:element>
```

This code, while being completely accurate and workable, is unnecessary. Here's an easier way (see Example B–15):

EXAMPLE B–15 The right way

```
<xsd:simpleType name="phoneNumber">
<xsd:restriction base="xsd:string">
    <xsd:pattern value="(\d{3})\s\d{3}-\d{4}" />
</xsd:restriction>
</xsd:simpleType>

<xsd:element name="workPhone" type="phoneNumber" />
<xsd:element name="cellPhone" type="phoneNumber" />
<xsd:element name="fax" type="phoneNumber" />
```

How the Code Works

Ah, much better. We begin by creating a simple type called "phoneNumber" without attaching it to any specific element. We just create the type without immediately doing anything with it. We then set the three elements, giving them each the phone number type.

That's about it for simple types. Now you're ready for elements that can contain other elements as well as attributes. These are the complex types.

Complex Types

Any element that contains an attribute or other elements is a complex-type element. It doesn't matter how simple it is. Even `<a b="1"/>` is a complex-type element because it contains an attribute.

Elements Within Elements

Let's begin by looking at elements that contain other elements. We'll start with something simple:

```
<order>
    <clothesType>jeans</clothesType>
    <quantity>14</quantity>
</order>
```

Example B–16 contains the XML Schema to define such a thing:

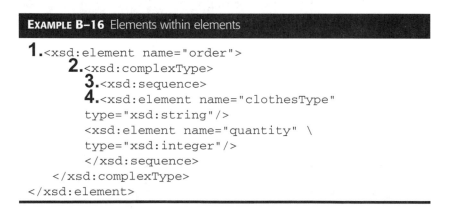

EXAMPLE B–16 Elements within elements

```
1.<xsd:element name="order">
    2.<xsd:complexType>
      3.<xsd:sequence>
      4.<xsd:element name="clothesType"
      type="xsd:string"/>
      <xsd:element name="quantity" \
      type="xsd:integer"/>
      </xsd:sequence>
  </xsd:complexType>
</xsd:element>
```

How the Code Works

1. We start in a familiar way, creating an element call "order."

2. Instead of declaring that a simpleType definition follows, we say a complexType is coming. Notice that there are no predetermined complexType types, like there were for simple types.
3. The sequence element states that the following elements are to appear inside the order element in the following sequence.
4. Here, we set the two elements, clothesType and quantity, as string and integer, respectively.

You can also determine the cardinality of any included elements (cardinality is the number of times something can appear). This is set by using the minOccurs and maxOccurs attributes in the xsd:element element. Table B–1 shows us how this compares to determining cardinality with DTDs.

TABLE B–1 Setting cardinality with XML Schema and DTD

XML SCHEMA	DTD EQUIVALENT
`minOccurs=0` `maxOccurs="unbounded"`	`element*`
`minOccurs="0"` `maxOccurs="1"`	`element?`
`minOccurs="1"` `maxOccurs="unbounded"`	`element+`

Default:
`minOccurs="1"`
`maxOccurs="1"`
	`Element`

Fortunately, XML Schema offers us more choices than just using the sequence element. For more flexibility, you can use xsd:choice and xsd:all.

XSD:CHOICE

xsd:choice is useful if you have a number of elements that could appear in your XML document, but not all of them have to. See Example B–17.

EXAMPLE B–17 Choice from a list of elements

```
<xsd:element name="singleItemOrder">
<xsd:complexType>
   <xsd:choice>
     <xsd:element name="shirt" type="xsd:string" />
     <xsd:element name="sweatshirt"
     type="xsd:string"/>
     <xsd:element name="mugs" type="xsd:integer"/>
   </xsd:choice>
</xsd:complexType>
</xsd:element>
```

How the Code Works

The syntax for using `xsd:sequence` and `xsd:choice` is exactly the same. In this example, the XML could have one of three elements, `<shirt>`, `<sweatshirt>`, or `<mugs>`, inside `<singleItemOrder>` , but not all three.

Element groups that are choices or sequences can be nested within each other, as in Example B–18.

EXAMPLE B–18 Nested groups of elements

```
<xsd:element name="multipleItemOrder">
<xsd:complexType>
   <xsd:choice>
     <xsd:sequence>
       <xsd:element name="shirt"
             type="xsd:string"/>
       <xsd:element name="jeans"
             type="xsd:string"/>
     </xsd:sequence>
     <xsd:choice>
       <xsd:element name="hats" type="xsd:string"/>
       <xsd:element name="skirts"
             type="xsd:string"/>
     </xsd:choice>
     <xsd:element name="hats" type="xsd:integer"/>
   </xsd:choice>
</xsd:complexType>
</xsd:element>
```

How the Code Works

There are a few things going on here. The multipleItem-Order element can contain one of a few different things:

1. The sequence of <shirt> and <sweatshirt>,
2. A choice between <mugs> and <martiniGlasses>, or
3. The single element <hats>.

Only one of these options is valid.

XSD:ALL

`xsd:all` behaves exactly the same as `xsd:sequence`, except that the elements don't have to appear in any predetermined order. Example B–19 shows how.

EXAMPLE B–19 Ignoring order in a sequence

```
<xsd:element name="completeOrder">
<xsd:complexType>
   <xsd:all>
        <xsd:element name="shirt" type="xsd:string"
            minOccurs="0" maxOccurs="unbounded"/>
        <xsd:element name="sweatshirt"
            type="xsd:string"
            minOccurs="0" maxOccurs="unbounded"/>
        <xsd:element name="mugs" type="xsd:string"
            minOccurs="0" maxOccurs="100"/>
        <xsd:element name="hats" type="xsd:string"
            minOccurs="0" maxOccurs="50"/>
   </xsd:all>
</xsd:complexType>
</xsd:element>
```

How the Code Works

The XML spawned by the code above could have the four elements (`shirt`, `sweatshirt`, `mugs`, and `hats`) appear in any order.

That's enough for nesting elements. On to attributes!

Attributes

When you define an attribute, you can also decide how it is to be used. For example, is it required or optional? Does it have a default value? You can determine these things with the `use` attribute in the `xsd:attribute` XML Schema element:

```
<xsd:attribute name="hat" type="xsd:string" use="required">
```

This code determines that the `hat` attribute must exist in the indicated element (the indicated element isn't in this line of code—we'll get to that soon). Table B–2 contains a list of all the other values.

TABLE B–2 Defining how attributes are to be used

ITEM	DESCRIPTION
`Use="required"`	Attribute must be present
`Use="optional"`	Attribute may or may not be present. This is the default value, so you don't need to use this one.
`Use="prohibited"`	Attribute is forbidden from being present in the XML.
`use="fixed" value="`*`mandatoryValue`*`"`	If the attribute is present in the XML document, it must have the value of *`mandatoryValue`*. If the attribute is not present, then no value is set.
`use="default" value="`*`defaultValue`*`"`	If the attribute is not present in the XML document, the parser in instructed to insert it and give it a value of *`defaultValue`*. If the attribute is present, then its value overrides *`defaultValue`*.

ATTRIBUTES AND ELEMENTS

To incorporate attributes into an element that contains nested elements, the attribute declarations must come last, after all the element declarations. There's no real reason for this, other than that it forces some organization on your code, like in Example B–20.

EXAMPLE B–20 Attributes and nested elements

```
<xsd:element name="order">
<xsd:complexType>
   <xsd:sequence>
     <xsd:element name="shirts" type="xsd:string"/>
     <xsd:element name="hats" type="xsd:string"/>
     <xsd:element name="jeans" type="xsd:string"/>
     <xsd:element name="skirts" type="xsd:string"/>
   </xsd:sequence>
   <xsd:attribute name="orderDate"
          type="xsd:date"/>
   <xsd:attribute name="custID" type="xsd:string"/>
</xsd:complexType>
</xsd:element>
```

How the Code Works

All we did was tack on a couple xsd:attribute tags to the end of the complextype definition. Here's what the resulting XML could look like:

```
<order orderDate="2002-03-23" source="PDA">
    <shirts>9 red</shirts>
    <sweatshirts>7 purple</sweatshirts>
    <mugs>3 travel</mugs>
    <hats>37 sombrero</hats>
</order>
```

Attributes and Text

Say that instead of combining attributes and nested elements, you'd like to combine attributes and simple text, like this:

```
<shirt quantity="4">XL purple</shirt>
```

This looks like a simple type element with an attribute. That's all it is, but the addition of that attribute automatically makes `<shirt>` a complex type element.

The code to accomplish this is surprisingly complicated. Have a look at Example B–21.

EXAMPLE B–21 Combining attributes and text

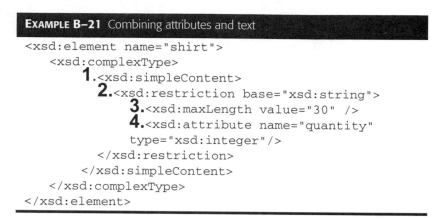

```
<xsd:element name="shirt">
   <xsd:complexType>
      1.<xsd:simpleContent>
        2.<xsd:restriction base="xsd:string">
            3.<xsd:maxLength value="30" />
            4.<xsd:attribute name="quantity"
            type="xsd:integer"/>
        </xsd:restriction>
      </xsd:simpleContent>
   </xsd:complexType>
</xsd:element>
```

How the Code Works

1. Here's something new. (Notice this is xsd:simpleContent, not xsd:simpleType.) In order to allow this element to contain text, we must wrap the simple-type restrictions and attribute declarations with a xsd:simpleContent. This XML Schema element is only necessary when your element contains attributes and text, but no other elements.
2. We can use xsd:restriction the same as if we were inside a xsd:simpleType. That means you can restrict the text inside this element in the ways you could if it was a simple-type element.
3. Here we constrain the number of characters in the text to 30. This is the same xsd:maxLength we saw in the last chapter.
4. Finally, inside the xsd:restriction, we have the attribute declaration. This isn't really a restriction on the text, but this is where the statement goes. It's a little counterintuitive, but it works.

What happens when you don't want to restrict the text? If that's the case, then you don't need to use xsd:restriction, right? In this case, we use a new XML Schema element called xsd:extension, which is the theoretical opposite of xsd:restriction: It adds to the element instead of subtracts. Example B–22 shows the code you'd use if you didn't want to restrict the text in any way.

EXAMPLE B–22 Using xsd:extension

```
<xsd:element name="shirt">
   <xsd:complexType>
       <xsd:simpleContent>
         <xsd:extension base="xsd:string">
             <xsd:attribute name="quantity"
                 type="xsd:integer"/>
         </xsd:extension>
       </xsd:simpleContent>
   </xsd:complexType>
</xsd:element>
```

That's right, we added an attribute using both xsd:restriction and xsd:extension. It's odd, but take a deep breath and make peace with it.

Attributes, Text, and Nested Elements

Combining attributes, text, and nested elements is pretty simple. Let's say you want to produce this XML:

```
<order orderDate="2001-04-18">To ship overnight:
<shirt>9 purple XL</shirt> and <mugs>7 Roadrunner
style</mugs> to Fairfax, CA</order>
```

Example B–23 contains the XML Schema that would spawn such a thing:

EXAMPLE B–23 Attributes, text, and elements

```
<xsd:element name="order">
<xsd:complexType mixed="true">
   <xsd:sequence>
     <xsd:element name="shirts" type="xsd:string"/>
     <xsd:element name="mugs" type="xsd:string"/>
   </xsd:sequence>
   <xsd:attribute name="orderDate" type="xsd:date"/>
</xsd:complexType>
</xsd:element>
```

How the Code Works

Did you notice the mixed="true" attribute in xsd:complexType? It means that the complex type contains text, attributes, and nested elements. That's all you need to include text along with the attributes and elements. Makes more sense than the xsd:simpleContent thing you had to deal with earlier, doesn't it?

Creating Custom Complex Types

Much like simple types, you can create your own custom complex types and use them later in your code. Example B–24 has us define both simple and complex types.

EXAMPLE B–24 Custom complex types

```
<!-- define simple types -->
<xsd:simpleType name="colorType">
   <xsd:restriction base="xsd:string">
     <xsd:enumeration value="red"/>
     <xsd:enumeration value="green"/>
     <xsd:enumeration value="black"/>
     <xsd:enumeration value="orange"/>
   </xsd:restriction>
</xsd:simpleType>

<xsd:simpleType name="sizeType">
   <xsd:restriction base="xsd:string">
     <xsd:enumeration value="L"/>
     <xsd:enumeration value="XL"/>
     <xsd:enumeration value="XXL"/>
   </xsd:restriction>
</xsd:simpleType>


<!-- define complex type -->
1.<xsd:complexType name="sizeColorType">
   <xsd:sequence>
     <xsd:element name="size" type="sizeType"/>
     <xsd:element name="color" type="colorType"/>
   </xsd:sequence>
   <xsd:attribute name="quantity"
           type="xsd:integer"/>
```

EXAMPLE B–24 Custom complex types (Continued)

```
</xsd:complexType>


<!-- define elements -->
2.<xsd:element name="shirt" type="sizeColorType"/>
<xsd:element name="jeans" type="sizeColorType"/>
```

How the Code Works

1. To create a custom complex type, simply add a name attribute, and don't place the xsd:complexType inside any other XML Schema element.
2. Here's where we call our custom complex type and apply it to both the shirt and sweatshirt elements.

Here's an example of some XML based on the XML Schema above:

```
<shirt>
    <size>M</size>
    <color>red</color>
</shirt>
<jeans>
    <size>XL</size>
    <color>orange</color>
</jeans>
```

Referencing Elements and Attributes

You've probably noticed that XML Schema code isn't as readable as a DTD. The more you add to an XML Schema, the harder it gets to read, as elements and types are nested deeper and deeper into each other. A sufficiently complex document is especially difficult to read and almost impossible to debug. Luckily, XML Schema provides a way for you to modularize your code so it's easier to read, understand, and debug.

XML Schema allows you to define an element or attribute and then refer to it later. We do this to an element in Example B–25.

EXAMPLE B–25 Referring to an element

```
1.<xsd:element name="shirt" type="xsd:string"/>

<xsd:element name="shirt_list">
   <xsd:complexType>
       <xsd:sequence>
         2.<xsd:element ref="shirt"
                maxOccurs="unbounded"/>
       </xsd:sequence>
   </xsd:complexType>
</xsd:element>
```

How the Code Works

1. Here's where we define the simple-type element shirt.
2. We now place this element inside the shirt_list element by referring to it using the ref attribute. Imagine that we're making a clone of the shirt element and moving it to another place.

You can make as many clones of elements as you want, and each clone has its own cardinality (that is, its own `minOccurs` and `maxOccurs`).

Attributes have the same flexibility, and the syntax is the same, as Example B–26 indicates.

EXAMPLE B–26 Referring to an attribute

```
<xsd:attribute name="quantity"
   type="xsd:nonNegativeInteger"/>

<xsd:complexType name="quantityAttrType">
   <xsd:attribute ref="quantity"/>
</xsd:complexType>

<xsd:element name="mugs" type="quantityAttrType"/>
<xsd:element name="hats" type="quantityAttrType"/>
```

How the Code Works

In this chunk of code, we create an attribute called quantity. When we create a custom complex type called quantityAttr-

Type, we call (or clone) quantity and then attach that complex type to two elements. In this way, we can easily and quickly attach attributes to elements.

New Complex Types Based on Existing Types

It's possible to create a new custom complex type by using an existing complex type as a template, as shown in Example B–27. This can be useful if you have many related complex types to deal with in your data. I know the complexity of this is getting a little crazy, but hang in there—if you've made it this far, you can handle this last bit.

EXAMPLE B–27 Creating a new custom type

```
<!-- define simple types -->
<xsd:simpleType name="colorType">
   <xsd:restriction base="xsd:string">
     <xsd:enumeration value="red"/>
     <xsd:enumeration value="green"/>
     <xsd:enumeration value="purple"/>
     <xsd:enumeration value="orange"/>
   </xsd:restriction>
</xsd:simpleType>

<xsd:simpleType name="sizeType">
   <xsd:restriction base="xsd:string">
     <xsd:enumeration value="L"/>
     <xsd:enumeration value="XL"/>
     <xsd:enumeration value="XXL"/>
   </xsd:restriction>
</xsd:simpleType>


<!-- define complex types -->
1.<xsd:complexType name="sizeColorType">
   <xsd:sequence>
     <xsd:element name="size" type="sizeType"/>
     <xsd:element name="color" type="colorType"/>
   </xsd:sequence>
   <xsd:attribute ref="quantity"/>
</xsd:complexType>
```

EXAMPLE B–27 Creating a new custom type (Continued)

```
2.<xsd:complexType name="shirtDescType">
   3.<xsd:complexContent>
      4.<xsd:extension base="sizeColorType">
          <xsd:sequence>
          <xsd:element name="material"
                type="xsd:string" />
          <xsd:element name="collar"
                type="xsd:string" />
          <xsd:element name="sleeve"
                type="xsd:string" />
        </xsd:sequence>
    </xsd:extension>
</xsd:complexContent>
</xsd:complexType>

<!--define attribute -->
<xsd:attribute name="quantity"
type="xsd:nonNegativeInteger"/>

<!-- define element -->
<xsd:element name="shirt" type="shirtDescType"/>
```

How the Code Works

1. sizeColorType is the complex type that we'll be using as a template later on. It contains two elements: size and color.
2. This is the complex type that we'll build on top of size-ColorType.
3. This is a new XML Schema element: xsd:complexContent. Remember how xsd:simpleContent was used to combine text and attributes? Here's its older brother.
4. To bring the template complex type into the one we're building, we use xsd:extension and call the template type as the base to build from. Since we're building on top of the complex type template (we're adding to it, extending it), we use xsd:extension. If we were creating a complex type that had elements that were more restricted than the complex type we're bringing in, we'd use xsd:restriction instead of xsd:extension.

This is a great way to both expand and modularize your code. It may seem a little odd, but try it and play around with it for a while and it'll become more intuitive.

Miscellaneous

There are a few more things to look at in XML Schema: named groups of elements and attributes, documenting your code (beyond comments), and including external files.

NAMED GROUPS OF ELEMENTS AND ATTRIBUTES

Another way for you to control the readability and infrastructure of your XML Schema document is to create reusable groups of elements and attributes. These groups are named by you, which allows you to refer to them elsewhere in the document. As with elements and attributes, calling these groups of elements or attributes is like cloning them and placing that clone wherever the reference is.

GROUPS OF ELEMENTS

You can create a group of elements at the root level of your XML Schema document and then refer to that group any number of times in that same document. Inside of that group, the list of elements must be a sequence, choice, or all. Example B–28 shows it in action.

EXAMPLE B–28 Named group of elements

```
<!-- define simple types -->
<xsd:simpleType name="colorType">
   <xsd:restriction base="xsd:string">
       <xsd:enumeration value="red"/>
       <xsd:enumeration value="yellow"/>
       <xsd:enumeration value="orange"/>
       <xsd:enumeration value="mauve"/>
   </xsd:restriction>
</xsd:simpleType>
<xsd:simpleType name="sizeType">
   <xsd:restriction base="xsd:string">
       <xsd:enumeration value="L"/>
```

EXAMPLE B–28 Named group of elements (Continued)

```
        <xsd:enumeration value="XL"/>
        <xsd:enumeration value="XXL"/>
    </xsd:restriction>
</xsd:simpleType>


<!-- define group -->
1.<xsd:group name="sizeColorGroup">
    <xsd:sequence>
        <xsd:element name="size" type="sizeType"/>
        <xsd:element name="color" type="colorType"/>
    </xsd:sequence>
</xsd:group>


<!-- define elements -->
<xsd:element name="shirt">
    <xsd:complexType>
        2.<xsd:group ref="sizeColorGroup"/>
    </xsd:complexType>
</xsd:element>

<xsd:element name="jeans">
    <xsd:complexType>
        3.<xsd:group ref="sizeColorGroup"/>
    </xsd:complexType>
</xsd:element>
```

How the Code Works

1. Creating a group is pretty simple. Inside the xsd:group element, place xsd:sequence, xsd:choice, or xsd:all. Then include your list of elements (you can even include another xsd:group if you want). You can't place an attribute inside of a group, though.
2. Here, we clone the sizeColorGroup and place that clone inside the shirt element.
3. We do the same thing to the sweatshirt element: clone the group sizeColorGroup and place it in sweatshirt.

We can also create groups of attributes in a similar way using the `xsd:attributeGroup` element.

GROUPS OF ATTRIBUTES

If we want to tweak our XML so that all the information about shirts and sweatshirts is contained within attributes, it might look like this:

```
<shirt quantity="2" color="purple" size="XL"
    material="cotton"/>
<sweatshirt quantity="1" color="orange" size="M"
    material="cotton"/>
```

Since these elements contain the same set of attributes, we can create a group of attributes and place that group into both the shirt and sweatshirt elements, as in Example B–29.

EXAMPLE B–29 Group of attributes

```
<!-- define simple types -->
<xsd:simpleType name="colorType">
   <xsd:restriction base="xsd:string">
        <xsd:enumeration value="purple"/>
        <xsd:enumeration value="orange"/>
        <xsd:enumeration value="blue"/>
        <xsd:enumeration value="grey"/>
   </xsd:restriction>
</xsd:simpleType>
<xsd:simpleType name="sizeType">
   <xsd:restriction base="xsd:string">
        <xsd:enumeration value="M"/>
        <xsd:enumeration value="L"/>
        <xsd:enumeration value="XL"/>
   </xsd:restriction>
</xsd:simpleType>


<!-- define attribute group -->
1.<xsd:attributeGroup name="clothesAttrGroup">
   <xsd:attribute name="quantity"
type="xsd:nonNegativeInteger"/>
   <xsd:attribute name="color" type="colorType"/>
   <xsd:attribute name="size" type="sizeType"/>
   <xsd:attribute name="material" type="xsd:string"/>
</xsd:attributeGroup>
```

Example B–29 Group of attributes (Continued)

```
<!-- define elements -->
<xsd:element name="shirt">
   <xsd:complexType>
      2.<xsd:attributeGroup ref="clothesAttrGroup"/>
   </xsd:complexType>
</xsd:element>

<xsd:element name="sweatshirt">
   <xsd:complexType>
      3.<xsd:attributeGroup ref="clothesAttrGroup"/>
   </xsd:complexType>
</xsd:element>
```

How the Code Works

1. To define a group of attributes, use the xsd:attributeGroup element. Then simply list as many attributes (and only attributes) as you want.
2. Here's the first reference, much like other references you've seen, an xsd:attributeGroup element with a ref attribute.
3. Here's the reference for the sweatshirt element.

Annotation and Documentation

To officially add documentation to your XML Schema and it make more readable and decipherable, you embed an xsd:documentation element inside xsd:annotation, like this:

```
<xsd:annotation>
     <xsd:documentation>
     This schema is designed to validate any XML
document that contains order information from the
Stitch Store.
     </xsd:documentation>
</xsd:annotation>
```

You can place these elements anywhere in your document—anywhere it'd be helpful for you or another programmer to understand what's going on.

Including External Files

You can create your schema from several different documents, if you like, by using a couple of simple tags. To include an entire external schema, use the `xsd:include` element like so:

```
<xsd:include schemaLocation="filename.xsd"/>
```

Using this XML Schema element is just like copying and pasting the code from an external file into your file—it's a complete inclusion. However, you aren't allowed to redefine anything that's in the external file.

There is a way around this, though. If you call an external file using xsd:redefine, the external file is included, but you're given an opportunity to redefine any of the elements, attributes, types, or groups in that external file. Here's an example:

```
<xsd:redefine schemaLocation="shirts.xsd">
  <xsd:element name="shirt" type="newShirtType"/>
  <xsd:simpleType name="newColorType">
      <xsd:restriction base="xsd:string">
        <xsd:maxLength value="20"/>
      </xsd:restriction>
  </xsd:simpleType>
</xsd:redefine>
```

How the Code Works

All of your redefinitions have to be placed inside the xsd:redefine element, and they override anything that's inside the shirts.xsd file.

APPENDIX C

SOAP Compared with Other Distributed Object Technologies

SOAP is just a wire protocol, not an entire distributed object architecture. However, it can be useful to examine architectures like CORBA, COM, and RMI and compare them to SOAP.

Technology Aspects

There are many ways to examine and compare proprietary systems, but we'll focus on a few aspects: security, scalability, garbage collection and state management. All of the remote architectures have their own wire protocol, their own version of SOAP, if you will.

The three architectures we'll look at are CORBA, COM and RMI. We'll begin with SOAP, and then see how it compares.

SOAP

As we've seen, SOAP is just a wire protocol—it's a way to package information in order to send it to a remote machine. SOAP must be a part of a larger architecture. Let's review in Figure C–1 how SOAP encapsulates information.

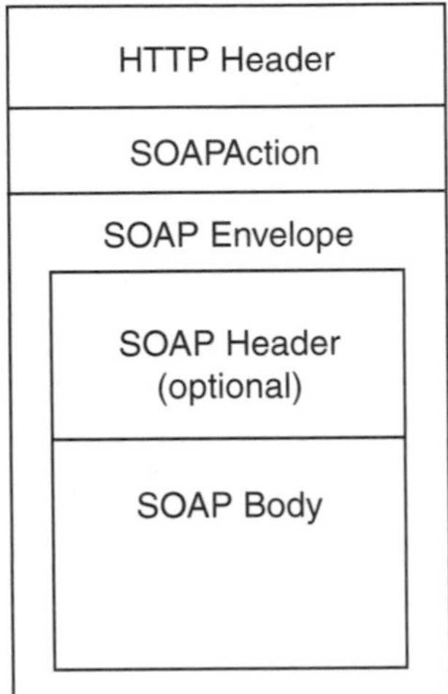

FIGURE C–1 How SOAP encapsulates information

SOAP and Security

SOAP does not implement security. In fact, SOAP deliberately ignores security and leaves it to the architecture to deal with it. The only aspect of SOAP that may help security measures is the presence of the SOAPAction field in the HTTP header. The presence of this field allows firewalls to correctly route these messages, but that's about it. Apart from the SOAP specification, you can add XML Signature to a SOAP header and send the message via SSL to increase security.

SOAP and Scalability

Scalability refers to an application's ability to handle ever-increasing numbers of connections. When does the application break: at five simultaneous connections or a hundred? How about 20,000? An architecture's ability to handle this sort of load is a measure of its scalability.

SOAP's measure of scalability depends on its inherently stateless nature. As a rule of thumb, the more stateless something is, the more scalable it tends to be. Since moving SOAP messages over HTTP is a completely stateless communication, SOAP is viewed as exceptionally scalable.

SOAP and Garbage Collection

Garbage collection is the practice of freeing up system resources from abandoned objects, clients, and servers that are no longer being used. If an application does not practice garbage collection, then the system's memory begins to fill and the application's response time dwindles until (possibly) the whole system crashes.

SOAP ignores garbage collection as thoroughly as it ignores security: completely and quite deliberately. The SOAP specification explicitly states that SOAP has nothing to do with garbage collection. An architecture that uses SOAP would have to implement its own garbage collection system.

SOAP and State Management

As stated above, SOAP does nothing to implement state management. It's possible to use the SOAP header to carry state information back and forth (a SOAP cookie? bleah), but no matter what you use, there's nothing in the SOAP specification that discusses SOAP.

CORBA

CORBA is a somewhat complex system involving a client knowing ahead of time the name of an object it wants to activate. It first calls that object's binding method, which causes the CORBA runtime to figure out exactly where the object is and has the server activate the object. The object activates, tells the server it's finished activating, and the server passes a reference to the object back to the client. Only then is the client free to invoke methods as it sees fit.

CORBA has its own wire protocol called General Inter-ORB Protocol (GIOP). There's even a specialization of GIOP that travels over TCP/IP called Internet Inter-ORB Protocol, or IIOP. Figure C–2 shows what the basic GIOP packet layout looks like.

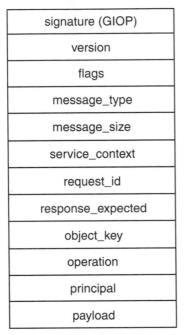

signature (GIOP)
version
flags
message_type
message_size
service_context
request_id
response_expected
object_key
operation
principal
payload

FIGURE C–2 GIOP package layout

In a general sense, CORBA is structured more like SOAP than DCOM. Also, CORBA is designed to be used by more than one operating system. For example, both IBM and Netscape have an implementation of CORBA.

CORBA also uses more layers than DCOM to accomplish its goals, which is a performance hit.

CORBA and Security

CORBA's chief security measure is SSL, which we saw in Chapter 4 when we covered HTTP. However, there is another option: CORBA has a secure protocol called SECIOP, which is a secure Inter-ORB protocol that provides a secure layer between GIOP and the ORB. CORBA doesn't contain an intrinsic security method for authentication or authorization.

CORBA and Scalability

CORBA uses a model that maintains state among connections, so it is not as scalable as a stateless model would be. However, CORBA does have a way to increase scalability: Instead of launching multiple processes to deal with object requests, CORBA can use multiple threads within a single process, which takes less memory than multiple processes do.

CORBA and Garbage Collection

CORBA's wire protocols, GIOP and IIOP, do not support garbage collection, but CORBA does. However, the exact method of garbage collection is vendor-specific.

CORBA and State Management

Since all CORBA 2.0 implementations are required to implement both GIOP and IIOP, CORBA allows developers a number of ways to maintain state across connections.

DCOM (Distributed Component Object Model)

COM is a way to create applications for Windows. When you use COM, you create individual modules that are stored as separate little programs. These modules are blocks of reusable code. They are DLL or EXE (often DLLs). DCOM is a way for components to interact across a network. Like SOAP, DCOM simply allows the server and client to talk to each other. Figure C–3 shows the various DCOM packets that are used (here are three of them).

DCOM and Security

DCOM was designed with deep security in mind, so it's very security-oriented. You are allowed to determine exactly what level of security is actually enforced. This has resulted in many security-setting errors when dealing with DCOM. Messages can be sent at any security level, from plain text (not secure) to encrypting both the header and the serialized arguments (darn secure), as well as a host of levels inbetween.

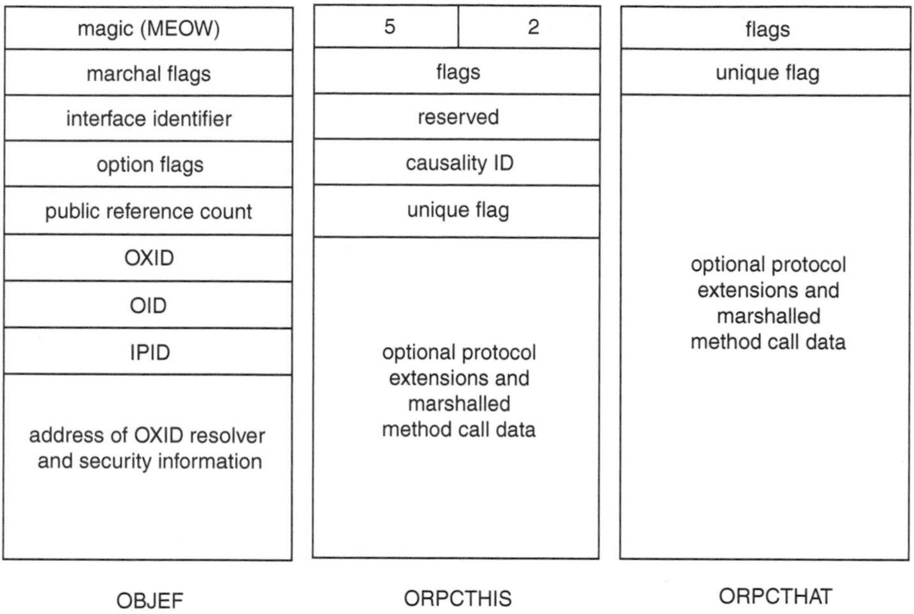

OBJEF
magic (MEOW)
marchal flags
interface identifier
option flags
public reference count
OXID
OID
IPID
address of OXID resolver and security information

ORPCTHIS	
5	2
flags	
reserved	
causality ID	
unique flag	
optional protocol extensions and marshalled method call data	

ORPCTHAT
flags
unique flag
optional protocol extensions and marshalled method call data

FIGURE C–3 DCOM packet

Not surprisingly, this level of security requires a number of round-trips, which creates a performance hit and tends to make DCOM slower than other options. However, if your system requires a high level of security, then DCOM's emphasis might be heartening.

DCOM and Scalability

DCOM is not considered scalable because of the amount of round-trips it requires and its garbage collection. In addition, to ensure that all participants involved in the remote invocation remain active and online, all the clients are required to ping the server at two-minute intervals. You can see how an increase of clients would increase the number of pings the server must deal with. The pinging is a part of DCOM's garbage collection, and you can disable it if you wish. This would increase scalability, but would hamper other aspects of DCOM's performance.

DCOM and Garbage Collection

DCOM keeps a tab on active objects by the pinging method mentioned above. If a client stops pinging the server, it is assumed that the client is no longer active and connected. The server then waits six minutes to see if the client will reinstate its pinging. After those six minutes, the server destroys the object that the client has activated and reclaims the system resources.

DCOM and State Management

One of the design goals of DCOM is that of object transparency. That is, the client doesn't know where the remote object is. As a result, state information is deeply ingrained (the pinging is an example of this). If you had to write a system that uses DCOM but was stateless, you would be sad—it's pretty difficult.

Java RMI

Java's answer to invoking remote methods is Java Remote Method Invocation (Java RMI). Java RMI is built on CORBA, so it's not entirely separate. The goal of Java RMI is to take the strong features of CORBA, but make them simpler to use. The good news is that Java RMI inherits some of the features of Java, which means garbage collection is taken care of.

The wire protocol for Java RMI is called JRMP (Java Remote Method Invocation Wire Protocol) An aspect of JRMP is its three sub-protocols: SingleOpProtocol, StreamProtocol, and MultiplexProtocol. SingleOpProtocol is used for a single text message, which allows the connection to be immediately closed. The other two protocols determine that more than one message follows the header and that the connection should remain open. MultiplexProtocol is used when client and server communicate over a single socket to conserve system resources.

Java RMI and Security

RMI inherits Java's security consciousness. There is also such a thing as RMI Security Manager to enable such things as dynamic class loading.

Java RMI and Scalability

Java RMI is relatively scalable, but it is variable. For example, if you spread the RMI Registry over several servers, scalability is increased. State can be maintained with the StreamProtocol and MultiplexProtocol, which decrease scalability.

Java RMI and Garbage Collection

Java RMI has strong garbage collection. This is expected, since garbage collection is natively built into Java. The way this works is that a client gets to lease an object from the server. The client must periodically renew this lease, or the server destroys the reference and frees up system resources.

Java RMI and State Management

As we've seen from above, Java can be both stateless and hold state, depending on which subprotocol is being used. However, you can also use an alternate protocol—Java is flexible enough to allow that.

APPENDIX D

Future Directions of SOAP—XML Protocol Working Group

The W3C has created a group called the XML Protocol Working Group, whose charter is to create a way for applications to communicate across the Internet using some form of XML. Yep, that's the same goal SOAP has. In fact, the XML Protocol Working Group is laboring to create something that does exactly what SOAP does. You might be asking, "Why bother?" I'm not sure. While the Working Group will definitely look closely at SOAP and XML-RPC in figuring out what the language should look like, and it will almost certainly look almost exactly like SOAP, no one can tell for sure. As of this writing, the Working Group is still deciding what the goals of this SOAP-like language should be—they definitely haven't gotten around to actually creating any sort of specification yet.

This means that at some point in the future, there will probably be a push to move away from SOAP and towards whatever language the XML Protocol Working Group comes up with.

An interesting note: This new specification will probably have the name XP. Sounds familiar, doesn't it?

APPENDIX E

Keeping Up-to-Date

SOAP is constantly evolving, as is the whole world of web services. Here are some Web sites that you might find useful in keeping up to date.

- Scripting News (focus on XML-RPC)—*www.scripting.com*
- SoapWare.org—*www.soapware.org*
- SOAPClient (news and code)—*www.soapclient.com*
- PocketSOAP—*www.pocketsoap.com*
- SOAP News—*soap.weblogs.com*
- Web Services (general)—*www.webservices.org*

That should keep you busy for a while.

APPENDIX F

SOAP Tools

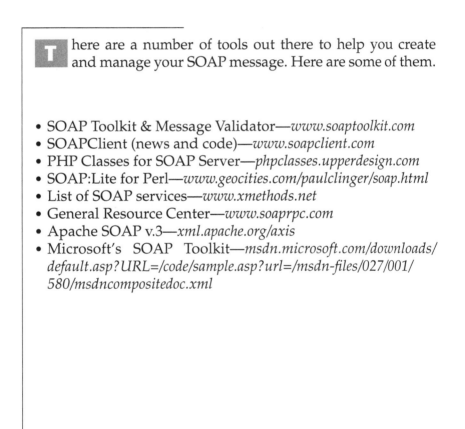

There are a number of tools out there to help you create and manage your SOAP message. Here are some of them.

- SOAP Toolkit & Message Validator—*www.soaptoolkit.com*
- SOAPClient (news and code)—*www.soapclient.com*
- PHP Classes for SOAP Server—*phpclasses.upperdesign.com*
- SOAP:Lite for Perl—*www.geocities.com/paulclinger/soap.html*
- List of SOAP services—*www.xmethods.net*
- General Resource Center—*www.soaprpc.com*
- Apache SOAP v.3—*xml.apache.org/axis*
- Microsoft's SOAP Toolkit—*msdn.microsoft.com/downloads/default.asp?URL=/code/sample.asp?url=/msdn-files/027/001/580/msdncompositedoc.xml*

APPENDIX G

UDDI API XML Schema

Here's what your UDDI better adhere to.

```
<?xml version = "1.0" encoding = "UTF-8"?>

<xsd:schema xmlns = "urn:uddi-org:api_v2"
       targetNamespace = "urn:uddi-org:api_v2"
       xmlns:xsd = "http://www.w3.org/2000/10/
XMLSchema"
       elementFormDefault = "unqualified"
       attributeFormDefault = "unqualified">
      <xsd:annotation>
        <xsd:documentation>UDDI Version 2.0 API
schema.  Release candidate 1, review draft 3</
xsd:documentation>
      </xsd:annotation>
      <!--shared attribute definitions -->

      <xsd:attribute name = "authorizedName" type =
"xsd:string">

        <xsd:annotation>
          <xsd:documentation>Returned on output,
ignored in input.  A persons name that is associated
with the publication of registered data.</
xsd:documentation>
```

```
        </xsd:annotation>
      </xsd:attribute>
      <xsd:attribute name = "bindingKey" type = "xsd:string">
        <xsd:annotation>
          <xsd:documentation>Multi-use.  Identifies the
bindingKey value associated with a bindingTemplate.  On
save, empty value implies that a new bindingTemplate key is
to be assigned.</xsd:documentation>
        </xsd:annotation>
      </xsd:attribute>
      <xsd:attribute name = "businessKey" type =
"xsd:string">
        <xsd:annotation>
          <xsd:documentation>Multi-use.  Identifies the
businessKey value associated with a businessEntity.  On
save, empty value implies that a new businessEntity key is
to be assigned.</xsd:documentation>
        </xsd:annotation>
      </xsd:attribute>
      <xsd:attribute name = "generic" use = "required" type =
"xsd:string">
        <xsd:annotation>
          <xsd:documentation>Signifies the UDDI registry
software version number.  On input, signifies the UDDI
version understood by the requesting caller.</
xsd:documentation>
        </xsd:annotation>
      </xsd:attribute>
      <xsd:attribute name = "keyName" type = "xsd:string">
        <xsd:annotation>
          <xsd:documentation>The name part of a name-value
pair.  In a keyedReference, these are purely descriptive
except when used with the uddi-org:general tModell, where
they are used as the Name part of a name value pair.  In
address, these are addressLine code-set field names</
xsd:documentation>
        </xsd:annotation>
      </xsd:attribute>
      <xsd:attribute name = "keyValue" type = "xsd:string">
        <xsd:annotation>
          <xsd:documentation>The value part of a name-value
pair. This is the value associated with the context
specified by the tModelKey value.  In address, these are
qualifierss on the field name.</xsd:documentation>
        </xsd:annotation>
```

```
      </xsd:attribute>
      <xsd:attribute name = "maxRows" type = "xsd:int">
        <xsd:annotation>
          <xsd:documentation>Used on input to limit the
maximum result size returned from inquiry API messages.</
xsd:documentation>
        </xsd:annotation>
      </xsd:attribute>
      <xsd:attribute name = "operator" type = "xsd:string">
        <xsd:annotation>
          <xsd:documentation>Ignored on input. Identifies the
UDDI registry that supplied the data (top level message
attribute) and the UDDI registry where the data is mastered
(entity level use).</xsd:documentation>
        </xsd:annotation>
      </xsd:attribute>
      <xsd:attribute name = "serviceKey" type = "xsd:string">
        <xsd:annotation>
          <xsd:documentation>Multi-use.  Identifies the
serviceKey value associated with a businessService.  On
save, empty value implies that a new businessService key is
to be assigned.</xsd:documentation>
        </xsd:annotation>
      </xsd:attribute>
      <xsd:attribute name = "sortCode" type = "xsd:string">
        <xsd:annotation>
          <xsd:documentation>Used to convey application
specific rules.  Typically a URN identifying the application
manufacturer, application, and version.  Ex. "urn:foo-
com:foocontactMgr:v-1-0"</xsd:documentation>
        </xsd:annotation>
      </xsd:attribute>
      <xsd:attribute name = "tModelKey" type = "xsd:string">
        <xsd:annotation>
          <xsd:documentation>A reference to a tModel. Usually
used to represent the context to understand the keyName and
keyValue values.</xsd:documentation>
        </xsd:annotation>
      </xsd:attribute>
      <xsd:attribute name = "truncated">
        <xsd:annotation>
          <xsd:documentation>Used on output only. Signifies
that results returned do not reflect the complete result set
possible.</xsd:documentation>
```

```
        </xsd:annotation>
        <xsd:simpleType>
          <xsd:restriction base = "xsd:NMTOKEN">
            <xsd:enumeration value = "true"/>
            <xsd:enumeration value = "false"/>
          </xsd:restriction>
        </xsd:simpleType>
      </xsd:attribute>
      <xsd:attribute name = "URLType">
        <xsd:annotation>
          <xsd:documentation>Used to specify the transport
type associated with a bindingTemplate.  If a given web
service or entry point represented by a binding has multiple
possible transports, a bindingTemplate should be added to
the same businessService for each transport, repeating all
of the same information except the transport type and the
accessPoint or hostingRedirector pointer.</
xsd:documentation>
        </xsd:annotation>
        <xsd:simpleType>
          <xsd:restriction base = "xsd:NMTOKEN">
            <xsd:enumeration value = "mailto"/>
            <xsd:enumeration value = "http"/>
            <xsd:enumeration value = "https"/>
            <xsd:enumeration value = "ftp"/>
            <xsd:enumeration value = "fax"/>
            <xsd:enumeration value = "phone"/>
            <xsd:enumeration value = "other"/>
          </xsd:restriction>
        </xsd:simpleType>
      </xsd:attribute>
      <xsd:attribute name = "useType" type = "xsd:string">
        <xsd:annotation>
          <xsd:documentation>Descriptive attribute. Used to
convey the intended use.  Suggested values are URN
identifying the intended use.  Ex. "urn:contact:technical"</
xsd:documentation>
        </xsd:annotation>
      </xsd:attribute>

      <!-- Element definitions begin -->

      <xsd:element name = "accessPoint">
        <xsd:annotation>
```

```
          <xsd:documentation>Data: present when a service is
directly accessible at a particular address (e.g. URL, etc).
Mutually exclusive with hostingRedirector.</
xsd:documentation>
        </xsd:annotation>
        <xsd:complexType>
          <xsd:simpleContent>
            <xsd:extension base = "xsd:string">
              <xsd:attribute ref = "URLType"/>
            </xsd:extension>
          </xsd:simpleContent>
        </xsd:complexType>
      </xsd:element>
      <xsd:element name = "address">
        <xsd:annotation>
          <xsd:documentation>An address.  Use the useType
attribute to signify purpose.  Use the sortCode attribute to
signify associated software make/product/version.  Use the
tModelKey to signify the context or namespace of keyName/
keyValue markeup on individual addressLine elements. </
xsd:documentation>
        </xsd:annotation>
        <xsd:complexType>
          <xsd:sequence>
            <xsd:element ref = "addressLine" minOccurs = "0"
maxOccurs = "unbounded"/>
          </xsd:sequence>
          <xsd:attribute ref = "useType"/>
          <xsd:attribute ref = "sortCode"/>
          <xsd:attribute ref = "tModelKey"/>
        </xsd:complexType>
      </xsd:element>
      <xsd:element name = "addressLine">
        <xsd:annotation>
          <xsd:documentation>A part of an address.  Order of
addressLine elements is not lax.  Use the optional keyName
keyValue attributes to specify field specific parsing hints.
These should be used in conjunction with the optional
tModelKey on the address structure to identify the namespace
or context of the address element.  These field hints are
not validated by UDDI registries.</xsd:documentation>
        </xsd:annotation>
        <xsd:complexType>
          <xsd:simpleContent>
            <xsd:extension base = "xsd:string">
```

```
              <xsd:attribute ref = "keyName"/>
              <xsd:attribute ref = "keyValue"/>
            </xsd:extension>
          </xsd:simpleContent>
        </xsd:complexType>
      </xsd:element>
      <xsd:element name = "assertionStatusItem">
        <xsd:annotation>
          <xsd:documentation>This is a report back to the
publisher of assertions - the status indicates whether the
handshake conditions (both key owners have asserted the same
facts) have been satisfied.  Only symmetric relationship
types require the agreement between parties.</
xsd:documentation>
        </xsd:annotation>
        <xsd:complexType>
          <xsd:sequence>
            <xsd:element ref = "fromKey"/>
            <xsd:element ref = "toKey"/>
            <xsd:element ref = "keyedReference"/>
            <xsd:element ref = "keysOwned"/>
          </xsd:sequence>
          <xsd:attribute name = "completionStatus" use =
"required" type = "xsd:string">
            <xsd:annotation>
              <xsd:documentation>See the UDDI V2 API
specification for valid values.</xsd:documentation>
            </xsd:annotation>
          </xsd:attribute>
        </xsd:complexType>
      </xsd:element>
      <xsd:element name = "authInfo" type = "xsd:string">
        <xsd:annotation>
          <xsd:documentation>This structure is used in all
publishing API messages.  It holds an authentication token
value.</xsd:documentation>
        </xsd:annotation>
      </xsd:element>
      <xsd:element name = "bindingKey" type = "xsd:string">
        <xsd:annotation>
          <xsd:documentation>This is the element form of
bindingKey.  Identifies the bindingKey value associated with
a bindingTemplate.</xsd:documentation>
        </xsd:annotation>
```

```
      </xsd:element>
      <xsd:element name = "bindingTemplate">
        <xsd:annotation>
          <xsd:documentation>Primary Data type: Describes an
instance of a web service in technical terms.</
xsd:documentation>
        </xsd:annotation>
        <xsd:complexType>
          <xsd:sequence>
            <xsd:element ref = "description" minOccurs = "0"
maxOccurs = "unbounded"/>
            <xsd:choice>
              <xsd:element ref = "accessPoint" minOccurs =
"0"/>
              <xsd:element ref = "hostingRedirector"
minOccurs = "0"/>
            </xsd:choice>
            <xsd:element ref = "tModelInstanceDetails"/>
          </xsd:sequence>
          <xsd:attribute ref = "serviceKey"/>
          <xsd:attribute ref = "bindingKey"/>
        </xsd:complexType>
      </xsd:element>
      <xsd:element name = "bindingTemplates">
        <xsd:annotation>
          <xsd:documentation>Service element.  Collection
accessor for bindingTemplate information.</
xsd:documentation>
        </xsd:annotation>
        <xsd:complexType>
          <xsd:sequence>
            <xsd:element ref = "bindingTemplate" minOccurs =
"0" maxOccurs = "unbounded"/>
          </xsd:sequence>
        </xsd:complexType>
      </xsd:element>
      <xsd:element name = "businessEntity">
        <xsd:annotation>
          <xsd:documentation>Primary Data type: Describes an
instance of a business or business unit.</xsd:documentation>
        </xsd:annotation>
        <xsd:complexType>
          <xsd:sequence>
```

```
            <xsd:element ref = "discoveryURLs" minOccurs =
"0"/>
            <xsd:element ref = "name" maxOccurs =
"unbounded"/>
            <xsd:element ref = "description" minOccurs = "0"
maxOccurs = "unbounded"/>
            <xsd:element ref = "contacts" minOccurs = "0"/>
            <xsd:element ref = "businessServices" minOccurs =
"0"/>
            <xsd:element ref = "identifierBag" minOccurs =
"0"/>
            <xsd:element ref = "categoryBag" minOccurs = "0"/
>
          </xsd:sequence>
          <xsd:attribute ref = "businessKey"/>
          <xsd:attribute ref = "operator"/>
          <xsd:attribute ref = "authorizedName"/>
        </xsd:complexType>
      </xsd:element>
      <xsd:element name = "businessEntityExt">
        <xsd:annotation>
          <xsd:documentation>Data: This structure is the
container for safely extending the businessEntity
information in private implementations of UDDI compatible
registries. Official operator nodes may not provide extended
data but must return a properly populated businessEntity
structure within this structure in response to a
get_businessDetailExt message.</xsd:documentation>
          <xsd:documentation>to support customization/
extensibility</xsd:documentation>
        </xsd:annotation>
        <xsd:complexType>
          <xsd:sequence>
            <xsd:element ref = "businessEntity"/>
            <xsd:any namespace = "##other" processContents =
"strict" minOccurs = "0" maxOccurs = "unbounded"/>
          </xsd:sequence>
        </xsd:complexType>
      </xsd:element>
      <xsd:element name = "businessInfo">
        <xsd:annotation>
          <xsd:documentation>Data - This element is used as a
short form of the BusinessEntityelement as a first pass
```

```
result set for "find businesses" queries.</
xsd:documentation>
        </xsd:annotation>
        <xsd:complexType>
          <xsd:sequence>
            <xsd:element ref = "name" maxOccurs =
"unbounded"/>
            <xsd:element ref = "description" minOccurs = "0"
maxOccurs = "unbounded"/>
            <xsd:element ref = "serviceInfos"/>
          </xsd:sequence>
          <xsd:attribute ref = "businessKey"/>
        </xsd:complexType>
      </xsd:element>
      <xsd:element name = "businessInfos">
        <xsd:annotation>
          <xsd:documentation>Accessor container for one or
more businessInfo structures</xsd:documentation>
        </xsd:annotation>
        <xsd:complexType>
          <xsd:sequence>

            <xsd:element ref = "businessInfo" minOccurs = "0"
maxOccurs = "unbounded"/>
          </xsd:sequence>
        </xsd:complexType>
      </xsd:element>
      <xsd:element name = "businessKey" type = "xsd:string">
        <xsd:annotation>
          <xsd:documentation>This is the element form of
businessKey.  Identifies the businessKey value associated
with a businessEntity.</xsd:documentation>
        </xsd:annotation>
      </xsd:element>
      <xsd:element name = "businessService">
        <xsd:annotation>
          <xsd:documentation>Primary Data type: Describes a
logical service type in business terms.</xsd:documentation>
        </xsd:annotation>
        <xsd:complexType>
          <xsd:sequence>
            <xsd:element ref = "name" maxOccurs =
"unbounded"/>
```

```
            <xsd:element ref = "description" minOccurs = "0"
maxOccurs = "unbounded"/>
            <xsd:element ref = "bindingTemplates"/>
            <xsd:element ref = "categoryBag" minOccurs = "0"/
>
          </xsd:sequence>
          <xsd:attribute ref = "serviceKey"/>
          <xsd:attribute ref = "businessKey"/>
        </xsd:complexType>
      </xsd:element>
      <xsd:element name = "businessServices">
        <xsd:annotation>
          <xsd:documentation>Service element.  Accessor
collection point for businessService data.</
xsd:documentation>
        </xsd:annotation>
        <xsd:complexType>
          <xsd:sequence>
            <xsd:element ref = "businessService" minOccurs =
"0" maxOccurs = "unbounded"/>
          </xsd:sequence>
        </xsd:complexType>
      </xsd:element>
      <xsd:element name = "categoryBag">
        <xsd:annotation>
          <xsd:documentation>Service element.  Used in
searching and categorization.</xsd:documentation>
        </xsd:annotation>
        <xsd:complexType>
          <xsd:sequence>
            <xsd:element ref = "keyedReference" minOccurs =
"0" maxOccurs = "unbounded"/>
          </xsd:sequence>
        </xsd:complexType>
      </xsd:element>
      <xsd:element name = "completionStatus" type =
"xsd:string">
        <xsd:annotation>
          <xsd:documentation>This is the element form of the
completionStatus attribute.</xsd:documentation>
        </xsd:annotation>
      </xsd:element>
      <xsd:element name = "contact">
        <xsd:annotation>
```

```
          <xsd:documentation>Data: a contact</
xsd:documentation>
        </xsd:annotation>
        <xsd:complexType>
          <xsd:sequence>
            <xsd:element ref = "description" minOccurs = "0"
maxOccurs = "unbounded"/>
            <xsd:element ref = "personName"/>
            <xsd:element ref = "phone" minOccurs = "0"
maxOccurs = "unbounded"/>
            <xsd:element ref = "email" minOccurs = "0"
maxOccurs = "unbounded"/>
            <xsd:element ref = "address" minOccurs = "0"
maxOccurs = "unbounded"/>
          </xsd:sequence>
          <xsd:attribute ref = "useType"/>
        </xsd:complexType>
      </xsd:element>
      <xsd:element name = "contacts">
        <xsd:annotation>
          <xsd:documentation>Service element: accessor for
one or more contacts.</xsd:documentation>
        </xsd:annotation>
        <xsd:complexType>
          <xsd:sequence>
            <xsd:element ref = "contact" minOccurs = "0"
maxOccurs = "unbounded"/>
          </xsd:sequence>
        </xsd:complexType>
      </xsd:element>
      <xsd:element name = "description" type = "xsd:string">
        <xsd:annotation>
          <xsd:documentation>A textual, short description.
When adorned with an xml:lang markup, signifies a
description in a specific language.</xsd:documentation>
        </xsd:annotation>
      </xsd:element>
      <xsd:element name = "discoveryURL">
        <xsd:annotation>
          <xsd:documentation>Data:  A url pointing to an
external (typed by convention) discovery doc.</
xsd:documentation>
        </xsd:annotation>
        <xsd:complexType>
```

```
          <xsd:simpleContent>
            <xsd:extension base = "xsd:string">
              <xsd:attribute ref = "useType"/>
            </xsd:extension>
          </xsd:simpleContent>
        </xsd:complexType>
      </xsd:element>
      <xsd:element name = "discoveryURLs">
        <xsd:annotation>
          <xsd:documentation>Service Element: accessor for
one or more discoveryURL elements</xsd:documentation>
        </xsd:annotation>
        <xsd:complexType>
          <xsd:sequence>
            <xsd:element ref = "discoveryURL" maxOccurs =
"unbounded"/>
          </xsd:sequence>
        </xsd:complexType>
      </xsd:element>
      <xsd:element name = "email">
        <xsd:annotation>
          <xsd:documentation>Data: an email address.</
xsd:documentation>
        </xsd:annotation>
        <xsd:complexType>
          <xsd:simpleContent>
            <xsd:extension base = "xsd:string">
              <xsd:attribute ref = "useType"/>
            </xsd:extension>
          </xsd:simpleContent>
        </xsd:complexType>
      </xsd:element>
      <xsd:element name = "errInfo">
        <xsd:annotation>
          <xsd:documentation>Supports the DispositionReport
structure. Provided for conveying text and structured error
code (alphanumeric) information.  Error message text is
contained by this element.</xsd:documentation>
        </xsd:annotation>
        <xsd:complexType>
          <xsd:simpleContent>
            <xsd:extension base = "xsd:string">
              <xsd:attribute name = "errCode" use =
"required" type = "xsd:string">
```

```
                <xsd:annotation>
                  <xsd:documentation>Returned on output.
Signifies error status in a dispositionReport.  See error
code appendix in the API specification.</xsd:documentation>
                </xsd:annotation>
              </xsd:attribute>
            </xsd:extension>
          </xsd:simpleContent>
        </xsd:complexType>
      </xsd:element>
      <xsd:element name = "findQualifier" type =
"xsd:string">
        <xsd:annotation>
          <xsd:documentation>This element modifies the
behavior of the find operations.  See the search qualifiers
appendix in the UDDI API specification.</xsd:documentation>
        </xsd:annotation>
      </xsd:element>
      <xsd:element name = "findQualifiers">
        <xsd:annotation>
          <xsd:documentation>Service Element: container/
accessor for findQualifiers</xsd:documentation>
        </xsd:annotation>
        <xsd:complexType>
          <xsd:sequence>
            <xsd:element ref = "findQualifier" minOccurs =
"0" maxOccurs = "unbounded"/>
          </xsd:sequence>
        </xsd:complexType>
      </xsd:element>
      <xsd:element name = "fromKey" type = "xsd:string">
        <xsd:annotation>
          <xsd:documentation>This is a place holder for a
businessKey value.  It is used in several messages and is
not intended to always represent a positional place in a
relationship.</xsd:documentation>
        </xsd:annotation>
      </xsd:element>
      <xsd:element name = "hostingRedirector">
        <xsd:annotation>
          <xsd:documentation>Data: present only when the
service is provisioned via remote hosting,load balancing,
etc.  Mutually exclusive with accessPoint.</
xsd:documentation>
```

```
        </xsd:annotation>
        <xsd:complexType>
          <xsd:attribute ref = "bindingKey"/>
        </xsd:complexType>
      </xsd:element>
      <xsd:element name = "identifierBag">
        <xsd:annotation>
          <xsd:documentation>Service element.  Used in
searching and categorization.</xsd:documentation>
        </xsd:annotation>
        <xsd:complexType>
          <xsd:sequence>
            <xsd:element ref = "keyedReference" minOccurs =
"0" maxOccurs = "unbounded"/>
          </xsd:sequence>
        </xsd:complexType>
      </xsd:element>
      <xsd:element name = "instanceDetails">
        <xsd:annotation>
          <xsd:documentation>Support element: used to contain
optional information about the way an instance of a web
service is implemented or varies from the general
specifications outlined in a specific tModel.  An individual
binding property.</xsd:documentation>
        </xsd:annotation>
        <xsd:complexType>
          <xsd:sequence>
            <xsd:element ref = "description" minOccurs = "0"
maxOccurs = "unbounded"/>
            <xsd:element ref = "overviewDoc" minOccurs = "0"/
>
            <xsd:element ref = "instanceParms" minOccurs =
"0"/>
          </xsd:sequence>
        </xsd:complexType>
      </xsd:element>
      <xsd:element name = "instanceParms" type =
"xsd:string">
        <xsd:annotation>
          <xsd:documentation>This is a general purpose field
for use in providing more specific information associated
with a tModel fingerprint component within a
bindingTemplate.  Depending on the meaning or concept
represented by the tModel reference (depends on the tModel
```

```
creator's intent), this element will hold data meaningful to
those who understand it's purpose based on that intent.</
xsd:documentation>
        </xsd:annotation>
      </xsd:element>
      <xsd:element name = "keyValue" type = "xsd:string">
        <xsd:annotation>
          <xsd:documentation>This is the element form of
keyValue.  See the attribute form description for more
information.</xsd:documentation>
        </xsd:annotation>
      </xsd:element>
      <xsd:element name = "keyedReference">
        <xsd:annotation>
          <xsd:documentation>Represents a namespace qualified
name-value pair.  Depending on use context, this structure
can be used within different convention frameworks. V2
CHANGE: On playback, a record saved without a keyName
attribute is returned without the attribute as well. The
behavior of saving without a tModelKey is promotion to the
keyword namespace by operator assignment of the
keyedReference to the uddi-org:general namespace.</
xsd:documentation>

        </xsd:annotation>
        <xsd:complexType>
          <xsd:attribute ref = "tModelKey"/>
          <xsd:attribute ref = "keyName"/>
          <xsd:attribute ref = "keyValue"/>
        </xsd:complexType>
      </xsd:element>
      <xsd:element name = "keysOwned">
        <xsd:annotation>
          <xsd:documentation>Used to report which keys
involved with an assertion are managed by the publisher who
is viewing the data.  This is a support element that is part
of the assertionStatusReport</xsd:documentation>
        </xsd:annotation>
        <xsd:complexType>
          <xsd:sequence>
            <xsd:element ref = "fromKey" minOccurs = "0"/>
            <xsd:element ref = "toKey" minOccurs = "0"/>
          </xsd:sequence>
        </xsd:complexType>
```

```
      </xsd:element>
      <xsd:element name = "name" type = "xsd:string">
        <xsd:annotation>
          <xsd:documentation>A textual representation of a
name.  When used with tModel, suggested format is URN.  With
other entities, more than one name may be supplied, as long
as each name is adorned with a unique xml:lang value to
signify the language that the name is expressed in.</
xsd:documentation>
        </xsd:annotation>
      </xsd:element>
      <xsd:element name = "overviewDoc">
        <xsd:annotation>
          <xsd:documentation>Support element - used to
contain an on-line description and a URL pointer to more in-
depth or external documentation.</xsd:documentation>
        </xsd:annotation>
        <xsd:complexType>
          <xsd:sequence>
            <xsd:element ref = "description" minOccurs = "0"
maxOccurs = "unbounded"/>
            <xsd:element ref = "overviewURL" minOccurs = "0"/
>
          </xsd:sequence>
        </xsd:complexType>
      </xsd:element>
      <xsd:element name = "overviewURL" type = "xsd:string">
        <xsd:annotation>
          <xsd:documentation>A uniform resource locator (URL)
that can be used to get more information or specifications</
xsd:documentation>
        </xsd:annotation>
      </xsd:element>
      <xsd:element name = "personName" type = "xsd:string">
        <xsd:annotation>
          <xsd:documentation>The name associated with a
contact.  Blank if no name applies.  For transliteration
purposes (e.g. romanization) the suggested approach is to
file multiple contacts.</xsd:documentation>
        </xsd:annotation>
      </xsd:element>
      <xsd:element name = "phone">
        <xsd:annotation>
```

```
          <xsd:documentation>Data: an telephone number.</
xsd:documentation>
        </xsd:annotation>
        <xsd:complexType>
          <xsd:simpleContent>
            <xsd:extension base = "xsd:string">
              <xsd:attribute ref = "useType"/>
            </xsd:extension>
          </xsd:simpleContent>
        </xsd:complexType>
      </xsd:element>
      <xsd:element name = "publisherAssertion">
        <xsd:annotation>
          <xsd:documentation>This is used in the
set_publisherAssertions message to specify a relationship
assertion.  See set_publisherAssertions before using this
element.</xsd:documentation>
        </xsd:annotation>
        <xsd:complexType>
          <xsd:sequence>

            <xsd:element ref = "fromKey"/>
            <xsd:element ref = "toKey"/>
            <xsd:element ref = "keyedReference"/>
          </xsd:sequence>
        </xsd:complexType>
      </xsd:element>
      <xsd:element name = "relatedBusinessInfo">
        <xsd:annotation>
          <xsd:documentation>Data - used in response to
get_relatedBusinesses.  This element is used to give brief
information about a related business and the shared
relationships.</xsd:documentation>
        </xsd:annotation>
        <xsd:complexType>
          <xsd:sequence>
            <xsd:element ref = "businessKey"/>
            <xsd:element ref = "name" maxOccurs =
"unbounded"/>
            <xsd:element ref = "description" minOccurs = "0"
maxOccurs = "unbounded"/>
            <xsd:element ref = "sharedRelationships"/>
          </xsd:sequence>
        </xsd:complexType>
```

```
      </xsd:element>
      <xsd:element name = "relatedBusinessInfos">
        <xsd:annotation>
          <xsd:documentation>Used to convey the
relatedBusiness information for a particular
businessEntity.</xsd:documentation>
        </xsd:annotation>
        <xsd:complexType>
          <xsd:sequence>
            <xsd:element ref = "relatedBusinessInfo"
minOccurs = "0" maxOccurs = "unbounded"/>
          </xsd:sequence>
        </xsd:complexType>
      </xsd:element>
      <xsd:element name = "result">
        <xsd:annotation>
          <xsd:documentation>Service Element: This structure
supports the dispositionReport structure.</
xsd:documentation>
        </xsd:annotation>
        <xsd:complexType>
          <xsd:sequence>
            <xsd:element ref = "errInfo" minOccurs = "0"/>
          </xsd:sequence>
          <xsd:attribute name = "keyType">
            <xsd:annotation>

              <xsd:documentation>Used to signify the type of
key associated with the result report.</xsd:documentation>
            </xsd:annotation>
            <xsd:simpleType>
              <xsd:restriction base = "xsd:NMTOKEN">
                <xsd:enumeration value = "businessKey"/>
                <xsd:enumeration value = "tModelKey"/>
                <xsd:enumeration value = "serviceKey"/>
                <xsd:enumeration value = "bindingKey"/>
              </xsd:restriction>
            </xsd:simpleType>
          </xsd:attribute>
          <xsd:attribute name = "errno" use = "required" type
= "xsd:int">
            <xsd:annotation>
```

```
                <xsd:documentation>Returned on output.  The
numeric equivalent of the errCode value.  0 signifies
success.</xsd:documentation>
              </xsd:annotation>
            </xsd:attribute>
          </xsd:complexType>
        </xsd:element>
        <xsd:element name = "serviceInfo">
          <xsd:annotation>
            <xsd:documentation>This structure is used as the
short form of a service for list purposes. V2 CHANGE:
multiple names allowed for internationalization support.</
xsd:documentation>
          </xsd:annotation>
          <xsd:complexType>
            <xsd:sequence>
              <xsd:element ref = "name" maxOccurs =
"unbounded"/>
            </xsd:sequence>
            <xsd:attribute ref = "serviceKey"/>
            <xsd:attribute ref = "businessKey"/>
          </xsd:complexType>
        </xsd:element>
        <xsd:element name = "serviceInfos">
          <xsd:annotation>
            <xsd:documentation>Accessor container for one or
more serviceInfo structures</xsd:documentation>
          </xsd:annotation>
          <xsd:complexType>
            <xsd:sequence>
              <xsd:element ref = "serviceInfo" minOccurs = "0"
maxOccurs = "unbounded"/>
            </xsd:sequence>
          </xsd:complexType>
        </xsd:element>
        <xsd:element name = "serviceKey" type = "xsd:string">
          <xsd:annotation>
            <xsd:documentation>The element form of the
serviceKey attribute.</xsd:documentation>
          </xsd:annotation>
        </xsd:element>
        <xsd:element name = "sharedRelationships">
          <xsd:annotation>
```

```
          <xsd:documentation>This is a collection of
relationship information.</xsd:documentation>
        </xsd:annotation>
        <xsd:complexType>
          <xsd:sequence>
            <xsd:element ref = "keyedReference" maxOccurs =
"unbounded"/>
          </xsd:sequence>
        </xsd:complexType>
      </xsd:element>
      <xsd:element name = "tModel">
        <xsd:annotation>
          <xsd:documentation>This structure defines a
metadata about a technology, specificationor namespace
qualified list (e.g. taxonomy, organizaton, etc.)</
xsd:documentation>
        </xsd:annotation>
        <xsd:complexType>
          <xsd:sequence>
            <xsd:element ref = "name"/>
            <xsd:element ref = "description" minOccurs = "0"
maxOccurs = "unbounded"/>
            <xsd:element ref = "overviewDoc" minOccurs = "0"/
>
            <xsd:element ref = "identifierBag" minOccurs =
"0"/>
            <xsd:element ref = "categoryBag" minOccurs = "0"/
>
          </xsd:sequence>
          <xsd:attribute ref = "tModelKey"/>
          <xsd:attribute ref = "operator"/>
          <xsd:attribute ref = "authorizedName"/>
        </xsd:complexType>
      </xsd:element>
      <xsd:element name = "tModelBag">
        <xsd:annotation>
          <xsd:documentation>Support element used in searches
by tModel key values</xsd:documentation>
        </xsd:annotation>
        <xsd:complexType>
          <xsd:sequence>
            <xsd:element ref = "tModelKey" maxOccurs =
"unbounded"/>
          </xsd:sequence>
```

```
        </xsd:complexType>
      </xsd:element>
      <xsd:element name = "tModelInfo">
        <xsd:annotation>
          <xsd:documentation>Data: This structure is used to
enumerate short form tModel information.</xsd:documentation>
        </xsd:annotation>
        <xsd:complexType>
          <xsd:sequence>
            <xsd:element ref = "name"/>
          </xsd:sequence>
          <xsd:attribute ref = "tModelKey"/>
        </xsd:complexType>
      </xsd:element>
      <xsd:element name = "tModelInfos">
        <xsd:annotation>
          <xsd:documentation>Support element - accessor
container for tModelInfo.</xsd:documentation>
        </xsd:annotation>
        <xsd:complexType>
          <xsd:sequence>
            <xsd:element ref = "tModelInfo" minOccurs = "0"
maxOccurs = "unbounded"/>
          </xsd:sequence>
        </xsd:complexType>
      </xsd:element>
      <xsd:element name = "tModelInstanceDetails">
        <xsd:annotation>
          <xsd:documentation>Support element used as a
container for tModel "fingerprint" within a web service
bindingTemplate metadata set.</xsd:documentation>
        </xsd:annotation>
        <xsd:complexType>
          <xsd:sequence>
            <xsd:element ref = "tModelInstanceInfo" minOccurs
= "0" maxOccurs = "unbounded"/>
          </xsd:sequence>
        </xsd:complexType>
      </xsd:element>
      <xsd:element name = "tModelInstanceInfo">
        <xsd:annotation>
          <xsd:documentation>Support element: used to contain
implementation instance specific information about
compatible specications (via tModel reference) and optional
```

```
settings details.  Think of these as binding properties.</
xsd:documentation>
        </xsd:annotation>
        <xsd:complexType>
          <xsd:sequence>
            <xsd:element ref = "description" minOccurs = "0"
maxOccurs = "unbounded"/>
            <xsd:element ref = "instanceDetails" minOccurs =
"0"/>
          </xsd:sequence>
          <xsd:attribute ref = "tModelKey"/>
        </xsd:complexType>
      </xsd:element>
      <xsd:element name = "tModelKey" type = "xsd:string">
        <xsd:annotation>
          <xsd:documentation>The element form of the
tModelKey attribute.</xsd:documentation>
        </xsd:annotation>
      </xsd:element>
      <xsd:element name = "toKey" type = "xsd:string">
        <xsd:annotation>
          <xsd:documentation>This is a place holder for a
businessKey value.  It is used in several messages and is
not intended to always represent a positional place in a
relationship.</xsd:documentation>
        </xsd:annotation>
      </xsd:element>
      <xsd:element name = "uploadRegister" type =
"xsd:string">
        <xsd:annotation>
          <xsd:documentation>A uniform resource locator
(URL).  Defined for historical purposes.  Not supported in
UDDI V1 and V2 operator registries.  May be used by private
registries to specifiy location of data to be imported into
a registry instance.</xsd:documentation>
        </xsd:annotation>
      </xsd:element>

      <!-- Message Definitions -->

      <xsd:element name = "add_publisherAssertions">
        <xsd:annotation>
          <xsd:documentation>Message - Request: This message
is used to add new assertions to the existing set of
```

```
assertions tracked on a per-publisher basis.</
xsd:documentation>
        </xsd:annotation>
        <xsd:complexType>
          <xsd:sequence>
            <xsd:element ref = "authInfo"/>
            <xsd:element ref = "publisherAssertion" maxOccurs
= "unbounded"/>
          </xsd:sequence>
          <xsd:attribute ref = "generic"/>
        </xsd:complexType>
      </xsd:element>
      <xsd:element name = "assertionStatusReport">
        <xsd:annotation>
          <xsd:documentation>Message - Response: This message
is a response to the get_assertionStatusReport message.  It
is a report of all complete and incomplete assertions and
serves an administrative use involving determinine if there
are any outstanding, incomplete assertions about
relationships involving businesses the publisher account is
associated with.</xsd:documentation>
        </xsd:annotation>
        <xsd:complexType>
          <xsd:sequence>
            <xsd:element ref = "assertionStatusItem"
minOccurs = "0" maxOccurs = "unbounded"/>
          </xsd:sequence>
          <xsd:attribute ref = "generic"/>
          <xsd:attribute ref = "operator"/>
        </xsd:complexType>
      </xsd:element>
      <xsd:element name = "authToken">
        <xsd:annotation>
          <xsd:documentation>Message - Response: used to
return an authentication token in response to a
"get_authToken" message.</xsd:documentation>
        </xsd:annotation>
        <xsd:complexType>
          <xsd:sequence>
            <xsd:element ref = "authInfo"/>
          </xsd:sequence>
          <xsd:attribute ref = "generic"/>
          <xsd:attribute ref = "operator"/>
        </xsd:complexType>
```

```
      </xsd:element>
      <xsd:element name = "bindingDetail">
        <xsd:annotation>
          <xsd:documentation>Message - Response: Returns one
or more bindingTemplate structures based on the input
passed.  This is the response to a get_bindingDetail
message.  Response to get_bindingDetail and save_binding
messages.</xsd:documentation>
        </xsd:annotation>
        <xsd:complexType>
          <xsd:sequence>
            <xsd:element ref = "bindingTemplate" minOccurs =
"0" maxOccurs = "unbounded"/>
          </xsd:sequence>
          <xsd:attribute ref = "generic"/>
          <xsd:attribute ref = "operator"/>
          <xsd:attribute ref = "truncated"/>
        </xsd:complexType>
      </xsd:element>
      <xsd:element name = "businessDetail">
        <xsd:annotation>
          <xsd:documentation>Message - Response: Returns one
or more businessEntity structures.  This is the natural
response to a get_businessDetail message and to a
save_business message.</xsd:documentation>
        </xsd:annotation>
        <xsd:complexType>
          <xsd:sequence>
            <xsd:element ref = "businessEntity" minOccurs =
"0" maxOccurs = "unbounded"/>
          </xsd:sequence>
          <xsd:attribute ref = "generic"/>
          <xsd:attribute ref = "operator"/>
          <xsd:attribute ref = "truncated"/>
        </xsd:complexType>
      </xsd:element>
      <xsd:element name = "businessDetailExt">
        <xsd:annotation>
          <xsd:documentation>Message - Response: The extended
businessDetail messages define an API that allows non-
operator UDDI registries to provide extended information via
a consistent API.  This message is the response to
get_businessDetailExt.</xsd:documentation>
        </xsd:annotation>
```

```
        <xsd:complexType>
          <xsd:sequence>
            <xsd:element ref = "businessEntityExt" maxOccurs
= "unbounded"/>
          </xsd:sequence>
          <xsd:attribute ref = "generic"/>
          <xsd:attribute ref = "operator"/>
          <xsd:attribute ref = "truncated"/>
        </xsd:complexType>
      </xsd:element>
      <xsd:element name = "businessList">
        <xsd:annotation>
          <xsd:documentation>Message - Response: This is a
report - a list of businesses in short form. This message is
the response to a find_businessEntity query.</
xsd:documentation>
        </xsd:annotation>
        <xsd:complexType>
          <xsd:sequence>
            <xsd:element ref = "businessInfos"/>
          </xsd:sequence>
          <xsd:attribute ref = "generic"/>
          <xsd:attribute ref = "operator"/>
          <xsd:attribute ref = "truncated"/>
        </xsd:complexType>
      </xsd:element>
      <xsd:element name = "delete_binding">
        <xsd:annotation>
          <xsd:documentation>Message - Request: This message
is used to delete information about a previously registered
bindingTemplate structure.</xsd:documentation>
        </xsd:annotation>
        <xsd:complexType>
          <xsd:sequence>
            <xsd:element ref = "authInfo"/>
            <xsd:element ref = "bindingKey" maxOccurs =
"unbounded"/>
          </xsd:sequence>
          <xsd:attribute ref = "generic"/>
        </xsd:complexType>
      </xsd:element>
      <xsd:element name = "delete_business">
        <xsd:annotation>
```

```
          <xsd:documentation>Message - Request: used to
delete information about a previously registered
businessEntity.</xsd:documentation>
        </xsd:annotation>
        <xsd:complexType>
          <xsd:sequence>
            <xsd:element ref = "authInfo"/>
            <xsd:element ref = "businessKey" maxOccurs =
"unbounded"/>
          </xsd:sequence>
          <xsd:attribute ref = "generic"/>
        </xsd:complexType>
      </xsd:element>
      <xsd:element name = "delete_publisherAssertions">
        <xsd:annotation>
          <xsd:documentation>Message - Request: This message
is used to delete specific assertions to the existing set of
assertions tracked on a per-publisher basis.</
xsd:documentation>
        </xsd:annotation>
        <xsd:complexType>
          <xsd:sequence>
            <xsd:element ref = "authInfo"/>
            <xsd:element ref = "publisherAssertion" maxOccurs
= "unbounded"/>
          </xsd:sequence>
          <xsd:attribute ref = "generic"/>
        </xsd:complexType>
      </xsd:element>
      <xsd:element name = "delete_service">
        <xsd:annotation>
          <xsd:documentation>Message - Request: used to
delete information about a previously registered
businessService structure.</xsd:documentation>
        </xsd:annotation>
        <xsd:complexType>
          <xsd:sequence>
            <xsd:element ref = "authInfo"/>
            <xsd:element ref = "serviceKey" maxOccurs =
"unbounded"/>
          </xsd:sequence>
          <xsd:attribute ref = "generic"/>
        </xsd:complexType>
      </xsd:element>
```

```
      <xsd:element name = "delete_tModel">
        <xsd:annotation>
          <xsd:documentation>Message - Request: used to Hide
information about a previously registered tModel.</
xsd:documentation>
        </xsd:annotation>
        <xsd:complexType>
          <xsd:sequence>
            <xsd:element ref = "authInfo"/>
            <xsd:element ref = "tModelKey" maxOccurs =
"unbounded"/>
          </xsd:sequence>
          <xsd:attribute ref = "generic"/>
        </xsd:complexType>
      </xsd:element>
      <xsd:element name = "discard_authToken">
        <xsd:annotation>
          <xsd:documentation>Message - Request: used to
deactivate an authentication token that was obtained by a
call to get_authToken.</xsd:documentation>
        </xsd:annotation>
        <xsd:complexType>
          <xsd:sequence>
            <xsd:element ref = "authInfo"/>
          </xsd:sequence>
          <xsd:attribute ref = "generic"/>
        </xsd:complexType>
      </xsd:element>
      <xsd:element name = "dispositionReport">
        <xsd:annotation>
          <xsd:documentation>Message - Response: This message
is used report the outcome of calls.  It is used within
error (fault) messages, and can stand alone when indicating
success.</xsd:documentation>
        </xsd:annotation>
        <xsd:complexType>
          <xsd:sequence>
            <xsd:element ref = "result" maxOccurs =
"unbounded"/>
          </xsd:sequence>
          <xsd:attribute ref = "generic"/>
          <xsd:attribute ref = "operator"/>
          <xsd:attribute ref = "truncated"/>
        </xsd:complexType>
```

```
      </xsd:element>
      <xsd:element name = "find_binding">
        <xsd:annotation>
          <xsd:documentation>Message - Request: This message
is used to search for summary results listing registered
bindingTemplate data within a businessService matching
specific criteria.</xsd:documentation>
        </xsd:annotation>

        <xsd:complexType>
          <xsd:sequence>
            <xsd:element ref = "findQualifiers" minOccurs =
"0"/>
            <xsd:element ref = "tModelBag"/>
          </xsd:sequence>
          <xsd:attribute ref = "generic"/>
          <xsd:attribute ref = "maxRows"/>
          <xsd:attribute ref = "serviceKey"/>
        </xsd:complexType>
      </xsd:element>
      <xsd:element name = "find_business">
        <xsd:annotation>
          <xsd:documentation>Message - Request: This message
is used to search for summary results listing registered
businessEntity data matching specific criteria. V2 CHANGE:
allows up to 5 xml:lang qualified names</xsd:documentation>
          <xsd:documentation>One of the arguments name,
identifierBag, categoryBag, tModelBag or discoveryURLs must
be supplied for data to be returned.</xsd:documentation>
        </xsd:annotation>
        <xsd:complexType>
          <xsd:sequence>
            <xsd:element ref = "findQualifiers" minOccurs =
"0"/>
            <xsd:element ref = "name" minOccurs = "0"
maxOccurs = "unbounded"/>
            <xsd:element ref = "identifierBag" minOccurs =
"0"/>
            <xsd:element ref = "categoryBag" minOccurs = "0"/
>
            <xsd:element ref = "tModelBag" minOccurs = "0"/>
            <xsd:element ref = "discoveryURLs" minOccurs =
"0"/>
          </xsd:sequence>
```

```
          <xsd:attribute ref = "generic"/>
          <xsd:attribute ref = "maxRows"/>

        </xsd:complexType>
      </xsd:element>
      <xsd:element name = "find_relatedBusinesses">
        <xsd:annotation>
          <xsd:documentation>Message - Request: This inquiry
API message is used to get information about businessEntity
data that are related to a particular businessEntity in a
particular way.  Only those relationships whose assertion
status is complete are reported.  No data is reported in the
response to this request unless the publisher of that
businessEntity and the publisher of the businessEntity key
passed in the inquiry have made relationship assertionst
that agree.</xsd:documentation>
        </xsd:annotation>
        <xsd:complexType>
          <xsd:sequence>
            <xsd:element ref = "findQualifiers" minOccurs =
"0"/>
            <xsd:element ref = "businessKey"/>
            <xsd:element ref = "keyedReference" minOccurs =
"0"/>
          </xsd:sequence>
          <xsd:attribute ref = "generic"/>
        </xsd:complexType>
      </xsd:element>
      <xsd:element name = "find_service">
        <xsd:annotation>
          <xsd:documentation>Message - Request: This message
is used to search for summary results listing registered
businessService data matching specific criteria. V2 CHANGE:
allows up to 5 xml:lang qualified names</xsd:documentation>
          <xsd:documentation>One of the arguments name,
identifierBag, categoryBag or tModelBag must be supplied for
data to be returned.</xsd:documentation>
        </xsd:annotation>
        <xsd:complexType>
          <xsd:sequence>
            <xsd:element ref = "findQualifiers" minOccurs =
"0"/>
            <xsd:element ref = "name" minOccurs = "0"
maxOccurs = "unbounded"/>
```

```
            <xsd:element ref = "categoryBag" minOccurs = "0"/
>
            <xsd:element ref = "tModelBag" minOccurs = "0"/>
          </xsd:sequence>
          <xsd:attribute ref = "generic"/>
          <xsd:attribute ref = "maxRows"/>
          <xsd:attribute ref = "businessKey"/>
        </xsd:complexType>
      </xsd:element>
      <xsd:element name = "find_tModel">
        <xsd:annotation>
          <xsd:documentation>Message - Request: used to
search for summary results listing registered tModel data
matching specific criteria.</xsd:documentation>

          <xsd:documentation>One of the arguments name,
identifierBag, or categoryBag must be supplied for data to
be returned.</xsd:documentation>
        </xsd:annotation>
        <xsd:complexType>
          <xsd:sequence>
            <xsd:element ref = "findQualifiers" minOccurs =
"0"/>
            <xsd:element ref = "name" minOccurs = "0"/>
            <xsd:element ref = "identifierBag" minOccurs =
"0"/>
            <xsd:element ref = "categoryBag" minOccurs = "0"/
>
          </xsd:sequence>
          <xsd:attribute ref = "generic"/>
          <xsd:attribute ref = "maxRows"/>
        </xsd:complexType>
      </xsd:element>
      <xsd:element name = "get_assertionStatusReport">
        <xsd:annotation>
          <xsd:documentation>Message - Request: This message
is used to request the current status of relationship and
reference information based on the relationship data defined
in the publisherAssertions message.</xsd:documentation>
        </xsd:annotation>
        <xsd:complexType>
          <xsd:sequence>
            <xsd:element ref = "authInfo"/>
```

```
          <xsd:element ref = "completionStatus" minOccurs =
"0"/>
        </xsd:sequence>
        <xsd:attribute ref = "generic"/>
      </xsd:complexType>
    </xsd:element>
    <xsd:element name = "get_authToken">
      <xsd:annotation>
        <xsd:documentation>Message - Request: used to
request an authentication token.  The response is an
authToken message.</xsd:documentation>
      </xsd:annotation>
      <xsd:complexType>
        <xsd:attribute ref = "generic"/>
        <xsd:attribute name = "userID" use = "required"
type = "xsd:string">
          <xsd:annotation>
            <xsd:documentation>Part of a user credential.
Used with get_authToken message.</xsd:documentation>
          </xsd:annotation>
        </xsd:attribute>
        <xsd:attribute name = "cred" use = "required" type
= "xsd:string">
          <xsd:annotation>
            <xsd:documentation>User credentials.  Typically
a password.  Can be a certificate or signed piece of data as
well.</xsd:documentation>
          </xsd:annotation>
        </xsd:attribute>
      </xsd:complexType>
    </xsd:element>
    <xsd:element name = "get_bindingDetail">
      <xsd:annotation>
        <xsd:documentation>Message - Request: Used to get
one or more bindingTemplate structures back based on the
identifiers passed.  Response is bindingDetail</
xsd:documentation>
      </xsd:annotation>
      <xsd:complexType>
        <xsd:sequence>
          <xsd:element ref = "bindingKey" maxOccurs =
"unbounded"/>
        </xsd:sequence>
        <xsd:attribute ref = "generic"/>
```

```
        </xsd:complexType>
      </xsd:element>
      <xsd:element name = "get_businessDetail">
        <xsd:annotation>
          <xsd:documentation>Message - Request: This message
is used to get the detailed information registered about
businessEntity data matching specific key value(s).</
xsd:documentation>
        </xsd:annotation>
        <xsd:complexType>
          <xsd:sequence>
            <xsd:element ref = "businessKey" maxOccurs =
"unbounded"/>
          </xsd:sequence>
          <xsd:attribute ref = "generic"/>
        </xsd:complexType>
      </xsd:element>
      <xsd:element name = "get_businessDetailExt">
        <xsd:annotation>
          <xsd:documentation>Message - Request: The extended
businessDetail messages define an  API that allows non-
operator UDDI registries to provide extended information via
a consistent API.  This message is the request that will
cause a businessDetailExt message to be returned.</
xsd:documentation>
        </xsd:annotation>
        <xsd:complexType>
          <xsd:sequence>
            <xsd:element ref = "businessKey" maxOccurs =
"unbounded"/>
          </xsd:sequence>
          <xsd:attribute ref = "generic"/>
        </xsd:complexType>
      </xsd:element>
      <xsd:element name = "get_publisherAssertions">
        <xsd:annotation>
          <xsd:documentation>Message - Request: This message
is used to get the complete set of assertion information
managed by a particular publisher.  The response is a
publisherAssertions message that contains the full assertion
set for the publisher associated with the authInfo token..</
xsd:documentation>
        </xsd:annotation>
        <xsd:complexType>
```

```
          <xsd:sequence>
            <xsd:element ref = "authInfo"/>
          </xsd:sequence>
          <xsd:attribute ref = "generic"/>
        </xsd:complexType>
      </xsd:element>
      <xsd:element name = "get_registeredInfo">
        <xsd:annotation>
          <xsd:documentation>Message - Request: This message
is used to support tool resynch by allowing a query to get
summarized information about registered businessEntity and
tModels for a given userID.  This API is intended to let
publishers determine what they've published.  As such,
authentication is required.  The response is a
registeredInfo message.</xsd:documentation>
        </xsd:annotation>
        <xsd:complexType>
          <xsd:sequence>
            <xsd:element ref = "authInfo"/>
          </xsd:sequence>
          <xsd:attribute ref = "generic"/>
        </xsd:complexType>
      </xsd:element>
      <xsd:element name = "get_serviceDetail">
        <xsd:annotation>
          <xsd:documentation>Message - Request: This message
is used to get the detailed information registered about
businessService data matching specific key value(s).</
xsd:documentation>
        </xsd:annotation>
        <xsd:complexType>
          <xsd:sequence>
            <xsd:element ref = "serviceKey" maxOccurs =
"unbounded"/>
          </xsd:sequence>
          <xsd:attribute ref = "generic"/>
        </xsd:complexType>
      </xsd:element>
      <xsd:element name = "get_tModelDetail">
        <xsd:annotation>
          <xsd:documentation>Message - Request: used to
request the details about one or more specific tModel
structures.  Results are returned in a tModelDetail
message.</xsd:documentation>
```

```
        </xsd:annotation>
        <xsd:complexType>
          <xsd:sequence>
            <xsd:element ref = "tModelKey" maxOccurs =
"unbounded"/>
          </xsd:sequence>
          <xsd:attribute ref = "generic"/>
        </xsd:complexType>
      </xsd:element>
      <xsd:element name = "publisherAssertions">
        <xsd:annotation>
          <xsd:documentation>Message - Response: response to
get_publisherAssertions request and the
set_publisherAssertions message.  Contains all of the
relationship assertions made by the requesting publisher.
This one structure contains all of the relationships
recorded by the publisher.</xsd:documentation>
        </xsd:annotation>
        <xsd:complexType>
          <xsd:sequence>
            <xsd:element ref = "publisherAssertion" minOccurs
= "0" maxOccurs = "unbounded"/>
          </xsd:sequence>
          <xsd:attribute ref = "generic"/>
          <xsd:attribute ref = "operator"/>
          <xsd:attribute ref = "authorizedName"/>
        </xsd:complexType>
      </xsd:element>
      <xsd:element name = "registeredInfo">
        <xsd:annotation>
          <xsd:documentation>Message - Response This
structure is used in the resynch process and is a response
to a get_registeredInfo message.</xsd:documentation>
        </xsd:annotation>
        <xsd:complexType>
          <xsd:sequence>
            <xsd:element ref = "businessInfos"/>
            <xsd:element ref = "tModelInfos"/>
          </xsd:sequence>
          <xsd:attribute ref = "generic"/>
          <xsd:attribute ref = "operator"/>
          <xsd:attribute ref = "truncated"/>
        </xsd:complexType>
      </xsd:element>
```

```
      <xsd:element name = "relatedBusinessesList">
        <xsd:annotation>
          <xsd:documentation>Message - Response: This is a
report - a list of related businesses in short form. This
message is the response to a find_relatedBusinesses query.</
xsd:documentation>
        </xsd:annotation>
        <xsd:complexType>
          <xsd:sequence>
            <xsd:element ref = "businessKey"/>
            <xsd:element ref = "relatedBusinessInfos"/>
          </xsd:sequence>
          <xsd:attribute ref = "generic"/>
          <xsd:attribute ref = "operator"/>
          <xsd:attribute ref = "truncated"/>
        </xsd:complexType>
      </xsd:element>

      <xsd:element name = "save_binding">
        <xsd:annotation>
          <xsd:documentation>Message - Request: This message
is used to save (add/update) information about one or more
bindingTemplate structures.</xsd:documentation>
        </xsd:annotation>
        <xsd:complexType>
          <xsd:sequence>
            <xsd:element ref = "authInfo"/>
            <xsd:element ref = "bindingTemplate" maxOccurs =
"unbounded"/>
          </xsd:sequence>
          <xsd:attribute ref = "generic"/>
        </xsd:complexType>
      </xsd:element>
      <xsd:element name = "save_business">
        <xsd:annotation>
          <xsd:documentation>Message - Request: used to save
(add/update) information describing one or more
businessEntity structures.  One of businessEntity or
uploadRegister is required.  Invalid if contains both or
neither type.</xsd:documentation>
        </xsd:annotation>
        <xsd:complexType>
          <xsd:sequence>
            <xsd:element ref = "authInfo"/>
```

```
            <xsd:element ref = "businessEntity" minOccurs =
"0" maxOccurs = "unbounded"/>
            <xsd:element ref = "uploadRegister" minOccurs =
"0" maxOccurs = "unbounded"/>
          </xsd:sequence>
          <xsd:attribute ref = "generic"/>
        </xsd:complexType>
      </xsd:element>
      <xsd:element name = "save_service">
        <xsd:annotation>
          <xsd:documentation>Message - Request: used to save
(add/update) information about one or more businessService
structures.</xsd:documentation>
        </xsd:annotation>
        <xsd:complexType>
          <xsd:sequence>
            <xsd:element ref = "authInfo"/>
            <xsd:element ref = "businessService" maxOccurs =
"unbounded"/>
          </xsd:sequence>
          <xsd:attribute ref = "generic"/>
        </xsd:complexType>
      </xsd:element>
      <xsd:element name = "save_tModel">
        <xsd:annotation>
          <xsd:documentation>Message - Request: used to
register or update a tModel.  One of tModel or
uploadRegister is required.  Invalid if contains both or
neither type.</xsd:documentation>
        </xsd:annotation>
        <xsd:complexType>
          <xsd:sequence>
            <xsd:element ref = "authInfo"/>
            <xsd:element ref = "tModel" minOccurs = "0"
maxOccurs = "unbounded"/>
            <xsd:element ref = "uploadRegister" minOccurs =
"0" maxOccurs = "unbounded"/>
          </xsd:sequence>
          <xsd:attribute ref = "generic"/>
        </xsd:complexType>
      </xsd:element>
      <xsd:element name = "serviceDetail">
        <xsd:annotation>
```

```
          <xsd:documentation>Message - Response: This message
is used to return full businessService details.</
xsd:documentation>
        </xsd:annotation>
        <xsd:complexType>
          <xsd:sequence>
            <xsd:element ref = "businessService" minOccurs =
"0" maxOccurs = "unbounded"/>
          </xsd:sequence>
          <xsd:attribute ref = "generic"/>
          <xsd:attribute ref = "operator"/>
          <xsd:attribute ref = "truncated"/>
        </xsd:complexType>
      </xsd:element>
      <xsd:element name = "serviceList">
        <xsd:annotation>
          <xsd:documentation>Message - Response: This message
is used to return results of a find_service request.</
xsd:documentation>
        </xsd:annotation>
        <xsd:complexType>
          <xsd:sequence>
            <xsd:element ref = "serviceInfos"/>
          </xsd:sequence>
          <xsd:attribute ref = "generic"/>
          <xsd:attribute ref = "operator"/>
          <xsd:attribute ref = "truncated"/>
        </xsd:complexType>
      </xsd:element>
      <xsd:element name = "set_publisherAssertions">
        <xsd:annotation>
          <xsd:documentation>Message - Request: This message
is used to save all relationship assertions information
managed by a particular publisher.  The response is a
publisherAssertions message containing all of the currently
registered assertions for an individual publisher account.</
xsd:documentation>
        </xsd:annotation>
        <xsd:complexType>
          <xsd:sequence>
            <xsd:element ref = "authInfo"/>
            <xsd:element ref = "publisherAssertion" minOccurs
= "0" maxOccurs = "unbounded"/>
          </xsd:sequence>
```

```
          <xsd:attribute ref = "generic"/>
        </xsd:complexType>
      </xsd:element>
      <xsd:element name = "tModelDetail">
        <xsd:annotation>
          <xsd:documentation>Message - Response:  returns all
exposed details about a tModel.  This is the response to a
get_tModelDetail message.</xsd:documentation>
        </xsd:annotation>
        <xsd:complexType>
          <xsd:sequence>
            <xsd:element ref = "tModel" maxOccurs =
"unbounded"/>
          </xsd:sequence>
          <xsd:attribute ref = "generic"/>
          <xsd:attribute ref = "operator"/>
          <xsd:attribute ref = "truncated"/>
        </xsd:complexType>
      </xsd:element>
      <xsd:element name = "tModelList">
        <xsd:annotation>
          <xsd:documentation>Message - Response: This is a
report - a list of tModels in short form. This message is
the response to a find_tModel query.</xsd:documentation>
        </xsd:annotation>
        <xsd:complexType>
          <xsd:sequence>
            <xsd:element ref = "tModelInfos"/>
          </xsd:sequence>
          <xsd:attribute ref = "generic"/>
          <xsd:attribute ref = "operator"/>
          <xsd:attribute ref = "truncated"/>
        </xsd:complexType>
      </xsd:element>
      <xsd:element name = "validate_values">
        <xsd:annotation>
          <xsd:documentation>This defines the SOAP 1.1 body
that will be used by operators who call third party
validation services.</xsd:documentation>
        </xsd:annotation>
        <xsd:complexType>
          <xsd:sequence>
            <xsd:element ref = "businessEntity" minOccurs =
"0" maxOccurs = "unbounded"/>
```

```
            <xsd:element ref = "businessService" minOccurs =
"0" maxOccurs = "unbounded"/>
            <xsd:element ref = "tModel" minOccurs = "0"
maxOccurs = "unbounded"/>
          </xsd:sequence>
          <xsd:attribute ref = "generic"/>
        </xsd:complexType>
      </xsd:element>

</xsd:schema>
```

APPENDIX H

The Original HTTP, as Defined in 1991

This document defines the Hypertext Transfer Protocol (HTTP) as originally implemented by the World Wide Web initiative software in the prototype released. This is a subset of the full HTTP protocol, and is known as HTTP 0.9.

No client profile information is transferred with the query. Future HTTP protocols will be back-compatible with this protocol.

This restricted protocol is very simple and may always be used when you do not need the capabilities of the full protocol, which is backwards compatible.

The definition of this protocol is in the public domain (see policy).

The protocol uses the normal internet-style telnet protocol style on a TCP-IP link. The following describes how a client acquires a (hypertext) document from an HTTP server, given an HTTP document address.

Connection

The client makes a TCP-IP connection to the host using the domain name or IP number, and the port number given in the address.

If the port number is not specified, 80 is always assumed for HTTP.

The server accepts the connection.

> **Note** HTTP currently runs over TCP, but could run over any connection-oriented service. The interpretation of the protocol below in the case of a sequenced packet service (such as DECnet(TM) or ISO TP4) is that the request should be one TPDU, but the response may be many.

Request

The client sends a document request consisting of a line of ASCII characters terminated by a CR LF (carriage return, line feed) pair. A well-behaved server will not require the carriage return character.

This request consists of the word "GET", a space, the document address, omitting the "http:," host, and port parts when they are the coordinates just used to make the connection. (If a gateway is being used, then a full document address may be given specifying a different naming scheme).

The document address will consist of a single word (i.e., no spaces). If any further words are found on the request line, they MUST either be ignored, or else treated according to the full HTTP spec.

The search functionality of the protocol lies in the ability of the addressing syntax to describe a search on a named index.

A search should only be requested by a client when the index document itself has been described as an index using the ISINDEX tag.

Response

The response to a simple GET request is a message in hypertext mark-up language (HTML). This is a byte stream of ASCII characters.

Lines shall be delimited by an optional carriage return followed by a mandatory line feed character. The client should not assume that the carriage return will be present. Lines may be of any length. Well-behaved servers should restrict line length to 80 characters, excluding the CR LF pair.

The format of the message is HTML—that is, a trimmed SGML document. Note that this format allows for menus and hit lists to be returned as hypertext. It also allows for plain ASCII text to be returned following the PLAINTEXT tag.

The message is terminated by the closing of the connection by the server.

Well-behaved clients will read the entire document as fast as possible. The client shall not wait for user action (output paging for example) before reading the whole of the document. The server may impose a timeout of the order of 15 seconds on inactivity.

Error responses are supplied in human-readable text in HTML syntax. There is no way to distinguish an error response from a satisfactory response except for the content of the text.

Disconnection

The TCP-IP connection is broken by the server when the whole document has been transferred.

The client may abort the transfer by breaking the connection before this, in which case the server shall not record any error condition.

Requests are idempotent. The server need not store any information about the request after disconnection.

APPENDIX I

SOAP 1.2 Working Draft

Here's the whole thing—the entire SOAP 1.2 specification, straight from the World Wide Web Consortium.

W3C Working Draft 9 July 2001

This version:

http://www.w3.org/TR/2001/WD-soap12-20010709/

Latest version:

http://www.w3.org/TR/soap12/

Editors:

Martin Gudgin (DevelopMentor)
Marc Hadley (Sun Microsystems)
Jean-Jacques Moreau (Canon)
Henrik Frystyk Nielsen (Microsoft Corp.)

Abstract

SOAP version 1.2 is a lightweight protocol for exchange of information in a decentralized, distributed environment. It is an XML based protocol that consists of four parts: an envelope that defines a framework for describing what is in a message and how to process it, a set of encoding rules for expressing instances of application-defined data types, a convention for representing remote procedure calls and responses and a binding convention for exchanging messages using an underlying protocol. SOAP can potentially be used in combination with a variety of other protocols; however, the only bindings defined in this document describe how to use SOAP in combination with HTTP and the experimental HTTP Extension Framework.

Status of this Document

This section describes the status of this document at the time of its publication. Other documents may supersede this document. The latest status of this document series is maintained at the W3C.

This is the first W3C Working Draft of the SOAP version 1.2 specification for review by W3C members and other interested parties. It has been produced by the XML Protocol Working Group (WG), which is part of the XML Protocol Activity.

The XML Protocol Protocol Working Group has, in keeping with its charter, produced a set of requirements and usage scenarios that have been published as a Working Draft. To better evaluate SOAP/1.1 against these requirements and usage scenarios, the Working Group has produced an abstract model and a glossary of terms and concepts used by the Working Group. In addition, the Working Group has produced an issues list that describes issues and concerns raised by mapping its requirements and the XMLP abstract model against the SOAP/1.1 specification as well as issues raised on the <xml-dist-app@w3.org> mailing list against SOAP/1.1.

The current name for this specification is SOAP version 1.2, this first Working Draft being based on SOAP/1.1 as per the Working Group's charter (see change log in appendix D)

Comments on this document should be sent to xmlp-comments@w3.org (public archives). It is inappropriate to send discussion emails to this address.

Discussion of this document takes place on the public <xml-dist-app@w3.org> mailing list (Archives) per the email communication rules in the XML Protocol Working Group Charter.

This is a public W3C Working Draft. It is a draft document and may be updated, replaced, or obsoleted by other documents at any time. It is inappropriate to use W3C Working Drafts as reference material or to cite them as other than "work in progress". A list of all W3C technical reports can be found at http://www.w3.org/TR/.

Table of Contents

1. Introduction

SOAP version 1.2 provides a simple and lightweight mechanism for exchanging structured and typed information between peers in a decentralized, distributed environment using XML. SOAP does not itself define any application semantics such as a programming model or implementation specific semantics; rather it defines a simple mechanism for expressing application semantics by providing a modular packaging model and encoding mechanisms for encoding application defined data. This allows SOAP to be used in a large variety of systems ranging from messaging systems to remote procedure calls (RPC).

SOAP consists of four parts:

1. The SOAP envelope (see section 4) construct defines an overall framework for expressing *what* is in a message, *who* should deal with it, and whether it is *optional* or *mandatory*.
2. The SOAP encoding rules (see section 5) defines a serialization mechanism that can be used to exchange instances of application-defined datatypes.
3. The SOAP RPC representation (see section 7) defines a convention that can be used to represent remote procedure calls and responses.
4. The SOAP binding (see section 6) defines a convention for exchanging SOAP envelopes between peers using an underlying protocol for transport.

To simplify the specification, these four parts are functionally orthogonal. In particular, the envelope and the encoding rules are defined in different namespaces.

This specification defines two SOAP bindings that describe how a SOAP message can be carried in HTTP [5] messages either with or without the experimental HTTP Extension Framework [6].

1.1 Design Goals

Two major design goals for SOAP are simplicity and extensibility. SOAP attempts to meet these goals by omitting features often found in messaging systems and distributed object systems such as:

- distributed garbage collection;
- boxcarring or batching of messages;
- objects-by-reference (which requires distributed garbage collection);
- activation (which requires objects-by-reference).

1.2 Notational Conventions

The keywords "MUST", "MUST NOT", "REQUIRED", "SHALL", "SHALL NOT", "SHOULD", "SHOULD NOT", "RECOMMENDED", "MAY", and "OPTIONAL" in this document are to be interpreted as described in RFC-2119 [2].

The namespace prefixes "env" and "enc" used in the prose sections of this document are associated with the SOAP namespace names "http://www.w3.org/2001/06/soap-envelope" and "http://www.w3.org/2001/06/soap-encoding" respectively.

The namespace prefixes "xs" and "xsi" used in the prose sections of this document are associated with the namespace names "http://www.w3.org/2001/XMLSchema" and "http://www.w3.org/2001/XMLSchema-instance" respectively, both of which are defined in the XML Schemas specification [10,11].

Note that the choice of any namespace prefix is arbitrary and not semantically significant.

Namespace URIs of the general form "http://example.org/..." and "http://example.com/..." represent an application-dependent or context-dependent URI [4].

This specification uses the augmented Backus-Naur Form (BNF) as described in RFC-2616 [5].

Editorial notes are indicated with yellow background (may not appear in all media) and prefixed with "Ednote".

1.3 Examples of SOAP Messages

The first example shows a simple notification message expressed in SOAP. The message contains the header block "alertcontrol" and the body block "alert" which are both application defined and not defined by SOAP. The header block contains the parameters "priority" and "expires" which may be of use to intermediaries as well as the ultimate destination of the message. The body block contains the actual notification message to be delivered.

EXAMPLE I–0 Sample SOAP Message containing a header block and a body block

```
<env:Envelope xmlns:env="http://www.w3.org/2001/06/
soap-envelope">
 <env:Header>
  <n:alertcontrol xmlns:n="http://example.org/
alertcontrol">
   <n:priority>1</n:priority>
   <n:expires>2001-06-22T14:00:00-05:00</n:expires>
  </n:alertcontrol>
 </env:Header>
 <env:Body>
  <m:alert xmlns:m="http://example.org/alert">
   <m:msg>Pick up Mary at school at 2pm</m:msg>
  </m:alert>
 </env:Body>
</env:Envelope>
```

SOAP messages may be bound to different underlying protocols and used in a variety of message exchange patterns. The following example shows SOAP used in connection with HTTP as the underlying protocol taking advantage of the request/response mechanism provided by HTTP (see section section 6).

Examples 1 and 2 show a sample SOAP/HTTP request and a sample SOAP/HTTP response. The SOAP/HTTP request contains a block called GetLastTradePrice which takes a single parameter, the ticker symbol for a stock. As in the previous example, the GetLastTradePrice element is not defined by SOAP itself. The service's response to this request contains a single parameter, the price of the stock. The SOAP Envelope element is the top element of the XML document representing the SOAP message. XML namespaces are used to disambiguate SOAP identifiers from application specific identifiers.

EXAMPLE I–1 Sample SOAP Message embedded in an HTTP Request

```
POST /StockQuote HTTP/1.1
Host: www.stockquoteserver.com
Content-Type: text/xml; charset="utf-8"
Content-Length: nnnn
SOAPAction: "http://example.org/2001/06/quotes"

<env:Envelope xmlns:env="http://www.w3.org/2001/06/
soap-envelope" >
 <env:Body>
  <m:GetLastTradePrice
        env:encodingStyle="http://www.w3.org/2001/
06/soap-encoding"
        xmlns:m="http://example.org/2001/06/
quotes">
    <symbol>DIS</symbol>
  </m:GetLastTradePrice>
 </env:Body>
</env:Envelope>
```

Example 2 shows the SOAP message sent by the StockQuote service in the corresponding HTTP response to the request from Example 1.

EXAMPLE I–2 Sample SOAP Message embedded in an HTTP Response

```
HTTP/1.1 200 OK
Content-Type: text/xml; charset="utf-8"
Content-Length: nnnn

<env:Envelope xmlns:env="http://www.w3.org/2001/06/
soap-envelope" >
 <env:Body>
  <m:GetLastTradePriceResponse
        env:encodingStyle="http://www.w3.org/2001/
06/soap-encoding"
        xmlns:m="http://example.org/2001/06/
quotes">
    <Price>34.5</Price>
  </m:GetLastTradePriceResponse>
 </env:Body>
</env:Envelope>
```

More examples are available in Appendix A.

1.4 SOAP Terminology

1.4.1 PROTOCOL CONCEPTS

SOAP

The formal set of conventions governing the format and processing rules of a SOAP message and basic control of interaction among applications generating and accepting SOAP messages for the purpose of exchanging information along a SOAP message path.

SOAP BINDING

The formal set of rules for carrying a SOAP message within or on top of another protocol (underlying protocol) for the purpose of transmission. Typical SOAP bindings include carrying a SOAP message within an HTTP message, or on top of TCP.

SOAP NODE

A SOAP node processes a SOAP message according to the formal set of conventions defined by SOAP. The SOAP node is responsible for enforcing the rules that govern the exchange of SOAP messages and accesses the services provided by the underlying protocols through SOAP bindings. Non-compliance with SOAP conventions can cause a SOAP node to generate a SOAP fault (see also SOAP receiver and SOAP sender).

1.4.2 DATA ENCAPSULATION CONCEPTS

SOAP MESSAGE

A SOAP message is the basic unit of communication between peer SOAP nodes.

SOAP ENVELOPE

The outermost syntactic construct or structure of a SOAP message defined by SOAP within which all other syntactic elements of the message are enclosed.

SOAP BLOCK

A syntactic construct or structure used to delimit data that logically constitutes a single computational unit as seen by a SOAP node. A SOAP block is identified by the fully qualified name of the outer element for the block, which consists of the namespace URI and the local name. A block encapsulated within the SOAP header is called a header block and a block encapsulated within a SOAP body is called a body block.

SOAP HEADER

A collection of zero or more SOAP blocks which may be targeted at any SOAP receiver within the SOAP message path.

SOAP BODY

A collection of zero, or more SOAP blocks targeted at the ultimate SOAP receiver within the SOAP message path.

SOAP FAULT

A special SOAP block which contains fault information generated by a SOAP node.

The following diagram illustrates how a SOAP message is composed.

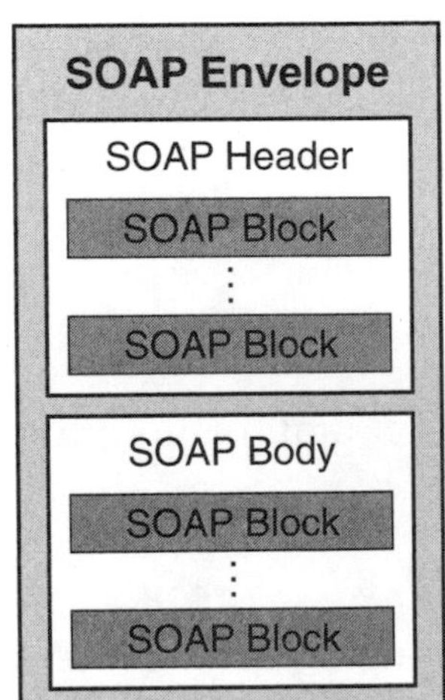

FIGURE I–1 Encapsulation model illustrating the parts of a SOAP message

1.4.3 MESSAGE SENDER AND RECEIVER CONCEPTS

SOAP SENDER

A SOAP sender is a SOAP node that transmits a SOAP message.

SOAP RECEIVER

A SOAP receiver is a SOAP node that accepts a SOAP message.

SOAP MESSAGE PATH

The set of SOAP senders and SOAP receivers through which a single SOAP message passes. This includes the initial SOAP sender, zero or more SOAP intermediaries, and the ultimate SOAP receiver.

INITIAL SOAP SENDER

The SOAP sender that originates a SOAP message as the starting point of a SOAP message path.

SOAP INTERMEDIARY

A SOAP intermediary is both a SOAP receiver and a SOAP sender, target-able from within a SOAP message. It processes a defined set of blocks in a SOAP message along a SOAP message path. It acts in order to forward the SOAP message towards the ultimate SOAP receiver.

ULTIMATE SOAP RECEIVER

The SOAP receiver that the initial sender specifies as the final destination of the SOAP message within a SOAP message path. A SOAP message may not reach the ultimate recipient because of a SOAP fault generated by a SOAP node along the SOAP message path.

1.4.4 DATA ENCODING CONCEPTS

SOAP DATA MODEL

A set of abstract constructs that can be used to describe common data types and link relationships in data.

SOAP DATA ENCODING

The syntactic representation of data described by the SOAP data model within one or more SOAP blocks in a SOAP message.

2. The SOAP Message Exchange Model

SOAP messages are fundamentally one-way transmissions from a SOAP sender to a SOAP receiver, but as illustrated above, SOAP messages are often combined to implement patterns such as request/response.

SOAP implementations can be optimized to exploit the unique characteristics of particular network systems. For example, the HTTP binding described in section 6 provides for SOAP response messages to be delivered as HTTP responses, using the same connection as the inbound request.

2.1 SOAP Nodes

A SOAP node can be the initial SOAP sender, the ultimate SOAP receiver, or a SOAP intermediary, in which case it is both a SOAP sender and a SOAP receiver. SOAP does not provide a routing mechanism, however SOAP does recognise that a SOAP sender originates a SOAP message which is sent to an ultimate SOAP receiver, via zero or more SOAP intermediaries.

A SOAP node receiving a SOAP message MUST perform processing, generate SOAP faults, SOAP responses, and if appropriate send additional SOAP messages, as provided by the remainder of this specification.

2.2 SOAP Actors and SOAP Nodes

In processing a SOAP message, a SOAP node is said to act in the role of one or more SOAP actors, each of which is identified by a URI known as the SOAP actor name. Each SOAP node MUST act in the role of the special SOAP actor named "http://www.w3.org/2001/06/soap-envelope/actor/next", and can additionally assume the roles of zero or more other SOAP actors. A SOAP node can establish itself as the ultimate SOAP receiver by acting in the (additional) role of the anonymous SOAP actor. The roles assumed MUST be invariant during the processing of an individual SOAP message; because this specification deals only with the processing of individual SOAP messages, no statement is made regarding the possibility that a given piece of software might or might not act in varying roles when processing more than one SOAP message.

While the purpose of a SOAP actor name is to identify a SOAP node, there are no routing or message exchange semantics associated with the SOAP actor name. For example, SOAP Actors MAY be named with a URI useable to route SOAP messages to an appropriate SOAP node. Conversely, it is also appropriate to use SOAP actor roles with names that are related more indirectly to message routing (e.g. "http://example.org/banking/anyAccountMgr") or which are unrelated to routing (e.g. a URI meant to identify "all cache management software"; such a header might be used, for example, to carry an indication to any concerned software that the containing SOAP message is idempotent, and can safely be cached and replayed.)

2.3 Targeting SOAP Header Blocks

SOAP header blocks carry optional env:actor attributes (see section 4.2.2) that are used to target them to the appropriate SOAP node(s). SOAP header blocks with no env:actor attribute and the SOAP body are implicitly targeted at the anonymous SOAP actor, implying that they are to be processed by the ultimate SOAP receiver. We refer to the (implicit or explicit) value of the SOAP actor attribute as the SOAP actor for the corresponding SOAP block (either a SOAP header block or a SOAP body block).

We say that a SOAP block is targeted to a SOAP node if the SOAP actor (if present) on the block matches (see [8]) a role played by the SOAP node, or in the case of a SOAP block with no actor attribute (including SOAP body blocks), if the SOAP node has assumed the role of the anonymous SOAP actor.

2.4 Understanding SOAP Headers

We presume that specifications for a wide variety of header functions will be developed over time, and that each SOAP node MAY include the software necessary to implement one or more such extensions. We say that a SOAP header block is understood by a SOAP node if the software at that SOAP node has been written to fully conform to and implement the semantics conveyed by the fully qualified name of the outer-most element of that block.

When a SOAP header block is tagged with a SOAP mustUnderstand attribute with a value of "1", the targeted SOAP node MUST: either process the SOAP block according to the semantics conveyed by the fully qualified name of the outermost element of that block; or not process the SOAP message at all, and fail (see section 4.4).

2.5 Processing SOAP Messages

This section sets out the rules by which SOAP messages are processed. Unless otherwise stated, processing must be semantically equivalent to performing the following steps separately, and in the order given. Note however that nothing in this specification should be taken to prevent the use of optimistic concurrency, roll back, or other techniques that might provide increased flexibility in processing order as long as all SOAP messages, SOAP faults and application-level side effects are equivalent to those that would be obtained by direct implementation of the following rules.

1. Generate a single SOAP mustUnderstand fault if one or more SOAP blocks targeted at the SOAP node carry the attribute env:mustUnderstand="1" and are not understood by that node. If such a fault is generated, any further processing MUST NOT be done.
2. Process SOAP blocks targeted at the SOAP node, generating SOAP faults if necessary. A SOAP node MUST process SOAP blocks identified as env:mustUnderstand="1". A SOAP node MAY process or ignore SOAP blocks not so identified. In all cases where a SOAP

block is processed, the SOAP node must understand the SOAP block and must do such processing in a manner fully conformant with the specification for that SOAP block. Faults, if any, must also conform to the specification for the processed SOAP block. It is possible that the processing of particular SOAP block would control or determine the order of processing for other SOAP blocks. For example, one could create a SOAP header block to force processing of other SOAP header blocks in lexical order. In the absence of such a SOAP block, the order of processing is at the discretion of the SOAP node. SOAP nodes can make reference to any information in the SOAP envelope when processing a SOAP block. For example, a caching function can cache the entire SOAP message, if desired.

If the SOAP node is a SOAP intermediary, the SOAP message pattern and results of processing (e.g. no fault generated) MAY require that the SOAP message be sent further along the SOAP message path. Such relayed SOAP messages MUST contain all SOAP header blocks and the SOAP body blocks from the original SOAP message, in the original order, except that SOAP header blocks targeted at the SOAP intermediary MUST be removed (such SOAP blocks are removed regardless of whether they were processed or ignored). Additional SOAP header blocks MAY be inserted at any point in the SOAP message, and such inserted SOAP header blocks MAY be indistinguishable from one or more just removed (effectively leaving them in place, but emphasizing the need to reinterpret at each SOAP node along the SOAP message path.)

3. Relation to XML

All SOAP messages are encoded using XML (see [7] for more information on XML).

A SOAP application SHOULD include the proper SOAP namespace on all elements and attributes defined by SOAP in messages that it generates. A SOAP application MUST be able to process SOAP namespaces in messages that it receives. It

MUST discard messages that have incorrect namespaces (see section 4.4) and it MAY process SOAP messages without SOAP namespaces as though they had the correct SOAP namespaces.

SOAP defines the following namespaces (see [8] for more information on XML namespaces):

- The SOAP envelope has the namespace identifier "http://www.w3.org/2001/06/soap-envelope"
- The SOAP serialization has the namespace identifier "http://www.w3.org/2001/06/soap-encoding"
- The SOAP mustUnderstand fault namespace identifier "http://www.w3.org/2001/06/soap-faults"
- The SOAP upgrade namespace identifier "http://www.w3.org/2001/06/soap-upgrade"

Schema documents for these namespaces can be found by dereferencing the namespace identifiers.

A SOAP message MUST NOT contain a Document Type Declaration. A SOAP message MUST NOT contain Processing Instructions. [7]

SOAP uses the local, unqualified "id" attribute of type "ID" to specify the unique identifier of an encoded element. SOAP uses the local, unqualified attribute "href" of type "anyURI" to specify a reference to that value, in a manner conforming to the XML Specification [7], XML Schema Specification [11], and XML Linking Language Specification [9].

With the exception of the SOAP mustUnderstand attribute (see section 4.2.3) and the SOAP actor attribute (see section 4.2.2), it is generally permissible to have attributes and their values appear in XML instances or alternatively in schemas, with equal effect. That is, declaration in a DTD or schema with a default or fixed value is semantically equivalent to appearance in an instance.

4. SOAP Envelope

A SOAP message is an XML document that consists of a mandatory SOAP envelope, an optional SOAP Header, and a mandatory SOAP Body. This XML document is referred to as a SOAP message for the rest of this specification. The namespace identifier for the elements and attributes defined in this section is "http://www.w3.org/2001/06/soap-envelope". A SOAP message contains the following:

- A SOAP envelope. This is the top element of the XML document representing the SOAP message.
- A SOAP Header. This is a generic mechanism for adding features to a SOAP message in a decentralized manner without prior agreement between the communicating parties (a SOAP sender, a SOAP receiver, and possibly one or more SOAP intermediaries). SOAP defines a few attributes that can be used to indicate who should deal with a feature and whether it is optional or mandatory (see section 4.2)
- A SOAP Body. This is a container for mandatory information intended for the ultimate SOAP receiver (see section 4.3). SOAP defines a SOAP fault for reporting errors.

The grammar rules are as follows:

1. SOAP envelope
   - The element name is "Envelope".
   - The element MUST be present in a SOAP message
   - The element MAY contain namespace declarations as well as additional attributes. If present, such additional attributes MUST be namespace-qualified. Similarly, the element MAY contain additional sub-elements. If present these sub-elements MUST be namespace-qualified and MUST come immediately after the SOAP Body.
2. SOAP Header (see section 4.2)
   - The element name is "Header".
   - The element MAY be present in a SOAP message. If present, the element MUST be the first immediate child element of a SOAP envelope.
   - The element MAY contain a set of SOAP header blocks, each being an immediate child element of the SOAP Header. All immediate child elements of the SOAP Header MUST be namespace-qualified.
3. SOAP Body (see section 4.3)
   - The element name is "Body".

- The element MUST be present in a SOAP message and MUST be an immediate child element of a SOAP Envelope. It MUST come immediately after the SOAP Header, if present. Otherwise, it MUST be the first immediate child element of the SOAP envelope.
- The element MAY contain a set of SOAP body blocks, each being an immediate child element of the SOAP Body. Immediate child elements of the SOAP Body MAY be namespace-qualified. At most one child element MAY be a SOAP fault. The SOAP fault is used to carry error information (see section 4.4).

4.1.1 SOAP ENCODINGSTYLE ATTRIBUTE

The SOAP encodingStyle global attribute can be used to indicate the serialization rules used in a SOAP message. This attribute MAY appear on any element, and is scoped to that element's contents and all child elements not themselves containing such an attribute, much as an XML namespace declaration is scoped. There is no default encoding defined for a SOAP message.

The attribute value is an ordered list of one or more URIs identifying the serialization rule or rules that can be used to deserialize the SOAP message indicated in the order of most specific to least specific. Example 3 shows three sample values for the encodingStyle attribute.

EXAMPLE I–3 Example values for the encodingStyle attribute

```
encodingStyle="http://www.w3.org/2001/06/soap-
encoding"
encodingStyle="http://example.org/encoding/
restricted http://example.org/encoding/"
encodingStyle=""
```

The serialization rules defined by SOAP in section 5 are identified by the URI "http://www.w3.org/2001/06/soap-encoding". SOAP messages using this particular serialization SHOULD indicate this using the SOAP encodingStyle attribute. In addition, all URIs syntactically beginning with "http://www.w3.org/2001/06/soap-encoding" indicate conformance with the SOAP encoding rules defined in section 5 (though with potentially tighter rules added).

A value of the zero-length URI ("") explicitly indicates that no claims are made for the encoding style of contained elements. This can be used to turn off any claims from containing elements.

4.1.2 ENVELOPE VERSIONING MODEL

SOAP does not define a traditional versioning model based on major and minor version numbers. A SOAP message MUST contain a SOAP envelope associated with the "http://www.w3.org/2001/06/soap-envelope" namespace. If a SOAP message is received by a SOAP node in which the SOAP envelope is associated with a different namespace, the SOAP node MUST treat this as a version error and generate a VersionMismatch SOAP fault (see section 4.4). A SOAP VersionMismatch fault message MUST use the SOAP/1.1 envelope namespace "http://schemas.xmlsoap.org/soap/envelope/" (see Appendix C).

4.2 SOAP Header

SOAP provides a flexible mechanism for extending a SOAP message in a decentralized and modular way without prior knowledge between the communicating parties. Typical examples of extensions that can be implemented as SOAP header blocks are authentication, transaction management, payment, etc.

The SOAP Header is encoded as the first immediate child element of the SOAP envelope. All immediate child elements of the SOAP Header are called SOAP header blocks.

The encoding rules for SOAP header blocks are as follows:

1. A SOAP header block is identified by its fully qualified element name, which consists of the namespace URI and the local name. All immediate child elements of the SOAP Header MUST be namespace-qualified.
2. The SOAP encodingStyle attribute MAY be used to indicate the encoding style used for the SOAP header blocks (see section 4.1.1).
3. The SOAP actor attribute (see section 4.2.2) and SOAP mustUnderstand attribute (see section 4.2.3) MAY be used to indicate which SOAP node will process the

SOAP header block, and how it will be processed (see section 4.2.1).

4.2.1 USE OF HEADER ATTRIBUTES

The SOAP Header attributes defined in this section determine how a SOAP receiver should process an incoming SOAP message, as described in section 2. A SOAP sender generating a SOAP message SHOULD only use the SOAP Header attributes on immediate child elements of the SOAP Header. A SOAP receiver MUST ignore all SOAP Header attributes that are not applied to an immediate child element of the SOAP Header.

An example is a SOAP header block with an element identifier of "Transaction", a "mustUnderstand" value of "1", and a value of 5, as shown in Example 4.

EXAMPLE I–4 Example header with a single header block

```
<env:Header xmlns:env="http://www.w3.org/2001/06/
soap-envelope" >
  <t:Transaction xmlns:t="http://example.org/2001/
06/tx" env:mustUnderstand="1" >
    5
  </t:Transaction>
</env:Header>
```

4.2.2 SOAP ACTOR ATTRIBUTE

EdNote: This section partially overlaps with section 2. We expect this to be reconciled in a future revision of the specification.

A SOAP message travels from an initial SOAP sender to an ultimate SOAP receiver, potentially passing through a set of SOAP intermediaries along a SOAP message path. Both intermediaries as well as the ultimate SOAP receiver are identified by a URI.

Not all parts of a SOAP message may be intended for the ultimate SOAP receiver. They may be intended instead for one or more SOAP intermediaries on the SOAP message path. However, a SOAP intermediary MUST NOT forward further a SOAP header block intended for it. This would be considered as a breach of contract, the contract being only between the SOAP node which generated the SOAP header block, and the SOAP intermediary itself. However, the SOAP intermediary MAY instead insert a similar SOAP header block, which effectively sets up a new contract between that SOAP intermediary and the SOAP node at which the SOAP header block is targeted.

The SOAP actor global attribute can be used to indicate the SOAP node at which a particular SOAP header block is targeted. The value of the SOAP actor attribute is a URI. The special URI "http://www.w3.org/2001/06/soap-envelope/actor/next" indicates that the SOAP header block is intended for the very first SOAP node that processes the message. This is similar to the hop-by-hop scope model represented by the Connection header field in HTTP.

Omitting the SOAP actor attribute indicates that the SOAP header block is targeted at the ultimate SOAP receiver.

This attribute MUST appear in the SOAP message itself in order to be effective, and not in an eventual corresponding XML Schema (see section 3 and 4.2.1).

4.2.3 SOAP MUSTUNDERSTAND ATTRIBUTE

EdNote: This section partially overlaps with section 2. We expect this to be reconciled in a future revision of the specification.

The SOAP mustUnderstand global attribute can be used to indicate whether the processing of a SOAP header block is mandatory or optional at the target SOAP node. The target SOAP node itself is defined by the SOAP actor attribute (see section 4.2.2). The value of the SOAP mustUnderstand attribute is either "1" or "0". The absence of this attribute is semantically equivalent to its presence with the value "0", which means processing the block is optional.

When a SOAP header block is tagged with a SOAP mustUnderstand attribute with a value of "1", the targeted SOAP node MUST: either process the SOAP block according to the semantics conveyed by the fully qualified name of the outermost element of that block; or not process the SOAP message at all, and fail (see section 4.4).

The SOAP mustUnderstand attribute allows for robust evolution. Elements tagged with the SOAP mustUnderstand attribute with a value of "1" MUST be presumed to somehow modify the semantics of their parent or peer elements. Tagging elements in this manner assures that this change in semantics will not be silently (and, presumably, erroneously) ignored by those who may not fully understand it.

This attribute MUST appear in the SOAP message itself in order to be effective, and not in an eventual corresponding XML Schema (see section 3 and 4.2.1).

4.3 SOAP Body

The SOAP Body element provides a simple mechanism for exchanging mandatory information intended for the ultimate SOAP receiver of a SOAP message. Typical uses of SOAP Body include marshalling RPC calls and error reporting.

The SOAP Body element is an immediate child element of a SOAP envelope. If a SOAP Header is present then the SOAP Body MUST immediately follow the SOAP Header, otherwise it MUST be the first immediate child element of the SOAP envelope.

All immediate child elements of the SOAP Body are called SOAP body blocks, and each SOAP body block is encoded as an independent element within the SOAP Body.

The encoding rules for SOAP body blocks are as follows:

1. A SOAP body block is identified by its fully qualified element name, which consists of the namespace URI and the local name. Immediate child elements of the SOAP Body element MAY be namespace-qualified.
2. The SOAP encodingStyle attribute MAY be used to indicate the encoding style used for the SOAP body blocks (see section 4.1.1).

SOAP defines one particular SOAP body block, the SOAP fault, which is used for reporting errors (see section 4.4).

4.3.1 RELATIONSHIP BETWEEN SOAP HEADER AND BODY

While both SOAP Header and SOAP Body are defined as independent elements, they are in fact related. The relationship between a SOAP body block and a SOAP header block is as follows: a SOAP body block is semantically equivalent to a SOAP header block targeted at the anonymous actor and with a

SOAP mustUnderstand attribute with a value of "1". The anonymous actor is indicated by omitting the actor attribute (see section 4.2.2).

4.4 SOAP Fault

The SOAP fault is used to carry error and/or status information within a SOAP message. If present, the SOAP fault MUST appear as a SOAP body block and MUST NOT appear more than once within a SOAP Body.

The SOAP Fault defines the following four sub-elements:

FAULTCODE

The faultcode element is intended for use by software to provide an algorithmic mechanism for identifying the fault. The faultcode MUST be present in a SOAP fault and the faultcode value MUST be a qualified name as defined in [8], section 3. SOAP defines a small set of SOAP fault codes covering basic SOAP faults (see section 4.4.1)

FAULTSTRING

The faultstring element is intended to provide a human readable explanation of the fault and is not intended for algorithmic processing. The faultstring element is similar to the 'Reason-Phrase' defined by HTTP (see [5], section 6.1). It MUST be present in a SOAP fault and SHOULD provide at least some information explaining the nature of the fault.

FAULTACTOR

The faultactor element is intended to provide information about which SOAP node on the SOAP message path caused the fault to happen (see section 2). It is similar to the SOAP actor attribute (see section 4.2.2) but instead of indicating the target of a SOAP header block, it indicates the source of the fault. The value of the faultactor attribute is a URI identifying the source. SOAP nodes that do not act as the ultimate SOAP receiver MUST include the faultactor element in the SOAP fault. The ultimate SOAP receiver MAY use the faultactor element to indicate explicitly that it generated the fault (see also the detail element below).

DETAIL

The detail element is intended for carrying application specific error information related to the SOAP Body. It MUST be present when the contents of the SOAP Body could not be processed successfully. It MUST NOT be used to carry error information about any SOAP header blocks. Detailed error information for SOAP header blocks MUST be carried within the SOAP header blocks themselves, see section 4.4.2 for an example.

The absence of the detail element in the SOAP fault indicates that the fault is not related to the processing of the SOAP Body. This can be used to find out whether the SOAP Body was at least partially processed by the ultimate SOAP receiver before the fault occurred, or not.

All immediate child elements of the detail element are called detail entries, and each detail entry is encoded as an independent element within the detail element.

The encoding rules for detail entries are as follows (see also example 10):

1. A detail entry is identified by its fully qualified element name, which consists of the namespace URI and the local name. Immediate child elements of the detail element MAY be namespace-qualified.
2. The SOAP encodingStyle attribute MAY be used to indicate the encoding style used for the detail entries (see section 4.1.1).

4.4.1 SOAP FAULT CODES

The SOAP faultcode values defined in this section MUST be used in the SOAP faultcode element when describing faults defined by this specification. The namespace identifier for these SOAP faultcode values is "http://www.w3.org/2001/06/soap-envelope". Use of this space is recommended (but not required) in the specification of methods defined outside of the present specification.

The default SOAP faultcode values are defined in an extensible manner that allows for new SOAP faultcode values to be defined while maintaining backwards compatibility with existing SOAP faultcode values. The mechanism used is very similar to the 1xx, 2xx, 3xx etc basic status classes classes defined in HTTP (see [5] section 10). However, instead of integers, they are defined as XML qualified names (see [8] section 3). The character "." (dot) is used as a separator of SOAP faultcode values indicating that what is to the left of the dot is a more generic fault code value than the value to the right. This is illustrated in Example 5.

EXAMPLE I–5 Example of an authentication fault code

```
Client.Authentication
```

The faultcode values defined by SOAP are listed in the following table.

NAME	MEANING
`VersionMismatch`	The processing party found an invalid namespace for the SOAP envelope element (see section 4.1.2)
`MustUnderstand`	An immediate child element of the SOAP Header element that was either not understood or not obeyed by the processing party contained a SOAP mustUnderstand attribute with a value of "1" (see section 4.2.3)
`Client`	The Client class of errors indicate that the message was incorrectly formed or did not contain the appropriate information in order to succeed. For example, the message could lack the proper authentication or payment information. It is generally an indication that the message should not be resent without change. See also section 4.4 for a description of the SOAP Fault detail sub-element.
`Server`	The Server class of errors indicate that the message could not be processed for reasons not directly attributable to the contents of the message itself but rather to the processing of the message. For example, processing could include communicating with an upstream SOAP node, which did not respond. The message may succeed at a later point in time. See also section 4.4 for a description of the SOAP Fault detail sub-element.

4.4.2 MUSTUNDERSTAND FAULTS

When a SOAP node generates a MustUnderstand fault, it SHOULD provide, in the generated fault message, header blocks as described below which detail the qualified names (QNames, per the XML Schema Datatypes specification) of the particular header block(s) which were not understood.

Each such header block has a local name of Misunderstood and a namespace name of "http://www.w3.org/2001/06/soap-faults". Each block has an unqualified attribute with a local name of qname whose value is the QName of a header block which the faulting node failed to understand.

For example, the message shown in Example 6 will result in the fault message shown in Example 7 if the recipient of the initial message does not understand the two header elements `abc:Extension1` and `def:Extension2`.

EXAMPLE I–6 SOAP envelope that will cause a SOAP MustUnderstand fault if Extension1 or Extension2 are not understood

```
<env:Envelope xmlns:env='http://www.w3.org/2001/06/
soap-envelope'>
  <env:Header>
    <abc:Extension1 xmlns:abc='http://example.org/
2001/06/ext'
                              env:mustUnderstand='1' />
    <def:Extension2 xmlns:def='http://example.com/
stuff'
                              env:mustUnderstand='1' />
  </env:Header>
  <env:Body>
  . . .
  </env:Body>
</env:Envelope>
```

EXAMPLE I–7 SOAP fault generated as a result of not understanding Extension1 and Extension2 in Example 6

```
<env:Envelope xmlns:env='http://www.w3.org/2001/06/
soap-envelope'
     xmlns:f='http://www.w3.org/2001/06/soap-
faults' >
  <env:Header>
    <f:Misunderstood qname='abc:Extension1'

xmlns:abc='http://example.org/2001/06/ext' />
    <f:Misunderstood qname='def:Extension2'

xmlns:def='http://example.com/stuff' />
  </env:Header>
  <env:Body>
    <env:Fault>
      <faultcode>MustUnderstand</faultcode>
      <faultstring>One or more mandatory headers
not understood</faultstring>
    </env:Fault>
  </env:Body>
</env:Envelope>
```

Note that there is no requirement that the namespace prefix returned in the value of the qname attribute match the namespace prefix of the original header element. Provided the prefix maps to the same namespace name the faulting node may use any prefix.

Note also that there is no guarantee that each MustUnderstand error contains ALL misunderstood header QNames. SOAP nodes MAY generate a fault after the first header block that causes an error containing details about that single header block only, alternatively SOAP nodes MAY generate a combined fault detailing all of the MustUnderstand problems at once.

5. SOAP Encoding

The SOAP encoding style is based on a simple type system that is a generalization of the common features found in type systems in programming languages, databases and semi-structured data. A type either is a simple (scalar) type or is a compound type constructed as a composite of several parts, each with a type. This is described in more detail below. This section defines rules for serialization of a graph of typed objects. It operates on two levels. First, given a schema in any notation consistent with the type system described, a schema for an XML grammar may be constructed. Second, given a type-system schema and a particular graph of values conforming to that schema, an XML instance may be constructed. In reverse, given an XML instance produced in accordance with these rules, and given also the original schema, a copy of the original value graph may be constructed.

The namespace identifier for the elements and attributes defined in this section is "http://www.w3.org/2001/06/soap-encoding". The encoding samples shown assume all namespace declarations are at a higher element level.

Use of the data model and encoding style described in this section is encouraged but not required; other data models and encodings can be used in conjunction with SOAP (see section 4.1.1).

5.1 Rules for Encoding Types in XML

XML allows very flexible encoding of data. SOAP defines a narrower set of rules for encoding. This section defines the encoding rules at a high level, and the next section describes the encoding rules for specific types when they require more detail. The encodings described in this section can be used in conjunction with the mapping of RPC calls and responses specified in Section 7.

To describe encoding, the following terminology is used:

1. A "value" is a string, the name of a measurement (number, date, enumeration, etc.) or a composite of several such primitive values. All values are of specific types.
2. A "simple value" is one without named parts. Examples of simple values are particular strings, integers, enumerated values etc.

3. A "compound value" is an aggregate of relations to other values. Examples of Compound Values are particular purchase orders, stock reports, street addresses, etc.
4. Within a compound value, each related value is potentially distinguished by a role name, ordinal or both. This is called its "accessor." Examples of compound values include particular Purchase Orders, Stock Reports etc. Arrays are also compound values. It is possible to have compound values with several accessors each named the same, as for example, RDF does.
5. An "array" is a compound value in which ordinal position serves as the only distinction among member values.
6. A "struct" is a compound value in which accessor name is the only distinction among member values, and no accessor has the same name as any other.
7. A "simple type" is a class of simple values. Examples of simple types are the classes called "string," "integer," enumeration classes, etc.
8. A "compound type" is a class of compound values. An example of a compound type is the class of purchase order values sharing the same accessors (shipTo, totalCost, etc.) though with potentially different values (and perhaps further constrained by limits on certain values).
9. Within a compound type, if an accessor has a name that is distinct within that type but is not distinct with respect to other types, that is, the name plus the type together are needed to make a unique identification, the name is called "locally scoped." If however the name is based in part on a Uniform Resource Identifier, directly or indirectly, such that the name alone is sufficient to uniquely identify the accessor irrespective of the type within which it appears, the name is called "universally scoped."
10. Given the information in the schema relative to which a graph of values is serialized, it is possible to determine that some values can only be related by a single instance of an accessor. For others, it is not possible to make this determination. If only one accessor can reference it, a value is considered "single-reference". If referenced by more than one, actually or potentially, it is

"multi-reference." Note that it is possible for a certain value to be considered "single-reference" relative to one schema and "multi-reference" relative to another.

11. Syntactically, an element may be "independent" or "embedded." An independent element is any element appearing at the top level of a serialization. All others are embedded elements.

Although it is possible to use the xsi:type attribute such that a graph of values is self-describing both in its structure and the types of its values, the serialization rules permit that the types of values MAY be determinate only by reference to a schema. Such schemas MAY be in the notation described by "XML Schema Part 1: Structures" [10] and "XML Schema Part 2: Datatypes" [11] or MAY be in any other notation. Note also that, while the serialization rules apply to compound types other than arrays and structs, many schemas will contain only struct and array types.

The rules for serialization are as follows:

1. All values are represented as element content. A multi-reference value MUST be represented as the content of an independent element. A single-reference value SHOULD not be (but MAY be).
2. For each element containing a value, the type of the value MUST be represented by at least one of the following conditions: (a) the containing element instance contains an xsi:type attribute, (b) the containing element instance is itself contained within an element containing a (possibly defaulted) enc:arrayType attribute or (c) or the name of the element bears a definite relation to the type, that type then determinable from a schema.
3. A simple value is represented as character data, that is, without any subelements. Every simple value must have a type that is either listed in the XML Schemas Specification, part 2 [11] or whose source type is listed therein (see also section 5.2).
4. A Compound Value is encoded as a sequence of elements, each accessor represented by an embedded element whose name corresponds to the name of the

accessor. Accessors whose names are local to their containing types have unqualified element names; all others have qualified names (see also section 5.4).

5. A multi-reference simple or compound value is encoded as an independent element containing a local, unqualified attribute named "id" and of type "ID" per the XML Specification [7]. Each accessor to this value is an empty element having a local, unqualified attribute named "href" and of type "uri-reference" per the XML Schema Specification [11], with a "href" attribute value of a URI fragment identifier referencing the corresponding independent element.
6. Strings and byte arrays are represented as multi-reference simple types, but special rules allow them to be represented efficiently for common cases (see also section 5.2.1 and 5.2.3). An accessor to a string or byte-array value MAY have an attribute named "id" and of type "ID" per the XML Specification [7]. If so, all other accessors to the same value are encoded as empty elements having a local, unqualified attribute named "href" and of type "uri-reference" per the XML Schema Specification [11], with a "href" attribute value of a URI fragment identifier referencing the single element containing the value.
7. It is permissible to encode several references to a value as though these were references to several distinct values, but only when from context it is known that the meaning of the XML instance is unaltered.
8. Arrays are compound values (see also section 5.4.2). SOAP arrays are defined as having a type of "enc:Array" or a type derived there from.

SOAP arrays have one or more dimensions (rank) whose members are distinguished by ordinal position. An array value is represented as a series of elements reflecting the array, with members appearing in ascending ordinal sequence. For multi-dimensional arrays the dimension on the right side varies most rapidly. Each member element is named as an independent element (see rule 2).

SOAP arrays can be single-reference or multi-reference values, and consequently may be represented as the content of either an embedded or independent element.

SOAP arrays MUST contain a "enc:arrayType" attribute whose value specifies the type of the contained elements as well as the dimension(s) of the array. The value of the "enc:arrayType" attribute is defined as follows:

```
arrayTypeValue    =    atype asize
Atype             =    QName *( rank )
rank              =    "[" *( "," ) "]"
asize             =    "[" #length "]"
length            =    1*DIGIT
```

The "atype" construct is the type name of the contained elements expressed as a QName as would appear in the "type" attribute of an XML Schema element declaration and acts as a type constraint (meaning that all values of contained elements are asserted to conform to the indicated type; that is, the type cited in enc:arrayType must be the type or a supertype of every array member). In the case of arrays of arrays or "jagged arrays", the type component is encoded as the "innermost" type name followed by a rank construct for each level of nested arrays starting from 1. Multi-dimensional arrays are encoded using a comma for each dimension starting from 1.

The "asize" construct contains a comma separated list of zero, one, or more integers indicating the lengths of each dimension of the array. A value of zero integers indicates that no particular quantity is asserted but that the size may be determined by inspection of the actual members.

For example, an array with 5 members of type array of integers would have an arrayTypeValue value of "int[][5]" of which the atype value is "int[]" and the asize value is "[5]". Likewise, an array with 3 members of type two-dimensional arrays of integers would have an arrayTypeValue value of "int[,][3]" of which the atype value is "int[,]" and the asize value is "[3]".

A SOAP array member MAY contain a "enc:offset" attribute indicating the offset position of that item in the enclosing array. This can be used to indicate the offset position of a partially represented array (see section 5.4.2.1). Likewise, an array member MAY contain a "enc:position" attribute indicating the position of that item in the enclosing array. This can be used to describe members of sparse arrays (see section 5.4.2.2). The value of the "enc:offset" and the "enc:position" attribute is defined as follows:

```
arrayPoint            =      "[" #length "]"
```

with offsets and positions based at 0.

9. A NULL value or a default value MAY be represented by omission of the accessor element. A NULL value MAY also be indicated by an accessor element containing the attribute xsi:null with value '1' or possibly other application-dependent attributes and values.

Note that rule 2 allows independent elements and also elements representing the members of arrays to have names which are not identical to the type of the contained value.

5.2 Simple Types

For simple types, SOAP adopts all the types found in the section "Built-in datatypes" of the "XML Schema Part 2: Datatypes" Specification [11], both the value and lexical spaces. Examples include:

TYPE	EXAMPLE
int	58502
Float	314159265358979E+1
negativeInteger	-32768
string	Louis "Satchmo" Armstrong

The datatypes declared in the XML Schema specification may be used directly in element schemas. Types derived from these may also be used. For example, for the following schema:

EXAMPLE I–7 Schema with simple types

```
<!-- schema document -->
<xs:schema xmlns:xs="http://www.w3.org/2001/
XMLSchema" >

  <xs:element name="age" type="xs:int" />
  <xs:element name="height" type="xs:float" />
  <xs:element name="displacement"
type="xs:negativeInteger" />
  <xs:element name="color" >
    <xs:simpleType base="xsd:string">
      <xs:restriction base="xs:string" >
        <xs:enumeration value="Green"/>
        <xs:enumeration value="Blue"/>
          </xs:restriction>
    </xs:simpleType>
  </xs:element>
</xs:schema>
```

The following elements would be valid instances:

EXAMPLE I–8 Message fragment corresponding to the schema in Example 8

```
<!-- Example instance elements -->
<age>45</age>
<height>5.9</height>
<displacement>-450</displacement>
<color>Blue</color>
```

All simple values MUST be encoded as the content of elements whose type is either defined in "XML Schema Part 2: Datatypes" Specification [11], or is based on a type found there by using the mechanisms provided in the XML Schema specification.

If a simple value is encoded as an independent element or member of a heterogenous array it is convenient to have an element declaration corresponding to the datatype. Because the

"XML Schema Part 2: Datatypes" Specification [11] includes type definitions but does not include corresponding element declarations, the enc schema and namespace declares an element for every simple datatype. These MAY be used.

EXAMPLE I–9

```
<enc:int xmlns:enc="http://www.w3.org/2001/06/soap-
encoding" id="int1">45</enc:int>
```

5.2.1 STRINGS

The datatype "string" is defined in "XML Schema Part 2: Datatypes" Specification [11]. Note that this is not identical to the type called "string" in many database or programming languages, and in particular may forbid some characters those languages would permit. (Those values must be represented by using some datatype other than xsd:string.)

A string MAY be encoded as a single-reference or a multi-reference value.

The containing element of the string value MAY have an "id" attribute. Additional accessor elements MAY then have matching "href" attributes.

For example, two accessors to the same string could appear, as follows:

EXAMPLE I–10 Two accessors for the same string

```
<greeting id="String-0">Hello</greeting>
<salutation href="#String-0"/>
```

However, if the fact that both accessors reference the same instance of the string (or subtype of string) is immaterial, they may be encoded as two single-reference values as follows:

EXAMPLE I–11 Two accessors for the same string

```
<greeting>Hello</greeting>
<salutation>Hello</salutation>
```

Schema fragments for these examples could appear similar to the following:

EXAMPLE I–12 Schema for Example 11

```
<xs:schema xmlns:xs="http://www.w3.org/2001/
XMLSchema"
           xmlns:enc="http://www.w3.org/2001/06/
soap-encoding" >

  <xs:import namespace="http://www.w3.org/2001/06/
soap-encoding" />

  <xs:element name="greeting" type="enc:string" />
  <xs:element name="salutation" type="enc:string" />

</xs:schema>
```

(In this example, the type enc:string is used as the element's type as a convenient way to declare an element whose datatype is "xsd:string" and which also allows an "id" and "href" attribute. See the SOAP Encoding schema for the exact definition. Schemas MAY use these declarations from the SOAP Encoding schema but are not required to.)

5.2.2 ENUMERATIONS

The "XML Schema Part 2: Datatypes" Specification [11] defines a mechanism called "enumeration." The SOAP data model adopts this mechanism directly. However, because programming and other languages often define enumeration somewhat differently, we spell-out the concept in more detail here and describe how a value that is a member of an enumerated list of possible values is to be encoded. Specifically, it is encoded as the name of the value.

"Enumeration" as a concept indicates a set of distinct names. A specific enumeration is a specific list of distinct values appropriate to the base type. For example the set of color names ("Green", "Blue", "Brown") could be defined as an enumeration based on the string built-in type. The values ("1", "3", "5") are a possible enumeration based on integer, and so on. "XML Schema

Part 2: Datatypes" [11] supports enumerations for all of the simple types except for boolean. The language of "XML Schema Part 1: Structures" Specification [10] can be used to define enumeration types. If a schema is generated from another notation in which no specific base type is applicable, use "string". In the following schema example "EyeColor" is defined as a string with the possible values of "Green", "Blue", or "Brown" enumerated, and instance data is shown accordingly.

EXAMPLE I–13 Schema with enumeration

```
<xs:schema xmlns:xs="http://www.w3.org/2001/
XMLSchema"

xmlns:tns="http://example.org/2001/06/samples"

targetNamespace="http://example.org/2001/06/
samples" >

  <xs:element name="EyeColor" type="tns:EyeColor" />
  <xs:simpleType name="EyeColor" >
    <xs:restriction base="xs:string" >
      <xs:enumeration value="Green" />
      <xs:enumeration value="Blue" />
      <xs:enumeration value="Brown" />
    </xs:restriction>
  </xs:simpleType>

</xs:schema>
```

EXAMPLE I–14 Message fragment corresponding to the schema in Example 13

```
<p:EyeColor xmlns:p="http://example.org/2001/06/
samples" >Brown</p:EyeColor>
```

5.2.3 ARRAY OF BYTES

An array of bytes MAY be encoded as a single-reference or a multi-reference value. The rules for an array of bytes are similar to those for a string.

In particular, the containing element of the array of bytes value MAY have an "id" attribute. Additional accessor elements MAY then have matching "href" attributes.

The recommended representation of an opaque array of bytes is the 'base64' encoding defined in XML Schemas [10][11], which uses the base64 encoding algorithm defined in 2045 [13]. However, the line length restrictions that normally apply to base64 data in MIME do not apply in SOAP. A "enc:base64" subtype is supplied for use with SOAP.

EXAMPLE I–15 Image with base64 encoding

```
<picture xmlns:xsi="http://www.w3.org/2001/
XMLSchema-instance"
         xmlns:enc="http://www.w3.org/2001/06/soap-
encoding"
         xsi:type="enc:base64" >
   aG93IG5vDyBicm73biBjb3cNCg==
</picture>
```

5.3 Polymorphic Accessor

Many languages allow accessors that can polymorphically access values of several types, each type being available at run time. A polymorphic accessor instance MUST contain an "xsi:type" attribute that describes the type of the actual value.

For example, a polymorphic accessor named "cost" with a value of type "xsd:float" would be encoded as follows:

EXAMPLE I–16 Polymorphic accessor

```
<cost xmlns:xsi="http://www.w3.org/2001/XMLSchema-
instance"
      xmlns:xs="http://www.w3.org/2001/XMLSchema"
          xsi:type="xs:float">29.95</cost>
```

as contrasted with a cost accessor whose value's type is invariant, as follows:

EXAMPLE I–17 Accessor whose value type is invariant

```
<cost>29.95</cost>
```

5.4 Compound types

SOAP defines types corresponding to the following structural patterns often found in programming languages:

STRUCT

A "struct" is a compound value in which accessor name is the only distinction among member values, and no accessor has the same name as any other.

ARRAY

An "array" is a compound value in which ordinal position serves as the only distinction among member values.

SOAP also permits serialization of data that is neither a Struct nor an Array, for example data such as is found in a Directed-Labeled-Graph Data Model in which a single node has many distinct accessors, some of which occur more than once. SOAP serialization does not require that the underlying data model make an ordering distinction among accessors, but if such an order exists, the accessors MUST be encoded in that sequence.

5.4.1 COMPOUND VALUES, STRUCTS AND REFERENCES TO VALUES

The members of a Compound Value are encoded as accessor elements. When accessors are distinguished by their name (as for example in a struct), the accessor name is used as the element name. Accessors whose names are local to their containing types have unqualified element names; all others have qualified names.

The following is an example of a struct of type "Book":

EXAMPLE I–18 Book structure

```
<e:Book xmlns:e="http://example.org/2001/06/books" >
   <author>Henry Ford</author>
   <preface>Prefactory text</preface>
   <intro>This is a book.</intro>
</e:Book>
```

And this is a schema fragment describing the above structure:

EXAMPLE I–19 Schema for Example 18

```
<xs:element name="Book"
            xmlns:xs='http://www.w3.org/2001/
XMLSchema' >
  <xs:complexType>
    <xs:sequence>
      <xs:element name="author" type="xs:string" />
      <xs:element name="preface" type="xs:string" />
      <xs:element name="intro" type="xs:string" />
    </xs:sequence>
  </xs:complexType>
</xs:element>
```

Below is an example of a type with both simple and complex members. It shows two levels of referencing. Note that the "href" attribute of the "Author" accessor element is a reference to the value whose "id" attribute matches. A similar construction appears for the "Address".

EXAMPLE I–20 Book with muli-reference addresses

```
<e:Book xmlns:e="http://example.org/2001/06/books" >
  <title>My Life and Work</title>
  <author href="#Person-1"/>
</e:Book>
<e:Person xmlns:e="http://example.org/2001/06/
books"
          id="Person-1" >
  <name>Henry Ford</name>
  <address href="#Address-2"/>
</e:Person>
<e:Address xmlns:e="http://example.org/2001/06/
books"
           id="Address-2" >
  <email>mailto:henryford@hotmail.com</email>
  <web>http://www.henryford.com</web>
</e:Address>
```

The form above is appropriate when the "Person" value and the "Address" value are multi-reference. If these were instead both single-reference, they SHOULD be embedded, as follows:

EXAMPLE I–21 Book with single-reference addresses

```
<e:Book xmlns:e="http://example.org/2001/06/books" >
   <title>My Life and Work</title>
   <author>
     <name>Henry Ford</name>
     <address>
       <email>mailto:henryford@hotmail.com</email>
       <web>http://www.henryford.com</web>
     </address>
   </author>
</e:Book>
```

If instead there existed a restriction that no two persons can have the same address in a given instance and that an address can be either a Street-address or an Electronic-address, a Book with two authors would be encoded as follows:

EXAMPLE I–22 Book with two authors having different addresses

```
<e:Book xmlns:e="http://example.org/2001/06/books" >
   <title>My Life and Work</title>
   <firstauthor href="#Person-1"/>
   <secondauthor href="#Person-2"/>
</e:Book>
<e:Person xmlns:e="http://example.org/2001/06/books"
          xmlns:xsi="http://www.w3.org/2001/
XMLSchema-instance"
          id="Person-1" >
   <name>Henry Ford</name>
   <address xsi:type="e:ElectronicAddressType">
       <email>mailto:henryford@hotmail.com</email>
       <web>http://www.henryford.com</web>
   </address>
</e:Person>
<e:Person xmlns:e="http://example.org/2001/06/books"
          xmlns:xsi="http://www.w3.org/2001/
XMLSchema-instance"
          id="Person-2">
   <name>Samuel Crowther</name>
   <address xsi:type="e:StreetAddressType">
       <street>Martin Luther King Rd</street>
       <city>Raleigh</city>
       <state>North Carolina</state>
   </address>
</e:Person>
```

Serializations can contain references to values not in the same resource:

EXAMPLE I–23 Book with external references

```
<e:Book xmlns:e="http://example.org/2001/06/books" >
   <title>Paradise Lost</title>
   <firstAuthor href="http://www.dartmouth.edu/
~milton/" />
</e:Book>
```

And this is a schema fragment describing the above structures:

EXAMPLE I–24 Schema for example 22

```
<xs:schema xmlns:xs="http://www.w3.org/2001/
XMLSchema"
           xmlns:tns="http://example.org/2001/06/
books"
targetNamespace="http://example.org/2001/06/books" >

  <xs:element name="Book" type="tns:BookType" />
  <xs:complexType name="BookType" >
    <xs:annotation>
          <xs:documentation>
            <info>
      Either the following group must occur or else
      the href attribute must appear, but not both.
                </info>
          </xs:documentation>
    </xs:annotation>
    <xs:sequence minOccurs="0" maxOccurs="1" >
      <xs:element name="title" type="xs:string" />
      <xs:element name="firstAuthor"
type="tns:PersonType" />
      <xs:element name="secondAuthor"
type="tns:PersonType" />
    </xs:sequence>
    <xs:attribute name="href" type="xs:anyURI" />
    <xs:attribute name="id" type="xs:ID" />
    <xs:anyAttribute namespace="##other" />
  </xs:complexType>

  <xs:element name="Person" type="tns:PersonType" />
  <xs:complexType name="PersonType" >
    <xs:annotation>
          <xs:documentation>
            <info>
      Either the following group must occur or else
      the href attribute must appear, but not both.
                </info>
          </xs:documentation>
        </xs:annotation>
```

EXAMPLE I–24 Schema for example 22 (Continued)

```
    <xs:sequence minOccurs="0" maxOccurs="1" >
      <xs:element name="name" type="xs:string" />
      <xs:element name="address"
type="tns:AddressType" />
    </xs:sequence>
    <xs:attribute name="href" type="xs:anyURI" />
    <xs:attribute name="id" type="xs:ID" />
    <xs:anyAttribute namespace="##other" />
  </xs:complexType>

  <xs:element name="Address" base="tns:AddressType" />
  <xs:complexType name="AddressType" abstract="true" >
    <xs:annotation>
          <xs:documentation>
            <info>
       Either one of the following sequences must
       occur or else the href attribute must
       appear, but not both.
                </info>
          </xs:documentation>
        </xs:annotation>
    <xs:choice>
          <xs:sequence minOccurs="0" maxOccurs="1" >
            <xs:element name="email"
type="xs:string" />
                <xs:element name="web"
type="xs:anyURI" />
          </xs:sequence>
          <xs:sequence minOccurs='0' maxOccurs='1' >
        <xs:element name="street" type="xs:string" />
        <xs:element name="city" type="xs:string" />
        <xs:element name="state" type="xs:string"/>
          </xs:sequence>
        </xs:choice>
    <xs:attribute name="href" type="xs:anyURI"/>
    <xs:attribute name="id" type="xs:ID"/>
    <xs:anyAttribute namespace="##other"/>
  </xs:complexType>

  <xs:complexType name="StreetAddressType">
    <xs:annotation>
          <xs:documentation>
            <info>
```

EXAMPLE I–24 Schema for example 22 (Continued)

```
        Either the second sequence in the following
        group must occur or else the href attribute
        must appear, but not both.
                </info>
          </xs:documentation>
        </xs:annotation>
        <xs:complexContent>
          <xs:restriction base="tns:AddressType" >
            <xs:sequence>
              <xs:sequence minOccurs="0"
maxOccurs="0" >
                <xs:element name="email"
type="xs:string" />
                    <xs:element name="web"
type="xs:anyURI" />
              </xs:sequence>
          <xs:sequence minOccurs="0" maxOccurs="1">
            <xs:element name="street"
type="xs:string" />
            <xs:element name="city"
type="xs:string" />
            <xs:element name="state"
type="xs:string"/>
          </xs:sequence>
                </xs:sequence>
        <xs:attribute name="href" type="xs:anyURI"/>
        <xs:attribute name="id" type="xs:ID"/>
        <xs:anyAttribute namespace="##other"/>
          </xs:restriction>
        </xs:complexContent>
  </xs:complexType>

  <xs:complexType name="ElectronicAddressType">
    <xs:annotation>
          <xs:documentation>
            <info>
        Either the first sequence in the following
        group must occur or else the href attribute
        must appear, but not both.
                </info>
          </xs:documentation>
        </xs:annotation>
```

EXAMPLE I–24 Schema for example 22 (Continued)

```
        <xs:complexContent>
          <xs:restriction base="tns:AddressType" >
            <xs:sequence>
          <xs:sequence minOccurs="0" maxOccurs="1">
            <xs:element name="email"
type="xs:string" />
            <xs:element name="web" type="xs:anyURI"
/>
          </xs:sequence>
                <xs:sequence minOccurs="0"
maxOccurs="0">
            <xs:element name="street"
type="xs:string" />
            <xs:element name="city"
type="xs:string" />
            <xs:element name="state"
type="xs:string"/>
          </xs:sequence>
              </xs:sequence>
            <xs:attribute name="href"
type="xs:anyURI"/>
        <xs:attribute name="id" type="xs:ID"/>
        <xs:anyAttribute namespace="##other"/>
          </xs:restriction>
        </xs:complexContent>
  </xs:complexType>

</xs:schema>
```

5.4.2 ARRAYS

SOAP arrays are defined as having a type of enc:Array or a derived type having that type in its derivation hierarchy (see also rule 8). Such derived types would be restrictions of the enc:Array type and could be used to represent, for example, arrays limited to integers or arrays of some user-defined enumeration. Arrays are represented as element values, with no specific constraint on the name of the containing element (just as values generally do not constrain the name of their containing element). The elements which make up the array can themselves can be of any type, including nested arrays.

The representation of the value of an array is an ordered sequence of elements constituting the items of the array. Within an array value, element names are not significant for distinguishing accessors. Elements may have any name. In practice, elements will frequently be named so that their declaration in a schema suggests or determines their type. As with compound types generally, if the value of an item in the array is a single-reference value, the item contains its value. Otherwise, the item references its value via an "href" attribute.

The following example is a schema fragment and an array containing integer array members:

EXAMPLE I–25 Schema declaring an array of integers

```
<xs:schema xmlns:xs="http://www.w3.org/2001/
XMLSchema"
           xmlns:enc="http://www.w3.org/2001/06/
soap-encoding" >
  <xs:import namespace="http://www.w3.org/2001/06/
soap-encoding" />
  <xs:element name="myFavoriteNumbers"
type="enc:Array" />
</xs:schema>
```

EXAMPLE I–26 Array conforming to the schema in Example 25

```
<myFavoriteNumbers xmlns:xs="http://www.w3.org/
2001/XMLSchema"

xmlns:enc="http://www.w3.org/2001/06/soap-encoding"
                  enc:arrayType="xs:int[2]" >
  <number>3</number>
  <number>4</number>
</myFavoriteNumbers>
```

In that example, the array myFavoriteNumbers contains several members each of which is a value of type xs:int. This can be determined by inspection of the enc:arrayType attribute. Note that the enc:Array type allows both unqualified element names and qualified element names from any namespace. These convey no type information, so when used they must either have an xsi:type attribute or the containing element must have a enc:arrayType attribute. Naturally, types derived from enc:Array may declare local elements, with type information.

As previously noted, the enc schema contains declarations of elements with names corresponding to each simple type in the "XML Schema Part 2: Datatypes" Specification [11]. It also contains a declaration for "Array". Using these, we might write:

EXAMPLE I–27 Using the enc:Array element

```
<enc:Array xmlns:enc="http://www.w3.org/2001/06/
soap-encoding"
           xmlns:xs="http://www.w3.org/2001/
XMLSchema"
           enc:ArrayType="xs:int[2]" >
  <enc:int>3</enc:int>
  <enc:int>4</enc:int>
</enc:Array>
```

Arrays can contain instances of any subtype of the specified arrayType. That is, the members may be of any type that is substitutable for the type specified in the arrayType attribute, according to whatever substitutability rules are expressed in the schema. So, for example, an array of integers can contain any type derived from integer (for example "int" or any user-defined derivation of integer). Similarly, an array of "address" might contain a restricted or extended type such as "internationalAddress". Because the supplied enc:Array type admits members of any type, arbitrary mixtures of types can be contained unless specifically limited by use of the arrayType attribute.

Types of member elements can be specified using the xsi:type attribute in the instance, or by declarations in the schema of the member elements, as the following two arrays demonstrate respectively:

EXAMPLE I–28 Array with elements of varying types

```
<enc:Array xmlns:enc="http://www.w3.org/2001/06/
soap-encoding"
           xmlns:xs="http://www.w3.org/2001/
XMLSchema"
```

EXAMPLE I–28 Array with elements of varying types (Continued)

```
xmlns:xsi="http://www.w3.org/2001/XMLSchema-
instance"
           enc:arrayType="xs:anyType[4]">
   <thing xsi:type="xs:int">12345</thing>
   <thing xsi:type="xs:decimal">6.789</thing>
   <thing xsi:type="xs:string">
      Of Mans First Disobedience, and the Fruit
      Of that Forbidden Tree, whose mortal tast
      Brought Death into the World, and all our
woe,
   </thing>
   <thing xsi:type="xs:anyURI">
      http://www.dartmouth.edu/~milton/
reading_room/
   </thing>
</enc:Array>
```

EXAMPLE I–29 Array with elements of varying types

```
<enc:Array xmlns:xs="http://www.w3.org/2001/
XMLSchema"
           xmlns:enc="http://www.w3.org/2001/06/
soap-encoding"
           enc:arrayType="xs:anyType[4]" >
   <enc:int>12345</enc:int>
   <enc:decimal>6.789</enc:decimal>
   <enc:string>
      Of Mans First Disobedience, and the Fruit
      Of that Forbidden Tree, whose mortal tast
      Brought Death into the World, and all our woe,
   </enc:string>
   <enc:anyURI>
      http://www.dartmouth.edu/~milton/
reading_room/
   </enc:anyURI >
</enc:Array>
```

Array values may be structs or other compound values. For example an array of "xyz:Order" structs:

EXAMPLE I–30 Arrays containing structs and other compound values

```
<enc:Array xmlns:enc="http://www.w3.org/2001/06/
soap-encoding"
           xmlns:xyz="http://example.org/2001/06/
Orders"
           enc:arrayType="xyz:Order[2]">
   <Order>
       <Product>Apple</Product>
       <Price>1.56</Price>
   </Order>
   <Order>
       <Product>Peach</Product>
       <Price>1.48</Price>
   </Order>
</enc:Array>
```

Arrays may have other arrays as member values. The following is an example of an array of two arrays, each of which is an array of strings.

EXAMPLE I–31 Array containing other arrays

```
<enc:Array xmlns:xs="http://www.w3.org/2001/
XMLSchema"
           xmlns:enc="http://www.w3.org/2001/06/
soap-encoding"
           enc:arrayType="xs:string[][2]" >
   <item href="#array-1"/>
   <item href="#array-2"/>
</enc:Array>
<enc:Array xmlns:xs="http://www.w3.org/2001/
XMLSchema"
           xmlns:enc="http://www.w3.org/2001/06/
soap-encoding"
           id="array-1"
           enc:arrayType="xs:string[2]">
   <item>r1c1</item>
   <item>r1c2</item>
   <item>r1c3</item>
</enc:Array>
<enc:Array xmlns:xs="http://www.w3.org/2001/
XMLSchema"
```

EXAMPLE I–31 Array containing other arrays (Continued)

```
           xmlns:enc="http://www.w3.org/2001/06/
soap-encoding"
           id="array-2"
           enc:arrayType="xs:string[2]">
   <item>r2c1</item>
   <item>r2c2</item>
</enc:Array>
```

The element containing an array value does not need to be named "enc:Array". It may have any name, provided that the type of the element is either enc:Array or is derived from enc:Array by restriction. For example, the following is a fragment of a schema and a conforming instance array:

EXAMPLE I–32 Schema for an array

```
<xs:schema xmlns:xs="http://www.w3.org/2001/
XMLSchema"
           xmlns:enc="http://www.w3.org/2001/06/
soap-encoding"
           xmlns:tns="http://example.org/2001/06/
numbers"

targetNamespace="http://example.org/2001/06/
numbers" >

  <xs:simpleType name="phoneNumberType" >
    <xs:restriction base="xs:string" />
  </xs:simpleType>

  <xs:element name="ArrayOfPhoneNumbers"
type="tns:ArrayOfPhoneNumbersType" />

  <xs:complexType name="ArrayOfPhoneNumbersType" >
    <xs:complexContent>
      <xs:restriction base="enc:Array" >
            <xs:sequence>
          <xs:element name="phoneNumber"
type="tns:phoneNumberType" maxOccurs="unbounded" />
            </xs:sequence>
        <xs:attributeGroup
```

EXAMPLE I–32 Schema for an array (Continued)

```
ref="enc:arrayAttributes" />
        <xs:attributeGroup
ref="enc:commonAttributes" />
      </xs:restriction>
    </xs:complexContent>
  </xs:complexType>

</xs:schema>
```

EXAMPLE I–33 Array conforming to the schema in Example 32

```
<abc:ArrayOfPhoneNumbers
xmlns:abc="http://example.org/2001/06/numbers"

xmlns:enc="http://www.w3.org/2001/06/soap-encoding"

enc:arrayType="abc:phoneNumberType[2]" >
   <phoneNumber>206-555-1212</phoneNumber>
   <phoneNumber>1-888-123-4567</phoneNumber>
</abc:ArrayOfPhoneNumbers>
```

Arrays may be multi-dimensional. In this case, more than one size will appear within the asize part of the arrayType attribute:

EXAMPLE I–34 Multi-dimensonal array

```
<enc:Array xmlns:xs="http://www.w3.org/2001/
XMLSchema"
           xmlns:enc="http://www.w3.org/2001/06/
soap-encoding"
           enc:arrayType="xs:string[2,3]" >
   <item>r1c1</item>
   <item>r1c2</item>
   <item>r1c3</item>
   <item>r2c1</item>
   <item>r2c2</item>
   <item>r2c3</item>
</enc:Array>
```

While the examples above have shown arrays encoded as independent elements, array values MAY also appear embedded and SHOULD do so when they are known to be single reference.

The following is an example of a schema fragment and an array of phone numbers embedded in a struct of type "Person" and accessed through the accessor "phone-numbers":

EXAMPLE I–34 Schema fragment for array of phone numbers embedded in a struct

```
<xs:schema xmlns:xs="http://www.w3.org/2001/
XMLSchema"
           xmlns:enc="http://www.w3.org/2001/06/
soap-encoding"
           xmlns:tns="http://example.org/2001/06/
numbers"

targetNamespace="http://example.org/2001/06/
numbers" >

  <xs:import namespace="http://www.w3.org/2001/06/
soap-encoding" />

  <xs:simpleType name="phoneNumberType" >
    <xs:restriction base="xs:string" />
  </xs:simpleType>

  <xs:element name="ArrayOfPhoneNumbers"
type="tns:ArrayOfPhoneNumbersType" />

  <xs:complexType name="ArrayOfPhoneNumbersType" >
    <xs:complexContent>
      <xs:restriction base="enc:Array" >
            <xs:sequence>
          <xs:element name="phoneNumber"
type="tns:phoneNumberType" maxOccurs="unbounded" />
            </xs:sequence>
        <xs:attributeGroup
ref="enc:arrayAttributes" />
        <xs:attributeGroup
ref="enc:commonAttributes" />
      </xs:restriction>
```

EXAMPLE I–34 Schema fragment for array of phone numbers embedded in a struct (Continued)

```
    </xs:complexContent>
  </xs:complexType>

  <xs:element name="Person">
    <xs:complexType>
          <xs:sequence>
        <xs:element name="name" type="xs:string" />
        <xs:element name="phoneNumbers"
type="tns:ArrayOfPhoneNumbersType" />
      </xs:sequence>
    </xs:complexType>
  </xs:element>

</xs:schema>
```

EXAMPLE I–35 Array of phone numbers embedded in a struct conforming to the schema in Example 34

```
<def:Person xmlns:def="http://example.org/2001/06/
numbers"
            xmlns:enc="http://www.w3.org/2001/06/
soap-encoding" >
   <name>John Hancock</name>
   <phoneNumbers
enc:arrayType="def:phoneNumber[2]">
       <phoneNumber>206-555-1212</phoneNumber>
       <phoneNumber>1-888-123-4567</phoneNumber>
   </phoneNumbers>
</def:Person>
```

Here is another example of a single-reference array value encoded as an embedded element whose containing element name is the accessor name:

EXAMPLE I–36 Single-reference array encoded as en embedded element

```
<xyz:PurchaseOrder
xmlns:xyz="http://example.org/2001/06/Orders" >
   <CustomerName>Henry Ford</CustomerName>
   <ShipTo>
```

EXAMPLE I–36 Single-reference array encoded as en embedded element

```
        <Street>5th Ave</Street>
        <City>New York</City>
        <State>NY</State>
        <Zip>10010</Zip>
    </ShipTo>
    <PurchaseLineItems xmlns:enc="http://www.w3.org/
2001/06/soap-encoding"
                       enc:arrayType="xyz:Order[2]">
        <Order>
            <Product>Apple</Product>
            <Price>1.56</Price>
        </Order>
        <Order>
            <Product>Peach</Product>
            <Price>1.48</Price>
        </Order>
    </PurchaseLineItems>
</xyz:PurchaseOrder>
```

5.4.2.1 PARTIALLY TRANSMITTED ARRAYS

SOAP provides support for partially transmitted arrays, known as "varying" arrays in some contexts [12]. A partially transmitted array indicates in an "enc:offset" attribute the zero-origin offset of the first element transmitted. If omitted, the offset is taken as zero.

The following is an example of an array of size five that transmits only the third and fourth element counting from zero:

EXAMPLE I–37 Array of size five that transmits only the third and fourth element

```
<enc:Array xmlns:enc="http://www.w3.org/2001/06/
soap-encoding"
           xmlns:xs="http://www.w3.org/2001/
XMLSchema"
           enc:arrayType="xs:string[6]"
           enc:offset="[3]" >
  <item>The fourth element</item>
  <item>The fifth element</item>
</enc:Array>
```

5.4.2.2 SPARSE ARRAYS

SOAP provides support for sparse arrays. Each element representing a member value contains a "enc:position" attribute that indicates its position within the array. The following is an example of a sparse array of two-dimensional arrays of strings. The size is 4 but only position 2 is used:

EXAMPLE I–38 Sparse array

```
<enc:Array xmlns:enc="http://www.w3.org/2001/06/
soap-encoding"
           xmlns:xs="http://www.w3.org/2001/
XMLSchema"
           enc:arrayType="xs:string[,][4]" >
   <enc:Array href="#array-1" enc:position="[2]" />
</enc:Array>
<enc:Array id="array-1"
           enc:arrayType="xs:string[10,10]" >
   <item enc:position="[2,2]">Third row, third
col</item>
   <item enc:position="[7,2]">Eighth row, third
col</item>
</enc:Array>
```

If the only reference to array-1 occurs in the enclosing array, this example could also have been encoded as follows:

EXAMPLE I–39 Another sparse array

```
<enc:Array xmlns:enc="http://www.w3.org/2001/06/
soap-encoding"
           xmlns:xs="http://www.w3.org/2001/
XMLSchema"
           enc:arrayType="xs:string[,][4]" >
  <enc:Array enc:position="[2]"
enc:arrayType="xs:string[10,10]" >
    <item enc:position="[2,2]">Third row, third
col</item>
    <item enc:position="[7,2]">Eighth row, third
col</item>
  </enc:Array>
</enc:Array>
```

5.4.3 GENERIC COMPOUND TYPES

The encoding rules just cited are not limited to those cases where the accessor names are known in advance. If accessor names are known only by inspection of the immediate values to be encoded, the same rules apply, namely that the accessor is encoded as an element whose name matches the name of the accessor, and the accessor either contains or references its value. Accessors containing values whose types cannot be determined in advance MUST always contain an appropriate xsi:type attribute giving the type of the value.

Similarly, the rules cited are sufficient to allow serialization of compound types having a mixture of accessors distinguished by name and accessors distinguished by both name and ordinal position. (That is, having some accessors repeated.) This does not require that any schema actually contain such types, but rather says that if a type-model schema does have such types, a corresponding XML syntactic schema and instance may be generated.

EXAMPLE I–40 Generic compound types

```
<xyz:PurchaseOrder xmlns:xyz="http://example.org/
2001/06/Orders" >
  <CustomerName>Henry Ford</CustomerName>
  <ShipTo>
    <Street>5th Ave</Street>
    <City>New York</City>
    <State>NY</State>
    <Zip>10010</Zip>
  </ShipTo>
  <PurchaseLineItems>
    <Order>
      <Product>Apple</Product>
      <Price>1.56</Price>
    </Order>
    <Order>
      <Product>Peach</Product>
      <Price>1.48</Price>
    </Order>
  </PurchaseLineItems>
</xyz:PurchaseOrder>
```

Similarly, it is valid to serialize a compound value that structurally resembles an array but is not of type (or subtype) enc:Array. For example:

EXAMPLE I–41 Compound value

```
<PurchaseLineItems>
    <Order>
        <Product>Apple</Product>
        <Price>1.56</Price>
    </Order>
    <Order>
        <Product>Peach</Product>
        <Price>1.48</Price>
    </Order>
</PurchaseLineItems>
```

5.5 Default Values

An omitted accessor element implies either a default value or that no value is known. The specifics depend on the accessor, method, and its context. For example, an omitted accessor typically implies a Null value for polymorphic accessors (with the exact meaning of Null accessor-dependent). Likewise, an omitted Boolean accessor typically implies either a False value or that no value is known, and an omitted numeric accessor typically implies either that the value is zero or that no value is known.

5.6 SOAP root Attribute

The SOAP root attribute can be used to label serialization roots that are not true roots of an object graph so that the object graph can be deserialized. The attribute can have one of two values, either "1" or "0". True roots of an object graph have the implied attribute value of "1". Serialization roots that are not true roots can be labeled as serialization roots with an attribute value of "1" An element can explicitly be labeled as not being a serialization root with a value of "0".

The SOAP root attribute MAY appear on any subelement within the SOAP Header and SOAP Body elements. The attribute does not have a default value.

6. Using SOAP in HTTP

This section describes how to use SOAP within HTTP with or without using the experimental HTTP Extension Framework. Binding SOAP to HTTP provides the advantage of being able to use the formalism and decentralized flexibility of SOAP with the rich feature set of HTTP. Carrying SOAP in HTTP does not mean that SOAP overrides existing semantics of HTTP but rather that SOAP over HTTP inherits HTTP semantics.

SOAP naturally follows the HTTP request/response message model by providing a SOAP request message in a HTTP request and SOAP response message in a HTTP response. Note, however, that SOAP intermediaries are NOT the same as HTTP intermediaries. That is, an HTTP intermediary addressed with the HTTP Connection header field cannot be expected to inspect or process the SOAP entity body carried in the HTTP request.

HTTP applications MUST use the media type "text/xml" according to RFC 2376 [3] when including SOAP messages in HTTP exchanges.

6.1 SOAP HTTP Request

Although SOAP might be used in combination with a variety of HTTP request methods, this binding only defines SOAP within HTTP POST requests (see section 7 for how to use SOAP for RPC and section 6.3 for how to use the HTTP Extension Framework).

6.1.1 THE SOAPACTION HTTP HEADER FIELD

The SOAPAction HTTP request header field can be used to indicate the intent of the SOAP HTTP request. The value is a URI identifying the intent. SOAP places no restrictions on the format or specificity of the URI or that it is resolvable. An HTTP client MUST use this header field when issuing a SOAP HTTP Request.

```
soapaction      =   "SOAPAction" ":" [ <"> URI-reference
                    <"> ]
URI-reference   =   <as defined in RFC 2396 [4]>
```

The presence and content of the SOAPAction header field can be used by servers such as firewalls to appropriately filter SOAP request messages in HTTP. The header field value of empty string ("") means that the intent of the SOAP message is provided by the HTTP Request-URI. No value means that there is no indication of the intent of the message.

Examples:

EXAMPLE I–42 Examples of values for SOAPAction

```
SOAPAction: "http://electrocommerce.org/
abc#MyMessage"
SOAPAction: "myapp.sdl"
SOAPAction: ""
SOAPAction:
```

6.2 SOAP HTTP Response

SOAP over HTTP follows the semantics of the HTTP Status codes for communicating status information in HTTP. For example, a 2xx status code indicates that the client's request including the SOAP component was successfully received, understood, and accepted etc.

If an error occurs while processing the request, the SOAP HTTP server MUST issue an HTTP 500 "Internal Server Error" response and include a SOAP message in the response containing a SOAP fault (see section 4.4) indicating the SOAP processing error.

6.3 The HTTP Extension Framework

A SOAP message MAY be used together with the experimental HTTP Extension Framework [6] in order to identify the presence and intent of a SOAP HTTP request.

Whether to use the Extension Framework or plain HTTP is a question of policy and capability of the communicating parties. Clients can force the use of the experimental HTTP Extension Framework by using a mandatory extension declaration and the "M-" HTTP method name prefix. Servers can force the use of the HTTP Extension Framework by using the 510 "Not Extended" HTTP status code. That is, using one extra round trip, either party can detect the policy of the other party and act accordingly.

The extension identifier used to identify SOAP using the Extension Framework is

```
http://www.w3.org/2001/06/soap-envelope
```

6.4 SOAP HTTP Examples

EXAMPLE I–43 SOAP HTTP Request Using POST

```
POST /StockQuote HTTP/1.1
Content-Type: text/xml; charset="utf-8"
Content-Length: nnnn
SOAPAction: "http://electrocommerce.org/
abc#MyMessage"

<env:Envelope xmlns:env="http://www.w3.org/2001/06/
soap-envelope" >
  . . .
</env:Envelope>
```

EXAMPLE I–44 SOAP HTTP Response to Example 43

```
HTTP/1.1 200 OK
Content-Type: text/xml; charset="utf-8"
Content-Length: nnnn

<env:Envelope xmlns:env="http://www.w3.org/2001/06/
soap-envelope" >
  . . .
</env:Envelope>
```

EXAMPLE I–45 SOAP HTTP Request using the experimental HTTP Extension Framework

```
M-POST /StockQuote HTTP/1.1
Man: "http://www.w3.org/2001/06/soap-envelope";
ns=NNNN
Content-Type: text/xml; charset="utf-8"
Content-Length: nnnn
NNNN-SOAPAction: "http://electrocommerce.org/
abc#MyMessage"

<env:Envelope xmlns:env="http://www.w3.org/2001/06/
soap-envelope" >
  . . .
</env:Envelope>
```

EXAMPLE I–46 SOAP HTTP Response to Example 45

```
HTTP/1.1 200 OK
Ext:
Content-Type: text/xml; charset="utf-8"
Content-Length: nnnn

<env:Envelope xmlns:env="http://www.w3.org/2001/06/
soap-envelope" >
  . . .
</env:Envelope>
```

7. Using SOAP for RPC

One of the design goals of SOAP is to encapsulate remote procedure call functionality using the extensibility and flexibility of XML. This section defines a uniform representation of RPC invocations and responses.

Although it is anticipated that this representation is likely to be used in combination with the encoding style defined in section 5, other representations are possible. The SOAP encodingStyle attribute (see section 4.3.2) can be used to indicate the encoding style of the RPC invocation and/or the response using the representation described in this section.

Using SOAP for RPC is orthogonal to the SOAP protocol binding (see section 6). In the case of using HTTP as the protocol binding, an RPC invocation maps naturally to an HTTP request and an RPC response maps to an HTTP response. However, using SOAP for RPC is not limited to the HTTP protocol binding.

To invoke an RPC, the following information is needed:

- The URI of the target SOAP node
- A procedure or method name
- An optional procedure or method signature
- The parameters to the procedure or method
- Optional header data

SOAP relies on the protocol binding to provide a mechanism for carrying the URI. For example, for HTTP the request URI indicates the resource that the invocation is being made against. Other than it be a valid URI, SOAP places no restriction on the form of an address (see [4] for more information on URIs).

7.1 RPC and SOAP Body

RPC invocations and responses are both carried in the SOAP Body element (see section 4.3) using the following representation:

- An RPC invocation is modeled as a struct.
- The invocation is viewed as a single struct containing an accessor for each [in] or [in/out] parameter. The struct is both named and typed identically to the procedure or method name.
- Each [in] or [in/out] parameter is viewed as an accessor, with a name corresponding to the name of the parameter and type corresponding to the type of the parameter. These appear in the same order as in the procedure or method signature.
- An RPC response is modeled as a struct.
- The response is viewed as a single struct containing an accessor for the return value and each [out] or [in/out] parameter. The first accessor is the return value followed by the parameters in the same order as in the procedure or method signature.
- Each parameter accessor has a name corresponding to the name of the parameter and type corresponding to the type of the parameter. The name of the return value

accessor is not significant. Likewise, the name of the struct is not significant. However, a convention is to name it after the procedure or method name with the string "Response" appended.

- An invocation fault is encoded using a SOAP fault (see section 4.4). If a protocol binding adds additional rules for fault expression, those MUST also be followed.

As noted above, RPC invocation and response structs can be encoded according to the rules in section 5, or other encodings can be specified using the encodingStyle attribute (see section 4.1.1).

Applications MAY process invocations with missing parameters but also MAY return a fault.

Because a result indicates success and a fault indicates failure, it is an error for an RPC response to contain both a result and a fault.

7.2 RPC and SOAP Header

Additional information relevant to the encoding of an RPC invocation but not part of the formal procedure or method signature MAY be expressed in the RPC encoding. If so, it MUST be expressed as a header block.

An example of the use of a header block is the passing of a transaction ID along with a message. Since the transaction ID is not part of the signature and is typically held in an infrastructure component rather than application code, there is no direct way to pass the necessary information with the invocation. By adding a header block with a fixed name, the transaction manager on the receiving side can extract the transaction ID and use it without affecting the coding of remote procedure calls.

8. Security Considerations

Not described in this document are methods for integrity and privacy protection. Such issues will be addressed more fully in a future version(s) of this document.

9. References

9.1. Normative references

[2] IETF "RFC 2119: Key words for use in RFCs to Indicate Requirement Levels", S. Bradner, March 1997. Available at http://www.ietf.org/rfc/rfc2119.txt

[3] IETF "RFC 2376: XML Media Types", E. Whitehead, M. Murata, July 1998. Available at http://www.ietf.org/rfc/rfc2376.txt

[4] IETF "RFC 2396: Uniform Resource Identifiers (URI): Generic Syntax", T. Berners-Lee, R. Fielding, L. Masinter, August 1998. Available at http://www.ietf.org/rfc/rfc2396.txt

[5] IETF "RFC 2616: Hypertext Transfer Protocol -- HTTP/1.1", R. Fielding, J. Gettys, J. C. Mogul, H. Frystyk, T. Berners-Lee, January 1997. Available at http://www.ietf.org/rfc/rfc2616.txt

[6] IETF "RFC 2774: An HTTP Extension Framework", H. Nielsen, P. Leach, S. Lawrence, February 2000. Available at http://www.ietf.org/rfc/rfc2774.txt

[7] W3C Recommendation "Extensible Markup Language (XML) 1.0 (Second Edition)", Tim Bray, Jean Paoli, C. M. Sperberg-McQueen, Eve Maler, 6 October 2000. Available at http://www.w3.org/TR/2000/REC-xml-20001006

[8] W3C Recommendation "Namespaces in XML", Tim Bray, Dave Hollander, Andrew Layman, 14 January 1999. Available at http://www.w3.org/TR/1999/REC-xml-names-19990114/

[9] W3C Proposed Recommendation "XML Linking Language (XLink) Version 1.0", Steve DeRose, Eve Maler, David Orchard, 20 December 2000. Available at http://www.w3.org/TR/2000/PR-xlink-20001220/

[10] W3C Recommendation "XML Schema Part 1: Structures", Henry S. Thompson, David Beech, Murray Maloney, Noah Mendelsohn, 2 May 2001. Available at http://www.w3.org/TR/2001/REC-xmlschema-1-20010502/

[11] W3C Recommendation "XML Schema Part 2: Datatypes", Paul V. Biron, Ashok Malhotra, 2 May 2001. Available at http://www.w3.org/TR/2001/REC-xmlschema-2-20010502/

9.2. Informative references

[12] Transfer Syntax NDR, in Open Group Technical Standard "DCE 1.1: Remote Procedure Call", August 1997. Available at http://www.opengroup.org/public/pubs/catalog/c706.htm

[13] IETF "RFC2045: Multipurpose Internet Mail Extensions (MIME) Part One: Format of Internet Message Bodies", N. Freed, N. Borenstein, November 1996. Available at http://www.ietf.org/rfc/rfc2045.txt

A. SOAP Envelope Examples

A.1 Sample Encoding of Call Requests

EXAMPLE I–47 Similar to Example 1 but with a Mandatory Header

```
POST /StockQuote HTTP/1.1
Host: www.stockquoteserver.com
Content-Type: text/xml; charset="utf-8"
Content-Length: nnnn
SOAPAction: "http://example.org/2001/06/quotes"

<env:Envelope
  xmlns:env="http://www.w3.org/2001/06/soap-
envelope" >
   <env:Header>
       <t:Transaction
           xmlns:t="http://example.org/2001/06/tx"

env:encodingStyle="http://www.w3.org/2001/06/soap-
encoding"
           env:mustUnderstand="1" >
               5
       </t:Transaction>
   </env:Header>
   <env:Body >
       <m:GetLastTradePrice

env:encodingStyle="http://www.w3.org/2001/06/soap-
encoding"
             xmlns:m="http://example.org/2001/06/
quotes" >
           <m:symbol>DEF</m:symbol>
       </m:GetLastTradePrice>
   </env:Body>
</env:Envelope>
```

EXAMPLE I–48 Similar to Example 1 but with multiple request parameters

```
POST /StockQuote HTTP/1.1
Host: www.stockquoteserver.com
Content-Type: text/xml; charset="utf-8"
Content-Length: nnnn
SOAPAction: "http://example.org/2001/06/quotes"

<env:Envelope xmlns:env="http://www.w3.org/2001/06/
soap-envelope" >
   <env:Body>
       <m:GetLastTradePriceDetailed

env:encodingStyle="http://www.w3.org/2001/06/soap-
encoding"
             xmlns:m="http://example.org/2001/06/
quotes" >
           <Symbol>DEF</Symbol>
           <Company>DEF Corp</Company>
           <Price>34.1</Price>
       </m:GetLastTradePriceDetailed>
   </env:Body>
</env:Envelope>
```

A.2 Sample Encoding of Response

EXAMPLE I–49 Similar to Example 2 but with a Mandatory Header

```
HTTP/1.1 200 OK
Content-Type: text/xml; charset="utf-8"
Content-Length: nnnn

<env:Envelope xmlns:env="http://www.w3.org/2001/06/
soap-envelope" >
   <env:Header>
       <t:Transaction
xmlns:t="http://example.org/2001/06/tx"
xmlns:xsi="http://www.w3.org/2001/XMLSchema-instance"
xmlns:xs="http://www.w3.org/2001/XMLSchema"
                      xsi:type="xs:int"
                      env:encodingStyle="http://
www.w3.org/2001/06/soap-encoding"
```

EXAMPLE I–49 Similar to Example 2 but with a Mandatory Header (Continued)

```
                              env:mustUnderstand="1" >
           5
       </t:Transaction>
   </env:Header>
   <env:Body>
       <m:GetLastTradePriceResponse

env:encodingStyle="http://www.w3.org/2001/06/soap-
encoding"
             xmlns:m="http://example.org/2001/06/
quotes" >
           <Price>34.5</Price>
       </m:GetLastTradePriceResponse>
   </env:Body>
</env:Envelope>
```

EXAMPLE I–50 Similar to Example 2 but with a Struct

```
HTTP/1.1 200 OK
Content-Type: text/xml; charset="utf-8"
Content-Length: nnnn

<env:Envelope xmlns:env="http://www.w3.org/2001/06/
soap-envelope" >
   <env:Body>
       <m:GetLastTradePriceResponse

env:encodingStyle="http://www.w3.org/2001/06/soap-
encoding"
             xmlns:m="http://example.org/2001/06/
quotes" >
           <PriceAndVolume>
               <LastTradePrice>34.5</
LastTradePrice>
               <DayVolume>10000</DayVolume>
           </PriceAndVolume>
       </m:GetLastTradePriceResponse>
   </env:Body>
</env:Envelope>
```

EXAMPLE I–51 Similar to Example 2 but Failing to honor Mandatory Header

```
HTTP/1.1 500 Internal Server Error
Content-Type: text/xml; charset="utf-8"
Content-Length: nnnn

<env:Envelope xmlns:env="http://www.w3.org/2001/06/
soap-envelope">
   <env:Body>
       <env:Fault>
           <faultcode>env:MustUnderstand</
faultcode>
           <faultstring>SOAP Must Understand
Error</faultstring>
       </env:Fault>
   </env:Body>
</env:Envelope>
```

EXAMPLE I–52 Similar to Example 2 but Failing to handle Body

```
HTTP/1.1 500 Internal Server Error
Content-Type: text/xml; charset="utf-8"
Content-Length: nnnn

<env:Envelope xmlns:env="http://www.w3.org/2001/06/
soap-envelope" >
  <env:Body>
    <env:Fault>
      <faultcode>env:Server</faultcode>
      <faultstring>Server Error</faultstring>
      <detail>
        <e:myfaultdetails xmlns:e="http://
example.org/2001/06/faults" >
          <message>My application didn't work</
message>
          <errorcode>1001</errorcode>
        </e:myfaultdetails>
      </detail>
    </env:Fault>
 </env:Body>
</env:Envelope>
```

B. Acknowledgements

This document is the work of the W3C XML Protocol Working Group.

Members of the Working Group are (at the time of writing, and by alphabetical order): Yasser al Safadi (Philips Research), Vidur Apparao (Netscape), Don Box (DevelopMentor), David Burdett (Commerce One), Charles Campbell (Informix Software), Alex Ceponkus (Bowstreet), Michael Champion (Software AG), David Clay (Oracle), Ugo Corda (Xerox), Paul Cotton (Microsoft Corporation), Ron Daniel (Interwoven), Glen Daniels (Allaire), Doug Davis (IBM), Ray Denenberg (Library of Congress), Paul Denning (MITRE Corporation), Frank DeRose (TIBCO Software, Inc.), Brian Eisenberg (Data Channel), David Ezell (Hewlett-Packard), James Falek (TIBCO Software, Inc.), David Fallside (IBM), Chris Ferris (Sun Microsystems), Daniela Florescu (Propel), Dan Frantz (BEA Systems), Dietmar Gaertner (Software AG), Scott Golubock (Epicentric), Rich Greenfield (Library of Congress), Martin Gudgin (Develop Mentor), Hugo Haas (W3C), Marc Hadley (Sun Microsystems), Mark Hale (Interwoven), Randy Hall (Intel), Gerd Hoelzing (SAP AG), Oisin Hurley (IONA Technologies), Yin-Leng Husband (Compaq), John Ibbotson (IBM), Ryuji Inoue (Matsushita Electric Industrial Co., Ltd.), Scott Isaacson (Novell, Inc.), Kazunori Iwasa (Fujitsu Software Corporation), Murali Janakiraman (Rogue Wave), Mario Jeckle (Daimler-Chrysler Research and Technology), Eric Jenkins (Engenia Software), Mark Jones (AT&T), Jay Kasi (Commerce One), Jeffrey Kay (Engenia Software), Richard Koo (Vitria Technology Inc.), Jacek Kopecky (IDOOX s.r.o.), Alan Kropp (Epicentric), Yves Lafon (W3C), Tony Lee (Vitria Technology Inc.), Michah Lerner (AT&T), Richard Martin (Active Data Exchange), Noah Mendelsohn (Lotus Development), Nilo Mitra (Ericsson Research Canada), Jean-Jacques Moreau (Canon), Masahiko Narita (Fujitsu Software Corporation), Mark Needleman (Data Research Associates), Eric Newcomer (IONA Technologies), Henrik Frystyk Nielsen (Microsoft Corporation), Mark Nottingham (Akamai Technologies), David Orchard (JamCracker), Kevin Perkins (Compaq), Jags Ramnaryan (BEA Systems), Andreas Riegg (Daimler-

Chrysler Research and Technology), Hervé Ruellan (Canon), Marwan Sabbouh (MITRE Corporation), Shane Sesta (Active Data Exchange), Miroslav Simek (IDOOX s.r.o.), Simeon Simeonov (Allaire), Nick Smilonich (Unisys), Soumitro Tagore (Informix Software), James Tauber (Bowstreet), Lynne Thompson (Unisys), Patrick Thompson (Rogue Wave), Randy Waldrop (WebMethods), Ray Whitmer (Netscape), Volker Wiechers (SAP AG), Stuart Williams (Hewlett-Packard), Amr Yassin (Philips Research) and Dick Brooks (Group 8760). *Previous members were:* Eric Fedok (Active Data Exchange) Susan Yee (Active Data Exchange) Alex Milowski (Lexica), Bill Anderson (Xerox), Ed Mooney (Sun Microsystems), Mary Holstege (Calico Commerce), Rekha Nagarajan (Calico Commerce), John Evdemon (XML Solutions), Kevin Mitchell (XML Solutions), Yan Xu (DataChannel) Mike Dierken (DataChannel) Julian Kumar (Epicentric) Miles Chaston (Epicentric) Bjoern Heckel (Epicentric) Dean Moses (Epicentric) Michael Freeman (Engenia Software) Jim Hughes (Fujitsu Software Corporation) Francisco Cubera (IBM), Murray Maloney (Commerce One), Krishna Sankar (Cisco), Steve Hole (MessagingDirect Ltd.) John-Paul Sicotte (MessagingDirect Ltd.) Vilhelm Rosenqvist (NCR) Lew Shannon (NCR) Henry Lowe (OMG) Jim Trezzo (Oracle) Peter Lecuyer (Progress Software) Andrew Eisenberg (Progress Software) David Cleary (Progress Software) George Scott (Tradia Inc.) Erin Hoffman (Tradia Inc.) Conleth O'Connell (Vignette) Waqar Sadiq (Vitria Technology Inc.) Tom Breuel (Xerox) David Webber (XMLGlobal Technologies) Matthew MacKenzie (XMLGlobal Technologies) and Mark Baker (Sun Microsystems).

This document is based on the SOAP/1.1 specification whose authors were: Don Box (Develop Mentor), David Ehnebuske (IBM), Gopal Kakivaya (Microsoft Corp.), Andrew Layman (Microsoft Corp.) Noah Mendelsohn (Lotus Development Corp.), Henrik Frystyk Nielsen (Microsoft Corp.), Satish Thatte (Microsoft Corp.) and Dave Winer (UserLand Software, Inc.).

We also wish to thank all the people who have contributed to discussions on xml-dist-app@w3.org.

C. Version Transition From SOAP/1.1 to SOAP Version 1.2

EdNote: The scope of the mechanism provided in this section is for transition between SOAP/1.1 and SOAP version 1.2. The Working Group is considering providing a more general transition mechanism that can apply to any version. Such a general mechanism may or may not be the mechanism provided here depending on whether it is deemed applicable.

The SOAP/1.1 specification says the following on versioning in section 4.1.2:

"SOAP does not define a traditional versioning model based on major and minor version numbers. A SOAP message MUST have an Envelope element associated with the "http://schemas.xmlsoap.org/soap/envelope/" namespace. If a message is received by a SOAP application in which the SOAP Envelope element is associated with a different namespace, the application MUST treat this as a version error and discard the message. If the message is received through a request/response protocol such as HTTP, the application MUST respond with a SOAP VersionMismatch faultcode message (see section 4.4) using the SOAP "http://schemas.xmlsoap.org/soap/envelope/" namespace."

That is, rather than a versioning model based on short-names (typically version numbers), SOAP uses a declarative extension model which allows a sender to include the desired features within the SOAP envelope construct. SOAP says nothing about the granularity of extensions nor how extensions may or may not affect the basic SOAP processing model. It is entirely up to extension designers be it either in a central or a decentralized manner to determine which features become SOAP extensions.

The SOAP extensibility model is based on the following four basic assumptions:

1. SOAP versioning is directed only at the SOAP envelope. It explicitly does not address versioning of blocks, encodings, protocol bindings, or otherwise.

2. A SOAP node must determine whether it supports the version of a SOAP message on a per message basis. In the following, "support" means understanding the semantics of the envelope version identified by the QName of the Envelope element:
   - A SOAP node receiving an envelope that it doesn't support must not attempt to process the message according to any other processing rules regardless of other up- or downstream SOAP nodes.
   - A SOAP node may provide support for multiple envelope versions. However, when processing a message a SOAP node must use the semantics defined by the version of that message.
3. It is essential that the envelope remains stable over time and that new features are added using the SOAP extensibility mechanism. Changing the envelope inherently affects interoperability, adds complexity, and requires central control of extensions—all of which directly conflicts with the SOAP requirements.
4. No versioning model or extensibility model can prevent buggy implementations. Even though significant work has been going into clarifying the SOAP processing model, there is no guarantee that a SOAP 1.2 implementation will behave correctly. Only extensive testing within the SOAP community and design simplicity at the core can help prevent/catch bugs.

The rules for dealing with the possible SOAP/1.1 and SOAP Version 1.2 interactions are as follows:

1. Because of the SOAP/1.1 rules, a compliant SOAP/1.1 node receiving a SOAP Version 1.2 message will generate a VersionMismatch SOAP fault using an envelope qualified by the "http://schemas.xmlsoap.org/soap/envelope/" namespace identifier.
2. A SOAP Version 1.2 node receiving a SOAP/1.1 message may either process the message as SOAP/1.1 or generate a SOAP VersionMismatch fault using the "http://schemas.xmlsoap.org/soap/envelope/" namespace identifier. As part of the SOAP VersionMis-

match fault, a SOAP Version 1.2 node should include the list of envelope versions that it supports using the SOAP upgrade extension identified by the "http://www.w3.org/2001/06/soap-upgrade" identifier.

The upgrade extension contains an ordered list of namespace identifiers of SOAP envelopes that the SOAP node supports in the order most to least preferred. Following is an example of a VersionMismatch fault generated by a SOAP Version 1.2 node including the SOAP upgrade extension:

EXAMPLE I–53 VersionMismatch fault generated by a SOAP Version 1.2 node, and including a SOAP upgrade extension

```
<env:Envelope xmlns:env="http://
schemas.xmlsoap.org/soap/envelope/">
  <env:Header>
    <V:Upgrade xmlns:V="http://www.w3.org/2001/06/
soap-upgrade">
      <envelope qname="ns1:Envelope"
xmlns:ns1="http://www.w3.org/2001/06/soap-
envelope"/>
    </V:Upgrade>
  </env:Header>
  <env:Body>
    <env:Fault>
      <faultcode>env:VersionMismatch</faultcode>
      <faultstring>Version Mismatch</faultstring>
    </env:Fault>
  </env:Body>
</env:Envelope>
```

Note that existing SOAP/1.1 nodes are not likely to indicate which envelope versions they support. If nothing is indicated then this means that SOAP/1.1 is the only supported envelope.

D. Change Log

D.1 SOAP Specification Changes

DATE	AUTHOR	DESCRIPTION
20010629	MJG	Amended description of routing and intermediaries in Section 2.1
20010629	JJM	Changed "latest version" URI to end with soap12
20010629	JJM	Remove "previous version" URI
20010629	JJM	Removed "Editor copy" in <title>
20010629	JJM	Removed "Editor copy" in the title.
20010629	JJM	Added "Previous version" to either point to SOAP/ 1.1, or explicitly mention there was no prior draft.
20010629	JJM	Pre-filed publication URIs.
20010629	JJM	Incorporated David's suggested changes for the examples in section 4.1.1 to 4.4.2
20010629	JJM	Fixed some remaining typos.
20010629	MJH	Fixed a couple of typos.
20010628	MJG	Made various formatting, spelling and grammatical fixes.
20010628	MJG	Moved soap:encodingStyle from soap:Envelope to children of soap:Header/soap:Body in examples 1, 2, 47, 48, 49 and 50
20010628	MJG	Changed text in Section 2.1 from 'it is both a SOAP sender or a SOAP receiver' to 'it is both a SOAP sender and a SOAP receiver'
20010628	MJG	Fixed caption on Example 24
20010628	MJH	Fixed a couple of capitalisation errors where the letter A appeared as a capital in the middle of a sentence.
20010628	MJH	Updated figure 1, removed ednote to do so.
20010622	HFN	Removed the introductory text in terminology section 1.4.3 as it talks about model stuff that is covered in section 2. It was left over from original glossary which also explained the SOAP model.

DATE	AUTHOR	DESCRIPTION
20010622	HFN	Moved the definition of block to encapsulation section in terminology
20010622	HFN	Removed introductory section in 1.4.1 as this overlaps with the model description in section 2 and doesn't belong in a terminology section
20010622	HFN	Removed reference to "Web Characterization Terminology & Definitions Sheet" in terminology section as this is not an active WD
20010622	HFN	Added revised glossary
20010622	HFN	Added example 0 to section 1.3 and slightly modified text for example 1 and 2 to make it clear that HTTP is used as a protocol binding
20010622	MJG	Added http://example.com/... to list of application/ context specific URIs in section 1.2
20010622	MJG	Updated examples in section 4.1.1 to be encodingStyle attributes rather than just the values of attributes
20010622	MJG	Added table.norm, td.normitem and td.normtext styles to stylesheet. Used said styles for table of fault code values in section 4.4.1
20010622	MJG	In Appendix C, changed upgrade element to Upgrade and env to envelope. Made envelope unqualified. Updated schema document to match.
20010622	MJG	Moved MisunderstoodHeader from envelope schema into seperate faults schema. Removed entry in envelope schema change table in Appendix D.2 that refered to additon of said element. Modified example in section 4.4.2 to match. Added reference to schema document to section 4.4.2
20010622	MJH	Added binding as a component of SOAP in introduction. Fixed a couple of typos and updated a couple of example captions.
20010622	MJG	Made BNF in section 6.1.1 into a table.
20010622	MJG	Made BNFs in section 5.1 clause 8 into tables. Added associated 'bnf' style for table and td elements to stylesheet

DATE	AUTHOR	DESCRIPTION
20010622	MJG	Amended text regarding namespace prefix mappings in section 1.2
20010622	MJG	Added link to schema for the http://www.w3.org/2001/06/soap-upgrade namespace to Appendix C. Updated associated ednote.
20010622	MJG	Added reference numbers for XML Schema Recommendation to text prior to schema change tables in Appendix D.2 and linked said numbers to local references in this document
20010622	MJG	Reordered entries in schema change classification table in Appendix D.2
20010622	MJG	Changed type of mustUnderstand and root attributes to standard boolean and updated schema change tables in Appendix D.2 accordingly
20010622	JJM	Manually numbered all the examples (53 in total!)
20010622	JJM	Added caption text to all the examples
20010622	JJM	Replaced remaining occurrences of SOAP/1.2 with SOAP Version 1.2 (including <title>)
20010621	HFN	Added ednote to section 4.2.2 and 4.2.3 that we know they have to be incorporated with section 2
20010621	HFN	Added version transition appendix C
20010621	HFN	Applied new styles to examples
20010621	HFN	Changed term "transport" to "underlying protocol
20010621	HFN	Changed example URNs to URLs of the style http://example.org/...
20010621	MJH	Updated the Acknowledgements section.
20010621	JJM	Added new style sheet definitions (from XML Schema) for examples, and used them for example 1 and 2.
20010621	JJM	Incorporated David Fallside's comments on section Status and Intro sections.
20010620	HFN	Changed the status section
20010620	HFN	Changed title to SOAP Version 1.2 and used that first time in abstract and in body

DATE	AUTHOR	DESCRIPTION
20010620	HFN	Removed question from section 2.4 as this is an issue and is to be listed in the issues list
20010620	HFN	Moved change log to appendix
20010615	JJM	Renamed default actor to anonymous actor for now (to be consistent)
20010615	JJM	Fixed typos in section 2
20010614	JJM	Updated section 2 to adopt the terminology used elsewhere in the spec.
20010613	MJH	Updated mustUnderstand fault text with additions from Martin Gudgin.
20010613	MJH	Added schema changes appendix from Martin Gudgin.
20010613	MJH	Added mustUnderstand fault text from Glen Daniels.
20010612	MJH	Fixed document <title>.
20010612	MJH	Moved terminology subsection from message exchange model section to introduction section.
20010612	MJH	Fixed capitalisation errors by replacing "... A SOAP ..." with "... a SOAP ..." where appropriate.
20010612	MJH	Removed trailing "/" from encoding namespace URI.
20010612	MJH	Fixed links under namespace URIs to point to W3C space instead of schemas.xmlsoap.org.
20010612	MJH	Removed some odd additional links with text of "/" pointing to the encoding schema following the text of the encoding namespace URI in several places.
20010611	MJH	Incorporated new text for section 2.
20010611	JJM	Changed remaining namespaces, in particular next.
20010609	JJM	Changed the spec name from XMLP/SOAP to SOAP.
20010609	JJM	Changed the version number from 1.1 to 1.2.
20010609	JJM	Changed the namespaces from http://schemas.xmlsoap.org/soap/ to http://www.w3.org/2001/06/soap-.
20010609	JJM	Replaced the remaining XS and XE prefixes to env and enc, respectively.

DATE	AUTHOR	DESCRIPTION
20010601	MJH	Updated the examples in section 1, 6 and appendix A with text suggested by Martin Gudgin to comply with XML Schema Recommendation.
20010601	JJM	Updated the examples in section 4 and 5 with text suggested by Martin Gudgin, to comply with XML Schema Recommendation.
20010531	HFN	Removed appendices C and D and added links to live issues list and separate schema files.
20010531	MJH	Added this change log and updated schemas in appendix C to comply with XML Schema Recommendation.

D.2 XML Schema Changes

The envelope and encoding schemas have been updated to be compliant with the XML Schema Recomendation[10,11]. The table below shows the categories of change.

CLASS	MEANING
Addition	New constructs have been added to the schema
Clarification	The meaning of the schema has been changed to more accurately match the specification
Deletion	Constructs have been removed from the schema
Name	The schema has been changed due to a datatype name change in the XML Schema specification
Namespace	A namespace name has been changed
Semantic	The meaning of the schema has been changed
Style	Style changes have been made to the schema
Syntax	The syntax of the schema has been updated due to changes in the XML Schema specification

The table below lists the changes to the envelope schema.

CLASS	DESCRIPTION
Namespace	Updated to use the http://www.w3.org/2001/XMLSchema namespace
Namespace	Value of targetNamespace attribute changed to http://www.w3.org/2001/06/soap-envelope
Clarification	Changed element and attribute wildcards in Envelope complex type to namespace="##other"
Clarification	Changed element and attribute wildcards in Header complex type to namespace="##other"
Clarification	Added explicit namespace="##any" to element and attribute wildcards in Body complex type
Clarification	Added explicit namespace="##any" to element and attribute wildcards in detail complex type
Clarification	Added an element wildcard with namespace="##other" to the Fault complex type
Name	Changed item type of encodingStyle from uri-reference to anyURI
Name	Changed type of actor attribute from uri-reference to anyURI
Name	Changed type of faultactor attribute from uri-reference to anyURI
Semantic	Added processContents="lax" to all element and attribute wildcards
Semantic	Changed type of the mustUnderstand attribute from restriction of boolean that only allowed 0 or 1 as lexical values to the standard boolean in the http://www.w3.org/2001/XMLSchema namespace. The lexical forms 0, 1, false, true are now allowed.
Style	Where possible comments have been changed into annotations
Syntax	Changed all occurences of maxOccurs="*" to maxOccurs="unbounded"
Syntax	Added <xs:sequence> to all complex type definitions derived implicitly from the ur-type
Syntax	Added <xs:sequence> to all named model group definitions

The table below lists the changes to the encoding schema.

CLASS	DESCRIPTION
Namespace	Updated to use the http://www.w3.org/2001/XMLSchema namespace
Namespace	Value of targetNamespace attribute changed to http://www.w3.org/2001/06/soap-encoding
Semantic	Changed type of the root attribute from restriction of boolean that only allowed 0 or 1 as lexical values to the standard boolean in the http://www.w3.org/2001/XMLSchema namespace. The lexical forms 0, 1, false, true are now allowed.
Addition	Added processContents="lax" to all element and attribute wildcards
Syntax	Changed base64 simple type to be a vacuous restriction of the base64Binary type in the http://www.w3.org/2001/XMLSchema namespace
Syntax	Updated all complex type definitions with simple base types to new syntax
Syntax	Added <xs:sequence> to all complex type definitions derived implicitly from the ur-type
Syntax	Added <xs:sequence> to all named model group definitions
Deletion	Removed the timeDuration datatype
Addition	Added duration datatype derived by extension from the duration datatype in the http://www.w3.org/2001/XMLSchema namespace.
Deletion	Removed the timeInstant datatype
Addition	Added dateTime datatype derived by extension from the dateTime datatype in the http://www.w3.org/2001/XMLSchema namespace.
Addition	Added gYearMonth datatype derived by extension from the gYearMonth datatype in the http://www.w3.org/2001/XMLSchema namespace.
Addition	Added gYear datatype derived by extension from the gYear datatype in the http://www.w3.org/2001/XMLSchema namespace.

CLASS	DESCRIPTION
Addition	Added gMonthDay datatype derived by extension from the gMonthDay datatype in the http://www.w3.org/2001/XMLSchema namespace.
Addition	Added gDay datatype derived by extension from the gDay datatype in the http://www.w3.org/2001/XMLSchema namespace.
Addition	Added gDay datatype derived by extension from the gDay datatype in the http://www.w3.org/2001/XMLSchema namespace.
Deletion	Removed the binary datatype
Addition	Added hexBinary datatype derived by extension from the hexBinary datatype in the http://www.w3.org/2001/XMLSchema namespace.
Addition	Added base64Binary datatype derived by extension from the base64Binary datatype in the http://www.w3.org/2001/XMLSchema namespace.
Deletion	Removed the uriReference datatype
Addition	Added anyURI datatype derived by extension from the anyURI datatype in the http://www.w3.org/2001/XMLSchema namespace.
Addition	Added normalizedString datatype derived by extension from the normalizedString datatype in the http://www.w3.org/2001/XMLSchema namespace.
Addition	Added token datatype derived by extension from the token datatype in the http://www.w3.org/2001/XMLSchema namespace.
Clarification	Added explicit namespace="##any" to all element and attribute wildcards which did not previously have an explicit namespace attribute
Style	Where possible comments have been changed into annotations

In addition several changes occured in the names of datatypes in the XML Schema specification and some datatypes were removed. The following table lists those changes.

DATATYPE	CLASS	DESCRIPTION
timeDuration	Renamed	New name is duration
timeInstant	Renamed	New name is dateTime
recurringDuration	Removed	The recurringDuration datatype no longer exists.
recurringInstant	Removed	The recurringInstant datatype no longer exists.
binary	Removed	The binary datatype has been replaced by the hexBinary and base64Binary datatypes.
month	Renamed	New name is gYearMonth
timePeriod	Removed	The timePeriod datatype no longer exists
year	Renamed	New name is gYear
century	Removed	The century datatype no longer exists
recurringDate	Renamed	New name is gMonthDay
recurringDay	Renamed	New name is gDay

Last Modified: $Date: 2001/07/09 13:39:15 $ UTC

SOAP Glossary

A

API

Application Program Interface. A set of routines, protocols, and tools for building software applications. A good API makes it easier to develop a program by providing all the building blocks. A programmer puts the blocks together.

Asynchronous

A one-way message. A client requests something of the server, and then doesn't wait for an answer—it continues on its merry way, listening for when the server finally does respond.

B

Binding

Formal rules for carrying a SOAP message within or on top of another protocol for purpose of transmission. Examples: SOAP floats on top of HTTP. Or it can be carried along with BEEP. In WSDL, binding means connecting the abstract description of a message with its data format and transport protocol.

Boxcar

Combining a bunch of method calls in a row, where everything has to work.

C

Canonicalize

Canonicalization is a method that breaks an XML document or fragment down into its logical parts. For example, let's say we have two XML documents that contain the same information but there are small differences, like the attributes are in a different order. The two documents are not byte-for-byte identical, because the attributes are in slightly different places, but their information is the same. However, if both of the documents were canonicalized, and those canonical forms were compared, they would be identical. Why? Because the canonical form of an XML document contains its basic information, and since the two documents contain the same information, their canonical forms would be identical. In fact, the W3C has accepted the Canonical XML as a full recommendation (*www.w3.org/TR/2001/REC-xml-c14n-20010315*).

COM

Component Object Model. A method of building Windows applications.

Cookie

A variable set by a server to live on a user's local machine. Used to maintain state over an HTTP connection.

CORBA/IIOP

Another distributed object architecture, like DCOM or Java's RMI. IIOP is the Internet wire protocol for CORBA.

core validation

In XML Signature, the process of validating both the signature over SignedInfo and each Reference digest within the SignedInfo element.

D

DCOM

Distributed Component Object Model. A way of sharing COM objects across a network. Very security-conscious, but not very scalable.

detached signature

A digital signature that's in a different place than the digital content it's signing. That is, the signature is in a file separate from the content it's associated with.

Digest

An encoded piece of text.

Disco

Microsoft's first effort to create a standard way to find (or discover) Web services. This was abandoned in favor of UDDI.

Discovery

Describes remote procedure interfaces. In other words, there have not been ways to automatically query those interfaces for their capabilities.

DLL Hell

Having to constantly manually replace DLLs as you made revisions to them, but having existing apps required the older version of the DLL, so that errors appear when the new DLL is put into place.

E

embedded elements

Anything that isn't an independent element.

Encode

To translate data from one format to another. In this book, encoding acts much the same as serialization does, except that encoding is more specific. It stands for how the input parameters are specifically turned into XML—what sort of rules are used to, say, place an array in XML?

Endpoint

Network service—where the application lives—the remote method.

enveloping signature

An XML digital signature that is over the information that's in the same document as the signature.

Extensibility

The ability to make up your own tags.

F

frequent client

A client that makes many requests of an HTTP server.

G

garbage collection

Releasing memory that was allotted to objects that are no longer in use.

H

Hooking

Modifying a request from the header.

HTTP

Hypertext Transfer Protocol—a wire protocol designed to transfer text HTML documents, associated images, and other files.

I

independent element

Child elements of the main SOAP envelope element (e.g., get head and body elements). Also, an element one level deeper than the scoping element.

Interop

Short for interoperability.

IP

Internet Protocol. The protocol responsible for forwarding packets to their destination.

ISAPI

Short for Internet Server API—it's an API for IIS.

K

Key

A specific method for encoding data; a secret value shared by two or more entities that are sending and received coded messages to each other.

L

Library

Just a chunk of code designed to be used by many programmers, right?

loosely coupled

Two separate systems connected in such a way that they don't really know, or care, who they're talking to. Loose coupling is often achieved by using a common language as an intermediary.

N

node, SOAP

An application that processes a SOAP message/packet according to the specification.

O

out-of-band

External information.

P

Packet

The final chunk of data that is sent from point A to point B by the network layer. For example, the actual bits that Ethernet sends across the wire.

Persistence

Allowing a TCP connection to remain open while multiple HTTP requests are made.

Pipelining

Making multiple HTTP requests without waiting for a server response.

Polymorphism

The ability to appear in may forms. Refers to a language's ability to process objects differently based on their data type.

public key cryptography

A method of encoding that uses a public key to encode data, but requires a secret, private key to decode the data. The reverse is also possible: A private key encodes the data, but only a public key is needed to decode it.

R

replay attack

Hacking scenario where an adversary copies a client's message to a server, and then resends that message to the server.

RMI

Remote Method Invocation.

round trip

A single request and response.

RPC

Remote Procedure Call. Calling a method/function on a remote host.

S

Serialization

Transforming binary data into text.

SOAP

Simple Object Access Protocol.

SOAP node

A SOAP server that can act as an ultimate SOAP server, or that can simply forward a SOAP message toward its destination.

SSL

Secure Sockets Layer. A technology created by Netscape to encrypt the messages passed via HTTP.

Stateless

No context is preserved from one connection to the next. In other words: request-respond amnesia.

Streaming

The client starts reading before the server finishes writing.

Struct

Data type that looks like a recordset or an associative array. For example, name.first="Jake", name.last="Fish".

Synchronous

Where a client requests something from the server, and then waits until the server responds. This is how HTTP works. The request must happen during the connection in which the request is made.

T

TCP

Transmission Control Protocol. The protocol responsible for making sure all packets arrive where they should and in the right order.

tunneling

Moving from point A to point B over HTTP.

W

Web services

Any number of applications that use each other's functions and methods, even though the applications are at different nodes across the Internet.

wire protocol

A set of instructions and rules for formatting data in order to move it across a network.

WSDL

Web Services Description Language.

X

XMI

XML message interfaces (part of HailStorm)—really just a set of SOAP messages.

XML

Extensible Markup Language.

XML payload

The input parameters for the method call in XML form. That is, the actual important part of the message that SOAP is wrapped around.

Index

P

R

S

Y

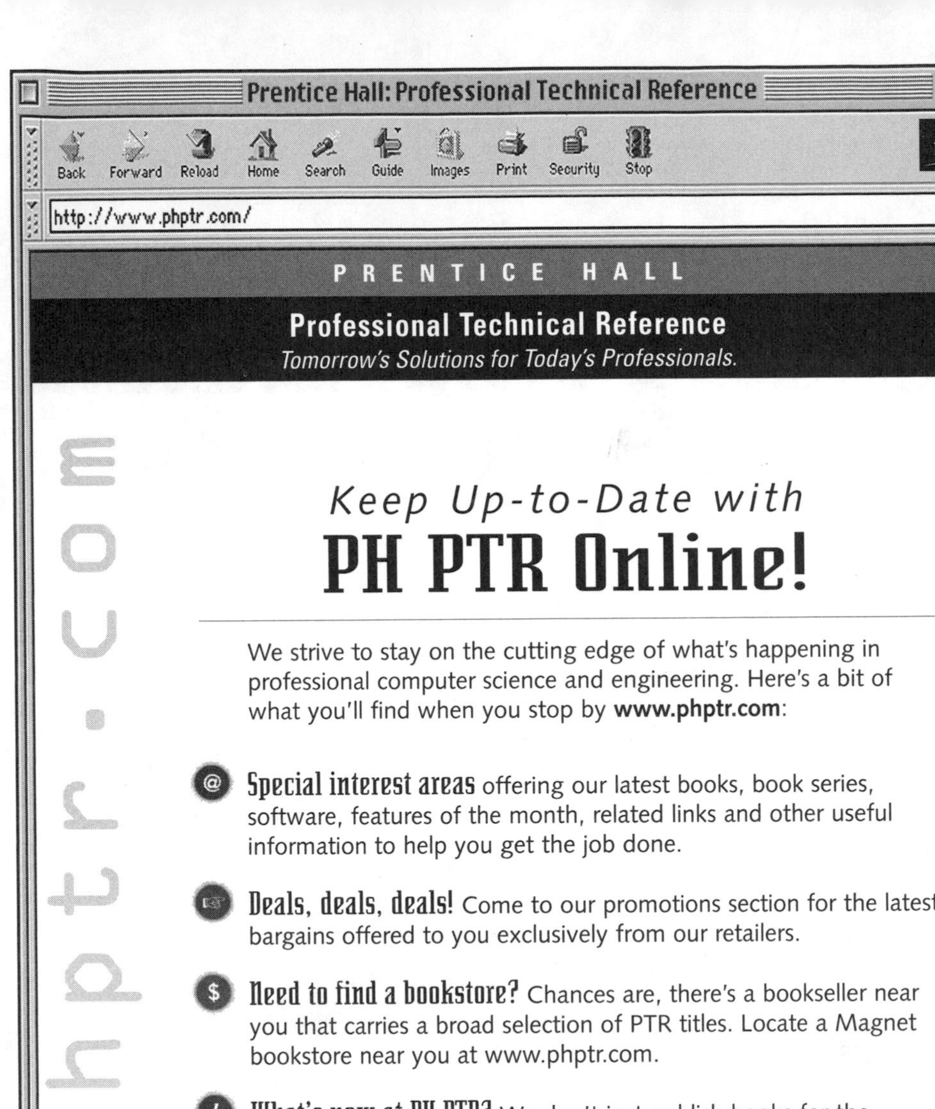

Keep Up-to-Date with

PH PTR Online!

We strive to stay on the cutting edge of what's happening in professional computer science and engineering. Here's a bit of what you'll find when you stop by **www.phptr.com**:

- **Special interest areas** offering our latest books, book series, software, features of the month, related links and other useful information to help you get the job done.
- **Deals, deals, deals!** Come to our promotions section for the latest bargains offered to you exclusively from our retailers.
- **Need to find a bookstore?** Chances are, there's a bookseller near you that carries a broad selection of PTR titles. Locate a Magnet bookstore near you at www.phptr.com.
- **What's new at PH PTR?** We don't just publish books for the professional community, we're a part of it. Check out our convention schedule, join an author chat, get the latest reviews and press releases on topics of interest to you.
- **Subscribe today! Join PH PTR's monthly email newsletter!**

Want to be kept up-to-date on your area of interest? Choose a targeted category on our website, and we'll keep you informed of the latest PH PTR products, author events, reviews and conferences in your interest area.

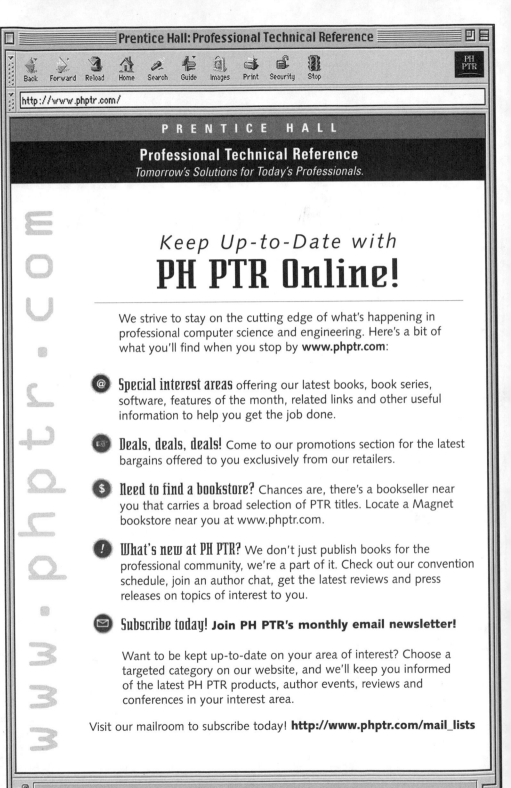

Visit our mailroom to subscribe today! **http://www.phptr.com/mail_lists**